BUSINESS LAW THE EASY WAY

by

Robert W. Emerson, J.D.

Professor of Business Law
University of Florida

BARRON'S

Dedication

*In memory of my father, Leonidas Polk Bills Emerson,
and for my mother, Gloria Bell Emerson.*

All inquiries should be addressed to:
Barron's Educational Series, Inc.
250 Wireless Boulevard
Hauppauge, New York 11788

Library of Congress Card No. 93-21028

International Standard Book No. 0-8120-4760-5

Library of Congress Cataloging-in-Publication Data

Emerson, Robert W.
   Business law the easy way / by Robert W. Emerson.
      p. cm. — (Easy way)
   Includes bibliographical references and index.
   ISBN 0-8120-4760-5
   1. Business law—United States. I. Title. II. Series.
KF889.6.E44 1994
346.73'07—dc20
[347.3067]   93-21028
                                              CIP

PRINTED IN THE UNITED STATES OF AMERICA
4567   100   987654321

PREFACE

In an introductory course on law, the student confronts a complex maze of principles and terms. This book will make learning that material much easier. Barron's *Business Law the Easy Way* provides a readily understandable explanation of business law and regulatory topics. It serves as a practical guide to the law for both businesspeople and students. Not only does it simply yet thoroughly discuss and explain the law, but its information is easily accessible. There is a glossary of close to a thousand words, and there is also a very detailed index. Helpful cross references are included throughout the text.

Business Law the Easy Way is thorough. It covers nearly every law school subject, but in a way designed to meet the needs of laypersons, particularly students in graduate school, college, or even advanced high school classes. It explains all of the material found in a one- or two-semester business law course (including essentially all business law topics studied by accounting students), and it also clarifies the other material often found in courses that introduce laypersons to the legal environment of business or the legal system generally. I have drawn upon my experience as both a practicing attorney and a professor in order to explain and illustrate the key concepts in law, including such areas as contracts, commercial paper, sales, secured transactions, the Uniform Commercial Code, litigation, torts, warranties, product liability, agency, partnerships, corporations, franchises, administrative and constitutional law, securities regulation, antitrust law, consumer protection, creditor-debtor relations, labor and employment law, environmental law, real estate, personal property, and other subjects.

Many years of teaching lead me to believe that *Business Law the Easy Way* can be a useful primary text, supplemental book, or recommended study guide for most business law/legal environment courses. It is eminently "teachable" for busy professors, teachers, and lawyer-lecturers, particularly those who seek a text covering "all of the basics" so that they are free to develop key topics in their own way.

Business Law the Easy Way embodies my teaching experience and philosophy, as well as my day-to-day advice to business owners, managers, and employees. I thank the many students and businesspeople whose questions and problems over the years have helped me to develop this practical guide to the law. Readers' comments and suggestions are most welcome.

Gainesville, Florida
April 1994

Robert W. Emerson

Table of Contents

Chapter 1

Law and the Legal System

NATURE AND ORIGIN OF LAW

The origin of law is obscure. In its most primitive form, law rested on brute power—the ability of one individual to control others through strength. Then, the *lex talionis*, the law of retaliation (an eye for an eye, a tooth for a tooth), arose from injured individuals' impulse for revenge. As society progressed, however, it became necessary to create rules governing both the behavior of individuals toward one another and the conduct of individuals toward society as a whole.

Laws therefore were enacted for different purposes:

- **Public law** prohibits certain kinds of behavior that society finds objectionable. It includes constitutional, administrative, and criminal law. Public law concerns *an individual's relationship with society*.
- **Private law** is intended to compensate an injured party and to prevent or end disputes. Thus, private law includes tort law, the law of private injury, and contract law. Private law governs *an individual's relationship with another individual*.

JURISPRUDENCE (THE SCIENCE OR PHILOSOPHY OF LAW)

One school of thought, sometimes referred to as "legal realism," defines law as that which a judge will decide concerning issues brought to him or her. However, there are other schools of thought with very different views on the law. "Legal positivism" defines law as simply a command from a sovereign (e.g., a king's decree, a legislature's statute, a judge's order). "Natural law" theorists believe that absolute moral rules can be found in a higher law and that any human law to the contrary is not law at all.

There is a close relationship between law and morality, and conduct that a reasonable person deems moral and right is unlikely to collide with law. Thus, since law reflects morality, strict control over all members of society should not be necessary. (Most people follow the law because it is in keeping with their own moral philosophy.)

SYSTEMS OF LAW

There are currently two major legal systems in use in the Western world:

1. **Civil Law (Code law—found in most of Europe and Latin America):** The main goal of Civil Law (whose origins can be traced to the Roman Empire) is

to establish a body of legal rules in one systematic code. In this system, judicial decisions (case law) are not a source of law, although they may be useful to judges in deciding cases.

2. **Common law (Case law—found in most English-speaking countries)**: England did not follow Civil Law. Instead, English judges resolved disputes on a case-by-case basis, using precedents set in similar previous cases as their guide. Since the United States was a British colony, an understanding of English common law is vital to the study of American law.

Sir William Blackstone's *Commentaries*, published just before the American Revolution, is considered the best text on English law as it existed when the United States gained its independence. According to Blackstone, common law is an "ancient collection of unwritten maxims and customs." American common law contains not only this collection inherited from England, but also all subsequent case law as it has developed over time.

As common law developed, judges followed precedents when confronted with new cases. The requirement that courts follow their own precedents is based on the legal principle of *stare decisis* or "stand by the decision." *Stare decisis* binds all of the lower courts of a jurisdiction to judgments rendered by the highest court in that same jurisdiction. *Stare decisis* is not absolute; a decision of the highest court can be amended either by that court changing its mind or by legislative mandate. In the absence of a precedent, a court may follow its own sense of justice or fairness, with due regard for prevailing custom or morality.

Unless changes are constitutionally prohibited, the legislature may enact laws known as *statutes* to modify the common law. These statutes, subject to judicial interpretation, are collected into codes. Along with case law, the codes form the law that courts generally apply. (Common law codes should not be confused with Civil Law codes. In common law, a code is merely the collection of statutes passed by the legislature; a Civil Law code is intended to be a comprehensive statement of the entire law.)

After England's conquest by William the Conqueror (A.D. 1066), Norman kings created—alongside the developing common law—an independent, but parallel, system of justice known as *equity*. Based on concepts of fair play, equity cases have no juries, and the equity system covers injunctive relief (court-ordered restraining orders), specific contract performance, contract modification, and parts of family law. Though the equity system no longer exists as a separate system of justice, many of the principles and maxims of equity have been merged into the common law.

Substantive and Procedural Law

It is crucial to any study of law, including American business law, to be able to distinguish between two types of law:

1. **Substantive law** defines legal rights and obligations in regard to a specific subject, such as contracts, torts, crimes, or property.
2. **Procedural law** is concerned with the enforcement of substantive law in a court of law. Rules of procedure are intended to promote justice.

Theoretically, there would be 50 bodies of law (combined case and statutory law) among the 50 states in the United States. Actually, however, there is great interdependence, conscious parallelism, and a disciplined effort to develop uniform legislation among the states. The *Uniform Commercial Code (UCC)*, adopted in 49 states and partly in Louisiana, is the most successful of the proposed uniform laws. However, even the UCC has not completely achieved uniformity. State legislatures can make changes, and courts are free to give independent and varying interpretations of existing laws.

COURTS

There are two main court systems in the United States: the federal and the state systems. The hierarchical structure of federal courts is comparable to that of the various state court systems. Therefore, as an example, we will look at the federal judiciary.

At the bottom rung are the U.S. *district courts*, which are trial courts. In each state there is at least one federal district court. If a party wishes to appeal the district court's judgment, he or she brings the case before the *appeals court*, which is the circuit court for that district. Each circuit court generally covers the federal district courts in several states. (The one exception is Washington, D.C., which, because of its heavy volume of work, has its own circuit.)

Lastly, appeals from circuit court decisions (or from holdings of the highest court of a state) *may* be heard by the *U.S. Supreme Court*. In a few cases, a party has an absolute right of appeal. In most cases, though, it is solely up to the Supreme Court whether to hear an appeal. Usually the case must involve a federal question (e.g., about the U.S. Constitution or a federal statute).

There are other types of specialized courts, too, such as federal bankruptcy courts, state landlord-tenant courts, and state small claims courts. However, the general trial courts, with juries available, remain the main arena for most important cases.

The power of a court system to hear and decide a case is called *jurisdiction*. The federal courts are limited to hearing cases specifically placed within their power by the U.S. Constitution or other laws. *Subject-matter jurisdiction* is the judicial power to decide the issues in a case. Federal courts decide *federal questions*, which are cases involving the federal Constitution, statutes, or treaties. In such cases, federal court jurisdiction is *exclusive*, but in some areas it is *concurrent*, that is, state courts can also hear cases on these subjects.

In addition to federal questions, Congress has provided another form of subject-matter jurisdiction to the federal courts: *diversity jurisdiction*. This means that when opposing parties in a civil lawsuit are citizens of different states, a matter based on state law (and normally brought before a state court) can be heard in a federal court *if* one of the parties requests it *and if* the amount of the controversy exceeds $50,000. Corporations are treated as "citizens" of both their place of incorporation and their principal business location; for partnerships, however, courts look to the citizenship of each general partner.

If a defendant wishes to transfer a case from one state to another, or from state court to federal court, his request will be for *removal*. Such requests must be made at the beginning of the case and are only granted if the correct jurisdiction lies in another court. State courts are generally open to hear any type of case, unless it is precluded by the U.S. Constitution or federal statutes or treaties. *Most common law areas—such as torts, contracts, crimes—tend to be brought before state courts.*

In addition to subject-matter jurisdiction, for each particular case, a court needs jurisdiction over the litigants themselves. *Personal (in personam) jurisdiction* is the judicial power over the parties in a case. By filing a lawsuit, the *plaintiff* voluntarily submits to the court's personal jurisdiction. Personal jurisdiction over the *defendant* requires that the defendant work or live in the state in which the lawsuit was filed, or have other clear-cut ties to the state. In addition, states have passed "long-arm statutes," which extend personal jurisdiction for the courts over people or corporations in certain specified circumstances.

When a court has authority over the subject matter and parties of a lawsuit, it has jurisdiction. However, there still may be problems with *venue*, the place (usually the county) where the case will be tried. Proper venue is defined by statute and is usually based on the notion of convenience to the parties, especially the defendant.

Obviously, the law varies from state to state. The doctrine of *stare decisis* does not require one state to follow another state's precedents. When disputes arise out of transactions occurring in more than one state, the issue is covered by a body of law known as *conflict of laws* (or choice of laws). Thus, while a court will almost always apply its own procedural law, it must look to conflict-of-laws principles to choose between different substantive laws:

- For *torts* (e.g., accident cases), the applicable law is usually that where the injury occurred.
- For *contracts*, courts generally look to the law intended (expressly or implicitly) by the parties to the contract.
- In *criminal cases*, courts apply their own substantive and procedural laws, regardless of where the acts were committed; however, almost all criminal prosecutions take place in the same state where the alleged crime occurred.

Once a court renders a judgment, the U.S. Constitution's "full faith and credit" clause requires that other states recognize the validity of that judgment as it specifically affects the rights and parties subject to that judgment. This does not mean that other states must adopt the reasoning on which a decision is based; one state's precedents are *not* binding on another state. The clause simply means that the judgment must be honored by other states' courts.

ATTORNEYS

Modern attorneys operate in two main areas: the law office and the courtroom. All practicing attorneys must have a general command of legal principles. In addition, attorneys must be *able to find specific and detailed application of legal principles* within the large body of case law and statute law. Thus, as a business law student, you must become familiar with the kinds of research materials that exist.

Statutory law is found in a state code or in the federal code. These codes are cross-referenced to other statutes and key cases interpreting and applying the same statute in question.

Case law is collected in the opinions of the appellate courts of the states and the United States. Opinions of trial courts are usually not published, except for federal trial courts. Case law may also be found in legal encyclopedias, textbooks, and computer data banks such as WESTLAW and LEXIS.

Businesses rely on attorneys not only when they are sued, but also to prevent problems. The hope is to improve business practices and thus reduce the risks of lawsuits and other fines or legal expenses.

A lawyer has several functions: investigator, drafter, negotiator, advisor, and advocate. A lawyer has a duty to advise against illegal actions, but also must maintain confidences shared during the course of an attorney/client relationship.

Except for in-house counsel (lawyers who are employees of a business, perhaps in a company's legal department), the businessperson usually contacts an attorney rather than vice versa. The *attorney/client privilege* permits clients to keep matters discussed with their attorneys confidential. This privilege can be waived by a client; for example, the client may divulge attorney/client communications to a third party. Also, because the attorney/client privilege depends on *confidential* communications, it does not extend to statements made in the presence of, or letters sent to, persons besides the attorney and the client.

Each state has ethical codes of conduct governing lawyers. In general, the attorney must:

1. only take cases that he or she can handle competently;
2. zealously advocate the client's cause, while remaining faithful to the attorney's own obligation as an officer of the court not to undermine the overall purposes of the system;
3. keep the client reasonably informed (e.g., concerning settlement offers);
4. abide by the attorney/client privilege; and
5. take measures to protect the client when withdrawing from a case.

Occasionally, attorney/client conflicts stem from what the attorney believes are her ethical obligations. Frank discussions between the attorney and the client are usually necessary and may resolve such differences.

The businessperson's basic knowledge of the legal system can play an important role in the lawyer's attempts to resolve problems. There is no substitute for professional advice, but the businessperson's limited knowledge can help him realize when the services of a lawyer are necessary, and what assistance the attorney and the client can mutually provide to one another.

LITIGATION

Procedural law is very complicated and varies from court to court. There are federal rules of procedure, and each state court system also has its own rules. Appellate courts have different rules from trial courts, and even courts in the same jurisdiction may have different local rules. Furthermore, criminal and civil cases follow different rules. Nevertheless, most cases follow a general pattern of procedure.

The person who initiates the lawsuit is called the *plaintiff*. The person sued is the *defendant*. In equity cases, the parties are instead called the *petitioner* and the *respondent*, respectively. In a criminal case there is no plaintiff; instead, the criminal defendant is opposed by the state itself, often referred to as "the prosecution" or "the people."

The papers required to bring the issues in a lawsuit before the court are termed the *pleadings*. To begin the action, the plaintiff's lawyer files a *complaint* with the clerk of a trial court with the proper jurisdiction and venue. The complaint contains a brief description of the facts, the basis of the suit, and a request for remedies.

An official then serves a *summons* and a copy of the complaint on the defendant. An affidavit is usually filed attesting to the fact that the defendant received the summons and complaint. The summons notifies the defendant that he or she must file an *answer* to the complaint with both the court and the plaintiff's attorney within a certain time period. The summons also tells the defendant that failure to file an answer will lead to a judgment by default for the plaintiff.

An answer, however, is not the defendant's only choice. He may file a *motion to dismiss*, sometimes called a *demurrer*, in which he contends that, even if the plaintiff's allegations are true, there is no legal basis for finding the defendant liable.

The answer generally admits or denies each of the various allegations set forth in the complaint. It may include *affirmative defenses*, that is, allegations of facts that, if proved by the defendant, defeat the plaintiff's claim. Generally, a complaint or answer may be amended unless a statute or rule specifically prohibits such amendment, or unless the amendment is made at such a later date that its acceptance as a new pleading would be grossly unfair to the other party.

When answering the complaint, or shortly thereafter, the defendant may file a *counterclaim,* which is a reverse complaint: one by the defendant against the plaintiff. Two other claims are (1) *cross claims,* brought by a plaintiff against one or more co-plaintiffs, or more likely, by a defendant against one or more co-defendants; and (2) *third-party claims,* whereby a defendant brings a new party into a lawsuit. In addition, large numbers of plaintiffs may join together in a *class action.*

Besides the motion to dismiss, many other types of *motions,* or requests to the court, may be made before the case goes to trial. The most important motion is the motion for *summary judgment.* It may be filed at any time by either the plaintiff or the defendant. Summary judgment is to be awarded if the judge decides that (1) there is no genuine issue as to material (potentially determinative) facts; and (2) when the law is applied to these facts, one party is clearly entitled to a verdict in her favor. Summary judgment may be granted on all or part of a lawsuit. The summary judgment may also be used to limit or eliminate certain types of damages, such as punitive damages.

Before there is a trial, each party is entitled to obtain information from other parties and other potential witnesses. These pretrial procedures are known as *discovery.*

Discovery may serve several purposes:
1. By providing parties with access to evidence that might otherwise be hidden, it prevents surprises at the trial.
2. It may narrow the issues at the trial (i.e., some questions may be resolved).
3. It preserves witnesses' testimony prior to trial (important witnesses may be unavailable at trial, their memories may fade, or their testimony may change).
4. It may place the case in a position for summary judgment.
5. It may lead to pretrial settlement, as both parties see their strengths and weaknesses.

The main methods of discovery are depositions, interrogatories, requests for admissions, and the production of documents.

DEPOSITIONS

A *deposition* is sworn testimony by one of the parties or any other witness, usually recorded and transcribed by a notary public. The testimony is ordinarily taken in response to oral questions from the parties' attorneys, although it can be in response to written questions.

INTERROGATORIES

Interrogatories are written questions to be answered in writing, and under oath, by another party (generally the opposing party). Unlike depositions, interrogatories can be directed only toward the parties themselves. Their usefulness is further reduced by the fact that the answering party's attorney can prepare the answers. However, interrogatories usually cost less than depositions, and their scope can be broader.

REQUESTS FOR ADMISSIONS

Requests for admissions are, like interrogatories, made and answered in writing and can be directed only to another party. The requesting party asks the other side to admit particular facts or acknowledge that certain documents are genuine. Admissions are conclusive. Thus, this method can save trial time because the parties have already agreed on some matters.

PRODUCTION OF DOCUMENTS

Parties may be required to produce, for inspection and copying, all their documents that may be relevant to the case. A deposition may include document production by the witness as well.

TRIAL

The trial issues can be narrowed via a *pretrial conference.* Although judges may use these conferences to encourage settlement, the main purpose is to ensure that the trial will proceed as smoothly as possible: Witnesses, exhibits, areas of dispute, and agreed upon facts are all identified ahead of time.

The next step is the trial itself. A jury trial is available in criminal cases and in most civil lawsuits. The major exceptions are (1) certain cases (e.g., divorce) that are historically based on equity, and (2) administrative agency proceedings.

The plaintiff or the defendant can ask for a trial by jury; this right is usually waived if not requested in the plaintiff's complaint or the defendant's answer.

A jury trial involves a *petit jury* (usually 12 members, though some states allow as few as six). The petit jury decides whether the defendant is guilty in criminal cases, or liable in civil cases. In federal courts and most state courts, the jury's decision must be unanimous. The federal courts and most states also have *grand juries* (approximately 18 to 24 jurors), which, under the guidance of prosecutors, decide whether an individual should be charged with a crime (indicted).

In *jury selection*, the first step in the trial, prospective jurors are questioned by the attorneys for both sides and by the judge. This examination is known as *voir dire.* Any number of potential jurors can be kept off the panel *for cause* (e.g., bias), and the attorneys for each side also have the right to reject a few (generally about three) without offering a reason, i.e., by *peremptory challenge*.

After the jury has been selected, the next step is the presentation of *opening statements*, where each attorney presents what he or she expects to prove.

The *plaintiff*'s case is then presented. Witnesses, called by the plaintiff's attorney, testify in response to the questions: first *direct examination* by the attorney who called them, and then *cross-examination* by the opposing attorney. Other evidence that could help the plaintiff's case is offered at this time. At the end of the plaintiff's case, the defendant may move for dismissal of the case, or for a *directed verdict*. The directed verdict will be granted by the judge if the plaintiff has failed to prove one or more elements of her case. If the judge grants the motion, the jury is instructed by the judge to find for the defendant.

If the trial continues, the next step is the *defendant's case*. This follows the same procedure as the plaintiff's case, but offers witnesses and evidence for the defense. When the defendant's case is complete, the plaintiff may move for a directed verdict in his favor. Also, in jury trials, this may be the proper time for the defendant to request a directed verdict.

Finally, in the *summation*, each attorney has the opportunity to review the testimony and other evidence and make closing arguments.

Throughout the trial, the judge makes legal rulings on evidence and other matters. Generally, only after the summations does he instruct the jury concerning the law that is applicable to the case and the various verdicts that the jury may render.

The jury then retires and tries to resolve all the *fact* (not legal) issues. As stated before, in federal courts and in most states, it is only when all members agree that the jury renders a *verdict*. In a nonjury trial, the judge makes the decision.

In reaching a verdict, consideration of evidence is governed by the *burden of proof* (persuasion). This refers to:

- A party's obligation, when asserting fact, to *come forward* with evidence establishing this fact.

- The necessity for one party to *persuade* the trier of fact (the judge or jury) that his or her contentions are supported by a *preponderance of the evidence*—that his or her version of the facts is, at the very least, slightly more believable than the opposition's. However, other allegations demand a higher standard of persuasion than a preponderance of the evidence (e.g., in a criminal case, the prosecution must prove the defendant's guilt beyond a reasonable doubt). If both sides are equally as believable, then the defendant generally wins.

Even after the jury returns its verdict, the losing party may ask the judge to enter judgment for her, *notwithstanding* the verdict for the other side. This is a motion for judgment *non obstante veredicto*, or *judgment notwithstanding the verdict (J.N.O.V.)*. This is a rare and serious measure, and the judge's interpretation of the evidence at trial must meet very high standards.

Either attorney can request that the trial court grant a *new trial*, usually for one or more of the following reasons:

1. erroneous interpretations of the substantive law,
2. erroneous admission or exclusion of evidence,
3. insufficient evidence or a verdict contrary to law,
4. excessive or inadequate damages award,
5. jury misconduct or other irregularities, and
6. newly discovered evidence.

Often these grounds, particularly (1) through (4), serve as the basis for an appeal requesting reversal or a new trial.

APPEAL

Each party to a lawsuit generally is entitled to one *appeal*, held in an appellate court. Consideration of further appeals is discretionary. Appellate courts do not hold trials; there are no witnesses or juries. The court simply reviews the record of the trial and the briefs submitted by the parties' attorneys. A *brief* is a written argument supported by citations of prior court decisions, statutes, or other authorities.

The attorneys may present short oral arguments of key points. They must also answer searching questions from the judges. When the court reaches a decision, it issues a written opinion that can provide future guidance in similar cases.

Opinions, in whole or in part, may affirm the original judgment (the most frequent result), reverse the judgment, instruct the lower court to issue a new judgment, or remand (i.e., send back) the case to the lower court for further proceedings. Decisions other than to affirm are almost always based on a trial court's errors of law. Mere belief that the jury or judge did not draw the correct factual conclusions is insufficient grounds for reversal.

ALTERNATIVE DISPUTE RESOLUTION

The vast majority of disputes are settled out of court. Most do not even reach the point where a suit is filed. If a complaint is filed, settlement usually occurs before trial. Several factors may spur compromise, such as (1) anxiety about going to court, (2) the time and expense of lawsuits, (3) concern about bad publicity, (4) the need for a quicker resolution, (5) uncertainty as to the outcome, and (6) a desire to maintain good business or personal relationships with the other party.

Alternative Dispute Resolution (ADR) is becoming a very popular option in order to avoid going to court. The two most frequently used out-of-court dispute resolution methods are mediation and arbitration. Both involve neutral third parties who are often familiar with, or even experts in, the disputed subjects.

In *mediation*, a third party (mediator) helps the disputing parties settle the case. Mediators cannot impose a settlement on the parties, but often can effect compromise. Mediation is increasingly used in settling labor disputes and in resolving consumer complaints, and some laws mandate mediation.

However, mediation cannot accomplish very much when the parties are unwilling to compromise. In such cases, *arbitration* may be more useful. *Unlike a mediator, an arbitrator has the power to make a final, binding decision.*

A dispute usually goes to arbitration because a contract either requires it or permits a party to request it. In certain instances, a law may mandate arbitration. Parties seeking to avoid arbitration usually will not be able to because of enforcement by both state and federal legislation. Arbitration is often a shorter, cheaper, and less formal version of litigation.

Once arbitration is completed, grounds for appeal are extremely limited. Courts are to overturn an arbitration award only if (1) it went beyond the matters submitted to the arbitrator(s), or (2) the arbitrator(s) failed to follow statutory requirements, or (3) the award arose out of fraud or corruption. *Clearly, an arbitration award is even less susceptible to reversal than is a court judgment.* Because arbitration usually saves money and time, often promotes less hostile relations than litigation, and can, when necessary, submit complex issues to experts, arbitration agreements are routinely placed in many business contracts.

QUESTIONS

Identify each of the following:

affirmative defenses
alternative dispute resolution
answer
appeal
appeals court
arbitration
attorney/client privilege
attorneys
brief
burden of proof
case law
Civil Law
class action
common law
complaint
concurrent jurisdiction
conflict of laws
counterclaim
cross claims
cross-examination
defendant
depositions
direct examination
directed verdict

discovery
district courts
equity
"federal questions" jurisdiction
"full faith and credit" clause
grand jury
interrogatories
J.N.O.V.
jurisdiction
jurisprudence
legal positivism
legal realism
lex talionis
long-arm statutes
mediation
motion to dismiss
natural law
opening statement
peremptory challenge
personal jurisdiction
petit jury
petitioner
plaintiff

pleadings
pretrial conference
private law
procedural law
production of documents
public law
removal
requests for admissions
respondent
stare decisis
statutes
statutory law
subject-matter jurisdiction
substantive law
summary judgment
summation
summons
Supreme Court
third-party claims
Uniform Commercial Code
venue
voir dire

Answer these Review Questions:

1. How does common law differ from Civil Law?
2. Why should a definition of law emphasize enforcement?
3. Why is it difficult to make law "uniform" by enacting uniform statutes?
4. Is substantive law more important than procedural law?
5. What are the three main levels of courts in the federal judiciary?
6. State the difference between the functions of a trial court and an appeals court.
7. What is the key constitutional question concerning "long-arm" personal jurisdiction?
8. Distinguish jurisdiction from venue.
9. What state's substantive laws usually govern a tort case?
10. What are the four main methods of discovery?
11. Who usually has the burden of persuasion?
12. Name at least five reasons why disputes are compromised.

Apply Your Knowledge:

1. If, after you lose at trial, your lawyer forgets to file your appeal within the required period of time, is that the end of your substantive rights in that case?
2. Jenny Jones wants to sue Bob Breach for breach of contract. Jenny lives in New York, and Bob lives in California. The contract was signed at a business meeting in Los Angeles. Bob has not left California for years, nor has he ever done any business elsewhere.
   (a) In what court can Jenny sue Bob?
   (b) In what court does Jenny's right to sue depend on the amount in controversy?
   (c) Why is it unlikely that Jenny can sue anywhere else?
   (d) What happens if the contract states that it is to be governed by New York law? Discuss both personal jurisdiction and conflict of laws.
   (e) Assume that New York gives defendants a longer time to answer a complaint than does California. Which time period can Bob use to try to have the case thrown out as being too late?
3. Bob refuses to answer Jenny's complaint. Jenny obtains a judgment, including a damages award, by default. Bob moves to another state, one which generally does not enforce the type of contract that Jenny and Bob had. May Jenny use the new state's courts to collect her money (damages award) against that state's new resident, Bob?
4. Bob does not leave California. He answers the complaint and files a motion for summary judgment, with an affidavit that says he has never met anyone named Jenny Jones, that there was no contract, and that the signature on the contract is not his. Will Bob win? What is the standard for granting a summary judgment?

ANSWERS

Answers to Review Questions:

1. Common law emphasizes precedent (past court decisions), while Civil Law emphasizes the wording of statutes (the code). Civil Law attempts to set forth the entire law on a subject, but common law accepts that gaps in the law must be filled by judicial interpretations of the law.
2. If law is not enforced, it has little effect on society. When governments enact numerous laws but fail to enforce them, citizens lose their respect for the law, and social order is weakened.

3. Each of the 50 states is a sovereign state with the right to define and carry out its own laws, subject only to constitutional limits. Even when so-called uniform laws are passed by a legislature, judges may interpret those laws differently.

4. Yes, inasmuch as one needs to have substantive law in order to "have a case." But procedural law is very important, too. Incorrect or improper procedures can deprive a person of the ability to have his or her substantive rights vindicated. While procedural law usually is more flexible than substantive law, that flexibility is limited. One usually must follow the rules (procedure) in order to obtain justice (have one's substantive rights upheld).

5. District courts, circuit courts, the U.S. Supreme Court.

6. Trial courts hear witnesses and decide factual disputes. Both trial and appellate courts interpret the law, but usually it is only the appellate court whose interpretations may well be published and serve as precedent, or at least guidance, for other courts. Appeals courts review lower court decisions on the record established at trial (they do not hear new evidence), and their review is focused much more on the law than the facts. (Trial court *factual* findings are only overturned in extreme cases—where the higher court finds no basis whatsoever for a factual determination.)

7. Whether the defendant had enough "contacts" within the state so that requiring him or her to defend a lawsuit there does not violate due process of law.

8. Jurisdiction involves a court's power over the issues (subject-matter jurisdiction) and parties (personal jurisdiction) in a case. Once jurisdiction has been established, venue is merely a matter of deciding whether a particular locale (e.g., county) is a proper place to bring the lawsuit.

9. The state where the injury occurred.

10. Depositions, interrogatories, requests for admissions, and production of documents.

11. The plaintiff.

12. (1) anxiety about going to court; (2) the time and expense of lawsuits; (3) concern about bad publicity; (4) the need for a quicker resolution; (5) uncertainty as to the outcome; (6) a desire to maintain good business or personal relationships with the other party.

Answers to "Apply Your Knowledge":

1. Yes, in that you cannot force the court to hear your case simply because your authorized agent—your attorney—made a mistake. Cases must end at some point, and so the procedural law is rather inflexible about letting people open up a case after the time to appeal has already passed. (Moreover, how fair would it be to the winning party if it could never be certain that in fact the case was now fully resolved?)

   Note, though, that you might have another, new case: a case against your attorney for legal malpractice. (See Chapter 3 on negligence by professionals.)

2. (a) California state court. (b) Jenny can sue in the federal court in California if she contends that the damages from the alleged breach of contract were more than $50,000 (diversity jurisdiction). (c) It appears that Bob would not be subject to any other state's (e.g., New York's) long-arm jurisdiction; thus, no personal jurisdiction. (d) No probable effect on personal jurisdiction. Under basic conflict-of-laws principles, though, the California court must interpret the contract according to New York law, as that was the law intended by the contracting parties. (e) The time period for the state in which Bob is sued (California). Statutes of limitations are not substantive law, but are a matter of procedural law (so the court applies its own state law).

3. Yes. The prior judgment is entitled to "full faith and credit" in another state.
4. It is very unlikely that Bob will win his summary judgment motion. Such motions can be granted only if there is (1) no genuine issue about the material facts, and (2) entitlement to judgment on the law applicable to the material facts.

   Jenny's complaint probably sets forth enough facts to show that there is a material factual dispute between the parties about whether there was a contract and whether Bob was a party to it. But because pleadings themselves (e.g., complaints) are not evidence in the way that an affidavit, testimony, or other sworn statements are, Jenny should file her own affidavit countering Bob's contentions or showing why his points are irrelevant (e.g., she acted through an agent and therefore never met Bob). Another reason for Jenny to file is as a practical matter, to oppose all erroneous, potentially harmful claims by an opponent.

Chapter 2

Constitutional and Administrative Law

ESSENTIAL PRINCIPLES

Eight important sources of law in the United States are:
1. The U.S. Constitution.
2. Federal statutes and treaties.
3. Executive orders.
4. The 50 state constitutions.
5. State statutes.
6. Local ordinances.
7. The rules and rulings of federal, state, and local agencies.
8. Decisions by federal and state courts.

The first six sources are roughly in the order of importance. Agency and court actions, however, are found throughout the hierarchy, from interpretations of constitutions to statutes to regulations, and from federal to state to local laws.

The U.S. Constitution dictates the organization, powers, responsibilities, and limits of the federal government, as each state's constitution does at the state level. Under the Supremacy Clause (Article VI, Section 2, of the Constitution), the U.S. Constitution is the supreme law of the land. Thus, federal and state judges are bound by the U.S. Constitution; any law that violates the Constitution is void.

Statutes are laws enacted by the U.S. Congress or a state legislature. Ordinances are passed by municipal governments, such as a city or county, and concern local issues like zoning. Regulations are rules issued by an administrative agency governing procedure or conduct in a specific field.

GOVERNMENTAL POWERS

There are three branches of government: legislative, executive, and judicial. Each branch of government has a major area of responsibility:
- **Legislative branch.** Congress (the federal legislature) *makes* the laws. If both the Senate and the House of Representatives approve a bill, the bill is then sent to the President. If he signs it, the bill becomes law; if he vetoes it, the bill may still become law if it receives a two-thirds vote of both houses.
- **Executive branch.** The President (chief executive) *enforces* the laws. The President has broad powers in both domestic and foreign affairs. In foreign relations, the President may enter into agreements with other nations without Congressional approval and make treaties with the approval of only two-thirds of the Senate. As commander-in-chief, the President may oversee military affairs.

13

- **Judicial branch.** The courts (judiciary) *pass on the constitutionality* of laws enacted by the federal and state legislatures. The judiciary also *interprets* the law, using two guidelines:
  1. the "plain meaning rule," which is the customary meaning of the words in a law; and
  2. the legislative history of a bill, which is the purpose for which it was created.

Courts "make law" in the sense that, under the principle of *stare decisis*, judicial decisions may serve as precedent when similar cases arise.

There is a system of *checks and balances* among the three branches. Overlapping powers make it possible for each branch to restrain the other two. The President can veto bills passed by Congress and is responsible for selecting federal judges. Congress may override the President's veto with a two-thirds vote, and may refuse to confirm the President's nominees for federal judgeships and other high-level positions. Congress may also conduct hearings and demand testimony from executive branch officials as well as other persons outside of the government. The judiciary may limit or void laws by the President or Congress. In turn, Congress may limit the scope of judicial review or increase the number of federal judges.

The discussion of governmental powers applies also in the state context. Each state government has three branches, with powers and checks and balances similar to those found at the federal level.

Congress has only those legislative powers that are granted to it by the U.S. Constitution. These powers may be granted either expressly *(enumerated powers)* or implicitly. The Constitution leaves other powers, known as *reserved powers*, to the states. In essence, if the Constitution does not proclaim that it is a federal power, and if Congress has not otherwise tried to control that area of the law, then a subject tends to be left to the states. Examples include divorce law and the common law of torts and contracts.

Sometimes the absence of Congressional action permits states to act although Congress could *preempt* (bar) state action. Courts ultimately determine the validity of state laws possibly impinging upon federal powers. To do this, the court first must decide:

- whether the state law conflicts with a federal law, and
- whether Congress intended to preempt legislation in that area. If the answer to either question is "yes," the state law is void.

Article 1, Section 8, of the U.S. Constitution expressly grants a number of legislative powers. Section 8 also states that Congress may create laws "necessary and proper" for carrying out any of the government's enumerated powers under the Constitution. Implied powers under this *necessary and proper clause* include laws that do not violate the Constitution, as long as they serve to advance a legislative goal within the scope of the Constitution.

Some of the enumerated powers in Section 8 include:

- **Power to regulate interstate commerce**—In almost all cases, courts have not questioned Congressional motives and have upheld this legislation under the *affectation doctrine*: As long as the activity sought to be regulated affects interstate commerce, it is within Congressional authority to do so.

  Regulation of commerce tends to be a power shared by the federal and state governments. As long as the state interest in a particular subject outweighs any burdens imposed on interstate commerce, state regulation that is (1) about a local concern, (2) does not discriminate against out-of-state business, and (3) is the least burdensome method for achieving state goals will usually be allowed. (However, if it chooses to do so, Congress almost always can intervene and preempt state action whenever the state law has some effect on interstate commerce.)

- **Power to tax**—Courts generally uphold any taxing measure by Congress so long as the measure is revenue-producing, not simply a punishment.
- **Power to spend for the general welfare**—In implementing its spending power, Congress may require state and local governments to meet certain conditions. This may be accomplished under a "carrot and stick" approach: While a state or local entity's failure to comply may be punished ("the stick"), the state and local governments that meet the necessary conditions imposed by Congress are eligible for needed revenue ("the carrot").

CIVIL LIBERTIES

Two fundamental rights in the U.S. Constitution are found in the Fourteenth Amendment: due process and equal protection.

The *due process* provision protects persons from being "deprived of life, liberty, or property, without due process of law" and states the steps that must be followed to ensure a "fundamentally fair" process (e.g., notice, a hearing, an unbiased factfinder, the opportunity to present evidence and to cross-examine witnesses, and a right of appeal). Due process may require not only *procedural* protections, but also, occasionally, fundamental *substantive* rights.

Under the *equal protection* provision, no person may be denied "equal protection under the laws." Equal protection does not prohibit all differences in the treatment of persons, but requires that the differences be *reasonable*. For most cases involving regulation of business and for other ordinary cases, *equal protection* just requires that differential treatment be reasonable and related to a permissible, governmental purpose (the "rational basis" test). There is a strict scrutiny test when cases involve "suspect" classifications (such as racial, religious, or nationality minorities) or basic rights (voting, marriage, privacy, court access, interstate travel). Equal protection is violated unless the differential treatment is as narrow as possible and is necessary to achieve a compelling governmental interest.

Both corporations and individuals are covered under the due process and equal protection clauses. The Fourteenth Amendment not only restricts state governmental acts that infringe upon those rights, but also expressly grants Congress the power to enforce its provisions by passing any legislation necessary. Furthermore, the Fifth Amendment's due process provision restricts the federal government from taking acts that might violate due process or equal protection.

Courts have had a larger role than Congress in enforcing the Fourteenth Amendment. U.S. Supreme Court decisions have served to incorporate almost all of the fundamental rights in the Bill of Rights (U.S. Constitution, First through Tenth Amendments) into the due process clause of the Fourteenth Amendment. These "incorporated" Bill of Rights provisions, which were always available to individuals challenging the federal government, are thus available against state governments via the Fourteenth Amendment.

Some other fundamental rights include freedom of expression (even advertising receives some First Amendment protection), compensation under eminent domain (Fifth Amendment), protection from laws impairing contract obligations, and freedom from (1) *ex post facto* laws (laws making past actions criminal that were not defined as criminal when they occurred), and (2) *bills of attainder* (laws intended to single out an individual and/or punish him without benefit of a trial).

ADMINISTRATIVE AGENCIES

Since our society is so complex and is always changing, it is virtually impossible for legislatures and courts to handle every problem that arises. Therefore, legislatures, through *enabling acts,* have established administrative agencies, where the government—federal, state, or local—delegates some of its authority to these agencies. Most enabling acts establish standards for an agency to follow so as to administer a particular area of the law. The agency then develops the necessary expertise in that particular field so as to render sound decisions in individual cases.

Most important federal agencies have a combination of legislative, judicial, and executive powers. Some agencies are directly under the supervision of one of the three branches of government, usually the executive branch. However, there are also a large number of independent agencies that are free from outside control. Examples at the national level include the Federal Communications Commission, Federal Reserve Board, Federal Trade Commission, Interstate Commerce Commission, National Labor Relations Board, and Securities and Exchange Commission.

The actions of an administrative agency must conform with:
- constitutional law,
- relevant statutes governing administrative procedure (e.g., the federal Administrative Procedure Act),
- objectives in the agency's own enabling act, and
- rules of the agency itself.

Agencies perform all or some of seven functions: (1) advising, (2) reviewing, (3) supervising, (4) rule-making, (5) investigating, (6) prosecuting, and (7) adjudicating. When performing its rule-making function, the administrative agency usually must give notice of a proposed rule, so that affected parties have the opportunity to ask questions or make comments before the rule is passed.

In much the same way that courts have the power to review legislative enactments, courts also have the power to review rules made by administrative agencies. However, in the area(s) of law in which an agency has expertise, the court will rarely overturn the agency's decisions unless they are clearly erroneous, without any supporting evidence, biased against or in favor of a party, or beyond the agency's powers.

ADMINISTRATIVE PROCEDURE

Agencies' exercise of judicial functions must comport with due process under the Fifth and Fourteenth Amendments. This requires that notice be given and a hearing held before the agency whenever a person is to be deprived of life, liberty, or property. Examples of those administrative deprivations that require a hearing include revocation of parole; revocation or suspension of a motor vehicle license or of a professional or business operating license; cessation or reduction of welfare, unemployment, or social security benefits; termination of parental custodial rights; and—usually—the firing of a public employee.

The adoption of rules, as well as the holding of hearings, is governed by federal and state Administrative Procedure Acts. The rules of evidence are relaxed under these acts, and the hearing officer may take a more active, inquisitive role than traditional judges. However, basic fairness is still of the utmost importance. Each party has a right to counsel, can state her case, and is permitted to cross-examine opposing witnesses. In addition, though the agency may have discretion in deciding on the format of hearings, it must, like a court, render decisions based solely on the evidence presented. In cases involving administrative law, there is no right to trial by jury. However, a dissatisfied party may appeal for judicial review of the case based on the hearing record.

Many agencies have *administrative law judges* who are separate from the investigatory or prosecutory personnel. Some agencies may provide for appeals within the agency itself, at an intermediate review stage, and an appeal to the board or commission at the top of the agency. Some states have created independent offices of administrative hearings in order to separate agencies' judicial functions from the executive, enforcement functions. This is seen as a way to better assure the citizen of an unbiased due process hearing.

The *exhaustion of remedies doctrine* states that an appellant must use all available agency procedures before complaining to a court of law. However, there are some areas of the law where, in rare circumstances, the exhaustion of remedies doctrine may be discarded: (1) the case involves fundamental constitutional guarantees, such as the right to free speech; (2) the agency is deadlocked; (3) irreparable harm is likely to occur without court relief; or (4) the enabling act or other statutes and rules do not require first an appeal within the agency.

QUESTIONS

Identify each of the following:

administrative agency	equal protection	ordinance
affectation doctrine	executive branch	preempt
checks and balances	exhaustion of remedies	reserved powers
constitution	judicial branch	rule
due process	legislative branch	*stare decisis*
enabling act	"necessary and	statute
enumerated powers	proper" clause	

Answer these Review Questions:

1. Name the three branches of government.
2. For each of the three branches of the federal government, name checks that it has on the powers of the other branches.
3. What constitutional provision gives Congress the authority to create laws for carrying out the government's enumerated and implied powers?
4. Name three Congressional powers specifically enumerated in the U.S. Constitution.
5. Name two fundamental rights set forth in the Fourteenth Amendment to the U.S. Constitution.
6. Name the seven general functions that may be performed by an administrative agency.
7. What is an ordinance?
8. Name three independent federal administrative agencies.

9. What doctrine states that an appellant must use all available agency procedures before turning to a court of law?

Apply Your Knowledge:

1. Suppose that a dissatisfied customer brings his complaint against XYZ, Inc., to the state legislature, which passes a law making illegal XYZ's past sales arrangement with the customer. In addition, with no trial scheduled, XYZ's sales license is to be suspended for three months. What should XYZ do?

2. Congress has enacted the Occupational Safety and Health Act (OSHA) to deal with most occupational hazards and unsanitary conditions. Fearing the dangers of secondhand smoke to employees of local businesses, Safetown's board of commissioners wants to enact some legislation to eliminate smoking at work. What legislation may the commissioners enact?

3. In BadState, a state statute prohibits businesses from contributing to charities and imposes a fine on those that do. A fine was imposed on Goody2shoes, Inc., for allegedly contributing to a charity, but when Goody2shoes requested a hearing date, it was denied. On what grounds should the law be challenged?

4. A statute placed a substantial tax on employers who knowingly hired underage children. Is this tax constitutional?

5. Scott Sneaky wants the state legislature to pass a law that would benefit his business. A friend has told him to go to a state administrative agency to obtain a ruling that would serve essentially the same purpose, and (Scott hopes) would avoid the publicity that would probably kill the chance for a new law in his favor. Assuming there are no constitutional problems with Scott's plan, will it succeed?

6. At an administrative hearing, the administrative law judge (ALJ) based her decision on inadmissible evidence, unauthenticated records, and the ALJ's own knowledge of customs in the industry. She also talked about the case while on the telephone with one of the parties. The ALJ allowed testimony from all witnesses but permitted cross-examination of only the witnesses who were also parties. In announcing her opinion, the ALJ failed to state the reasons for her decision. What problems are there with the ALJ's conduct?

ANSWERS

Answers to Review Questions:

1. (1) the legislative branch; (2) the judicial branch; (3) the executive branch.
2. *Executive*: veto bills; select federal judges.
   Legislative: override President's veto; refuse to confirm President's nominees; limit the scope of judicial review; increase the number of federal judges.
   Judiciary: limit or void laws.
3. The "necessary and proper" clause of Article I, Section 8.
4. The power to regulate interstate commerce; the power to tax; the power to spend for the general welfare.
5. Due process and equal protection.
6. (1) advising; (2) reviewing; (3) supervising; (4) rule-making; (5) investigating; (6) prosecuting; (7) adjudicating.
7. An ordinance is a law passed by a local governmental body below the state level and dealing with a local concern.
8. Three of these: The Federal Communications Commission, Federal Reserve Board, Federal Trade Commission, Interstate Commerce Commission, National Labor Relations Board, and Securities and Exchange Commission.
9. The exhaustion of remedies doctrine.

Answers to "Apply Your Knowledge":

1. XYZ should challenge the law in the courts. The law appears to be *ex post facto* and a bill of attainder, both of which are prohibited by the U.S. Constitution.

2. Perhaps none. The commissioners must follow the federal law. If the subject of office smoking has been preempted (by OSHA), no state or local government can pass laws in this area.

3. Violation of equal protection: The law treats businesses, including individuals and corporations, differently from other persons, and this different treatment is neither reasonable nor related to a permissible, governmental purpose. Violation of due process: The Fourteenth Amendment's due process clause protects persons from being "deprived of life, liberty, or property, without due process of law" and states the steps that must be followed to ensure a "fundamentally fair" process. Here, Goody2shoes was denied a hearing, and therefore its due process rights were violated.

4. No. A valid tax must be designed to raise money, not to punish. This is an invalid penalty because it applied only to employers who hired under-age children. A valid tax would have applied to all employers of children rather than just intentional wrongdoers whom Congress wished to punish.

5. It is difficult to say. The agency rule-making process may be less publicized, and thus Scott may be able to get the new rule passed. However, there are two factors that could prevent Scott from succeeding: (1) this area of the law may not yet be delegated to an agency in the enabling act, and therefore may still be handled by the legislature; and (2) the administrative agency may have to give notice of the proposed rule, so that affected parties get the opportunity to ask questions or make comments before the rule is passed. Thus, publicity or opposition is in fact possible.

6. The improper activities were (1) talking about the case with one party (on the telephone) while the other party was not present, (2) not allowing cross-examination of all witnesses, and (3) failing to state her findings of fact or some other reason for her decision. A more relaxed approach than in court cases—thus letting in otherwise inadmissible evidence, unauthenticated records, and the ALJ's own expertise—is often found at the administrative level.

Chapter 3

Crimes and Torts

NATURE OF CRIMES

A *crime* is a public wrong, committed with intent or by negligence, for which the law provides punishment or recompense to society. American criminal law is primarily codified law, based on statutes and regulations rather than merely on past judicial decisions. The same act or omission may be a crime under both federal law and state law. For instance, murder, a state crime, may also be a federal crime (e.g., a violation of the victim's civil rights) and thus be prosecuted in separate criminal cases in each of the two court systems.

Classification of Crimes

The three classes of common law crimes are *treason, felonies, and misdemeanors.*

Treason is a violation of allegiance toward one's country or sovereign, especially the betrayal of one's own country by waging war against it or by consciously and purposely acting to aid its enemies. Treason against the United States, the only crime defined in the U.S. Constitution, is a comparatively rare charge.

The distinction between a felony and a misdemeanor is usually found within each state's criminal code. Felonies are more serious crimes, punishable by imprisonment. Murder (which can carry the death penalty in most states), arson, rape, armed robbery, and tax evasion are felonies. Misdemeanors are generally punishable only by fines or, at most, a brief stay in the local jail. Simple assault, disorderly conduct, and trespass are usually classified as misdemeanors. Three other ways of categorizing crimes are these:

- **White-collar:** nonviolent crimes, perpetrated by people in positions of trust, usually against businesses or governments.
  Examples: embezzlement, mail fraud, bribery, forgery, antitrust law violations, and fraud concerning consumers, credit cards, securities, insurance, bankruptcy, and bank loans.
- **Organized:** crime by groups in the "business" of crime, such as the Mafia.
- **Victimless:** crimes that are sometimes considered to have no specific victims (just society as a whole).
  Examples: prostitution, gambling.

Criminal Intent and Causation

In most cases, a crime must include both a criminal act *(actus reus)* and a criminal intent *(mens rea).*

Example: No *Actus Reus*

Dave Deviant thinks about assaulting Veronica Victim, but does nothing about it. No crime, not even attempted assault.

Example: No *Mens Rea*

Ida Innocent, through no intent, negligence, or other fault of her own, collides with Veronica Victim and kills her. No crime.

Usually, a person is presumed to intend the natural consequences of what he or she knowingly does. Moreover, in a felonious action, the doer may be deemed responsible for even unwanted results.

Example: Unintended Harm

Dennis Devil, maliciously attempting to throw a brick through Ida Innocent's window, instead hits Ida. Dennis is guilty of criminal assault and battery, although he intended a lesser, property crime.

Example: Unintended Victim

Brenda Bad puts poison in Ivan Innocent's coffee. However, Todd Toughluck drinks the coffee instead and is injured. Brenda is guilty of criminal assault and battery on Todd, although she meant *him* no harm. Her intent to injure Ivan is transferable.

Only certain *specific-intent* crimes (e.g., burglary and arson) require proof of intent to commit that particular crime.

Note that the law distinguishes between *intent* and *motive*. Intent involves an express or implied desire to perform a particular act; it is a state of mind preceding or accompanying the act. Motive is the overall goal that prompts a person's actions, and good or bad motives may be taken into account in assessing punishment.

CRIMINAL PROCEDURE

Pretrial Stages

A criminal case passes through several phases before trial. First, the crime is reported and investigated. Then, if there is *probable cause*, that is, reasonable grounds—something more than mere suspicion—to believe that a particular person committed the crime, that person can be arrested. A warrant for arrest is necessary unless the pressure of time requires immediate action (e.g., before the suspect flees).

Finally, criminal charges must be lodged against the defendant. Depending on the state, the charges, usually called either an *indictment* (by a grand jury) or an *information* (by a magistrate or police officer), must be based on probable cause, preponderance of evidence, or prosecutor's evidence that supports a belief in the defendant's guilt.

Burden of Proof

A civil plaintiff merely needs a preponderance of the evidence; the judge or jury need only find that the evidence favors the plaintiff over the defendant.

A successful criminal prosecution requires proof of guilt beyond a reasonable doubt.

Absolute proof is not mandatory; the prosecution need not eliminate *all* doubts—merely all *reasonable* doubts.

A verdict of "not guilty" does not necessarily mean that the judge or jury believes the defendant to be innocent. It is simply a finding that there was insufficient evidence to prove guilt beyond a reasonable doubt.

Evidence

The law of evidence is the study of the legal regulation of proof and persuasion at trial, the means by which alleged matters of fact are established or disproved. In a trial, the evidence presented to the court and the jury is the sole means by which each party presents his or her case. Rules of evidence are designed to exclude irrelevant, unreliable, or unfairly prejudicial matters, especially in jury cases.

The judge's or jury's verdict is to be based solely on the evidence properly brought out at trial. Otherwise proper, highly relevant evidence may be excluded because it was obtained in violation of a defendant's constitutional rights.

CRIMINAL DEFENSES

Good *defenses* arise when one or more elements of a specific crime are absent (the defined terms are not met) or the prosecutor has fallen short of the level of proof required in a criminal case. The following are some general defenses to crimes:

Duress may excuse the commission of a crime while under an immediate and inescapable threat of serious bodily harm or death. The threatened harm must be more serious than the harm to be caused by the crime.

Entrapment is a criminal defense if the criminal act was induced by the government, with criminal intent originating from the police. If, however, the accused was predisposed to commit the crime, then entrapment is not a defense.

Immunity from prosecution is sometimes extended to actual or potential criminal defendants, usually to induce testimony and information from them. So long as the person receiving immunity cannot be prosecuted for her statements, that person cannot assert the Fifth Amendment privilege against self-incrimination.

Infancy bars criminal liability for children who are under a certain age or who do not understand that a particular act is wrong.

Insanity is a defense if the alleged crime occurred while the defendant lacked the mental capacity to have a *criminal* intent. A person is not criminally accountable for his acts if he is so diseased or defective in mind when committing an act as to be incapable of (1) understanding the nature of the act or (2) distinguishing right from wrong with respect to the act.

Intoxication (use of alcohol or other drugs) is a complete criminal defense only when *involuntary*; a person, by force, by mistake, or by some situation beyond his control, ingests or injects an intoxicating substance.

Mistake of fact is ignorance of an important fact.

Example: Mistake of Fact

If Nora Nearsighted walks off with Tammy True's child (who bears some resemblance to Nora's own tot), and Nora returns the child as soon as she discovers her mistake, Nora is not guilty of kidnapping.

Mistake of law is the criminal defense that a person honestly did not know that she was breaking the law and (1) the law wasn't published or otherwise made public, or (2) the person relied on an erroneous but official statement of the law; otherwise, ignorance of the law is no excuse.

Self-defense (or defense of others) permits people to use the degree of non-deadly force that seems necessary to protect themselves (or others) from criminal force. Deadly force (likely to result in death or serious injury) is also permitted if (1) an attacker is using unlawful force, (2) the victim did not initiate or provoke the attack, and (3) the victim reasonably believes that she will otherwise suffer death or serious bodily injury. Some jurisdictions allow deadly force whenever it appears necessary to prevent a felony within a home.

COMPARISON TO TORTS

A *tort* is a private wrong, a trespass against a person or his property, for which damages award or other judicial remedy may be sought. Most torts arise from either an intentional, wrongful action or from a negligent action. Many torts are also crimes, and most crimes involve tortious acts. Thus a single action may result in two trials: a criminal trial and a tort (civil) trial.

Comparison of Crimes and Torts

CRIME	TORT
1. A public wrong against society	1. A private wrong against individuals or businesses
2. "Plaintiff" (prosecutor) is the state (offended person is usually a witness)	2. Plaintiff is an individual or a business
3. Mostly statutory law	3. Mostly common law
4. Prosecutor's burden of proof: guilty beyond a reasonable doubt	4. Plaintiff's burden of proof: preponderance of evidence
5. Consent rarely a defense	5. Consent usually a defense
6. No damages are necessary	6. Damages must be shown
7. Basis for criminal guilt: an intentional act, and sometimes gross negligence or recklessness	7. Basis for tort liability: an intentional act, negligence, or strict liability

INTENTIONAL TORTS

To constitute an *intentional tort,* the defendant's act must be expressly or implicitly intended; the resulting harm need not be intended, but must have been reasonably foreseeable. The wrongful acts generally involve some sort of interference with the plaintiff's personal well-being or his property interests.

Interference with the Person

Assault: arousing in another individual the fear of an immediate harmful or offensive contact with his or her body. Words alone are insufficient; they must be accompanied by some act.
Examples: threats while raising fists, reaching toward what seems to be a concealed weapon.

Battery: unjustified contact with someone else's body or anything connected to it (purse, chair, cane, etc.). The contact may be direct (e.g., a slap) or due to a force put into motion by the defendant (e.g., shooting a bullet that strikes the plaintiff). Example: a masseuse suddenly shaves a customer's head.

False arrest: detention of the plaintiff, without his or her permission, under the falsely asserted authority of the defendant. No physical barrier, force, or threat of force is necessary.
Example: an insurance investigator posing as a police officer searches a person and detains him for questioning.

False imprisonment: wrongful use of force, physical barriers, or threats of force to restrain the plaintiff's freedom of movement.
Example: a merchant forcibly detains a suspected shoplifter without reasonable cause for suspicion.

Intentional infliction of mental (emotional) distress: disturbance of the plaintiff's peace of mind by the defendant's outrageous conduct. Although damages are not limited to bodily injury, usually some physical harm must be shown.
Examples: extreme actions by bill collectors, extensive cursing, and threats of future violence.

Invasion of privacy: interference with a person's right to be left alone. The right to solitude can be invaded in four different ways: (1) public disclosure of private facts; (2) publication of information placing a person in a false light; (3) intrusion upon a person's private life; or (4) unauthorized appropriation of name or likeness (e.g., picture) for commercial purposes. The first three must be disclosures or intrusions highly offensive to a reasonable person. Truth is no defense.
Examples: publishing information obtained from the psychiatric files of a business competitor; making, and selling for profit, baseball cards without the permission of the ballplayers pictured.

Interference with Business Relations

Abusive discharge: modification of the common law doctrine that "at will" employees (ones without a set term of employment) may be terminated for any reason.
Example: a firing that stems from the worker's notifying authorities about criminal activities being carried on in the workplace.

Disparagement: false injurious statements about a product or a competitor's reputation.
Example: stating falsely to customers that a competitor's products contain carcinogens.

Interference with contract: an intentional tort with three requirements: (1) valid contract exists, (2) a third party knows about the contract, and (3) the third party intentionally and unjustifiably causes one of the contracting parties to breach the contract, or otherwise unjustifiably prevents performance of the contract.

Interference with prospective economic advantage: a tort with roughly the same three requirements as interference with contract.
Example: Gary Greedy has his employees stand outside a competitor's store to divert customers to Greedy's shop.

Unfair competition: this tort concerns trying to "pass off" goods or services upon the public as if they were the goods or services of another, more reputable business or product.
Examples: deceitful advertising injures a competitor; bribery of a competitor's employees.

Interference with Property

Conversion: unauthorized, unjustified exercise of control over another's personal property. There are two requirements: defendant must (1) appropriate the property to his own use, and (2) indefinitely withhold its possession from the plaintiff or destroy it.
Examples: acts of arson, robbery, or embezzlement; taking someone else's umbrella, coat, or other personal property and keeping it after discovering that fact.

Nuisance: an act that unlawfully interferes with a person's possession of or ability to use his or her property. *Private nuisance*—the defendant's watering his lawn so much that the plaintiff's land is flooded. *Public nuisance*—interfering with the general right to health, safety, peace, comfort, or morals, and including, for example, smoking in nonsmoking areas.

Trespass to personal property: unjustified interference with the plaintiff's possessory interest (e.g., use) in personal property.
Example: without permission, a person takes someone else's lawn mower, cuts her own lawn with it, and then returns the machine.

Trespass to real property: unauthorized entry onto the plaintiff's land, either by a person or by something the person caused to enter the land.
Examples: throwing rocks or trash onto another's land.

Other Intentional Torts

Abuse of process: the use of a court process for a purpose for which it is not intended. (Such a process could be use of an injunction.)

Defamation: a false communication, oral (slander), written, or otherwise recorded (libel), by the defendant to a third person that harms the plaintiff's reputation.
Example: an employee tells her boss that another employee, whom she names, is a bigot, has repeatedly cheated on his income tax returns, and takes three-hour lunches; the employee telling these tales knows or should know that they are false.

Fraud (deceit, misrepresentation): a misstatement or omission of a material fact that the defendant either knows to be false or recklessly makes while knowing that the information is incomplete. "Material" means any representation that would influence any reasonable person in the plaintiff's situation. Matters of opinion and circumstances in which a person is "puffing," such as in attempting to make a sale, are not actionable in court. (For more on fraud, see Chapter 4.)

Infringement of intellectual property rights (copyrights, patents, trademarks): See Chapter 12.

Malicious prosecution: the instigation of criminal proceedings against someone for an improper purpose and without probable cause, with those proceedings terminating decisively in the criminal defendant's favor (e.g., by acquittal or dismissal for lack of evidence).

Negligent misrepresentation: incorrect statements of opinion or fact made by persons who breached a duty to exercise reasonable care in ascertaining the truth: such persons may include accountants, lawyers, title examiners, or others supplying the plaintiff with business guidance.

NEGLIGENCE

In a tort case arising out of negligence, the plaintiff must show four things: (1) there was a duty imposed on the defendant in favor of the plaintiff, (2) the defendant breached (violated) that duty, (3) the breach was the actual as well as proximate (natural and foreseeable) cause of the harm, and (4) the plaintiff suffered damages.

<u>Example: Tort of Negligence</u>

Suppose that a building collapses, and X thus wants to sue architect Y for negligence. To win, X must prove that (1) Y designed or was responsible for the design of the building; (2) Y had a duty to design, or review the design, in accordance with reasonable standards of her profession; (3) this duty, owed to present and future passersby, people in the building, and persons with property in or near the building, covered X; (4) the duty was breached by Y; (5) if Y had exercised due care, the building would not have collapsed; and (6) the collapse damaged X or his property.

The defendant's duty is to act reasonably, as would an ordinary, reasonable person in those same circumstances. The harm that the defendant's alleged negligence caused need not be likely when the defendant breached his or her duty of care, but it must at least be foreseeable. If the harm was so remote in time or place or chain of events that it could not be foreseen, then there is no *proximate cause*, and thus a claim for negligence fails.

DEFENSES TO TORTS

The following are some general defenses to torts:

Act of God is a defense to negligence when natural forces such as lightning, earthquakes, or hurricanes are the proximate cause of injury. However, when a person negligently created a situation whereby a foreseeable act of God could cause damage, no defense is available to foreseeable damages.

Assumption of risk is a defense to negligence. It applies when the plaintiff knowingly and voluntarily exposed himself or herself to the danger that caused the injury.

Comparative negligence means that liability for injuries resulting from negligent acts is shared by all persons who were negligent, including the injured party, on a basis proportionate to each person's carelessness. For example, if the plaintiff's damages are $100,000 and a jury finds that she was 30 percent at fault, while it assesses the defendant with 70 percent of the blame, then the plaintiff recovers $70,000. (Under the doctrine of contributory negligence, the plaintiff gets nothing if he was at all negligent, no matter how much more the defendant was negligent.)

Consent is a defense to all torts and few crimes. When the criminal law forbids an act against the victim's will, consent makes the act no crime at all. If Ms. Able is a mentally competent adult who consented to sexual intercourse with Mr. Baker, no crime of forcible rape has occurred.

Contributory negligence means that the plaintiff was negligent and that negligence contributed to her injuries. The defendant is freed from liability even if the defendant's negligence was much greater than the plaintiff's.

Duress means that an immediate threat of serious harm or death deprived the defendant of the intent needed to commit an intentional tort. Thus, duress is a good defense to intentional torts.

Immunity is a tort defense that may limit or outright bar recovery against governments, public officers, or other defendants specifically protected by statutes (e.g., charities).

Infancy and *insanity* and *intoxication* may be criminal defenses for children, the mentally ill, and intoxicated persons, but these defenses rarely protect people from tort liability. The law is more concerned with compensating the injured than with determining moral guilt. In negligence cases a child's standard of care (duty) is based on her intelligence and experience rather than the usual objective standard (the ordinary, reasonable person).

Privilege is an immunity existing under law and sometimes constituting a defense in, for example, cases involving interference with contract, interference with prospective economic advantage, or defamation. Free competition, for instance, may protect certain business interferences, such as labor strikes. Also, attorneys' and judges' statements at trial and legislators' comments in a legislative debate are protected from claims of defamation.

Self-defense in tort cases is judged by the "reasonable man" standard: If the defendant reasonably believes himself to be in danger and responds reasonably, there is a defense. The defense may also work concerning reasonable actions to protect others.

Statutes of limitations are statutorily defined periods of time within which a legal action must be brought. A lawsuit brought after that time is barred by the statute of limitations; the defendant wins.

Superseding (intervening) causes break the causal connection in torts between the defendant's act and the plaintiff's damages. As a general rule, they offer a defense based on lack of either an actual cause (causation in fact) or a proximate cause.

Example: Superseding (Intervening) Cause

Annie Absentminded leaves her grocery cart in a crowded, badly lit parking lot. Tom Thief places it in the back of his car and drives off. A half-mile later, the cart falls out and strikes Peter Pedestrian. Annie's negligence as to the cart would not render her liable to Peter; Tom's actions are a superseding cause of the accident.

STRICT LIABILITY

Under the doctrine of *strict liability*, the defendant is liable for the plaintiff's injuries despite the absence of negligence or intentional, wrongful acts. If the defendant was engaged in abnormally dangerous activities (e.g., blasting with dynamite, crop dusting, keeping wild animals), courts and legislatures have decided that she should bear the cost of any harm done. As in other areas of liability without fault (e.g., product liability, workers' compensation), the strict liability of some manufacturers is based on the belief that these defendants are in a better position to shoulder the costs of injury than are potential plaintiffs.

PRODUCT LIABILITY

The tort liability of a seller of goods typically arises from negligence or strict liability. (Intentional harmful action could form the basis for liability, but is an extremely rare factor in product liability cases.)

Negligence is the failure to follow some generally accepted standard of care. Thus, if manufactured goods explode, if cosmetics cause injury to the face or eyes, if plaintiff becomes ill upon consuming defendant's canned soup, a negligence case must demonstrate, first, some standard of care generally applicable in the manufacture of such goods, and, second, failure by the defendant to rise to the level of such standard of care.

Under the principle known as *res ipsa loquitur* ("the thing speaks for itself"), evidence of negligence is presumed if (1) the product was under the exclusive control of defendant at the time of its manufacture, and (2) injuries such as those suffered by plaintiff do not ordinarily happen in the absence of negligence. Thus, in the exploding bottle case (a soft drink bottle exploding as it is being placed in a grocery cart), *res ipsa loquitur* may force the manufacturer to introduce evidence showing that it was *not negligent* when making and bottling the drink.

As for strict liability concerning harm caused by products, the general elements of a case are set forth in the Second Restatement of Torts § 402A (used by most courts): (1) the product was sold in a defective condition; (2) as such, it was unreasonably dangerous; (3) the seller is in the business of selling such a product; (4) the product reached the user without substantial change; and (5) the defect caused harm to the plaintiff. A *defect* simply means that the goods were not in the condition that an ordinary consumer might reasonably expect. The defect may be in the product's design or its labeling (e.g., absence of adequate warnings) as well as its manufacture.

QUESTIONS

Identify each of the following:

abuse of process	indictment	negligence
abusive discharge	infancy	negligent
act of God	information	misrepresentation
actus reus	infringement of	organized crime
assault	intellectual property	privilege
assumption of risk	insanity	probable cause
battery	intent	product liability
burden of proof	intentional infliction of	*res ipsa loquitur*
comparative negligence	mental distress	self-defense
consent	intentional tort	statutes of limitations
contributory negligence	interference with	strict liability
conversion	contract	superseding causes
crime	interference with	tort
defamation	prospective	treason
disparagement	economic advantage	trespass
duress	intoxication	unfair competition
entrapment	invasion of privacy	victimless crime
evidence	malicious prosecution	white-collar crime
false arrest	*mens rea*	
false imprisonment	misdemeanors	
felonies	mistake of fact	
fraud	mistake of law	
immunity	motive	

Answer these Review Questions:

1. What is the level of evidence necessary at each of the four stages of criminal procedure: investigation, arrest, lodging of charges, and trial?
2. What are the rules of evidence intended to do?
3. What effect may U.S. Constitutional rights have on the use of evidence at trial?

4. Name two methods by which crimes can be classified.
5. Name several white-collar crimes.
6. How is intent transferable?
7. Distinguish intent from motive.
8. Compare the law of crimes and torts concerning burdens of proof, damages, consent, sources of law, and types of acts required for guilt or liability.
9. List (a) six intentional torts involving interference with the person, (b) five concerning interference with business relations, and (c) four involving interference with property.
10. What are the four basic elements of the tort of negligence?
11. What are four defenses to negligence that are not defenses to intentional torts or crimes?

Apply Your Knowledge:

1. You believe that Sid Sick has been molesting your eight-year-old child. However, a jury has acquitted Sid of all criminal charges. (a) Can you sue Sid? (b) How would a civil suit be different from the criminal case?
2. One of your employees may have embezzled thousands of dollars from your company. What may you do to stop her, to investigate her, to convict her?
3. Sol Silly was your embezzling worker. Alas, he may not be "quite right in the head."
   (a) In a criminal prosecution, what defense may his attorney raise?
   (b) What if Sol's problems stemmed from alcoholism?
   (c) What if Sol claims that he stole out of love for a woman that he thought was Mother Teresa, a woman who took most of his money and encouraged him to steal more?
   (d) If you were a prosecutor, would you give Sol immunity to testify against "Teresa"?
   (e) What torts have been committed?
4. How would the finding of "guilty, but insane" (instead of "not guilty by reason of insanity") change the criminal law?
5. Late at night, Lucy Luscious stops Sam Susceptible on a sidewalk in a bad section of town where many pornographic movies and similar entertainment are available. Hitching up her tight skirt a notch as she sits on a bench, Lucy asks for the time. Sam gives it. Lucy asks Sam to light her cigarette. He does. Lucy asks Sam to sit down and join her for a smoke. He sits. While talking to Sam, Lucy puts on rouge and more bright red lipstick. Sam offers her money for sexual services. Lucy flashes her police badge and arrests Sam for solicitation.
   (a) What defense might Sam raise?
   (b) Will Sam's defense succeed?
   (c) What tort has been committed?
6. Wanda Worker suspects that her employer, Crass Conglomerates, Inc., may have rigged prices with its main supposed competitor. She raises questions with her superior, Bonita Boss, who fires Wanda. Wanda's union goes on strike in protest. The strike prevents Crass from meeting its existing contracts or making new ones. Moreover, a shotgun, albeit unloaded, has been pointed at strikebreakers by union member Vera Vigilante.

   Crass management orders an investigation of the union leaders. Thus Crass manages to photograph and distribute pictures of the union's treasurer, Linda Leader, leaving a video club with several X-rated films, the titles plainly visible. Linda has countered by falsely telling Crass customers that certain Crass "super-balsam" products are actually made of very cheap papier-mache.

What torts have been committed, and by whom?

7. Explain whether Alfred must disclose to Bette every problem that he has had with a machine he is selling to Bette.

8. For several months Doris Dirt has allowed her garbage to accumulate in her backyard, next to a school playground. Little William Wanderer, age four, sees what to him seems to be a nice toy among the trash. Upon coming closer, William is bitten by a rat.

    William screams and then faints. His nearby mother calls an ambulance, which, on the way to the scene, jumps a curb and strikes Pedro Pedestrian, seriously injuring him.

    William requires a series of rabies shots. Except for some bad dreams, he apparently recovers.

    (a) Discuss the lawsuits based on negligence that William and his parents may bring against Doris.

    (b) Whom may Pedro sue, and on what grounds?

    (c) Who besides Doris may be liable for negligence?

9. In a negligence case, a jury decides that the plaintiff suffered $500,000 damages and assesses the blames for plaintiff's injuries at 25 percent for plaintiff and 75 percent for defendant. State the plaintiff's damages award under (a) comparative negligence, and (b) contributory negligence.

10. Workers from a moving company are delivering furniture to an apartment. While Heidi Hapless is walking by, a table crashes through a window of the apartment and lands on her foot, causing injury. What Latin term may Heidi invoke in seeking to prove her case against the movers?

Answers

Answers to Review Questions:

1. Investigation: no level; arrest: probable cause; charges: probable cause, preponderance of evidence, or prosecutor's evidence supports a belief in guilt; trial: guilt proved beyond a reasonable doubt.

2. To streamline the trial and exclude irrelevant, unreliable, or unfairly prejudicial matters.

3. The violation of constitutional rights may necessitate the restriction or barring of otherwise admissible evidence.

4. Classification as either felony or misdemeanor, and classification according to the type of harm caused.

5. Embezzlement, mail fraud, bribery, forgery, antitrust law violations, and fraud concerning consumers, credit cards, securities, insurance, bankruptcy, and bank loans.

6. If one knowingly commits a criminal or tortious act, one is presumed to intend the natural consequences of that act. Furthermore, if the consequences occur to someone not intended as the victim, or if the consequences are different from those intended, the law may transfer the *mens rea* or tortious intent from what was intended to what actually occurred.

7. Intent is the *mens rea*—knowledge of the act's wrongfulness—that accompanies a wrongful act. Motive is the overall purpose, good or bad, for which the act is done. Intent is an essential element in proving a crime or intentional tort. Motive is not.

8. Crimes: proof of guilt beyond a reasonable doubt, damages not required, consent usually no defense, mainly statutory law, and guilt arises only through intentional or grossly negligent acts.

Torts: preponderance of evidence, damages required, consent a defense, mainly common law, and liability based on intentional acts, negligence, or no-fault (strict liability).

9. (a) Assault, battery, false arrest, false imprisonment, intentional infliction of mental (emotional) distress, and invasion of privacy; (b) abusive discharge, disparagement, interference with contract, interference with prospective economic advantage, and unfair competition; (c) conversion, nuisance, trespass to personal property, and trespass to real property.

10. Duty, breach of duty, causation, and damages.

11. Act of God, assumption of risk, comparative negligence, and contributory negligence.

Answers to "Apply Your Knowledge":

1. (a) Yes. Double jeopardy applies only to the filing of the same *criminal* charges. You would be filing a civil suit. (b) The burden of proof for you, the plaintiff, would be only a preponderance of evidence, not—as it was for the prosecutor in the criminal case—proof of guilt beyond a reasonable doubt. There are other differences, of course; for instance, some evidence may be more easily admitted in a civil trial.

2. Contact the authorities. Do not be overzealous; that may lead to charges of malicious prosecution, abusive discharge, defamation, etc. However, to tolerate embezzlement by sending the embezzler on to another employer (without telling the new employer anything) may subject you to a civil suit from the new employer.

3. (a) Insanity. (b) Does alcoholism lead to an involuntary or voluntary intoxication defense? Although intoxication may cause personal anguish, it is difficult to see how it could justify intentional acts of fraud rather than mere recklessness. Even if it could, assuming that Sol has any moments of lucidity when he realizes what he has done, he will probably be held accountable for failing to act in order to stop the embezzling and otherwise correct matters. (c) Sol's infatuation with "Teresa" may be evidence of insanity, but it would not be duress. (d) If you consider Sol to be relatively innocent compared to Teresa, you may decide that Sol's aid is needed to convict Teresa. Immunity may be necessary to secure Sol's assistance. (e) Sol: conversion; Teresa: conversion (using Sol as her agent), perhaps fraud upon Sol.

4. It would remove the element of *mens rea*; since an insane person lacks criminal intent, finding him guilty means that his act is treated as a crime *per se.*

5. (a) Entrapment. (b) Not if Sam initially had the predisposition to solicit Lucy. Yes, if his *mens rea* was induced by Lucy. The key question is: Was Lucy's conduct the sort that would have caused an "innocent" man, one without the predisposition toward solicitation, to do what Sam did? (c) None. There is no tort equivalent to the crime of solicitation. Even if Sam's act was tortious, could Lucy or any other individual prove damages?

6. If Crass has rigged prices, then it and the other price-riggers have engaged in antitrust violations and unfair competition. Depending on other facts, this activity may constitute interference with contracts or prospective economic advantage.

   Wanda may have a claim for abusive discharge.

   While strikes are privileged conduct (hence, no interference with contracts or prospective economic advantage), Vera's act is probably an assault upon the strikebreakers who saw it and—with reason—believed that the shotgun was loaded.

For distributing the photographs of Linda leaving the video club with several X-rated videos, Crass is likely liable for invasion of privacy (public disclosure of private facts, intrusion upon a person's private life), and perhaps also liable for intentional infliction of mental or emotional distress. So long as the photos are an accurate representation of the facts (Linda was holding those videos), truth acts as a defense to a claim of defamation.

Linda's statements to the customers seem to be disparagement (trade libel). That Crass has provoked Linda's ire is no defense; her remedy is to sue Crass, not counter its torts with her own.

7. In most cases, there is no duty to volunteer information. Even if there were such a duty (for example, because Alfred knowingly permitted Bette to misconstrue his silence), proving fraud requires more: proof that (1) the nondisclosure was of a material fact, (2) Alfred intended that Bette rely on the nondisclosure, (3) Bette justifiably did rely on the nondisclosure, and (4) Bette was damaged because of the nondisclosure.

8. (a) Clearly Doris' allowing her garbage to accumulate over several months breached a duty of care. The key question is proximate cause.

William should be able to obtain a damages award against Doris for the physical and emotional harm that he suffered. It is *foreseeable* that rodents might gather in a festering pile of garbage and that a rat might bite someone nearby. If William were an adult or older child, he might be deemed contributorily or comparatively negligent, or to have assumed the risk, but for a four-year-old his actions seem reasonable. Moreover, the foreseeability of injury to a child is heightened by the close presence of a playground.

William's parents should be able to recover from Doris for their expenses in having William transported, examined, and treated. Damages would include any of their costs that directly and proximately follow from the injury. William's mother may also sue for trauma suffered, particularly if she saw her child being bitten; questions of duty, proximate cause, and actual damages, though, may undermine such a claim.

(b) While ambulances often have to travel fast, Pedro may show that, in these circumstances, climbing the curb amounted to negligent driving. If, however, the ambulance company is part of a governmental or charitable agency, immunity may serve as a partial or absolute defense.

Pedro's claim against Doris appears to be too indirect. Few, if any, courts would find proximate cause between Doris' negligence (accumulation of the garbage) and the force causing Pedro's injuries (the moving ambulance). There is no foreseeability. Also, superseding cause may be a defense.

(c) William's mother: Doris may claim that William's mother was herself negligent in supervising William. But even if the mother were contributorily or comparatively negligent, that defense would not bar *William's* suit (just the mother's claim). (However, Doris might file a third-party claim [see Chapter 1] against the mother to receive a contribution from her for any damages Doris must pay to William.)

Pedro presumably has no claim against William or his mother for negligence because William's going to get a toy and the mother's allegedly poor supervision of William both were no more the *proximate* cause of Pedro's harm than was Doris' negligent accumulation of garbage. Also, the calling of an ambulance did not foreseeably lead to Pedro's injuries, nor was it breaching a duty of care in the first place.

9. (a) 75 percent of $500,000 ($375,000); (b) Nothing.

10. *Res ipsa loquitur*.

Chapter 4

Contract Formation

THE ELEMENTS OF A CONTRACT

A *contract* is a legally enforceable agreement. It has four essential elements: (1) mutual assent (meeting of the minds), as shown by a valid offer and acceptance; (2) consideration (something of value given in exchange for a promise or an act); (3) capacity of the parties to the contract; and (4) legality of the contract's subject matter and purpose. Each of these concepts will be fully explained in this chapter or in Chapter 5.

Once a valid contract has been made, that contract is as binding upon the parties as any statute or any other law. A party cannot withdraw from the contract without the agreement of the other party. In effect, a "private law" has been created between the parties.

Most people enter into numerous contracts every day. Each purchase of goods or services almost always constitutes a contract, and each understanding as to one's rights or duties (e.g., Joe must mow Ms. Smith's lawn by Friday, and he expects a $25 payment in return) also is often a contract. It usually does not matter that the agreement is oral or is based on conduct; mere informality—the lack of a written document—usually has no legal effect on a contract. (For more on this point, see the discussion of the Statute of Frauds in Chapter 5.)

CONTRACT CLASSIFICATION

Contracts can be classified by how they are formed, how they are performed, and whether they are enforceable.

Type of Formation

An *express contract* is stated in words, written or oral. This contract is consciously and overtly formed.

An *implied contract* (implied-in-fact contract) is manifested entirely or mainly by the conduct of the parties. The test is: Would a reasonable person, if aware of the conduct, infer that a contract exists?

A *quasi-contract* (implied-in-law contract) is not really an agreement. Instead, a court creates an equitable remedy to avoid the *unjust enrichment* of one party at the expense of another. While there has been no meeting of the minds, the court acts in the interest of fairness to require compensation of a party rendering services, furnishing goods, or otherwise acting for another party's benefit (e.g., a nurse who rendered assistance to an unconscious accident victim). The appropriate level of compensation (*quantum meruit*) is determined by the court's own estimate of what is fair, not simply by what a party seeks or has charged others.

Testing the Parties' Intent

Since judges and juries are not mind readers, the parties' meeting of the minds must be manifest in word or in actions. Thus, if the parties' words, actions, or both would convince a reasonable person that there was a meeting of the minds, then the law concludes that a contract existed. This is known as an *objective test*, one not based on the subjective intent of the individual parties, but on what objectively appears to be the case, looking at the parties' words and actions in their entire context. (When documents contain contradictions or ambiguities, print tends to give way to type, and handwritten words supersede both print and type.)

Type of Performance

A *bilateral contract* involves two promises—one party's promise in return for the other party's promise.

Example: Mary promises to pay George $300 if George promises to prepare Mary's tax return.

A *unilateral contract* contains a promise by one party and an act by the other.

Example: Peter promises to help Jane with her homework if Jane provides him with five candy bars. Peter makes a promise, but asks for more than a promise from Jane—he wants the conduct itself (turning over the candy, not simply promising to do so). The Uniform Commercial Code (UCC) may permit the parties to a sales contract to convert a unilateral contract into a bilateral one (see Chapter 7).

An *executed contract* has been fully performed by both parties. In an *executory contract* something remains to be done by one or both parties. The difference is usually not of any legal significance except insofar as (1) courts may opt for different measures of damages or other remedies in the event of a breach, depending upon what remains to be done under the contract; and (2) trustees/executors in bankruptcy or probate have some latitude in rejecting executory contracts, but not executed contracts, made by the bankrupt party or the decedent.

Whether It Is Enforceable

A *valid contract* meets all legal requirements and can be enforced, in a court if necessary, by either party.

An *unenforceable contract* fails to meet a legal requirement and cannot be enforced by either party. Examples include agreements that violate the Statute of Frauds (see Chapter 5) or whose breach occurred so long ago as to be beyond the statute of limitations.

A *void contract* is, in the eyes of the law, something that never really was a contract; neither party can enforce it. An agreement to commit a crime is, for example, void.

A *voidable contract* binds only one party. The other party, because he or she is a minor, because he or she agreed under duress, or for some other reason, has the option to withdraw from the contract or to enforce it. (Of course, in some cases, both parties may be minors or both may have some other reason for seeking to void the contract; but in most instances only one side has the right to undo the contract.)

OFFER AND ACCEPTANCE

Offer—from the Offeror to the Offeree

An offer must (1) indicate a clear *intent* to enter into a contract; (2) be sufficiently *definite* so that a court can determine the parties' intent; and (3) be *communicated* to the other party. Unless circumstances indicate otherwise, use of the word *offer* does tend to indicate the presence of an offer; however, no specific wording, not even the word *offer,* is necessary.

Advertisements, catalogs, brochures, announcements, and requests for bids rarely are offers. Instead, they are "invitations to deal": The reader is asked to make an offer. Only when an advertisement, for example, is quite specific, and directed toward an identified or identifiable person or group, can contractual intent be inferred. Therefore, if a store advertised, "First five people on Labor Day to purchase a leather briefcase get a free calculator and deluxe pen," there seems to be sufficient specificity (first five persons, who are required to take certain actions) for courts to infer an offer.

To be definite, an offer need not state every term. Many unstated terms may be understood by the parties, suggested by the overall circumstances, or simply be matters of common sense. For instance, it is generally implied that payments, deliveries, and overall completion of a contract are to occur reasonably promptly, and that payments should be by cash, unless otherwise approved. For sales of goods, Article 2 of the Uniform Commercial Code provides that one or more terms may be left open, for a court to fill in later, if necessary. Even price may be omitted under Article 2; all that is needed is a clear intent to make a contract (with essential terms covered, such as subject matter and quantity).

The End of an Offer

Offers may specify how long they remain open. Offers expire before then if they are rejected by the offeree, if the offeree makes a counteroffer (thus implicitly rejecting the offer), if the terms of the offer become illegal (a statute or court decision bans the proposed contract), or if either the offeror or offeree dies or becomes incompetent.

Offers that do not specify an expiration time expire after the passage of a reasonable time. What is reasonable depends on the type of contract. Offers to sell perishables (e.g., food) or items that frequently fluctuate in price (e.g., securities) tend to die quickly, while there may be a far longer "reasonable" time period for keeping open the offers in a more stable market (e.g., real estate).

Offers are almost always freely revocable. That is, the offeror can withdraw the offer at any time before it is accepted by the offeree. There are four exceptions to the easy right of withdrawal: (1) options, (2) unilateral contracts, (3) merchants' firm written offers, and (4) promissory estoppel.

An *option* commits the offeror to keep his offer open for a specified time period, in return for a paid amount from the offeree. It is an excellent device to give offerees more time to think over and investigate a proposal, as well as to raise money or otherwise prepare to accept the offer. Suppose that Ollie Offeror offers to sell his car to Olga Offeree for $15,000, agrees to hold this offer open for five days, and is paid $50 by Olga to keep the offer open. Olga has an option. She may or may not decide to exercise the option (accept Ollie's offer to sell the car for $15,000).

Either way, the $50 remains Ollie's; unless the option contract expressly so provides, the $50 is not credited toward the $15,000 purchase price.

Because a *unilateral contract* calls for acceptance by an offeree's conduct, not merely her return promise, some courts permit revocation until the offeree has substantially performed. Other courts, however, do not permit revocation once the offeree has plainly started to perform (even though there is not yet an acceptance until the performance is substantially completed).

UCC § 2-205 provides that a *merchant's firm written offer* to buy or sell goods cannot be revoked during the term specified in the offer, or, if no time is specified, for a reasonable period (but in either case the period of irrevocability cannot exceed three months). Such offers must be person-specific, evincing a definite intent to be bound, and signed by the merchant. (So, again, advertisements typically would not constitute a type of offer.)

When a promise is made without calling for a return promise or action by the other party, but the promising party knows or should know that the other party will reasonably rely to its detriment upon the promise, then courts may find *promissory estoppel*. Even though it is not even an offer to make a contract, let alone a contract, courts find it unfair to let the promising party revoke.

<u>Example:</u> Paul promises to make a large charitable contribution to his church, and he knows (or should know) that the church vestry—in reliance upon these funds expected from Paul—will commit the church to various building contracts. Paul cannot withdraw his offer; he is estopped from doing so.

Acceptance—from the Offeree to the Offeror

An acceptance must be *clear* and *unqualified* (without conditions or reservations). An attempt to modify the offer is not an acceptance; it is a counteroffer. Here is an example.

> Offeror: It's yours for $15.
> Offeree: I accept, at $10.
> Offeror: Nope, forget it.
> Offeree: Okay, $15 it is.

The offeree first made a counteroffer and thus rejected the offer. He could not later accept the dead, original offer. All his last statement could be is an offer (not an acceptance)—something for the original offeror to now accept or reject.

An acceptance must also be *in the manner, if any, required by the offer*. Any time requirement (e.g., "acceptance must be received by noon on November 15") must be met. Under the common law, special status is accorded to an acceptance via the same method of transmittance as the offer: Thus, the mailed offer is accepted when the accepting letter is placed in the mailbox, the hand-delivered offer is accepted when the return acceptance is handed to the courier, and any other offer is transformed into a binding contract the moment an offeree sends her acceptance via the same method as was the offer. Any method of acceptance *different* from the method used to transmit the offer is only a valid acceptance upon the offeror's receiving it. UCC § 2-206(1)(a) simplifies this approach for sales contracts by finding that any reasonable method of acceptance, unless in violation of the offer's requirements, is as effective as any other method.

Acceptance of a Unilateral Offer

The traditional approach to a unilateral offer requires acceptance by conduct. Under UCC § 2-206(1)(b), though, an offer to pay for goods upon the offeree's shipping them to the offeror may be accepted either by performance (shipping the goods) or by a promise to perform; therefore, the offeree can convert a unilateral offer (the promise to pay for an act, for instance, shipping the goods) to a bilateral contract. While the offeree may still choose to accept by acting rather than promising to act, *the offeree should still inform the offeror of her intentions before commencing to act*; that is a requirement for sales contracts (UCC § 2-206(2)).

The "Mailbox Rule" in Operation

Because offers are not revoked until the revocation is received by the offeree, but a mailed offer is accepted as soon as the acceptance is mailed, one can have the following situation:

Offer mailed December 1.
Revocation mailed December 2.
Acceptance mailed December 3.
Revocation received December 4.
Acceptance received December 5.

The acceptance took effect on December 3, a day before the revocation would have had an effect. Because the offeror is the master of his own offer, he can prevent such a problem by specifying in the offer that acceptances are no good until received, that an acceptance must be received by a certain date and time to be effective, and that an acceptance must be in a certain manner (e.g., via fax, telephone, certified mail, telegram, or some other method).

Silence as Acceptance

Usually, silence is not acceptance. The offeror cannot impose a duty upon the offeree to decline an offer unless (1) the parties already agreed that silence will constitute acceptance (record and book clubs use this approach for future shipments to customers, who must pay for them or return them); (2) in the parties' previous dealings, or perhaps by custom in the industry, silence constituted acceptance; or (3) circumstances indicate a quasi-contract (unjust enrichment). Whenever in doubt, the conscientious businessperson should send a written rejection to the offeror.

CONSIDERATION

In the early English common law, a written contract was binding if under *seal*. Nowadays, other than when there are notary seals or corporate seals, and for certain formal documents such as deeds to real estate, sealed contracts are rare, with the seals themselves quaint and of little legal significance.

Presently, in almost all contracts, both parties must furnish consideration. This is something of value given in exchange for something else of value (*quid pro quo*—"something for something"). Any alteration of one's legal rights can be consideration; promises, actions, refraining from action—each can constitute consideration.

Courts very rarely strike down a contract because they believe that the consideration is inadequate or unequal. In equity cases, where fairness and overall justice are often of greater concern than legal substance, the relative value of each party's consideration may be examined more carefully than in other cases, but even there the courts are unlikely to overturn a "deal" unless the disparity is egregious.

Some promises or actions either are themselves lacking in consideration or are unsupported in consideration by the other side. For example, the promise to make a gift is one-sided. The other party is not providing something in return. This lack of a bargained-for exchange means that there is no contract.

Each of the following is *not* consideration: (1) performance of pre-existing duties, (2) illusory promises, (3) moral obligations, and (4) past consideration.

If a person already has a contract or some other duty requiring a particular performance, then another agreement promising to perform the same duty lacks consideration. Thus, for example, a reward offered for capturing a criminal generally cannot be collected by policemen who are already duty-bound because of their jobs.

As for an *illusory promise,* the promisor's offer is simply to do something if he "wishes" to do so, or words to that effect. The promisor is not really bound because the fulfillment of his promise is within the promisor's own discretion (e.g., "I'll hire you if I need you"—the promisor implicitly retains the right to say whether he needs the offeree).

Moral obligations are what one *ought* to do. Unless there is a legal requirement, these obligations are only ethical in nature, not mandatory. For instance, unless you are the legal guardian of a loved one, you typically have no duty to pay for that person's medical treatment or to pay her other debts.

Lastly, past consideration was performed without expectation of obtaining something in return from the other party (e.g., Sally Swim saves Dave Drowning's life). If the other party (here, Dave) should afterward promise some compensation for the benefit received, this promise would not be binding because it was not bargained for in the current transaction (Sally's rescue of Dave was in the past).

Even if consideration is not present, courts may find *promissory estoppel* (see the section, *The End of an Offer*, earlier in this chapter). When a promisor knows or should know that the other party will reasonably rely to its detriment upon a promise, the promisor may be bound even though the other party furnished no consideration. This equitable principle may be used, for instance, to compel employers to pay certain promised bonuses, even though nothing was required of the would-be recipients of these bonuses (no consideration). Promissory estoppel could thus be invoked if an employee reasonably took action, or refrained from action, based upon the promise of a bonus (e.g., did not go to work for another business), and the promisor knew or should have known that the employee would rely upon the bonus promise.

CONDUCT INVALIDATING MUTUAL ASSENT

An agreement may not exist, even though words or actions seem to prove otherwise. Genuine, mutual assent is lacking.

There are six reasons why mutual assent (a meeting of the minds) may be missing: mistake, fraud, innocent misrepresentation, duress, undue influence, and unconscionability.

Mistake

The most frequent circumstance barring a real meeting of the minds is mistake. For a mistake to be legally significant, it must concern a basic or *material* feature of the contract. That is, it goes to the heart of the matter. Any mistake about the nature of the subject matter itself would be material. If parties agree on the sale of a cow they both believe to be pregnant, but the cow is, in fact, barren, the parties are mistaken about a fundamental aspect of the agreement—the nature of the item being sold.

If facts are unknown, and both parties take their chances, each believing that he or she has some advantage, then no mistake results if the purchased goods or services turn out to be more valuable or less valuable than one of the parties anticipated. *Judgments* about value, even if ultimately wrong, are *not legally significant mistakes*.

Generally, there is no binding contract if a material mistake is *mutual*. Either side can rescind (cancel) the contract, and the parties are restored to their situation from before the contract was formed (termed, the *status quo ante*). Therefore, any money paid or goods delivered are returned to the original owner. (In the above example of the barren cow, there is a mutual mistake of fact, and either party can rescind.)

If only one side is mistaken (*unilateral mistake*), the contract is valid unless the nonmistaken party knew, or should have known, about the mistake. *A basic principle of contract law is that between two innocent (not intentionally misbehaving) parties, the mistaken one should bear the burden of her own ignorance or carelessness.* Thus, if Flora fails to read what she signs, or Otto overlooks an obvious defect, or Ned neglects to examine a display, they likely will be bound by what they objectively agreed to, even though they subjectively—and mistakenly—believed their contract was different.

But what if the other party knows of or suspects the mistake? For example, if Bart Buyer believes that a property contains 85 acres when it actually contains only 50 acres, Sarah Seller should correct Bart's misapprehension, if she is aware of it. For such cases of *palpable unilateral mistake*, the contract is voidable by the mistaken party.

In the earlier common law, the principle of *caveat emptor* ("buyer beware") held purchasers accountable for anything they could have discovered with a complete, extremely careful and meticulous inspection. Modern law, influenced by consumer protection legislation, equity concepts of fairness, and UCC provisions such as implied warranties, is more generous to mistaken buyers; now, in some instances, the seller has a duty to tell the buyer of potential defects or other problems. If the seller does not, an unobservant buyer may be allowed to withdraw from the contract.

Fraud

Unlike most cases of mistake, fraud involves *intentional wrongdoing*. When a party enters into a contract because of the other party's dishonest conduct, the innocent party has no legal obligation under the contract—there was no true "meeting of the minds."

FACTS AND MATERIALITY

Matters pertaining to value and matters asserted as opinion generally are not factual in nature and thus are *not* grounds for a fraud claim. Courts understand that it may be customary for parties to engage in some "puffing," some exaggeration or deprecation of the worth of a prospective deal. (However, if an opinion is offered by an expert, in her field of expertise [or by someone claiming to be an expert], then the other side may treat that opinion as a statement of fact.)

The Elements of Fraud

1. Misrepresentation of a material fact.
2. Knowingly made (scienter).
3. With intent to defraud (induce reliance).
4. Justifiably relied upon.
5. Causing injury to the plaintiff.

(All five must occur)

Even if the misrepresentation involves facts, those facts must be important. A *material* fact is one that is significant enough to be a deal maker or breaker. That is, for fraud in the contractual setting, a material fact causes parties to reach an agreement they otherwise would not have reached. Two examples of material representations are a contract to sell a car, specifying that the car has passed the required state inspections, and a contract to sell a painting, specifying that the famous impressionist painter Pierre Auguste Renoir painted it.

Misrepresentations may be by words (oral or written) or by conduct.

KNOWLEDGE (SCIENTER)

One can be liable for fraud although technically ignorant of the fact that one's statements were false. Knowledge, in the eyes of the law, extends beyond actual knowledge to include what one ought to have known. Thus, careless indifference to the truth (e.g., making statements without knowing their truth or falsehood) may satisfy the knowledge element necessary to prove fraud. This broad concept of knowledge is known as *scienter*.

INTENT TO DEFRAUD (INDUCE RELIANCE)

Because it is too easy for dishonest defendants to say that they had no intention to induce reliance or cause harm, the intent to defraud is presumed if there was scienter; the burden is on the alleged defrauder to show an absence of intent.

JUSTIFIABLE RELIANCE

If a seller lies, and the buyer should recognize the lie, there is no justifiable reliance—hence, no fraud.

Example: A homeowner tells prospective buyers that his house has five bedrooms and four bathrooms when it has only three bedrooms and two bathrooms. Any buyer who visits, or has the opportunity to visit, the property simply cannot succeed on a fraud claim based upon the homeowner's misrepresentation; reliance is unjustified.

Example: Justifiable Reliance

A carpet installer tells a potential customer that he has been installing carpets for over 20 years when, in fact, he just came out of retirement to start an entirely new career in carpet sales and servicing. Presumably, the customer, in deciding whether to hire the installer, may reasonably rely upon such a statement unless it is plainly suspect (e.g., the installer appears to be only about 18 years old, far too young to have such experience).

CAUSING INJURY

Fraud means more than merely lying; harm must occur. For example, if a misrepresentation concerns matters other than the intended use of the goods, it is unlikely to have caused any injury. If Cleo tells Monty that certain camping equipment Monty wants to use solely in Georgia would keep Monty warm even atop Mount Everest, and in fact it would not, then fraud cannot be proven unless Monty shows how this misrepresentation genuinely harmed him. (The lie seems to have no impact upon the equipment's usefulness to Monty. The question may be: Is the equipment worth less, such as for resale, in its true condition than in its misrepresented condition?)

REMEDIES FOR FRAUD

A defrauded party can rescind the contract, or he or she can affirm the contract and sue in tort to recover damages. For example, if Sid Seller misrepresents a car's mileage by turning back the odometer, Bob Buyer may rescind the contract (return the car and get back the purchase price) or he may keep the car and recover damages for the lessened value of the car. Damages would be the difference in value between what Sid misrepresented the car to be (a car with lower mileage) and what Bob actually received. *Fraud even leaves the perpetrator susceptible to a punitive damages judgment as well as the possibility of criminal charges.*

Negligent Misrepresentation

If a misrepresentation lacks the fraud elements of scienter and intent, the injured party only has the option to rescind the contract. There is no tort of fraud (only negligent misrepresentation), and no damages award is available.

Example: Irma, who knows little about rugs, bought a rug for $1,000 at an auction and was given a certificate stating that the rug was a genuine Aubusson. Soon thereafter, Irma sold the rug, as an Aubusson, to Barbara, whose insurance agent called an appraiser. This expert pronounced the rug a fake worth at most $200. Because Irma had been assured that the rug was an Aubusson and had innocently misrepresented it as such to Barbara, with no intent to defraud, Barbara cannot recover damages but can return the rug to Irma for a full refund. (Irma may then attempt to recover from her seller, either for fraud or innocent misrepresentation, depending on the facts.)

Duress

Duress is coercion, either physical or mental, that deprives a person of free will. A contract made under compelling physical force (e.g., at gunpoint) is void. More typically, claims of duress involve alleged mental coercion that leaves the contract voidable by the innocent party. Four kinds of threats made against the contracting party are generally considered duress:

1. Threat of harm to his or her body or property, or to his or her family members' physical well-being or property.
2. Threat of personal or family social disgrace.

3. Threat of extreme economic loss *if* the loss will occur by intentional actions of the allegedly coercive party, such as cutting off needed supplies (not simply economic losses because of a general downturn in the industry).
4. Threat of criminal prosecution.

While private parties may not use the potential for criminal charges as a lever to extract private gains (more favorable contract terms), there usually is nothing improper about threatening to sue someone and using that threat to come to a settlement agreement. Only if the coercive party actually knows that his threatened lawsuit would be without any basis does that threat render a resulting contract voidable.

Undue Influence

Undue influence occurs when one party takes advantage of another by reason of a superior position in a close or confidential relationship. Such confidential relationships include attorney and client, clergyman and parishioner, doctor and patient, trustee and beneficiary, husband and wife, guardian and ward, agent and principal. Whichever person occupies the superior position (the position of trust) is a type of *fiduciary*, who should be acting in the other person's interest. Any contract that is actually for the fiduciary's benefit, and not for the other person's, is presumed to be tainted with undue influence and therefore voidable.

Examples: Probable Undue Influence

A client wins a large judgment in a lawsuit and then lends a portion of the award to her attorney.

A dying patient deeds over valuable property to her doctor.

A husband, hospitalized because of a serious illness, signs insurance releases for the sole benefit of his wife, upon her advice.

To overcome suspicion, the fiduciary should fully disclose to the other party his private interest and potential gain. The disclosure should be in writing and before independent witnesses. If possible, the fiduciary should ensure that the other party obtain independent advice concerning any proposed contract or gift that will benefit the fiduciary.

Unconscionability

An otherwise valid contract may be voided because of gross inequality in the parties' bargaining positions while forming the contract *and* extremely one-sided terms favoring the more powerful party. Fine print and fast talk may serve as some evidence of unconscionability. Disparities in skill, education, job background, access to experts, and economic status are often factors in determining unconscionability.

One type of contract that frequently leads to claims of unconscionability is the *adhesion contract*. This is a standardized agreement presented to a consumer on a take-it-or-leave-it basis, leaving her no opportunity to bargain or to obtain the desired goods or services without signing the printed form exactly as it is.

Note: If the consumer could easily have obtained the same goods or services from another provider without being subjected to a similar adhesion contract, and if the consumer knew or should have known of that option, then many courts will find no unconscionability. In effect, the consumer had some bargaining leverage, even if she did not use it. We thus see that *unconscionability is not an easy out from contract obligations*. The burden of proof is high, and the law imposes a duty to resist high-handed, aggressive tactics before entering a contract, if that is at all practical.

Summing Up

A contract's four essential elements are: (1) mutual assent, as shown by a valid offer and acceptance, (2) consideration, (3) capacity of the parties to the contract, and (4) legality of the contract's subject matter and purpose.

Contracts can be classified by how they are formed (express or implied), how they are performed (unilateral or bilateral, executed or executory), and whether they are enforceable (valid, unenforceable, void, or voidable). If the parties' words, actions, or both would convince a reasonable person that there was a meeting of the minds, then the law concludes that a contract existed. This is known as an *objective test* of contractual intent. In interpreting a contract, courts consider the parties' words and actions in their entirety.

An offer must: (1) indicate a clear *intent* to enter into a contract; (2) be sufficiently *definite* so that a court can determine the parties' intent; and (3) be *communicated* to the other party. Many unstated terms may be understood by the parties or suggested by the overall circumstances.

Advertisements, catalogs, brochures, announcements, and requests for bids rarely are offers, but are instead invitations for the reader to make an offer.

An offer lasts for the period of time stated or, if no time is stated, for a reasonable time depending on the type of contract. It may expire before then if the offeree makes a counteroffer or otherwise rejects it, if the offer becomes illegal, or if either party dies or becomes incompetent.

The offeror can withdraw his offer at any time before it is accepted. The four main exceptions are: (1) options, (2) merchants' firm written offers, (3) promissory estoppel, and (4) according to some courts, unilateral contracts if the offeree has started to perform.

An acceptance must be clear, unqualified, and in the manner, if any, required by the offer. To avoid problems under the "mailbox rule," the offer should state that an acceptance: (1) is not valid until received, (2) must be received by a certain date and time, or (3) must be via a certain method of transmittal.

Under UCC § 2-206(1)(b), an offeree can convert a unilateral offer (the promise to pay for an act in return for the shipping of goods) to a bilateral contract. Offerees must inform the offeror of their intentions before commencing to act (UCC § 2-206(2)).

Silence is not acceptance unless: (1) the parties have already agreed that silence will constitute acceptance; (2) in the parties' previous dealings, or perhaps by custom in the industry, silence constitutes acceptance; or (3) circumstances indicate a quasi-contract (unjust enrichment).

Consideration is something of value given in exchange for something else of value (*quid pro quo*). Promises, actions, or refraining from action can be consideration.

Courts very rarely strike down a contract because they believe that the consideration is inadequate or unequal. These do *not* constitute consideration: (1) promises to make a gift, (2) performance of pre-existing duties, (3) illusory promises, (4) moral obligations, and (5) past consideration.

When a promisor knows or should know that the other party will reasonably rely to its detriment upon a promise, the promisor may be bound even though the other party furnished no consideration. That is known as promissory estoppel.

There are six reasons why mutual assent may be missing: mistake, fraud, innocent misrepresentation, duress, undue influence, and unconscionability.

A material mistake usually pertains to a fact, not to a matter of value or opinion. Either side can rescind (cancel) a contract when a material mistake is *mutual*. If only one side is mistaken (unilateral mistake), the contract is valid unless the nonmistaken party knew, or should have known, about the mistake. Modern law—influenced by consumer protection legislation, equity concepts of fairness, and UCC provisions such as implied warranties—sometimes places a duty upon sellers to tell buyers of potential defects or other problems.

Fraud is the intentional misrepresentation of a material fact, knowingly made (scienter) and with intent to defraud (induce reliance), such that the other party justifiably relies upon the misrepresentation and thus suffers damages. A defrauded party can rescind the contract or can affirm the contract and sue in tort to recover damages.

If a misrepresentation lacks the fraud elements of scienter and intent, the injured party can only rescind the contract (no damages tort suit is permitted for claims of innocent misrepresentation).

A contract made under compelling physical force is void because of duress. The mental coercion form of duress leaves a contract voidable due to threats of physical or property damage, threats of personal or family social disgrace, threats of extreme economic loss caused by the coercive party, and threats of criminal prosecution. If one has some basis for a lawsuit, threatening to sue does not generally constitute duress.

When one party (the fiduciary) takes advantage of another by reason of a superior position in a close or confidential relationship, any contract that is actually for the fiduciary's benefit, and not for the other person's, is presumed to be tainted with undue influence and therefore voidable.

An otherwise valid contract may be voided for unconscionability because of gross inequality in the parties' bargaining positions while forming the contract *and* extremely one-sided terms favoring the more powerful party. An adhesion contract (standardized agreement presented on a take-it-or-leave-it basis) may be unconscionable.

Questions

Identify each of the following:

acceptance	fraud	*scienter*
adhesion contract	implied-in-fact contract	seal
bilateral contract	innocent	unconscionability
caveat emptor	misrepresentation	undue influence
consideration	material mistake	unenforceable contract
contract	mutual mistake	unilateral contract
counteroffer	offer	unilateral mistake
duress	option	valid contract
executed contract	past consideration	void contract
executory contract	promissory estoppel	voidable contract
express contract	quasi-contract	
firm written offer	rescission	

Answer these Review Questions:

1. How can a unilateral offeree convert the contract into a bilateral contract? When should she do so?
2. When is an advertisement an offer?
3. Name three exceptions to the rule that offers can be withdrawn at any time before they are accepted.
4. What is the effect of a conditional acceptance?
5. What is the consideration for the promise in a unilateral contract?
6. When may a unilaterally mistaken party rescind the contract?
7. When can a faulty opinion permit a party to rescind its contract?
8. How is the modern law of mistake different from the strict common law notions of *caveat emptor*?
9. What remedy is available in cases of fraud that is not available for most other matters involving problems of mutual assent?
10. What type of duress causes a contract (a) to be void, (b) to be voidable?

Apply Your Knowledge:

1. How would you prove (a) an express contract, (b) an implied contract, (c) a quasi-contract?
2. Why is a lawsuit based on an implied contract more likely to produce greater damages and a larger verdict than one based on a quasi-contract?
3. You enter an expensive restaurant and are seated by the hostess. A waiter brings you plates, silverware, napkins, glasses of ice water, and bread and butter, which you consume. When you read the menu, you realize that the prices far exceed what you can afford, and you then make it clear that you do not intend to order a meal. What kind of contract do you have, if any?
4. In problem 3, you read the menu and place an order. Nothing is said about agreeing to pay. Is there a contract?
5. In problem 3, there is fine print at the bottom of the menu: "15 percent gratuity, $25 minimum charge per party." What is the effect, assuming that you order dinner but do not see the fine print?
6. You receive a letter from the Big Business Company (BBC) stating, ". . . and we will pay you for your services $30,000 for your first year." You respond by writing, "I like your offer, and I would accept for $35,000." Having heard no response, you write a second letter ten days later: "I accept your offer of

$30,000." (a) Is there a contract? (b) What if you hear nothing in response to the second letter?

7. Suppose that a long-term boarder at a farm is given a note from farmer Smith, stating: "I promise to pay you $100 a month in return for your performing the farm chores you have always done." Is this an enforceable contract?

8. Explain how careless statements can lead to a successful claim of fraud.

9. Larry Landowner has a 50-acre property near a large city.

   (a) An employee of the State Roads Commission tells a friend, Clara Clever, that the state plans a major road relocation next to Larry's property. This information is still unknown to the public.

   Clara persuades Larry to sell her the 50-acre property for $150,000, far less than it is worth considering the road that will be built nearby.

   (b) Clara knows that XYZ Chemical Company is seeking a plant site near the city, and she gets an option contract from Larry to purchase his land for $150,000 within the next year.

   If Clara says nothing to Larry about the plans outlined above, is there mistake? Fraud?

10. Nellie Naive is an elderly, naturalized American citizen with a marginal knowledge of English and a meager education. She owns a small shop, but is having trouble making ends meet. One of her neighbors, Sam Slick, a salesman, is aware of her difficulties. He offers to lend her $12,000 "on her home" if she will sign a "paper." The paper turns out to be a deed, and Nellie now seeks to have this conveyance set aside. Will she succeed?

11. Name seven confidential relationships in which undue influence could occur.

ANSWERS

Answers to Review Questions:

1. Under UCC § 2-206(1)(b), the offeree can respond as follows to an offer to buy goods that are to be shipped: "I accept your offer and hereby agree to perform the requested services." UCC § 2-206(2) makes clear that the offeree should do this before she expends any money or effort.

2. Only when definite and made very specifically to an identifiable person or group.

3. Options, merchants' firm written offers, cases involving promissory estoppel, and sometimes unilateral contracts that the offeree has started to perform.

4. It acts as a counteroffer to, and rejection of, the original offer.

5. Performance of the requested action.

6. Usually, he cannot rescind it. However, when the other party knew or should have known about the mistake, and thus had a duty to tell the mistaken party, the mistaken party may be able to rescind.

7. If the opinion was by a professional acting within his area of expertise, or by someone else claiming expertise in that subject, then it may be considered a statement of fact sufficient for claims of fraud or innocent misrepresentation.

8. In the earlier common law, the principle of *caveat emptor* held purchasers accountable for anything a careful buyer could have discovered. Modern law, though, sometimes requires that sellers tell buyers of potential defects or other problems. If sellers did not do so, an unobservant, mistaken buyer may be allowed to rescind his contract.

9. Defrauded parties may sue in tort for damages, including punitive damages.

10. (a) physical coercion; (b) mental coercion.

Answers to "Apply Your Knowledge":

1. (a) use the words of agreement, such as those found in a contract document; (b) look at all of the circumstances, such as the parties' conduct as well as words; (c) prove unjust enrichment of one party (that it would be unjust not to provide some form of compensation to the other party).

2. The implied contract is for the usual charge for services rendered, while the quasi-contract is for the *quantum meruit* level of "fairness" as determined by a judge. On the assumption that merchants or service-providers have more control over the charges they assess than they have over judicial calculations of a "fair" return, it seems likely that the former charges will, on average, be higher than the latter charges.

3. There is a quasi-contract for the food and water that you have consumed; the value of this food and water is unclear. It could also be argued that there is an implied, unilateral contract for the price of a dinner, because you may have entered the restaurant knowing what kind of establishment it purported to be. The question would then be: Since the restaurant did not substantially perform (furnish you with a dinner) and thus did not accept your implied unilateral offer (to pay for dinner), was there nonetheless a clear commencement to perform by the restaurant sufficient to bar you from withdrawing your unilateral offer? Individuals and courts may differ on this issue.

4. Yes. Ordering food from the menu creates an implied-in-fact contract to pay the menu price.

5. If this fine print somehow conflicted with the larger print elsewhere on the menu, or even with signs in the restaurant, then it could safely be ignored. That is also true if the fine print was illegible or somehow hidden. Otherwise, the fine print becomes part of the contract; you are not excused from this contractual obligation if a careful, reasonable person would have noticed it.

6. (a) No, inasmuch as your first letter is a counteroffer and a rejection of BBC's offer. Your second letter thus cannot revive the BBC offer but is instead an offer to the BBC on the same terms as the offer you previously killed. (b) Silence by BBC could possibly be an acceptance given that BBC started the communication process with its original offer. Most people would probably agree that BBC *should* make some sort of response to your second letter. How long BBC has and whether to hold it accountable *in contract law* if it remains silent is more debatable.

7. Yes, unless the statement "as you have always done" (or other evidence) indicates that the boarder has a pre-existing duty to do the chores. Then he would be furnishing no consideration in exchange for farmer Smith's promise.

   Perhaps doing the chores has always been part of the boarder's rent payment. However, if doing the chores has simply been a good deed, the boarder has no pre-existing duty to continue doing them, and his continuing to do them would constitute genuine consideration.

8. If the statements were made recklessly, with disregard for whether they were true, that may be sufficient to show that the speaker *should have known that* they were false. That the speaker did not know for a fact the statements were false is no defense. She may still have had the requisite scienter.

9. (a) Unilateral mistake by Larry. Clara knows that Larry is mistaken (that he knows nothing about the road to be built); and Larry cannot be held accountable for his mistake because this road information was unavailable to the public. Therefore, Larry can rescind the contract. He also may rescind or sue

for fraud, as a judge or jury could hold that Clara had inside information that she had a duty to disclose to Larry. (b) Neither mistake nor fraud. XYZ may or may not be interested in Larry's property; without any other facts, such as Clara's being a fiduciary for Larry, Clara seems to have no duty of disclosure to Larry.

10. Yes, it is quite likely. The extremely one-sided bargain and the parties' gross disparity in bargaining power and sophistication combine to indicate an unconscionable contract. In addition, this example may present a case of fraud or even, if there were a confidential relationship, a case of undue influence.

11. Attorney/client, clergyman/parishioner, doctor/patient, trustee/beneficiary, husband/wife, guardian/ward, agent/principal.

Chapter 5

Contract Problems and Defenses

CAPACITY

The third element of a valid contract is *capacity*. Capacity means each person has enough mental ability to understand the deal being made. If one (or both) of the parties cannot understand what is going on, that party cannot have the intent to form a contract. Therefore, no contract exists.

Three Types of People who may Lack Capacity
1. Minors.
2. The insane.
3. The intoxicated.

Minors

In most states a person must be 18 years old to make a contract; a few states require a person to be 21 years old. People under this age are *minors* and any contracts they make are voidable. A *voidable* contract is a valid contract until the minor disaffirms it; then it no longer exists. However, if the other person on the contract is an adult, that adult is bound by the contract, even though the minor is not.

Minors are not bound by their contracts. But, an adult who contracts with a minor is bound.

DISAFFIRMANCE

Disaffirmance is a minor's cancellation of a contract. Disaffirmance must occur before the minor reaches 18 or within a reasonable time after the eighteenth birthday. (Remember: Some states require the person to be 21 years old before a contract can be binding.)

Disaffirmance may be any act of cancellation made known to the other party. Most courts require the minor to return anything received under the contract that the minor still has, even if it is damaged. If the minor has used, lost, or otherwise disposed of the goods, the minor may still disaffirm. There is no obligation to make restitution or pay for the use of the goods.

FRAUD

A minor may disaffirm a contract even if the minor lied and claimed to be an adult. However, in some states, the minor may still have to pay the other party in a tort suit for this fraud (see Chapter 3). A minor is responsible for torts down to a very young age; however, parents are not responsible for their children's torts. If the minor committed fraud, the other party may be able to recover any losses. However, many states do not follow this rule since they feel it would provide a loophole through the protection needed by minors.

NECESSARIES

A minor must pay for any *necessaries* that the minor has used. A necessary is anything a person must have to live, such as food, shelter, clothing, medical services, and some types of schooling (e.g., vocational training). What is a necessary is determined on an individual basis; under the right circumstances, even a car may be a necessary.

Since the minor does not have the capacity to form a contract, any liability for the necessaries is based on unjust enrichment (quasi-contract, see Chapter 4). Minors only have to pay for the reasonable value of what they received; they do not have to pay the price agreed upon in the contract. Also, minors are not liable for anything they have not yet received (an executory contract, see Chapter 4).

Example: Necessaries

On his seventeenth birthday, Bob enters a six-month apartment lease and then lives in the apartment for three months. Bob must pay a reasonable rental rate for the three months actually used. Bob does not have to pay more than the reasonable value, regardless of how much he agreed to pay, and he does not have to pay for the additional three months on the lease.

RATIFICATION

Once a minor reaches 18, the minor may accept a previous contract and become bound by it. This is known as *ratification*. Once a contract has been ratified, it is effective from the time the minor originally agreed to it. Ratification may be express (by saying something like, "I accept the contract") or implied. Generally, making payments when due, continuing to enjoy the benefits of the agreement, or some other clear action within the scope of the agreement will usually imply acceptance and ratify the contract.

Insane People

Legal *insanity* is not necessarily the same thing as medical insanity. Any condition that affects the mind and the ability to understand may be legal insanity, especially if this condition is apparent to the other party.

A person who enters a contract while unable to understand its consequences has a voidable contract. The law treats insane people the same as it treats minors, with one exception: If the sane person acted in good faith, the insane person must restore whatever was received once the contract is disaffirmed.

If a person is insane in the medical sense, and has been declared insane in a court of law, all of that person's contracts are automatically void. A *void* contract is one that the law treats as never having existed. Such a person cannot contract for anything.

Intoxicated People: Alcohol or Other Drugs

Under certain conditions, a contract formed by an intoxicated person may not be binding. Those conditions are that the intoxication must (1) prevent the person from understanding the agreement, and (2) be apparent to the other party. If these two conditions are met, the intoxicated person has a voidable contract, but everything the intoxicated person received under the contract must be returned.

Aliens and Convicts

Aliens have the same rights as citizens to form contracts and enforce them in the U.S. courts, unless the alien is in the country illegally or is a citizen of a country at war with the United States.

Convicts may lose the right to vote or hold political office, but they have the same rights to form contracts and enforce them as everyone else.

Summing Up

A minor, a person under age 18, lacks the capacity to make a contract. Therefore, a minor can cancel a contract at any time during minority and for a reasonable time after the eighteenth birthday. A minor is, however, responsible for any necessaries consumed.

Although minors cannot be held to their contracts, they are responsible for their torts (down to a tender age), including frauds. Therefore, some courts hold a minor responsible for losses to the adult party in a contract because of the minor's misrepresentation of age (fraud).

If a minor accepts the contract after reaching the age of 18, the minor is then bound by it because of ratification.

Insanity is grounds for cancellation of a contract. If, however, the "insane" person has not been adjudicated insane and if the other party acted in good faith, the mentally impaired party must restore all value received in order to cancel.

A contract made by a person so intoxicated by alcohol or drugs that the person did not understand the nature of the agreement is voidable, if the intoxication was apparent to the other party.

LEGALITY OF THE SUBJECT MATTER

The subject matter of an agreement is whatever the agreement is about. For example, the subject matter of a contract to buy a car is the car.

If the subject matter of a contract is not legal, the contract is void; it simply does not exist in the eyes of the law.

There are two reasons why the subject matter of a contract may be illegal: statutes and public policy. Statutes are acts by legislative bodies such as Congress; public policy is a court's opinion about prevailing morality.

Agreements That Violate Statutes

Any contract to break a law is void and unenforceable in a court of law. For example, a wife's agreement with a hired killer to murder her husband is illegal and therefore unenforceable. In addition, if the killer backs out of the agreement after being paid, the wife cannot get her money back.

There are other statutes that may act indirectly on a contract and make it unenforceable. For example, states require many professionals, such as lawyers and doctors, to be licensed. A state's licensing system may be intended to protect people from incompetent or dishonest "professionals" (a *regulatory* measure), or simply to earn license fees or monitor the number of licenses granted (a *revenue* measure). If the licensing system is regulatory, a person without the required license cannot win a lawsuit to get paid for any work that requires a regulatory license. For example, a court will not make anyone pay a faith healer for medical services.

Agreements That Violate Public Policy

Public policy is the courts' opinion about prevailing morality. A restriction on competition, besides perhaps violating antitrust laws, may be against public policy and thus unenforceable. Those restrictions are permitted only if they are part of a valid contract (such as employment, or the sale of a business) and reasonably limited in subject matters, time, and geography. Another example of something that might violate public policy is an *exculpatory clause,* i.e., a part of the contract that says one of the parties will not be responsible for any negligence. Although exculpatory clauses do not always violate public policy, they may, especially if one party has much more bargaining power than the other.

The Effect of Illegality

Generally, illegal agreements *do not even have legal existence* except as possible evidence of a crime or tort. Exceptions to this rule are sometimes made for fairness (equity). For example, the innocent public, the disadvantaged party, a repentant party, or a party not as guilty of wrongful intent as the other, sometimes may sue to be put back in the same position as before the illegal agreement was made.

---

*An agreement may be illegal because it violates a statute or a public policy.
If an agreement is illegal, it does not have any legal existence and evidence of the
agreement generally cannot be introduced into a court of law.*

THE STATUTE OF FRAUDS

Statute of Frauds: *the statutory requirement that certain contracts must
have some writing as evidence of their existence.*

In 1677, to prevent frauds arising out of purely oral agreements, the British Parliament passed "An act for the Prevention of Frauds and Perjuries," generally called the Statute of Frauds. This statute required some written evidence to prove the existence of certain types of contracts that Parliament considered particularly subject to fraud.

When the American states adopted many of the laws of England in 1776, they adopted the Statute of Frauds. To this day many states still follow the old English Statute of Frauds as part of their common law, and follow the Uniform Commercial Code's (UCC) Statute of Frauds provision for sales contracts.

Scope of the Statute of Frauds

The Statute of Frauds and the UCC provision require six kinds of contracts to have some evidence in writing or they will not be enforceable:
1. The sale of land or an interest in land.
2. A contract that cannot be completed within one year after it is made.
3. The sale of goods for $500 or more (UCC).
4. A promise to pay the debt of another person.
5. A promise made in consideration of marriage.
6. A personal promise by the executor or administrator of an estate to pay a debt of the estate.

The meanings of the writings are, of course, subject to judicial interpretation.

THE SALE OF LAND OR AN INTEREST IN LAND

This category covers real estate sales contracts, leases, easements (rights of way), and any property attached more or less permanently to the real estate, such as buildings, trees, and crops. There is one important exception to the writing requirement: In most states, an oral lease for one year or less is valid.

A CONTRACT THAT CANNOT BE COMPLETED WITHIN ONE YEAR AFTER BEING MADE

A contract for five years, which may be canceled at any time with 90 days' notice, may be oral, since it is possible to complete the contract within a year. Similarly, a contract to work "for life" may be oral since a person may die within the year.

THE SALE OF GOODS FOR $500 OR MORE

This is a requirement of the UCC, and the writing must contain the quantity of goods sold. This requirement only covers fully unperformed (executory) contracts. Once the goods have been delivered or the money has been paid, the other party can enforce an oral contract in a court of law.

A PROMISE TO PAY THE DEBT OF ANOTHER PERSON

This involves two contracts: (1) A owes something to B, and (2) C promises B that C will pay if A does not. It is this second contract that is covered by the Statute of Frauds.

A PROMISE MADE IN CONSIDERATION OF MARRIAGE

This category does not apply to the engagement (the agreement to marry), which is not legally enforceable. Rather, it was intended to apply to dowries. A dowry is the agreement of a woman, or her parents, to pay the intended husband. Today, this rule also covers prenuptial agreements, since they are made in consideration of marriage.

A PERSONAL PROMISE BY THE EXECUTOR OR ADMINISTRATOR OF AN ESTATE TO PAY A DEBT OF THE ESTATE

This promise is like the agreement to pay the debt of another person, and a writing is required.

The Writing

CAUTION: The Statute of Frauds does not require the entire contract to be in writing. It requires only that there be some written evidence of the agreement. Several documents, letters, or notations may be used together to satisfy the writing requirement.

The writing must identify all the essential parts of the transaction. The essential parts may differ from transaction to transaction, but usually the writing must include the price or consideration, and the items being sold or the work being done. The writing must identify both parties, but only has to be signed by the party that denies there was a contract. As in most other rules requiring a signing, *any* signing will do: initials, a stamped or typed signature, a nickname, or the like.

The common law seeks to enforce agreements if possible. A court will enforce an agreement if there is reasonable evidence that the writing is adequate. Also the Statute of Frauds applies only to contracts that have not yet been completed (executory); a court will not cancel an agreement that has already been carried out by both parties. If only one of the parties has performed, the other may be liable under quasi-contract for the value of the benefits received (see Chapter 4). Also, a buyer of real estate may be able to enforce an oral agreement if the buyer has paid some of the purchase price *and* taken possession of the property.

THE PAROL EVIDENCE RULE

Parol Evidence: *evidence concerning a written agreement that is not part of the writing.*

The parol evidence rule prohibits either party from contradicting a fully written contract with evidence of any statement made before the signing. The reason for this rule is simple: If the parties wrote out their agreement, why should either of them be allowed to contradict what they wrote? However, this broad rule has broad exceptions, and courts are reluctant to withhold evidence of clear understandings.

The following types of evidence may be introduced concerning matter outside the written contract:

1. Evidence explaining, clarifying, or elaborating upon the agreement.
2. Evidence of later dealings between the parties, especially if there was further consideration in or reliance upon the later dealings.
3. Evidence that the parties did not intend the writing to be a contract, or evidence of any defense to the contract, such as lack of capacity, duress, fraud, or other factors that would make the contract void or voidable.
4. Evidence completing an incomplete written agreement.
5. Evidence that something must happen before the contract is to be enforced, and that this did not happen.
6. For a sale of goods: evidence of a custom (trade usage) or of the parties' prior repeated actions (course of dealing) in similar situations. (UCC § 2-202)

The Statute of Frauds requires written evidence for certain kinds of contracts: a contract for the sale of land or an interest in land, a contract that cannot be completed within a year after it was made, a provision by one person to pay debts of another, a promise made in consideration of marriage, or an executor's personal promise to pay a debt of the estate. In addition, the UCC requires written evidence for a contract for the sale of goods for $500 or more.

The writing does not have to be a fully written contract, but it must (1) include all the essential parts of the transaction, (2) have been signed by the party being sued, and (3) identify the other party to the agreement.

The parol evidence rule prohibits any extrinsic (outside) evidence that contradicts or alters a written agreement. Exceptions to the rule, however, are very broad.

PRIVITY AND THIRD PARTIES

Privity is the old common law requirement that a person must be one of the parties to the contract in order to have a legal interest in the contract. There are two very important exceptions to this requirement: First, parties can assign their rights in the contract. Second, sometimes if the parties to the contract intended to benefit an outside party, that outside party can sue to obtain the benefit.

Assignment of Rights

Each party to a contract has a right and a duty. For example, if Al and Barney have a contract for Barney to buy Al's hat for $20, then:

	Right	*Duty*
Al	to receive $20	to deliver hat
Barney	to receive hat	to deliver $20

Generally, a party to a contract can assign the rights in the contract. For example, Barney could assign to Dan his rights in the contract for Al's hat, and then Dan could buy Al's hat for $20. Al would have to sell his hat to Dan.

Whenever rights are assigned, the person to whom they are assigned (the *assignee*) is simply substituted for the person making the assignment (the *assignor*). In the example above, Dan, the assignee, has the same rights as Barney, the assignor. The assignee "stands in the shoes" of the assignor. Besides getting the assignor's rights, the assignee is subject to whatever defenses the other party could have raised against the assignor.

Suppose that someone purchases a boat and signs a contract of sale calling for certain payments. If the seller of the boat assigns to a bank the right to receive the payments, the bank (assignee) is substituted for the seller (assignor); the buyer must now make payments to the bank. If a dispute arises, any defense (breach of

contract, defects in the boat, or other claim) is as good against the bank (as~~~
as it would be against the seller (assignor).

RIGHTS THAT CANNOT BE ASSIGNED

The right to receive personal services cannot be assigned w~~~ut the oth~~~
ty's permission. Thus if Mark agrees to work in Nancy's store~~~ Nanc~~~
sells her store to Karen, Karen does not have the right to Mark's s~~~ces, even if
Nancy tried to assign the right to Karen.

Some rights are too personal to be assigned. For example, the righ~~~
negligence is not assignable. Many states also have restrictions on the r~~~ue for
sign wages.   as-

Any assignment that materially changes the obligations or risks of the~~~
party usually is not allowed unless the other party consents. For example,~~~
right to purchase goods on credit generally cannot be assigned because it is base~~~
on the credit worthiness of the original party. The assignee would have a different
credit rating than the assignor, so the creditor would not be getting the same deal.

PROHIBITING AN ASSIGNMENT

The contract may expressly forbid an assignment by either party or require the
other party's permission for an assignment. However, the trend in law is to limit
some "unreasonable" prohibitions on assignment.

Delegation of Duties

A delegation of duties is similar to an assignment of rights. Rights are assigned;
duties are delegated. Whether a party's duties under a contract can be delegated
to someone else must be examined on a case by case basis. Duties that do not require any personal skill can be delegated. But, if a party was chosen because of
talent, skill, reputation, standing, credit, or the like, that party cannot delegate the
duty to perform under the contract to someone else. Even if a duty normally
could be delegated, the contract can prohibit or limit any delegation.

A delegation does not relieve the delegating party of the obligation.

Example: Delegation (No Personal Skill)

Tom agrees to cut Jerry's lawn in exchange for $50. Tom delegates his duty to
cut the grass to Felix. If Felix does not cut Jerry's grass, Jerry can sue Tom.

Novation

A *novation* is an agreement among the two original contracting parties and a
third party that completely replaces one of the original parties. The replaced party
is completely out of the contract and has no more responsibility to perform.
Basically, a novation is two simultaneous agreements: First, the original two parties agree that their old contract no longer exists. Second, one of the original parties and a new third party make a new contract with the same terms as the
original contract. Simply agreeing to a delegation is not enough for a novation.

Example: Novation

In the example above, if Jerry, Tom, and Felix all agreed to a novation, then
Felix must cut Jerry's grass. If Felix does not cut the grass, Jerry only can sue Felix,
not Tom.

Third-Party Beneficiaries

The right of an assignee is one exception to the privity requirement; the other is the right of a third-party beneficiary. A *third-party beneficiary* is a person who benefits from a contract, but who is not an actual party to the contract. There are two categories of third-party beneficiaries who can sue to enforce a contract: the creditor beneficiary and the donee beneficiary. The modern trend combines the two into one classification called *intended beneficiaries.* The intent of the original parties governs the classification of the third-party beneficiary.

THE CREDITOR BENEFICIARY

A *creditor beneficiary* is a third-party beneficiary because one of the contracting parties is paying a debt owed to the creditor beneficiary.

Example: Creditor Beneficiary

Scott owes Terry $1,000. Scott agrees to pay by having Hank pave Terry's driveway. Scott and Hank form a contract. If Hank does not pave Terry's driveway, Terry, as a creditor beneficiary, can sue Hank to enforce Scott's contract. Terry also can sue Scott for the original $1,000, but Terry cannot get both the paving and the $1,000.

DONEE BENEFICIARY

A *donee beneficiary* is a third-party beneficiary through the gift of one of the contracting parties.

Example: Donee Beneficiary

Mr. Smith purchased life insurance that is payable to his wife, Mrs. Smith, when he dies. Mrs. Smith is the donee beneficiary. If Mr. Smith dies, and the insurance company refuses to pay, Mrs. Smith, as the donee beneficiary, can sue the insurance company to enforce her husband's contract.

INCIDENTAL BENEFICIARIES

Incidental beneficiaries are any third-party beneficiaries other than creditor beneficiaries and donee beneficiaries. Incidental beneficiaries cannot sue to enforce a contract, even though they get some benefit from it, because the contract was not made expressly for their benefit.

Summing Up

Privity is the requirement that only parties to the contract can sue to enforce the contract. There are two major exceptions: assignees of rights and third-party beneficiaries.

Most rights can be assigned, but some cannot (e.g., the right to receive personal services).

Duties that do not require any personal skill can be delegated, but other duties generally cannot.

Novation is a three-party agreement permitting one of the parties to be excused and another person to take the excused person's place.

There are two important types of third-party beneficiaries: creditor beneficiaries and donee beneficiaries.

QUESTIONS

Identify each of the following:

assignee	insanity	public policy
assignor	intended beneficiary	regulatory
capacity	minor	revenue
creditor beneficiary	necessaries	Statute of Frauds
disaffirmance	novation	third-party beneficiary
donee beneficiary	parol evidence	void
incidental beneficiary	privity	voidable

Answer these Review Questions:

1. How does the term *capacity* apply to both minors and insane persons?
2. What is the philosophical reason that an illegal contract is not enforceable in court?
3. Why should an intoxicated person not be given the same right to disaffirm a contract as a minor?
4. If an action (e.g., murder) is a crime because of a statute, will it usually also be a crime because of public policy?
5. What does the Statute of Frauds require?
6. Is an agreement to work for a person for the lifetime of that person subject to the Statute of Frauds?
7. What is the meaning of the sentence "The assignee 'stands in the shoes' of the assignor"?
8. Explain why a contract's incidental beneficiaries cannot sue on that contract.

Apply Your Knowledge:

1. Just after his seventeenth birthday, Murdock Minor signs a contract with Scholarship Books, Inc., for a correspondence course in geology. The cost of this course is $1,000, payable in 20 monthly installments of $50 each. There are 20 units, each completed monthly. Murdock completes 14 units and makes monthly payments promptly. In the fifteenth month, he seeks to rescind the contract. Can he do so?
2. Evan Eager telephoned the Ardent Cosmetic Company asking for a job as manager of sales. Ardent had advertised this job in a trade publication, stating, in part: "Exciting opportunity for sales manager with leading cosmetics manufacturer. $75,000 per year; two years to make good." The president of Ardent, Amy Ardent, agreed on the telephone to employ Evan, and he reported for duty the following Monday. Amy also wrote Evan, stating, "Glad you saw our ad in *Cosmetics World;* welcome aboard!" Amy fires Evan after six months, and he sues for 18 months' compensation. What will be the result?
3. Guana Fertilizer Company made a written contract with Rufus Rural to mine phosphate from the "Rural farm in Boise County, Idaho." The contract required Guana to pay a royalty of $35 per ton for all minable phosphate taken from the property.
   (a) Discuss whether parol evidence can be introduced for each of the following purposes: (1) to describe the location of the farm; (2) to define phosphate; (3) to state the depth to which Guana must dig to remove phosphate subject to the royalty.
   (b) Decide whether the royalty can be paid in Guana Company stock as opposed to cash.

4. Irene Instructor made an agreement to teach at a well-known university for one year at a salary of $40,000 per year. Discuss: (a) Irene's right to delegate her teaching position to her friend, Smith, a highly qualified and respected teacher in the same field; and (b) the university's right to assign this contract to a nearby university.

ANSWERS

Answers to Review Questions:

1. The term *capacity* relates to the ability of one mind to meet another mind. This ability may not yet be developed in a minor and may be clouded or confused by insanity.
2. A court of law cannot be a party to that which is unlawful.
3. An intoxicated person becomes intoxicated through her own freedom of action and is not within a class of persons whom society seeks to protect. Thus, unless the intoxication is evident to the other party, they are bound by a contract made while intoxicated.
4. Actions made criminal by statute are usually contrary to prevailing morality and, therefore, contrary to public policy. Murder, arson, robbery, and so forth are contrary to public policy. Some crimes (such as speeding, failure to file income tax returns, or failure to register securities being offered to the public) arguably are criminal only because they violate a statute.
5. The Statute of Frauds requires that there be *written evidence* of certain contracts. This written evidence does not need to be a full contract.
6. No. It is possible for this contract to be completed within one year.
7. The sentence simply means that the assignee has exactly the same rights as did the assignor. The other party to the contract does not have a better or worse position because the contract has been assigned.
8. An incidental beneficiary's benefit is too indirect and too remote. When persons make a contract, they should not have to worry about any person in the world bringing suit on their private agreement.

Answers to "Apply Your Knowledge":

1. Murdock has ratified the contract by continuing to take the course and making payments after his eighteenth birthday.
2. This two-year contract is covered by the Statute of Frauds. There is probably a good writing, since the ad contains the basic terms of the contract and Amy's letter is a signed document that can be read with the ad, thus meeting the requirements of the Statute of Frauds.
3. (a) Items (1), (2), and (3) are definable in court by parol evidence, since they do not contradict the terms of the contract. (b) Since the use of a dollar value suggests cash or the equivalent, Guana Company stock does not meet these requirements and would, therefore, contradict the writing.
4. (a) The teaching position cannot be delegated because teaching is a personal service and substitution is not permitted. (b) The same answer is true of the right to receive the teaching skill, since again the relationship between the employer and the employee is personal.

Chapter 6

Contracts: Discharge and Remedies

DISCHARGE

Discharge is a general legal term describing the end of a contract. This word is much broader than "performance," which is only one of several ways a contract may be discharged.

Discharge by Performance

When a contract is performed by both parties, it is discharged by *performance*. Every detail does not have to be completed for a contract to be performed; *substantial performance* is enough. For example, Barry Builder has a contract to build a house and plant a lawn for Owen Owner. If Builder completes the house, the contract is performed, even if he does not plant the lawn. However, Owner can subtract the cost of completing the work from the agreed-upon price.

However, if the contract is not substantially completed, that is, if the house itself is unfinished, Builder will only be paid for the value of the work actually done (quasi-contract, see Chapter 4). Of course, Builder would be responsible for his unperformed contract. Moreover, in many states, a contractor who willfully departs from the contract cannot win a lawsuit to be paid, even in quasi-contract.

A contract may be performed though minor details have not been completed. The performing party may win a suit on the contract, but the court will deduct the cost of completion.

For a contract to be performed, all the essential or fundamental parts of the contract must have been completed. The essential parts of the contract are usually its main provisions. If these have been completed, the contract has been substantially performed.

These essential or fundamental parts of a contract are called *conditions*.

Conditions *are the fundamental requirements of a contract that must be met by one party before the other party has an obligation.*

Conditions may be classified as either express or implied. They also may be classified as conditions precedent, concurrent, or subsequent.

EXPRESS CONDITIONS

Express conditions are conditions that the parties *deliberately* place in the contract.

Example: Express Condition

Dave agrees to cut Mr. Dodson's grass for $20. Dave's cutting the grass is an express condition of the contract.

IMPLIED CONDITIONS

Most contracts, whether written or oral, contain *implied conditions*. Implied conditions are not expressly stated by the parties, but implied from the nature of the transaction. Conditions may be implied in fact (reasonably assumed from the nature of the agreement), or implied by law.

Example: Implied Condition

Arnold agrees to sell his hat to Bert for $25. It may be implied in fact that the hat to be sold is the one Arnold is wearing. It may be implied in law that the $25 is to be cash, not a check.

TIME OF PERFORMANCE

The time of performance is usually not an implied condition. Therefore, if one party requires performance by a certain time, the contract should expressly say so. Thus, if the contract between Barry Builder and Owen Owner to build a house said "completion to be on or before September 1," but did not include a phrase such as "time being of the essence," Owner will be required to accept as substantial performance, completion that is a week or even a month late.

In contrast, time of completion could be considered an implied condition if the contract involves a peculiar or unusual situation. Thus, time of completion may be implied in a contract for highly perishable goods or for goods with rapidly fluctuating values, such as stocks and bonds.

SATISFACTORY PERFORMANCE

Satisfactory performance may be called for in a contract. This requirement may be for *subjective satisfaction* (a matter of personal taste) or *objective satisfaction* (a standard that can be proved). If the satisfaction is subjective, the performer is saying, "I guarantee that the contract will be completed to your taste," and personal satisfaction is a condition of the contract. Thus, if Ms. Painter contracts to paint a portrait of Mr. Model "to the satisfaction of Mr. Model," Model must be personally satisfied with the portrait before he has to pay under the contract. However, Model must exercise good faith if he rejects the painting; he cannot reject just because he changed his mind and no longer wants his picture painted.

If Barry Builder contracts to build Owen Owner's house "according to the attached plans," then Builder has agreed to an objective standard of satisfaction. If Builder complies with the plans, this objective standard of satisfaction is satisfied. Owner cannot unreasonably claim to be dissatisfied. In this case, satisfaction is not a matter of taste, and not a condition.

CONDITIONS PRECEDENT, CONCURRENT, AND SUBSEQUENT

A *condition precedent* is one that must be complied with, or must occur, before the other party becomes obligated to perform.

Example: A Condition Precedent

Betty Buyer agrees to buy Sheila Seller's property to open a book store, provided that Seller obtains the proper zoning by June 1. Seller must obtain the zoning before Buyer becomes obligated to buy the property.

Concurrent conditions require both parties to perform at the same time. Most contract conditions are concurrent: Arnold will give his hat to Bert when Bert gives him $25.

A *condition subsequent* removes the obligation of one or both parties: for example, a condition that the seller will be liable for defective goods if the buyer gives notice within 30 days of delivery that the goods are defective. Failure to give such notice releases the seller from any obligation for the defective goods.

Discharge by Breach of Condition

If a person fails in an important way to perform a condition of a contract, the other person will have no obligation under the contract—the contract will be discharged by *breach*. Of course, the person who failed to perform will be responsible for the other person's losses caused by the failure to perform, and the nonbreaching person will be responsible (in quasi-contract) for any value received.

If a failure to perform is only minor, then the contract has been substantially performed and is not discharged by breach. The person who substantially performed can be paid under the contract, but will have the cost of unfinished details deducted from the payment.

Discharge by Anticipatory Breach

Anticipatory breach occurs when one person finds out that the other person cannot or will not perform the contract. A clear, unambiguous action is required, for example, selling the contracted goods to someone else or even simply stating "I will not perform." When an anticipatory breach occurs, the nonbreaching person is released from any obligations under the contract and can immediately sue for breach of contract. There is no need to wait until performance was supposed to occur.

Discharge by Agreement of the Parties

Mutual Rescission

Since a contract is a mutual agreement, it can be ended at any time by another mutual agreement. *Mutual rescission* is a contract to end a contract. If no one has yet performed any of the contract, the mutual rescission requires no additional consideration. Parties may orally agree to end a contract even if the contract states "This contract shall not be modified except in writing."

Accord and Satisfaction

Accord and satisfaction change the performance required under a contract and thereby discharge the obligations of the original contract. The *accord* is the agreement to accept the new obligation; the *satisfaction* is the performance of the new obligation.

Example: Accord and Satisfaction

Arthur owes Beth $1,000, which he cannot pay. Beth agrees to forgive the debt if Arthur repairs the roof of her house. The agreement to accept the repair is the accord; the performance of the repair is the satisfaction.

Release or Waiver

One party may agree to excuse the other party from performing part, or all, of a contract. This does not require any consideration and is called a *release* or a *waiver*.

Discharge by Operation of Law

Four things could happen that would discharge the contract as a matter of law: subsequent illegality, impossibility, bankruptcy, and the statute of limitations.

SUBSEQUENT ILLEGALITY

As we saw in Chapter 5, an agreement to break a law is unenforceable in a court of law. This is true even if the performance was legal when the agreement was made. Some contracts that are legal when made become illegal because the legislature later passes a statute against such contracts. When this happens, the contract is discharged; neither party has to perform. For example, selling alcohol becomes illegal when a prohibition statute is passed, so a contract to sell alcohol is discharged by the statute.

Statutes that make certain acts illegal generally contain a *grandfather clause*, an exemption for conditions (including contracts) that existed before the statute was passed. If a grandfather clause exists, the contract is not discharged; both parties must still perform.

IMPOSSIBILITY

If performance becomes impossible, the contract is discharged by law. There are a number of occurrences that might make performance impossible, for example:

- In a personal services contract (e.g., services of a professional such as a lawyer or teacher), the death or incapacitating illness of the performer or, sometimes, the one who is to receive the services.
- Destruction of the subject matter of the contract (the goods being bought or sold).
- An act of government that makes performance illegal (subsequent illegality).
- "Acts of God" (natural occurrences such as floods or hurricanes that make performance impossible).

Some courts follow the principle of *strict impossibility*: The only impossibility excusing performance is absolute factual impossibility—the contract could not be performed at any cost. Other courts and the UCC follow a rule of *commercial impracticability*—if the contract cannot be performed except at excessive and unreasonable cost, the party subject to these extreme costs is excused from the contract. Courts following the impracticability rule require that some unforeseen contingency occurred, that such contingency was not planned for in the agreement, and that the custom in the business or trade of the contracting parties did not require that one party assume the risk of the contingency.

Example: Commercial Impracticability

An excavator agrees to build a cellar under an existing building for $5,000. Upon commencing work, the excavator finds underground springs at the site that greatly multiply the anticipated costs. Even though it might be possible to do the job at enormous loss, many courts would excuse the contractor from performance on the grounds of economic impracticability, or impossibility.

BANKRUPTCY

After a proceeding in a bankruptcy court, a debtor may be released from contractual obligations (see Chapter 11).

STATUTE OF LIMITATIONS

Sometimes a contract can no longer be enforced in a court of law because of the statute of limitations. The time limit varies from state to state but generally runs from two to six years. After the original obligation has thus expired, however, a new agreement to perform will revive the original obligation. No new consideration is needed, as the old consideration will be revived by the new promise to pay.

Discharge *means the end or completion of a contract.*

Summing Up

A contract may be discharged by substantial performance of the obligation, that is, substantially meeting the fundamental conditions of the agreement. These conditions may either be specifically agreed to in the contract or be implied. It is important in making a contract to use words of condition to describe the things that are most important to the parties.

A contract may be discharged by breach if one party fails in a material way to perform the obligations of the contract.

If a contract is not working out, it can be ended by agreement. In mutual rescission, this agreement may be written or oral; the only requirement is that there be a meeting of the minds to cancel.

In accord and satisfaction, the parties agree to substitute a new performance in place of, and in satisfaction of, the existing obligation. When one party has failed to perform a contract, or if there is dissatisfaction with the performance and fear of a suit by the other party, it is recommended that a release be obtained as protection from a later lawsuit.

A contract may be discharged by operation of law by four kinds of occurrences: subsequent illegality, impossibility, bankruptcy, and the statute of limitations.

Courts do not agree on the meaning of "impossibility."

DAMAGES

The damages award is a judge's order that the breaching party pay money to the nonbreaching party to compensate for any financial losses caused by a breach of contract.

Essential Elements of Plaintiff's Case in a Contract Suit

1. Proof of the existence of a contract.
2. Proof that the contract was breached by the defendant.
3. Proof that, as a result of defendant's breach, the plaintiff has been harmed (damages).

Whether the contract suit is brought by the plaintiff in a small claims court for $100, or by a giant corporation in federal court for $100 million, these three elements of proof are required.

Sometimes the damage to the plaintiff is so small as to be practically immeasurable. In that case, the plaintiff will receive only a token amount, such as $1 (called *nominal damages*), or the plaintiff's case may be dismissed altogether for lack of proof of injury. *De minimis non curat lex* ("the law does not concern itself with trifles"), frequently abbreviated simply as *de minimis*, is an important principle of the law and should be carefully considered before a person goes to court to avenge some perceived violation of principle, hurt feelings, or embarrassment.

Compensatory Damages

If there has been a breach of contract and this breach has caused measurable damages to the plaintiff, the court will try to compensate the plaintiff by awarding a sum of money sufficient to make the plaintiff "whole." This sum of money is called *compensatory damages*. Hammurabi's Code compensated the injured party by permitting him to injure the other party in the same manner; modern law places a monetary value on the injury and takes money from the wrongdoer as compensation for the injured party. The modern policy is to put the plaintiff in the same position as if the contract had been performed.

<u>Example: Compensatory Damages</u>

Smith contracted to sell a new automobile, model X, to Jones for $10,000. If Smith fails to sell that automobile to Jones, and Jones has not paid Smith but must pay $12,000 to some other seller for model X, the injury to Jones is $2,000. That amount of money from Smith will make Jones "whole," or will compensate him.

Three principles operate to limit compensatory damages.

Limitations on the Ability to Be Legally Compensated for Damages

1. Damages must be proved to a *reasonable certainty.*
2. Defendant is liable only for damages that were *reasonably foreseeable* at the time the contract was made or at the time the breach occurred.
3. Plaintiff must use every reasonable effort to *mitigate*, to avoid or minimize the damages.

CERTAINTY

The first principle, *reasonable certainty*, eliminates speculative losses. Suppose, for example, that ABC Contractors, Inc., has a contract with Glass Manufacturing Company to build a glass factory by February 1, time being of the essence. Suppose that the factory is completed two months late, and the Glass Company claims that it would have made profits of over $1 million during those two months. Unless there is a strong record of past performance upon which to rely, these lost profits are generally considered so uncertain that a court will not make ABC pay for them.

FORESEEABILITY

Foreseeability of the injury at the time the contract is formed or at the time of breach is the second limitation on compensatory damages. This principle is a reasonable guide for a party about to breach a contract: What will it cost to breach? This question can be answered only in terms of foreseen consequences. Suppose, for example, that a manufacturing company has a breakdown in its operations. It orders certain machinery parts from X Machine Company to be delivered in 24 hours. If the Machine Company is three days late in delivering the machine parts, the manufacturing company would have no basis for lost profits during the three-day period if loss of these profits would not have been *reasonably foreseeable* by X Machine Company at the time of the breach.

MITIGATION

The requirement of mitigation is the third limitation on compensatory damages. *Mitigation* means reduction to a minimum. It is the requirement that the injured party use reasonable efforts to minimize any loss.

If the plaintiff fails to mitigate the injury, a court may not award any of the damages that the plaintiff could have avoided (mitigated).

Examples: Mitigation Requirement
1. The duty of a wrongfully fired employee to find comparable employment at the best salary possible.
2. The duty of a landlord to find a new tenant to replace a tenant who broke the lease by moving before the end of the lease period.

Of course, the mitigating plaintiff is entitled to be repaid for the cost of mitigation. The fired employee is entitled to reasonable expenses moving to his new job. Both the fired employee and the landlord are entitled to reasonable advertising expenses. These direct costs of mitigation, which can reasonably be expected by the parties, are called *incidental damages* and are generally allowed to plaintiffs as part of their compensation.

Consequential Damages

Consequential damages are compensation for indirect injury, such as lost profits. Consequential damages are allowed as part of the compensatory damages if the breaching party knew or had reason to know of losses that would result from the breach. These indirect damages *can* include injury and lost profits caused by faulty performance *if* the principles of foreseeability, certainty, and mitigation are met. If, for example, an automobile with defective brakes is delivered to a buyer pursuant to a contract, injuries to that buyer and other persons caused by this defect may be the responsibility of the seller. Lost profits may be allowed if the breaching party knew or should have known that the other party expected such profits at the time the contract was made. Consequential damages are examined carefully under both the certainty and foreseeability tests, and their inclusion in a specific case is usually a matter for the jury to decide.

Liquidated Damages

The question of damages is not always a simple one. It is a good idea, therefore, to consider including a damage clause in the contract itself as a part of the meeting of the minds. Clauses specifying the dollar amount due upon breach are called *liquidated damage* clauses. When these clauses reflect the parties' reasonable effort (when the contract was made) to estimate damages, they are enforced by the courts, especially if the actual assessment of damages would prove difficult. However, if the clause is found to be a *penalty* (i.e., an unreasonable or arbitrary amount) for nonperformance or breach, it will not be enforced.

Punitive Damages

Punitive damages (to punish), sometimes called *exemplary damages* (to serve as an example), may be awarded in tort cases as punishment for the outrageous, malicious, and oppressive conduct of the defendant. Courts almost never allow punitive damages for breach of contract. However, when a breach of contract is accompanied by a tort (e.g., fraud), this tort may give rise to punitive damages. Also, the breach of contract may itself involve a tort, in which case the suit may have both contract and tort claims, the latter seeking punitive damages.

Example: A Suit with Both Contract and Tort Counts

Under a contract to deliver goods to the plaintiff's pier by barge, the defendant's barge captain negligently strikes the pier and destroys it. The suit may be both in contract (negligent performance) and tort (negligent destruction of property). If the captain were malicious (acted out of spite) or intoxicated (gross negligence), punitive damages also may be recovered.

EQUITABLE REMEDIES

Chapter 1 discussed the equity courts first established in England by the Norman kings. Certain extraordinary relief requiring the power of the king, such as specific performance of a contract or an injunction, were reserved to the king's equity courts; money damages were available in the regular English law courts. To this day, as in the old law, equity is used only as a last resort. If damages will suffice, the plaintiff must seek them instead.

Basic Principle of Law

Equitable remedies, such as specific performance of a contract or an injunction, will not be granted if a monetary award of damages will make the plaintiff "whole."

Specific Performance

Specific performance is a court order to the breaching party commanding the performance of the contract.

Two Kinds of Cases in Which Specific Performance Can Be Counted on for Relief

1. The subject matter of the contract is unique (not available in the marketplace).
2. The contract is for the sale of real estate. Since real estate is, in a sense, unique, the two categories can really be considered one.

Suppose Cindy has agreed to sell a new automobile, model Z, to Mindy for $10,000. If Cindy refuses to perform her contract of sale, Mindy cannot obtain specific performance in an equity suit. Mindy must buy model Z for the best obtainable price and sue Cindy for the difference in damages.

Suppose that the car, instead of being new model Z, was an irreplaceable antique. A court would then grant specific performance. The same result would apply to a sale of real estate. Either the buyer or the seller could get specific performance.

Specific performance is *not* available for a personal service contract. Courts cannot supervise the work to be done; moreover, forcing someone to perform personal service is too close to slavery.

Injunction

Injunction is a second equitable remedy available in certain situations. An *injunction* is a court order to a party to do, or refrain from doing, a specific thing. The court order may prohibit a breach of contract that has not yet occurred if the breach threatens "irreparable injury." For example, in an employment contract in which a person agrees not to work for a competitor after termination of employment, an injunction may be obtained to prevent the former employee from violating the agreement. In such a case the employer may suffer great injury if the employee works for a competitor even briefly, since the new employer may have full access to the first employer's business secrets through this breach of contract.

Two Other Equitable Remedies

If a judge can determine what the parties truly intended, but a written contract does not reflect the parties' intent, the judge may *reform* the contract. A *reformation* thus states the actual agreement of the parties. When reformation is impractical or the law of mistake otherwise prevents the rewriting of a contract, the judge may order a *rescission*. This equitable remedy means that the contract is canceled (rescinded).

Summing Up

The law does not concern itself with trifles, and litigation for principles that have no financial implication should be avoided. An award of monetary damages is the general goal of contract litigation.

The courts will award compensation for losses only if (1) damages can be proved with reasonable certainty, (2) they were reasonably foreseeable when the contract was made, and (3) the plaintiff used every reasonable effort to mitigate damages.

To receive consequential damages, the injury or lost profits must be foreseeable and reasonably certain.

A liquidated damage clause should be considered as a provision in every contract. This is an attempt to estimate the dollar loss should the contract be breached. If the amount is unreasonable, it is not enforceable.

Punitive damages are a tort remedy and not generally available in a suit involving a simple breach of contract. If, however, there is a tort aspect (e.g., fraud) to the contract suit, punitive damages may be claimed.

Equity actions—specific performance and injunction—are extraordinary relief and will not be allowed if monetary damages will make the plaintiff "whole." Specific performance may be obtained when the subject matter of the contract is unique or it is impossible to have satisfaction without the contract actually being performed. An injunction should be considered where irreparable damages will occur without a court ordering the other party to perform.

QUESTIONS

Identify each of the following:

accord and satisfaction
anticipatory breach
breach
compensatory damages
conditions
conditions concurrent
conditions precedent
conditions subsequent
consequential damages
damages
de minimis
discharge
exemplary damages
express conditions
grandfather clause

implied conditions
incidental damages
injunction
liquidated damages
mitigation
mutual rescission
objective satisfaction
punitive damages
reformation
release
rescission
specific performance
subjective satisfaction
substantial performance
waiver

Answer these Review Questions:

1. What is the difference between the words *discharge* and *performance?*
2. What damages can a performing party receive if: (a) a contract has been substantially, but not fully, performed, and (b) performance of a contract has barely begun and only a small benefit been given?
3. How can a contract be breached before the date of performance arises?
4. Are a party's contractual obligations discharged if performance becomes commercially "impracticable"?
5. Is a contract obligation wiped out by the passage of time provided in the statute of limitations?
6. There are three essential elements to a contract case in court. What are they, and which is most difficult to prove?
7. What limits are placed on compensatory damages?
8. When are consequential damages not allowed?
9. What prevents the parties, by mutual agreement, from placing a desired dollar amount of damages in their contract in case the contract is breached?
10. Name two equity remedies available in some breach of contract cases.

Apply Your Knowledge:

1. In a contract dated February 15, Wright agreed to build a drugstore on a lot owned by Peoples, near Washington, D.C. The drugstore was to be completed and ready for occupancy by January 1 of the following year. In September, a hurricane struck the Washington area and flooded the work site, where excavations had just been commenced. No further work was done, and Wright walked off the job. On December 1, Peoples declared Wright to be in breach of contract and employed Turner to complete the job. What damages are available to Wright and Peoples, respectively?
2. Singleton was transferred from employment in Dayton, Ohio, to Atlanta, Georgia. In June, he purchased an old house in Atlanta and made a contract with We Fix It to have the house ready for occupancy by September 1, time being of the essence. The contract contained a liquidated damage clause providing for damages to Singleton in the amount of $100 per day for each day, after September 1, required for completion. The house was not ready until

October 10. Is this damage clause enforceable if (a) the price of work was agreed to be $10,000, and (b) Singleton had a family that included two teenage children, and (c) the fair rental value of the house was $400 per month?

ANSWERS

Answers to Review Questions:

1. Discharge refers to any of the ways in which a contract may be completed or ended; performance is one way to discharge.
2. (a) If a contract has been substantially but not fully performed, the performing party is entitled to the contract amount minus the cost of completion. (b) If performance of the contract has barely begun, the performing party cannot recover on the express contract; he is entitled, however, to the fair value of the work performed (quasi-contract).
3. Anticipatory breach may occur before the date of performance arrives if one party signifies or implies that she cannot or will not perform.
4. Many courts will discharge contracted obligations as impossible if performance becomes commercially impracticable. However, some unforeseen contingency must occur that was not bargained for and that custom in the trade or business does not require one to assume. Other courts require *strict* impossibility and will not discharge obligations for mere impracticability.
5. The statute of limitations does not really wipe out the contractual obligation because it may be revived by renewal of the promise.
6. These three elements are (1) that there was a contract, (2) that the defendant breached it, and (3) that as a result of the breach, the plaintiff was damaged. Depending on the nature of the case, difficulty of proof varies. An implied-in-fact contract is sometimes hard to prove; where performance is complicated, breach may be difficult to show; damages are difficult to prove when bills were not rendered or accounts not kept.
7. The limits are (1) reasonable certainty, (2) reasonable foreseeability, and (3) mitigation of damage.
8. Consequential damages are not allowed if they were not reasonably foreseeable and reasonably certain.
9. The parties cannot agree upon an unreasonable, unconscionable amount of damages and call it liquidated damages. To be enforceable, the agreed-upon liquidated damages should be related in some way to the expected or anticipated loss that would occur upon breach.
10. Specific performance of contract and injunction to prevent breach of contract. Other remedies include reformation and rescission.

Answers to "Apply Your Knowledge":

1. Peoples is entitled to a completed drugstore for the same price as agreed upon by Wright. The "make whole" principle governs this case. Wright is entitled to the value of the work performed in quasi-contract, but this amount would no doubt be absorbed by Peoples' greater damages. The September storm, an "act of God," could excuse late performance, but Wright gave no notice—he merely walked off the job. Employment of Turner should have occurred early in order to mitigate damages; leaving the work unattended and uncompleted conflicts with the mitigation requirement. Compensatory damages are probably too uncertain; however, incidental damages caused by getting a new contractor to complete the work may be allowable.
2. Is $100 a day liquidated damages, or is it an unenforceable penalty? This $4,000 penalty for 40 days amounts to nearly half the price of the work. It is

also too large when compared with the fair rental value of the house ($400 per month). In all events, there should have been a ceiling (e.g., $1,000) on the $100 per day penalty; moreover, it should have been tied to some ascertainable dollar cost—rental of two hotel rooms, for example. Conclusion: This damage clause is an unenforceable penalty.

Chapter 7

Uniform Commercial Code— Article 2 (Sales Contracts)

SOME SPECIAL RULES

Article 2 of the UCC deals with contracts for the sale of personal property. In most cases, the code does not change the common law of contracts, but merely expands the law as it applies to sales. Furthermore, the courts have tended to extend some of the principles in Article 2 to all contracts generally.

Article 2 imposes higher standards of conduct on merchants than on nonmerchants. Section 2-104(1) defines a merchant as one "who deals in goods of the kind or otherwise by his occupation holds himself out as having knowledge or skill peculiar to the practices or goods involved in the transaction . . . "

A number of UCC provisions implement higher standards for merchants. For example:

1. § 2-103(1)(b): *Every* contract imposes on the parties an obligation of *good faith* (for merchants, good faith means honesty and adherence to commercial standards of fairness).
2. § 2-201(2): A written confirmation from one merchant to the other of an oral agreement satisfies the Statute of Frauds unless the recipient objects in writing within 10 days.
3. § 2-205: A written firm offer of a merchant to buy or sell goods is irrevocable even without consideration for up to three months.
4. § 2-207(2): Between merchants, an acceptance may vary the offer without being treated as a rejection, unless (1) the offer prohibits such varying, (2) the proposed terms materially alter the offer, or (3) the offeror objects within a reasonable time.
5. § 2-207(1) provides that, as to nonmerchants, an acceptance with new terms is an acceptance of the offer as made. The new terms are treated as proposals for additions to the contract unless the offeree specifies, as a condition, that they must be part of the agreement.
6. §§ 2-312(3) and 2-314(1): These provide for implied warranties of merchantability and ownership by merchants.

Under the UCC, an agreement for the sale of goods for $500 or more is subject to the Statute of Frauds. The Statute of Frauds requires that the principal terms of the agreement be stated in writing. The contract is only enforceable up to the quantity stated in the agreement and a reference to price is not necessary.

To interpret a contract, the intention of the parties must be found. Article 2 states that intent is shown by (1) the course of performance accepted or acquiesced in without objection (§ 2-208(1)), (2) a sequence of previous conduct between the parties . . . as establishing a common basis of understanding for interpreting their expressions and other conduct, and (3) practice or method of dealing . . . in a place, vocation, or trade.

NONSALES TRANSACTIONS

To better understand Article 2, it is necessary to have an overview of nonsales transactions. The law sets up three important categories of nonsales: bailments, leases, and gifts.

A *bailment* is a transfer of possession, care, and control of personal property by the owner or possessor (bailor) to another (bailee) for a limited time for a special purpose.

A *lease* is a transfer of possession by the owner (lessor) of real or personal property to another (lessee) for that person's use during a period of time for an agreed-upon consideration (rent).

A *gift* is a transfer of title by the owner of goods (donor) to another person (donee) without consideration. Whereas an executory (promised) gift is not an enforceable agreement, a fully executed (completed) gift will not be legally disturbed. An executed gift requires (1) delivery, (2) donor's intent to make a gift, and (3) donee's acceptance.

SALES AND THE TRANSFER OF TITLE

Both UCC § 2-106 and the common law of contracts agree that a *sale* of goods is the transfer of title from a seller to a buyer for a consideration known as the price. Generally, the law has been that the buyer can obtain no better title than what the seller had.

The UCC, though, recognizes three exceptions to this principle: In effect, the UCC thereby provides the buyer a better title than the seller had.

The first exception is where a person with a *voidable title* can pass a good title to a bona fide (honest) purchaser. For example, if B commits fraud to obtain goods from A, then B has voidable title to the goods (A can reclaim them from B); but once B has sold the goods to a bona fide purchaser, that purchaser has better title to the goods than B did, and A can no longer reclaim the goods. (A, of course, still has other claims she can make against B.)

The second exception is that when a person buys goods from a retailer in the regular course of the retailer's business, that person will get a good title even though the retailer has transferred a prior interest to others. The dealer may have previously sold or committed the goods to another person, for example, on lay-away; while that prior person has a claim against the dealer, he cannot obtain the goods from a bona fide, subsequent purchaser.

The third exception is where a person buys goods from a dealer and acquires a good title even though the goods purchased have been placed in the dealer's care by others. If goods were entrusted to the dealer for a special purpose (for example, repairs), but a bona fide purchaser reasonably believes the dealer owns the goods, then the purchaser obtains good title. Again, the original owner's remedy is against the dealer, not the innocent buyer.

RISK OF LOSS

Prior to the UCC, the risk of loss of goods being sold and delivered depended upon who had title at the time of loss. Today, if there are no contract provisions on risk of loss, the UCC establishes general principles for determining risk of loss, depending on whether the contract of sale and delivery is a shipment contract or a destination contract (UCC § 2-509).

A *shipment contract* passes the risk of loss to the buyer when the seller delivers the goods to a carrier. The carrier is deemed the agent of the buyer in any situation in which the contract does not include a requirement for the seller to deliver the goods to a specified destination.

Frequently, the use of certain shipping phrases creates a shipment contract:

1. FOB (free on board), sometimes with "point of origin," "seller's plant," or "manufacturing facility," together with the statement of FOB point, imposes the risk and cost of loss on the buyer at the FOB point, including the cost of shipment and loading at that point, the seller's factory. However, FOB car or vessel (statement of a different FOB point) requires the seller to load the goods into the buyer's carriage facilities.
2. FAS (free alongside ship) requires the seller to deliver the goods at his/her expense and risk to a specified ship and port.
3. CIF (cost, insurance, and freight) means that the price of the goods includes the cost of shipping and insuring the goods to the buyer's delivery point. These costs are thus passed to the seller.
4. C & F (cost and freight) means the same as CIF without the insurance obligation falling on the seller.

A *destination contract* passes the risk of loss to the buyer when the goods are delivered to the specified destination. The following terms create destination contracts:

- FOB destination: See item 1 above.
- Ex-ship: This term does not require that the contract name a specific vessel; risk and expense of loss are borne by the seller until the goods have actually been unloaded from the ship.
- No arrival, no sale (UCC §§ 2-324, 2-613): If the goods do not arrive, there is no contract; and neither buyer nor seller has an obligation to the other unless the seller has caused the nonarrival. If the goods arrive damaged or in violation of the contract, the seller is responsible.

Sometimes it is difficult or impossible to ascertain whether the contract is a shipment or a destination contract and there may be no terms in the contract providing for risk of loss. Section 2-509(3) provides that, if the seller is a merchant, he or she bears the risk of loss until delivery to the buyer; if the seller is not a merchant, risk of loss passes to the buyer when the goods are tendered for delivery (or become available to the buyer). This is another example of the higher duty imposed by the UCC on merchants.

Occasionally, a seller may deliver goods to a buyer for the buyer's inspection and approval (on trial) or for the buyer's resale (consignment), title remaining in the seller (consignor) and subject to the terms of a contract between the parties. Until approval, risk of loss remains with the seller. However, if the goods are delivered on consignment, risk of loss passes to the consignee, and this person may convey title freely to others.

Consigned goods may be seized or possessed by the consignee's creditors. The consignor may protect his or her interest in the goods by placing the public on notice of the consignor's ownership through proper filing of a notice of a security interest under the code, or placing a sign or other clearly visible statement of ownership where the goods are held for sale.

WARRANTIES

Code provisions concerning warranty are at the heart of contractually based product liability as it is imposed upon sellers.

There are two types of warranties: express and implied. Like express contracts, *express warranties* arise out of words or actions that establish a promise. Under the UCC (§ 2-313(1)), three kinds of representations express a promise of warranty:

1. *An affirmation of the fact of conformance.* This affirmation may be simply a statement that the goods will do a specified thing or serve a specified purpose.
2. *A description of the goods.* Such a description is a warranty that the goods are as described or specified.
3. *Reference to a sample or model.* This reference may be by picture, diagram, drawing, standard, or prototype. It expresses a warranty that the goods are as shown in the sample or model.

An *implied warranty* is implied by law and is based on the buyer-seller relationship. The implied warranty arises from the fact that the seller is selling goods to a buyer who has certain expectations. This warranty can be denied by a specific denial. However, in the absence of a disclaimer, implied warranties come under the code as a matter of law in two respects.

1. *Warranty of merchantability.* This warranty is imposed upon the merchant with respect to the goods that it is his or her business to sell. The UCC defines merchantability (§ 2-314(2)) as the assurance that the goods are fit for the ordinary purposes for which such goods are used. To bring suit under the implied warranty of merchantability, proof must be set forth that: (1) the goods were not salable at the time of sale, and (2) the plaintiff was injured because the goods failed to meet the merchantability standard (§ 2-314).
2. *Warranty of fitness.* The warranty of fitness differs from the warranty of merchantability in two major ways. First, it applies to both merchants and any other sellers of goods. Second, it warrants (in an implied way) that the goods will be fit for the buyer's particular purpose, which may or may not be the general purpose for which the goods were intended.

The UCC and the common law permit a seller to avoid both express and implied warranties through general contract principles. Through mutual agreement the parties may eliminate or modify the warranty obligation. This avoidance of warranty is a *disclaimer.*

The way for sellers to limit themselves from warranty obligations is by use of the words "as is," or "without warranty of any kind, whether express or implied." "As is" is particularly recommended as a simple, direct, and unambiguous statement of contractual understanding with regard to used or secondhand merchandise, or even new merchandise on sale.

In addition to the "as is" disclaimer, § 2-316 provides that there is no warranty if the buyer, before entering into the contract, examined the goods or refused to examine the goods when such examination would have revealed the defect. However, sellers must realize that disclaimers are most effective in contractual dealings between parties of equal bargaining power. In addition, their written disclaimers should be big, bold, and clear for the buyer to see and understand.

This will ensure that the buyer has had notice of the "no warranty" and thus proceeds at his or her own peril.

The Magnuson-Moss Act

This federal act was intended to provide consumers with greater protection from merchants. However, the act does not require that merchants give warranties, nor does it change the nature of implied warranties. It does, however, provide that, for items purchased for amounts in excess of $10, any warranty by the merchant shall be conspicuously designated as either a full or limited warranty.

The full warranty precludes the merchant-seller from disclaiming, modifying, or limiting the duration of an implied warranty and requires the merchant to remedy defects within a reasonable time and without charge. In contrast, the limited warranty may clearly state any limitations on consequential damages or on the duration of implied warranties. However, the act provides that the substance of an implied warranty may not be disclaimed or modified if the seller makes a written warranty or provides a service contract within 90 days of the time of sale.

PRIVITY

Privity requires that a person be a party to a contract to bring a suit on that contract. The majority view of courts is that persons on the same level of consumption as the buyer—guests, bystanders, family members—can sue the seller or manufacturer of the goods, even though there is no *horizontal privity* from the buyer or seller to these other persons, so long as the seller could reasonably anticipate that such persons would be exposed to, and might be injured by, the defective product. In addition, the buyer may seek redress not only from the person selling the goods, but from the manufacturer, the wholesaler, the distributor, and other persons in the chain of distribution where there is no privity.

PERFORMANCE

Performance of sales contracts is governed by Article 2, Part 5. Section 2-507(1) of the UCC requires that the seller of goods tender their delivery as a condition of the buyer's duties to accept them and, unless otherwise agreed, to pay for them. Section 2-511(1) requires that, unless otherwise agreed, the buyer's tender of payment is a condition to the seller's duty to tender and complete delivery of the goods.

The word *tender* means to make available. However, tender is a legal term with specific shades of meaning as defined by the code and the general law. In most contracts, whether shipment contracts or delivery contracts, including FOB place of shipment or buyer's plant and FAS seller's or buyer's port, the first tender must be made by the seller. The seller must make available the goods to the buyer unless the contract specifically requires that the buyer pay the seller prior to the seller's tender.

Common law provides that substantial performance of a contract is considered performance. The code modifies this rule with regard to the seller's obligation to make conforming goods available; the goods must be made available strictly in conformity with the contract. This is called the *perfect tender rule*. Substantial performance will not suffice. Section 2-601 of the UCC provides that, if the tender of delivery or if the goods "fail in any respect to conform to the contract," the buyer may (1) reject all the goods, (2) accept all, or (3) accept conforming goods and reject the rest. In addition, the seller must hold the goods for the buyer for a reasonable time; the goods must be tendered within a reasonable time; and tender must be made at the buyer's principal place of business, unless otherwise indicated in the contract.

In the absence of agreement between the parties, once the seller has made the goods available to the buyer, the buyer must pay for the goods prior to taking actual possession. Section 2-511 stipulates that payment is sufficient if in accordance with the ordinary course of business.

Section 2-513 of the UCC provides that the buyer has the right to inspect the goods prior to their acceptance and payment. Cost of inspection must be borne by the buyer unless the goods do not conform to the contract; then these expenses revert to the seller. It is important to note that a cash-on-delivery transaction does not provide the buyer with the right of inspection before paying for the goods. (§ 2-513(3)(a))

REMEDIES

MAKING THE PARTIES "WHOLE"

Section 1-106(1) of the UCC provides that the remedies provided for "shall be liberally administered to the end that the aggrieved party shall be put in as good a position as if the other party had fully performed. . . " The expression "liberally administered" requires the courts to vigorously attempt to make whole the injured party.

Section 2-718 provides for liquidated damage clauses in sales contracts. Section 2-719 permits the parties to exclude or limit consequential damages. However, when consumer goods are sold, such a limitation is considered unconscionable if it benefits the merchant.

BUYER'S BREACH

A buyer may breach a sales contract by (1) wrongfully refusing to accept the goods, (2) wrongfully returning the goods, (3) failing to pay for the goods when payment is due, or (4) expressing an unwillingness to go forward with the contract.

Upon the occurrence of a breach of contract, the seller is entitled to be made whole. The seller may cancel the contract, delay delivery of goods, resell the goods at fair market value, recover damages for any difference in price under UCC § 2-706, or recover damages for nonacceptance or repudiation.

SELLER'S BREACH

A seller may breach a sales contract by (1) failing to deliver the goods as agreed, (2) delivering goods that do not conform to the contract, or (3) expressing an unwillingness to go forward with the contract.

Section 2-712 states that upon a breach of contract by the seller, the buyer may cover his position by (1) purchasing other goods and recovering damages for any difference in price based on the difference between the contract price and the current market price (UCC § 2-713), (2) recovering damages for goods that do not comply with the contract, or (3) obtaining specific performance for unique goods.

QUESTIONS

Identify each of the following:

"as is"	gift	remedies
bailment	good faith	right of inspection
C & F	horizontal privity	risk of loss
CIF	implied warranties	sale
consigned goods	lease	shipment contract
destination contract	limited warranty	Statute of Frauds
disclaimer	Magnuson-Moss Act	tender
express warranties	merchant	voidable title
ex-ship	"no arrival, no sale"	warranty of fitness
FAS	nonmerchant	warranty of
firm offer	perfect tender rule	merchantability
FOB	performance	
full warranty	privity	

Answer these Review Questions:

1. State some examples of the higher standard of dealing imposed on merchants by the UCC.
2. Name two legal transactions that transfer possession of a good, but not the good's title.
3. How does the UCC permit a possessor of property to convey a better title than he or she has?
4. Does the UCC rely entirely upon contractual terms in determining risk of loss during the process of sale and delivery of goods?
5. What is the basis of a seller's contractual liability for defective goods? How can sellers protect themselves from this liability?
6. How does the Magnuson-Moss Act affect warranty law?
7. Is privity of contract required for a person to win a claim for breach of warranty?
8. How does the perfect tender rule change the common law rule of performance?

Apply Your Knowledge:

1. Chung, the purchasing manager for a paint company, mailed a purchase order to the Chromatic Can Corporation (CCC) for 50,000 cans. The order form Chung sent contained 27 printed conditions. The eighth condition stated: "Buyer may reject any defective goods within 30 days of delivery." The seller, CCC, sent a letter confirming the order, but the letter stated: "Any objection to goods shipped by CCC must be made in writing within 10 days of receipt of goods." Twelve days after her company received the cans, Chung sought to object to 10,000 of the cans as defective. Discuss the likely results.
2. Golly Gas Wells, Inc. and Paul Pipelines Corp. enter into a contract in which Golly agrees to sell natural gas to Paul. All essential terms other than price are specified in the contract. Golly is to set the price based on "the average price

then being obtained by gas producers in the state of Oklahoma for sales of gas in interstate commerce." Is the contract binding?

3. Gonzales takes a dress to ABC Dry Cleaners to be dry cleaned. She inadvertently leaves a very valuable, diamond-studded necklace in a pocket of the dress. ABC sells this necklace to a jewelry store. Can Gonzales recover the necklace from the jewelry store?

ANSWERS

Answers to Review Questions:

1. Merchants must not only be honest, but also must meet reasonable standards of fair dealing in their trade (such as a higher duty to disclose information to the other party to the contract, particularly uneducated or untrained buyers); their contracts are interpreted in accordance with methods of doing business in their trade; they are bound by firm written offers that they make; they are more likely to be subject to a contract despite the failure to comply with the ordinary principles of the Statute of Frauds.

2. Bailment and lease.

3. A person with a voidable title can pass a good title to a bona fide purchaser; a purchaser from a retailer who had earlier sold an interest in the goods to some other person can acquire a good title; a purchaser may obtain good title from a dealer in that type of goods, although the dealer was supposed to hold the goods for someone else.

4. No. If the terms of the contract are unclear about risk of loss, then the seller bears the risk until the goods are delivered to the buyer.

5. Express and/or implied warranties. By a disclaimer.

6. The Magnuson-Moss Act sets certain requirements for warranties. They must be either full warranties (without limitations) or limited warranties (with clearly stated limitations).

7. No. Parties usually are liable for a breach of warranty if they could have foreseen the existence of, and potential injury to, the purchaser of a defective good as well as others exposed to that defective good.

8. The common law rule of performance considers "substantial performance" as an acceptable performance. The perfect tender rule, however, requires absolute compliance with the contract before the tender is considered to have been performed.

Answers to "Apply Your Knowledge":

1. This question involves the application of "battle of the forms" principles to the different notice-of-defect provisions. Between two merchants (the paint company and CCC), UCC § 2-207(2) permits CCC's acceptance to vary the paint company's offer——in effect, to reduce the time limit for objecting about the goods from 30 to 10 days and add that the objection must be in writing. CCC's provision controls, and thus Chung's objection is too late, because presumably the offer (the paint company's order form) did not prohibit varying terms, the CCC provision did not materially alter the offer, and the paint company failed to object to the CCC provision within a reasonable time after receiving the acceptance (CCC's confirming letter).

2. If Golly acts in good faith while setting the price, the agreement is binding. Golly must make a sincere effort to determine the average price that conforms to the contractual provision. Golly should, to be safe from claims of bad faith, document how it has calculated the price.

3. If the jewelry store did not know about how ABC came to possess the necklace, then Gonzales cannot require the store to give her the necklace. The store presumably was a bona fide purchaser. While ABC's title was voidable, the store obtained a superior ownership interest in the necklace. (Gonzales, of course, may recover from ABC a lawsuit damages award equal to the value of the necklace.)

Chapter 8

Commercial Paper

NEGOTIABLE INSTRUMENTS AND THE UCC

Documents used to help exchange money or credit are termed *commercial paper*. There are two important aspects of commercial paper: promises and orders. A *promise* to pay money is when one party makes a written promise to pay another party a certain sum of money either on demand or at some definite point in the future. An *order* exists when there are *three parties*, and Party A orders Party B to pay a specific amount of money to Party C either on demand or at a certain time in the future.

Commercial paper developed out of society's need for alternate, safer, more practical methods of payment than using cash or commodities. It has also become one of our most common ways of extending credit.

Both purposes—cash substitution and credit extension—are possible via a special type of commercial paper: the *negotiable instrument*.

A negotiable instrument *is a written unconditional promise or order to pay a certain amount to another party either on demand or at a definite time. The most common form of negotiable instrument is the check.*

The Uniform Commercial Code, Articles 3 and 4

The American law of negotiable instruments is found in the Uniform Commercial Code, specifically Article 3 on commercial paper and Article 4 concerning bank deposits and collections. These articles are an attempt to make the nation's negotiable instruments law simpler and standardized. Since 1990, there have been some proposed revisions of these articles. However, since the original articles are still observed in most states, this book's references to the UCC will refer to the original Articles 3 and 4.

Types of Negotiable Instruments

Examples of negotiable instruments that are *promises to pay money* are promissory notes and bank certificates of deposit.

A *promissory note* is a written document in which a borrower agrees to repay his loan. It is a two-party instrument in which one person (the maker) makes an unconditional, written promise to pay another person (the payee) a certain sum of money either on demand or at some specified time in the future.

```
$10.02                                              Date: June 22, 199–

Ninety days after the above I promise to pay to the order of Steve Spurrier

-------------------------------ten dollars and 02/100----------------------------------

#5423                          Due: September 20, 199-    Name Ray Goff
```

Ray Goff is the maker, and Steve Spurrier is the payee.

A *certificate of deposit (CD)* is issued by a financial institution, such as a bank, as an acknowledgment that the institution has received the deposit of a specified sum of money. The institution promises to pay back to the depositor the sum deposited, plus interest at a stated rate, at a specified time in the future.

```
                        Certificate of Deposit
                                              Date: Aug. 22, 199–
             This is to certify that Bobby Bowden has deposited in
                  SEMINOLE NATIONAL BANK  $15.00
             Fifteen and no/100--------------------------dollars
             Payable to Bobby Bowden or order 6 months after date above
               with interest at a rate of 7% per annum from date above.

   Due:  February 22, 199–                         Chief O.
                                             President, Seminole Bank
```

Seminole National Bank is the maker, and depositor Bobby Bowden is the payee.

The second category of negotiable instruments, instead of a promise to pay, is an *order to pay money*, called a draft.

A *draft* is a *three-party instrument* in which one person (the *drawer*) orders a second person (the *drawee*) to pay a certain sum of money to a third person (the *payee*), or another person specified by the payee. The payment may be either on demand or at a particular time in the future.

A *check* is by far the most common type of negotiable instrument. It is a special type of draft in which the drawee is always a bank and the instrument is always payable on demand.

```
                                        Date:   Sept. 2, 199–
   Pay to the order of ___Daffy Duck___            $2.48
   Two and 48/100----------------------------dollars
   Porky's Bank
   For: Memorandum                          Wile E. Coyote
            012345666 70 114679
```

Daffy Duck is the payee, Wile E. Coyote is the drawer, and
Porky's Bank is the drawee.

NEGOTIABILITY

To be negotiable, an instrument must meet the following requirements of the UCC: It must (1) be written; (2) be signed by the drawer or maker; (3) contain an unconditional promise or order to pay a certain sum of money; (4) be payable on demand or at a definite time; and (5) be payable to order (specific person) or to bearer (the person in possession of the paper). These five requirements are strictly construed. If a requirement is missing, the instrument may be proof of a contract but it is not negotiable. While other forms of commercial paper, such as cash and investment securities, are easily transferred, only promissory notes, CDs, checks, and other drafts are *negotiable* instruments.

Requirements for Negotiability

SIGNATURE OF MAKER OR DRAWER

A "signature" is any name, word, or mark used for the purpose of authenticating a document. It does not have to be handwritten, but the signature does have to be on the instrument itself. The law presumes that a signature is genuine (made either by the person whom the document binds or with the consent of that person).

UNCONDITIONAL PROMISE OR ORDER TO PAY

Sometimes, conditions are associated with promises and orders. These conditions may include tying the payment to the occurrence of an event or to the performance of an agreement. The term *unconditional* means that the promise or order is not limited to or changed by an event or by a clause contained within the instrument.

Either of two types of statements can make an instrument conditional, and thus lead to *destroyed negotiability*. These statements that make an instrument nonnegotiable are (1) the instrument is subject to or governed by another agreement, and (2) the instrument is to be paid only out of a particular fund or source.

Many statements can be placed on an instrument without destroying its negotiability. These statements, allowing for *intact negotiability*, include those mentioning:

- the agreements that gave rise to an instrument;
- the instrument's consideration;
- a separate agreement;
- that the instrument matures according to a particular transaction;
- that acceleration (advancing the date of payment to a sooner, definite time) or prepayment (paying off early) rights are included in a separate agreement;
- that indorsement or cashing constitutes full satisfaction of the drawer's obligation;
- that the instrument is secured (but inclusion of the security agreement or mortgage in the instrument will make it conditional);
- that a confession of judgment is authorized upon default;
- that the instrument, if issued by a government, is to be paid out of a particular fund;
- that payment of the instrument by a partnership, incorporated association, trust, or estate is limited to the assets of that entity.

These statements are covered in UCC §§ 3-105, 3-112, and 3-119.

SUM CERTAIN IN MONEY

Sum certain generally means that the amount is expressly stated or readily verifiable from looking at the terms of the instrument (UCC § 3-106). The term *money* includes all means of exchange authorized by some government as a part of its currency. An instrument payable in any currency, domestic or foreign, can be considered negotiable. A specified interest rate, installment payments, particular discounts or additions, collection costs, and attorney fees do not render an amount "uncertain." (UCC § 3-106)

PAYABLE ON DEMAND OR AT A DEFINITE TIME

To be negotiable, an instrument must be either payable on demand (UCC § 3-108) or payable at a definite time (UCC § 3-109).

Even if an instrument does not state that it is a demand instrument, if it fails to state when payment is due it will be deemed a *demand instrument* (e.g., a check). It then becomes due (is to be paid) simply upon being presented for payment.

A *definite time instrument* may be payable:
- on or before a stated date;
- at a fixed period after a stated date;
- at a fixed period after sight (presentment);
- at a definite time subject to acceleration; or
- on a postponed date (extended to a definite, later date).

Payment time cannot be contingent upon a specified act or occurrence uncertain as to when it will occur, even though the act is certain to happen at some time (e.g., death).

PAYABLE TO ORDER (UCC § 3-110) OR TO BEARER (UCC § 3-111)

"To order" includes:
- pay to the order of A,
- pay to A or his/her assigns,
- pay to A or his/her order,
- pay to the order of A and/or B, and
- pay to A as the agent of B.

"To bearer" includes:
- pay bearer,
- pay to the order of bearer,
- pay A or bearer, and
- pay to the order of cash.

The way persons indorse an instrument can convert it from order to bearer paper, or vice-versa.

Rules of Construction

Negotiable instruments may be postdated, antedated, or undated (UCC § 3-114) and need not state the place where the instrument is drawn or payable (UCC § 3-112). The instrument's dates are presumed to be correct.

Rules of agency (see Chapter 9) apply. Thus, authorized agents may complete an instrument (UCC § 3-115).

When there are disputes concerning the terms of an instrument, precedence is taken in the following order: (1) handwriting; (2) typewriting; (3) print. Words take precedence over figures, but vice versa if the words are ambiguous.

A nonnegotiable instrument is not necessarily worthless. It may be proof of a valid contract.

Advantages of Negotiable Instruments over Ordinary Contracts

Most often, negotiable instruments are preferred over ordinary, nonnegotiable contracts. Although a negotiable instrument contains more formal requirements, it conveys to its holder rights superior to those of someone trying to enforce an ordinary contract (e.g., a nonnegotiable instrument).

Negotiable instruments are easier to enforce than ordinary contracts for many reasons. First, consideration in a negotiable instrument is presumed, whereas in an ordinary contract, it must be proved. Second, past consideration (e.g., a pre-existing debt) is sufficient for negotiable instruments, but it is not sufficient for ordinary contracts. Finally, while the assignee of an ordinary contract is subject to personal defenses under contract law, this is not true for a holder in due course (discussed later in this chapter).

NEGOTIATION

The main reason why negotiable instruments are so widely used is due to the easy, safe manner in which they can be transferred from one party to another. This transfer process, in which the transferee becomes a "holder," is known as *negotiation*.

A holder *possesses an instrument that passed to him or her via an unbroken chain of negotiation and was issued, drawn, or indorsed to bearer or to his or her order.*

Some forms of commercial paper are similar to cash in that they can be negotiated *merely by a change in possession*, that is, by "delivery." This type of negotiable instrument is known as *bearer paper*. This includes checks made out to "cash" or indorsed in blank (the holder's name is signed on the back without any further instruction, such as "Pay to the order of X" or "For deposit only"). Whoever holds the instrument, although perhaps not its lawful owner, may use it.

Another type of negotiation involves *order paper*. Order paper requires not only delivery, but the proper indorsement(s). An instrument payable to the order of Joe Smith is not negotiated to Barbara Brown until delivered to her with Joe Smith's indorsement. Without the indorsement, Barbara (and anyone else who acquires the instrument from her) is a mere transferee. To obtain payment, this mere transferee would have to prove that she in fact has title to the instrument, and that the instrument is valid. If Barbara is a holder (Joe indorsed the instrument), then the law assumes that she is entitled to be paid on the instrument (other parties have the burden to show she should not be paid).

INDORSEMENTS

An *indorsement* is the signature of the holder, written on a negotiable instrument, so that the title to the instrument and the holder's property interest in it are transferred to a new holder. An instrument may be indorsed on its front or back, or on an allonge (a paper physically attached to, and made a part of, the instrument).

There are several different types of indorsement.

Blank indorsements do not specify a particular indorsee. The instrument is merely signed by the indorser. This is equivalent to making the instrument payable to bearer.

Special indorsements specify to whom, or to whose order, the instrument is payable. Such an indorsement makes the instrument order paper.

<u>Example: Special Indorsement</u>

Willie Williams, the payee of a check, specifically indorses a check to Mary Jones by writing on the instrument, "Pay to the order of Mary Jones [signed] Willie Williams."

Willie could simply indorse, "Pay Mary Jones," and it would still be a special indorsement. It renders the instrument order paper (to Mary Jones), even though the front of the negotiable instrument should not be made out that way (or else the instrument would be nonnegotiable).

An instrument may have any number of blank and special indorsements. The most recent indorsement determines whether the instrument is bearer or order paper.

A third type of indorsement is a *restrictive indorsement*, of which there are four main classifications. Restrictive indorsements can be dependent upon certain conditions, can try to prohibit further transfer, can be designated for deposit or collection, or can be for the benefit of someone else.

Any indorsement, regardless of type, may have a *disclaimer*. This places subsequent holders on notice that the indorser disclaims liability on the instrument if it is not paid. The most frequent disclaimer is the phrase, "without recourse."

HOLDERS IN DUE COURSE

A special type of holder is a *holder in due course (HIDC)*. The HIDC is generally not subject to claims or personal defenses that could be raised by the original parties to the instrument. He takes possession and title free of most personal defenses that could be raised against the HIDC's transferor. (Payees can be HIDCs, but that is rare because payees usually deal directly with the maker or drawer, and *HIDC protection only occurs for personal defenses raised by persons "with whom the holder has not dealt"*—UCC § 3-305.)

Requirements for an HIDC

To be an HIDC, the holder must take a negotiable instrument for value in good faith and without notice that it is overdue, has been dishonored, or has defenses or claims against it (UCC § 3-302).

TAKING FOR VALUE

A holder takes an instrument for "value" to the extent that (1) the agreed-upon consideration has been performed, or (2) she acquires a security interest or lien on the instrument. "Value" does not arise, however, from security interests or liens obtained via legal proceedings, such as deficiency judgments.

<u>Example: Taking for Value</u>

Homer is to pay Bart $500 in order to receive a check from Marge to Bart in the same amount. If Homer pays Bart $500, then Homer can be an HIDC for the full amount of the check. If Homer gives less than the $500 agreed upon, however, then he can be an HIDC for only that amount he actually gave to Bart. It does not matter what consideration, if any, passed between prior parties, such as Marge and Bart.

Although an executory promise (to do something in the future) usually is good consideration for contracts, it is *not* the "value" necessary to make an HIDC. There *is* HIDC value when (1) a person takes an instrument as security or payment for a pre-existing claim, or (2) in order to obtain an instrument, persons exchange negotiable instruments. For example, Javier gives value by giving Connor a check in return for taking Connor's promissory note.

The following are *not* HIDC value: gifts, inheritances, promises (except binding ones to third parties), purchases via legal proceedings such as foreclosures, and bulk transfers not made in the ordinary course of business (UCC § 3-302).

GOOD FAITH

An instrument is taken in good faith if the person taking the instrument acts honestly (UCC § 1-201(19)). The holder must actually believe that the instrument is regular (genuine, authorized, and conforming with the law). While this is a subjective test (looking at the individual's beliefs, not what a reasonable person would think), an instrument may appear so irregular or some other problem may seem so obvious that courts presume a lack of good faith.

ABSENCE OF NOTICE

Because good faith is usually assumed, and "value" is generally easy to determine, most disputes about HIDC status concern alleged "notice" about a claim or defense.

Notice includes both what the holder actually knew as well as what she should have known from all the facts and circumstances (UCC § 1-201(25)). So notice is an objective test—what a reasonable holder should know. Obvious forgeries, significant alterations, incorrect indorsements, or blanks in material terms are themselves sufficient to suggest potential claims or defenses to the instrument. (Antedated or postdated instruments are *not*.)

To become an HIDC, the holder must not have had notice that: (1) the instrument is overdue (still unpaid after the due date, or, for demand instruments, after an unreasonable period of time, such as several months, or after a demand for payment was made); (2) the instrument has been dishonored (payment or acceptance of the instrument has been refused, usually by the drawee or maker); (3) the instrument's completion was unauthorized; (4) payments of principal (not just interest) on the instrument are in default; and (5) there are defenses against, or claims to, the instrument (awareness that the obligations of one or more parties are voidable or that the parties have been discharged).

<u>Example: Notice of a Defense</u>

Suppose that Guido Gullible pays Skeeter Skunk $5,000 in cash to obtain a check payable to Skunk in the amount of $6,000 and with the words "trustee for Wilhelmina Minor" written in boldface on the front of the check. The words seem to indicate that payment is intended for the benefit of Minor, but from the $1,000 discount and the fact that payment is in cash a person could reasonably infer that Skunk will keep the money for himself. Thus, Gullible seems to have notice of a defense. Without the discounted cash payment, Gullible probably could argue successfully that he neither knew nor should have known that Skunk was violating his duties as trustee.

THE SHELTER RULE

Non-HIDCs usually take whatever rights their transferrers had. Thus a transferee who is not an HIDC (e.g., someone who is given a gift—there is no value) but who takes the instrument from an HIDC, *or traces her title back to an HIDC*, acquires all the rights of an HIDC (UCC § 3-201(1)). This *shelter rule* furthers the transferability of instruments and the benefits of HIDC status.

<u>Example: The Shelter Rule</u>

Mike Maker is induced by Paul Payee's fraud to issue Payee a promissory note. Payee negotiates the note to Holden D. Course, who takes it for value, in good faith, and without notice that it is overdue, has been dishonored, or has defenses or claims to it. After the note becomes obviously overdue, Course negotiates it to Sally Safehaven.

Although Safehaven is clearly not an HIDC (she has notice that the note is overdue), Course was. Therefore, Safehaven takes all the HIDC rights that Course had, and she is free of Maker's personal defense (fraudulent inducement).

Two types of transferees cannot use the shelter rule:

1. Those who participated in fraud or illegality affecting the instrument.
2. Those who, as prior holders (before there was an HIDC), had notice of a defense or claim.

DEFENSES

The key to understanding the HIDC's special status is to distinguish between *"real" defenses*, which work against even HIDCs, and *"personal" defenses*, which do not. The HIDC, or someone taking possession under the shelter rule, is usually free of personal but not real defenses. Others take an instrument subject to both types of defenses.

"Real" Defenses

These include:

1. Fraud in the execution. The maker, drawer, or indorser is led to believe that he is signing something else—something other than an instrument. (If reasonably discoverable, this type of fraud is treated as a personal defense.)
2. Forgery (writing another person's name as if that person had done so) or other unauthorized signatures, unless the person whose name is signed consents to it or leads others to assume that it was authorized.
3. Other defenses sufficient to render a contract void, including extreme duress, illegality, and some cases of incapacity.
4. Discharge of the instrument, if the holder knew or should have known about the discharge.
5. Discharge in bankruptcy.
6. Statute of limitations.
7. Important changes to the instrument—those that give it a different legal effect. For instance, changing a $10 check to $10,000.

Personal Defenses

These include:

1. Lack or failure of consideration.
2. Fraud in the inducement. The maker, drawer, or indorser knows that she is signing an instrument for X amount; the fraud concerns misrepresentation about the consideration or other matters.
3. Ordinary contract defenses, such as another party's breach of contract.
4. Defenses rendering the contract voidable (e.g., undue influence, slight duress, infancy).
5. Violation of a restrictive indorsement (e.g., a prior transferee's cashing a check indorsed "for deposit only").
6. Nonbankruptcy discharges of which the holder has no notice.
7. Lack of agency.
8. Unauthorized completion of an instrument.
9. Nondelivery or unauthorized delivery of an instrument.

10. Acquisition of lost or stolen bearer instruments.
11. Certain "real" defenses when the party asserting the "real" defense was negligent.

LAWS TO PROTECT CONSUMERS

The HIDC's special status runs counter to the modern law's emphasis on consumer protection. If Connie Consumer buys an appliance by check, and the seller indorses the check in favor of an HIDC, then Connie must pay on that check even if under contract law she has several good reasons why she need not pay (these defenses are personal, not "real" defenses). Many states no longer permit parties to assume HIDC status against consumers with personal defenses, such as fraud in the inducement or failure of consideration. The Federal Trade Commission also has a rule requiring that a consumer credit contract include the following statement in extremely large, bold print:

NOTICE

ANY HOLDER OF THIS CONSUMER CREDIT CONTRACT IS SUBJECT TO ALL CLAIMS AND DEFENSES WHICH THE DEBTOR COULD ASSERT AGAINST THE SELLER OF GOODS OR SERVICES OBTAINED PURSUANT HERETO OR WITH THE PROCEEDS HEREOF.

This eliminates HIDC status for the debtor's/consumer's defenses and claims against the seller. The same type of statement appears on loan documents if the lending party, although not the seller itself, receives referrals from the seller or is otherwise affiliated with the seller.

LIABILITIES AMONG PARTIES

With negotiable instruments, a person may be liable on the underlying contract. The person also may be liable on the instrument itself *if* it contains his signature or the signature of an authorized agent.

The parties to an instrument are either primarily or secondarily liable. *Primary parties* are makers and acceptors (usually drawees), while *secondary parties* are drawers and indorsers.

The primary party is required to pay on an instrument (1) as it existed when it was drafted by the maker or accepted by the drawee, or (2) for an incomplete instrument later complete as authorized, the way the instrument was completed. A secondary party usually can assume that the primary party will pay on the instrument.

When the primary party has not paid, the secondary party will be required to pay if (1) the person seeking payment first demanded payment from the primary party, and (2) the secondary party received notice that the primary party refused to pay.

The amount on the front of a draft pegs the amount of a drawer's secondary liability. The indorser's secondary liability is for the amount stated at the time of her indorsement.

Secondary parties can avoid potential liabilities on an instrument by signing the words, "without recourse." The drawer or indorser is saying, "I make no guarantee that the primary party will pay; if he does not, I will not pay, either."

Three Main Types of Liability Based on the Instrument

The three main types of liability involve negligent persons, impostors or fictitious payees, and signers lacking capacity or authority.

NEGLIGENT PERSONS (UCC § 3-406)

If a person's negligence substantially contributes to a material alteration or an unauthorized signature, that person cannot use the alteration or signature as a defense against an HIDC or anyone else who honestly and reasonably pays the instrument (UCC § 3-406). Most states define negligence as failure to exercise ordinary care.

Examples of UCC § 3-406 negligence:

1. Upon receiving notice that forgeries are occurring, failure to act to prevent more forgeries.
2. Delivery of an instrument to the wrong person.
3. Failure to audit corporate books.
4. Negligence in permitting access to or use of a signature stamp or in failing to include a corporate designation (e.g., Corp., Inc., Co.) after a corporate name.

IMPOSTORS OR FICTITIOUS PAYEES (UCC § 3-405)

UCC § 3-405 says that indorsements in the payee's name are effective for negotiation purposes when:

1. An impostor induced the drawer or maker to issue the instrument to the impostor or her accomplice.
2. The payee was never intended to have an interest in the instrument, and the maker's or drawer's agent supplied the maker or drawer with the payee's name or simply signed the instrument on the maker's or drawer's behalf. (These are made-up accounts controlled by dishonest employees.)

UCC § 3-405's underlying policy is plain: It encourages the ready transfer of instruments, and it discourages carelessness by makers and drawers. Although a drawer or maker issues the instrument to an imposter or fictitious payee, the negotiation remains effective. Usually the maker's or drawer's only recourse is against the impostor or other persons who got him to issue the instrument.

SIGNERS WITHOUT CAPACITY OR AUTHORITY (UCC § 3-207)

Negotiation is effective even though it may be subject to rescission because of incapacity, illegality, duress, fraud, mistake, or breach of duty (UCC § 3-207). Furthermore, negotiation cannot be rescinded against an HIDC if the problem amounts to merely a personal defense, not a real defense. This is to be distinguished from blatantly unauthorized signatures, which simply do not constitute negotiation and thus cannot create holders, let alone HIDCs.

Example: Drawer's Forged Signature

Ira Innocent loses a check that he has not yet written. Fanny Forger finds it. She fills out the check, making it payable to the order of Paula Payee for $2,000 and signing Ira's name as drawer. Fanny, using her false identification cards as Paula Payee, obtains payment from Tammy Transferee, who takes it for value, in good faith, and without notice of the forgery.

May Tammy recover from Fanny? Yes. An unauthorized signature still operates as the signature of the unauthorized signer (UCC § 3-404(1)). May Tammy recover from Ira? Probably not. Ira's signature would be necessary to make the check negotiable and to make him liable on the instrument. Since Ira did not ratify the signature, it remains unauthorized and, having failed to receive a duly negotiated instrument, Tammy is not a holder, let alone an HIDC.

Example: Forged Indorsement

Madge Maker issues a note to the order of Patti Payee. Devon Devious steals the check, forges Patti's blank indorsement, and then himself indorses "without recourse" and to the order of Trujillo Transferee. Trujillo takes it for value, in good faith, and without notice of the forgery. He in turn gives an unqualified indorsement to Trixie Transferee, with the note being a gift for Trixie.

May Trixie recover from Devon? Yes. It does not matter that Devon indorsed "without recourse." Devon's forgery of Patti's signature leaves him accountable as if he were Patti (UCC § 3-404). Moreover, Devon is liable for breach of warranties (discussed later).

May Trixie recover from Trujillo? Yes, if Trixie indorses the instrument and the primary party (Madge Maker) refuses to pay. Besides breach of warranties, Trujillo is secondarily liable on the instrument because he failed to qualify his indorsement.

May Trixie recover from Madge or Patti? No. As Tammy in the preceding example is not a holder, so Trujillo here is not a holder. (The note is order paper to Patti, not properly negotiated by Patti.) Thus Trixie is a non-HIDC because she did not even take from a holder and because she gave no value. There is *no* indication that either Madge or Patti acted negligently and thus permitted Devon to steal the check and forge Patti's indorsement; hence, no remedy under UCC § 3-406.

Warranties on Presentment or Transfer

There is another basis for liability: *warranties.* Any person who receives payment or acceptance of an instrument, or who transfers an instrument and receives consideration, makes warranties. Under these, like other warranties (e.g., sales warranties under UCC §§ 2-312, 2-313, 2-314, and 2-315), a breaching party may be liable for damages (usually, the amount of the instrument).

Some warranties are imposed on the person who obtains payment or acceptance *and* all prior transferors. There are three such *presentment warranties:*

1. The person has good title to the instrument or is authorized to act for someone else with good title.
2. The person has no knowledge that the maker's or drawer's signature is unauthorized.
3. The instrument has not been materially altered. [Exceptions: these warranties may not be given by HIDCs to acceptors, makers, drawers, or drawees.]

Presentment warranties are given to any person who in good faith pays or accepts the instrument.

The other warranties are *warranties on transfer.* They are made by any person who transfers an instrument and receives consideration. (Sales agents and brokers, if they disclose that they are acting solely on behalf of someone else (the principal), can reduce the transfer warranties they give to simply good faith and authority to act on behalf of the principal.)

The five warranties on transfer are:

1. The person has good title to the instrument or is authorized to act for someone else with good title, and the transfer is otherwise rightful.
2. All signatures are genuine or authorized.
3. The instrument has not been materially altered.
4. The transferor has no knowledge of any insolvency proceeding concerning the maker, the acceptor, or (for an unaccepted instrument) the drawer.
5. No party's defense is good against the transferor. (Indorsing "without recourse" limits this warranty to a guarantee that the transferor does not *know* of such a defense.)

Transfer warranties go to the immediate transferee and, if the transfer is by indorsement, any subsequent holder taking the instrument in good faith.

One other major form of liability involves accommodation parties and guarantors. An *accommodation party* signs an instrument in some capacity to lend his credit status to another party to the instrument. Accommodation parties serve as sureties for the accommodated parties. Other parties may proceed against the accommodation party to collect what the accommodated party owes.

Indorsements with the words "payment guaranteed" or the like convert an indorser's secondary liability to primary liability. The holder may proceed directly against the indorser *(guarantor)* once the instrument falls due and is unpaid. When indorsements state "collection guaranteed," however, the guarantor is only liable after it becomes clear that going after the primary party (maker or acceptor) is useless. So, if Guarantor Greg does not want to be primarily liable for a note signed by Dead-Beat Dingham, Greg should plainly indicate that the guarantee extends simply to collection.

Discharge

A party's liability to pay an instrument may be discharged (terminated). A discharge generally is effective against all parties except an HIDC who lacked notice of the discharge when he or she took the instrument.

Discharge usually arises by payment or other satisfaction. However, some or all of the parties may be discharged of their liabilities upon:
- tender of payment (even though unaccepted);
- cancellations;
- impairment of reimbursement rights;
- fraudulent, material alterations;
- check certification;
- reacquisition of instrument by maker or drawer;
- unexcused delay on presentment;
- unexcused delay in notice of dishonor;
- draft-varying acceptance; or
- any act that discharges a simple contract to pay money.

BANK DEPOSITS, COLLECTIONS, AND THE BANK/CUSTOMER RELATIONSHIP—UCC ARTICLE 4

When someone deposits money in a checking account, the bank acquires title to the deposited money. In effect, the account holder is the bank's creditor, and the bank is the account holder's debtor. Because the bank owes money to the customer, it is subject to garnishment by the customer's creditors. Likewise, because the customer does not actually own the bank funds, she cannot assign the funds. All a customer can do is order the bank to make a payment (by writing a check: "Pay to the order of ... ").

The Bank's Duty to the Customer

The bank's primary duty to its customer is to honor his checks when the customer has sufficient funds on deposit. Banks are thus liable to their customers for *wrongful dishonor.* If the wrongful dishonor was unintentional, the customer can recover only his actual damages, which may include harm to credit or reputation, arrest for writing bad checks, or other consequential damages.

A second duty of the bank is to maintain customer signature cards and to be familiar with the depositor's authorized signature, so that forgeries may be detected before any payment is made.

The Customer's Duty to the Bank (UCC § 4-406)

The first duty of the customer is to maintain sufficient funds in an account to cover the checks that she expects to write. The customer is also responsible for doing her part to prevent forgeries or other unauthorized transactions. She must review bank statements, canceled checks, and other documents for alterations, unauthorized signatures, or other irregularities. A customer who promptly reviews her bank statements and is not otherwise negligent has the right to have her account recredited for checks bearing the customer's forged signature, any altered amounts, or one or more forged indorsements.

Generally if a customer's failure to review documents results in his not discovering and reporting an alteration or unauthorized signature, and the bank thereby suffers a financial loss, the customer is precluded from asserting a claim against the bank.

Example: Failure of Customer to Review Bank Statement

If Customer Clyde had reviewed the bank statement sent to him by Bob's Bank, he could have told Bob's Bank about a check forged by Fanny Fraud. Clyde is thus precluded from having his account recredited for that check if prompt reporting to Bob's Bank would have spared the bank a loss. Furthermore, if Fanny Fraud continues to practice her deceit, Clyde is barred from asserting against Bob's Bank these later forgeries. Clyde's diligence could have prevented these later problems because he would have put Bob's Bank on notice.

As under UCC § 3-405 (impostor/fictitious payee) and § 3-406 (drawer's negligence), the bank cannot take advantage of UCC § 4-406 bank customer negligence unless the bank itself was not negligent.

Rules Governing the Payment of Checks

The drawer's bank is the primary agent in the check collection process. Article 4 of the UCC sets forth specific rules governing the payment of checks:

- The bank need not (but may) pay *overdrafts* (checks for more than the amount in the customer's account). If the bank has specifically agreed to pay overdrafts, then it must do so.
- The bank can charge the customer's account for the full amount that it pays on an overdraft.
- The bank can refuse to pay *stale checks* (uncertified checks drawn more than six months before presentation of payment).
- The bank may supply necessary indorsements for its customer, except when the missing indorsement is that of the payee and the check expressly requires the payee to sign.
- If a customer dies or is declared by a court to be incompetent, the bank may continue to honor his checks until it receives notice of the death or incompetence and has had reasonable opportunity to respond. Even with a notice, the bank may pay or accept checks during the first ten days after death (unless it receives a stop-payment order from someone claiming an interest in the dead person's estate).

- The customer can order the bank not to pay a particular check, provided that the bank has enough time to react on the *stop-payment order*. These orders can be either oral or written, with oral orders effective for 14 days and written ones good for six months. Stop-payment orders are renewable, and a bank's failure to comply leaves it liable to the customer for any losses the customer sustains.

A bank and its customer may, by their contract, alter most of the Article 4 rules. However, they cannot void the bank's responsibility for its own dishonesty or negligence, or the measure of damages for such dishonesty or negligence.

CERTIFICATION OF CHECKS

Initially, a check is only as good as the credit of the drawer. To ensure payment, a payee should have the check certified. This prevents the drawee bank from denying liability; the *certified check* is the bank's guarantee that sufficient funds have been set aside to cover the check. A bank is not required to certify a check, and most banks are very cautious about doing so, because certification releases the drawer and the indorsers from liability and makes the drawee responsible for payment.

ALTERATIONS

When drawers are negligent (e.g., leave unreasonably large spaces while writing a check), then UCC § 3-406 may completely bar bank liability for payment if the check is altered (e.g., the amount is increased). These are the general rules when the drawer is *not* negligent:

- The bank bears a loss to the extent of the raised amount.
- The bank may charge the drawer's account for the original amount of the check.
- The bank may recover from the person who presented the check for payment (warranty liability).

Alterations before certification are deemed to have been accepted by the certifying bank.

ELECTRONIC FUNDS TRANSFER ACT

Electronic funds transfers (EFT) help banks replace the time- and paper-consuming check-collection process with something practically instantaneous. The most common EFT methods are automated teller machines, paycheck direct deposits/withdrawals, and point-of-sale terminals found in stores.

The Electronic Funds Transfer Act (1978) includes provisions specifying limits on customer liability for charges on lost or stolen bank cards, requiring receipts for computer terminal transactions, and mandating monthly statements of amount, date, name of retailer, and so forth for each electronic funds transfer.

QUESTIONS

Identify each of the following:

alterations	draft	negotiation
assignee	drawee	overdraft
assignor	drawer	payee
bearer paper	forgery	personal defenses
blank indorsement	good faith	primary party
certificate of deposit	guarantor	promissory note
certified check	holder in due course	real defenses
check	(HIDC)	secondary party
commercial paper	indorsement	shelter rule
discharge	maker	stale check
disclaimer	negotiable instrument	UCC Articles 3 & 4

Answer these Review Questions:

1. Name two purposes of commercial paper.
2. (a) Name the parties to a promissory note.
   (b) Name the parties to a draft.
3. How is a check different from other drafts?
4. Which usually requires greater formality (adherence to specific requirements for proper formation): a negotiable instrument or an ordinary contract?
5. What are the requirements for an instrument to be negotiable?
6. In disputes about the terms of an instrument, which usually takes precedence?
   (a) handwriting or typing
   (b) typing or print
   (c) handwriting or print
   (d) words or numerals
7. Define an HIDC.
8. Which type of defense works against even an HIDC?
9. State the three main types of liability between parties to a negotiable instrument.
10. Are banks subject to garnishment by a customer's creditors?
11. Give at least three proper reasons for dishonoring a check.
12. When can certification of a check be required?

Apply Your Knowledge:

1. Miss O'Hara obtains a loan of $300 from Mr. Butler, to whom she signs and dates a written "I owe you" (IOU) for $300. Soon thereafter, Butler expresses to O'Hara his resolute apathy as to her future whereabouts and seeks recovery of the $300 from O'Hara. Is the IOU a negotiable instrument? Is the IOU crucial, merely helpful, irrelevant, or in fact harmful to his case?
2. (a) Jerry Joker makes a note payable to Kid Kooke "five days after Nate Nerd's first kiss." Is the note negotiable?
   (b) What if Kid gets tired of waiting and plants one, a kiss, that is, on Nate?
3. An instrument from Ariel to the order of Cody is handed by Cody to Barbara.
   (a) What should Barbara request from Cody?
   (b) What may Barbara do if she is afraid that Ariel may not be good for the money and that a subsequent holder may seek the money from Barbara instead?
4. Jim pays Joan $50 for a check in the amount of $75. Can Jim be an HIDC? If so, for what amount?
5. Paul Payee indorses a negotiable instrument "to the order of Julia Jumper," who takes the instrument for value, in good faith, and without notice of claims or defenses to it. The instrument is not overdue, nor has it ever been dishonored, when Julia indorses it and gives it to Debbie Dole. Apparently, however, Paul has still not performed the services for which the instrument was issued. Now the issuer refuses to pay Debbie. Discuss.
6. Horace Holder presents to Big Bank a check, drawn by Big Bank accountholder Cory Careless to the order of Horace for the amount of $900, and containing all the proper signatures. Big Bank pays it although Cory's account contains only $750. Cory says that Big Bank should not have paid Horace.
   (a) Is Cory correct?
   (b) What may the bank do in regard to Cory and to Horace?
7. Gary Greedy wants to bring a certified check to his meeting with Robert Reelistate. However, Gary feels that he needs every last cent of interest he can get from his account. Are these conflicting goals?

8. During a three-month period, Boris Baddie forges Dudley Dewgood's signature on several checks, makes Dudley's supposed checks payable to Boris, and then cashes them. Dudley takes each month's bank statement and puts it in a box. Six months later, Dudley discovers Boris's fraud.
   (a) May Dudley recover from the bank?
   (b) What if the checks were themselves inartfully drawn copies, not the ones actually sent by the bank to its customers?

ANSWERS

Answers to Review Questions:

1. Extension of credit, money substitute.
2. (a) Maker, payee. (b) Drawer, drawee, payee.
3. The drawee of a check is always a bank, and a check, unlike some drafts, is payable on demand.
4. The negotiable instrument. Some special contracts (e.g., land transactions) must meet formal requirements to be enforceable. Generally, though, contracts do not require such formality.
5. It must be (1) in writing, (2) signed by the maker or drawer, (3) an unconditional promise or order to pay a sum certain in money, (4) without any other promise, order, obligation, or power except as permitted by UCC Article 3, (5) payable on demand or at a definite time, and (6) payable to order or to bearer.
6. (a) Handwriting. (b) Typing. (c) Handwriting. (d) Words.
7. A holder who has taken a negotiable instrument for value, in good faith, and without notice that it is overdue, has been dishonored, or has defenses or claims against it.
8. "Real" defenses. Only in cases of consumer protection does a personal defense have any likelihood of defeating an HIDC.
9. The underlying contract, contractual liability on the instrument, warranty liability.
10. Yes. In essence, the bank is a debtor of the customer/account holder.
11. Insufficient funds, improper or missing indorsement, unauthorized drawer's signature, stale check (over 6 months old).
12. Generally, never. It is the bank's option whether to certify.

Answers to "Apply Your Knowledge":

1. The IOU should be helpful. Although not a negotiable instrument, it is evidence of a loan from O'Hara to Butler.
2. (a) No. It is not payable at a definite time. (b) The note is still not a negotiable instrument. The happening of an uncertain event does not convert an indefinite as to time (hence nonnegotiable) instrument into a negotiable instrument. However, such a triggering event could make enforceable the contract that may underlie the nonnegotiable instrument.
3. (a) An indorsement. (b) When Barbara cashes the instrument, she should indorse it "without recourse."
4. Yes, if Jim meets the remaining HIDC requirements. If Jim had agreed to pay Joan more than $50 for the check, he can be an HIDC only to the extent that he has furnished consideration (here, $50). However, if $50 was the agreed-upon consideration, then Jim has fully met the "taking for value" element and—if he meets the other HIDC requirements—is fully an HIDC.
5. Debbie took the instrument from an HIDC, Julia. Nothing indicates that Debbie is an exception to the shelter rule. Therefore Debbie should be able to enforce the instrument against the issuer, who has raised only a personal defense.

6. (a) No. Banks generally have the option to pay overdrafts. (b) Big Bank may seek reimbursement from Cory for the remaining $150 (plus perhaps a penalty). It may charge Cory's account directly, assuming that more money is deposited.

   As for Horace, once Big Bank honored the check, its only recourse against him would be claims arising under Article 3. However, Horace may well be an HIDC.

7. Probably. When a check is certified, the bank usually withdraws the amount from the account *immediately.* Unless Gary's bank has some other arrangement, Gary will lose further interest on the amount of the check once he has the check certified. Of course, with ordinary checks, interest earnings are unaffected until the check is collected.

8. (a) Unless the bank itself was negligent, Dudley certainly cannot recover for checks drafted toward the end of the three-month period; by that time, if Dudley had examined his bank statements, he could have detected the fraud and put the bank on notice in order to prevent further forgeries. Even for the earlier checks, Dudley cannot recover if his prompt review of the bank statements would have left the bank able to prevent a loss (e.g., by getting the money back from Boris or some other party to the instrument). (b) If the bank was negligent, as in this case, Dudley's failure to examine does not matter. The bank's cashing of inartfully drawn copies constitutes the type of bank negligence that eliminates UCC § 4-406 preclusion of Dudley's claim.

Chapter 9

Agency, Partnerships, and Franchises

NATURE OF AGENCY AND OF AGENCY LAW

An *agency* is a legal relationship in which one person represents another and is authorized to act for him or her. The person who acts is the *agent*; the person for whom the agent acts is the *principal*. Both employees and independent contractors (discussed later in this chapter) may or may not be agents, and most nonpersonal duties, such as administrative, clerical, or mechanical tasks, can be delegated to an agent.

Agency law consists of all the rules, recognized and enforced by society, whereby one person acts for another. Without agency law, everyone would have to act directly for himself, and business would be severely crippled. Imagine not being able to send a representative, a messenger, or a salesman. Since corporations can act only indirectly through employees, officers, and agents, corporations could not function at all and would cease to exist.

The law of agency is mainly state common law. Neither federal law nor the Uniform Commercial Code deals expressly with the subject of agency.

THE AGENT/PRINCIPAL RELATIONSHIP

Creation of Agency

Most, but not all, agency relationships are created by contract. Since consideration is not required, however, there need not be a contract.

The agency relationship is always by the consent of both parties. Since either party can choose to no longer consent, an agency can be terminated by either the principal or the agent at any time; if there were also a contract, though, that may constitute a breach.

EXAMPLE OF AN AGENCY: A SIGNED POWER OF ATTORNEY

Aside from express agencies, created by the words of the parties, there are also agencies created by the parties' conduct (an implied agency, based on essentially the same principles as implied contracts—see Chapter 4). The other main methods by which an agency occurs are: (1) ratification (the would-be principal expressly or implicitly approves, after the fact, an unauthorized action); and (2) estoppel (the supposed principal's acts or failure to act leads a third party to the reasonable belief that someone was an agent). (A related concept, partnership by estoppel, is discussed later in this chapter.)

Duties of the Agent to the Principal

Whenever an agent is appointed by contract, the terms of the contract determine the duties of each party to the other. However, the duties of an agent may be modified by express agreement (either oral or written).

Because the law requires an agent to act in a fiduciary capacity, he or she owes a number of duties to the principal. The obligations of a *fiduciary* are very strict; failure of the fiduciary to account for money collected for her principal, *commingling* (mixing) of such money with the fiduciary's own, or taking the principal's property to use with the fiduciary's own may not only violate the agent's duty of loyalty toward the principal, but also often are *criminal* acts (embezzlement).

In keeping with this high degree of trust, the following additional duties are required of the agent (unless modified by contract):

1. **Duty to obey instructions.** The agent must carry out the principal's instructions. This duty involves no more than might be expected from any contract obligation. Bear in mind, however, that the agent may be undertaking duties of the highest and most complex nature: buying and selling, entering into contracts, and the like, all in the name of the principal. The agent is *personally liable* to the principal if she (1) causes the principal to become responsible for unauthorized contracts, (2) improperly delegates her duties to another, or (3) commits torts for which her principal may be responsible.

2. **Duty to act with skill.** An agent undertakes to act with the degree of skill ordinarily expected from others undertaking such employment. A business agent, a stockbroker, a manufacturer's representative, all undertake their agencies with the understanding that they will perform with accuracy and skill. Any case for breach of contract requires proof of (1) the proper standard of care or skill and (2) the agent's failure to meet that standard.

3. **Duty to avoid conflict of interest.** An agent who is acting for a principal cannot act for himself with respect to the same matter. An agent cannot engage in self-dealing ventures such as purchasing property for the principal while holding a personal interest in that property or selling the principal's goods to himself or to friends or relatives at a special or lower price. An attorney cannot act for conflicting parties in a lawsuit, or represent conflicting interests in any business transaction. This policy prohibits the agent from competing in business against the principal. Conflicts may be resolved by fully disclosing all facts to the concerned parties, followed by the principal's complete, informed consent to the actions taken or proposed by the agent.

4. **Duty to protect confidential information.** Obviously, the principal must be free to disclose all necessary information to her agent, including trade secrets and proprietary (owner) information. It is the agent's responsibility to safeguard this property from the general public, third parties, and the principal's competitors. Also, such proprietary and confidential information must be returned to the principal upon termination of the agency.

5. **Duty to notify.** Since the agent is, in some respects, an extension of the principal, he is the eyes and ears of the principal. Consequently, the agent must notify the principal of all pertinent information needed to evaluate a situation. In this way, the principal can make further decisions concerning his business and continue to give the agent proper guidance.

6. **Duty to account.** The contract of agency will specify times and rules of accounting. In all cases, the agent must maintain "an open book" for the principal to be able to assess the agent's work. At termination of the agency, all property must be accounted for and all income turned over to the principal in accordance with the original agency agreement.

Duties of the Principal to the Agent

If there is a contract, the principal's duties to the agent are governed by that contract. The primary duty is to compensate the agent for his services. If the contract is implied, the compensation is the agent's fee as understood by the parties or as reasonable in that field. If there is no contract, express or implied, and the agent did not agree to work for free, then the agent is entitled to compensation in quasi-contract calculated at the reasonable value (*quantum meruit*) of the services rendered.

The principal must (1) pay all expenses the agent incurred in carrying out his duties, (2) inform the agent of dangerous risks the principal has reason to know exist, and (3) for agents who are also employees, provide a place to work and access to the equipment, supplies, and accessories necessary to perform the work.

LIABILITY OF PRINCIPAL AND AGENT TO THIRD PARTIES

Liability of the Principal for Contracts Made by the Agent

The agent is a representative of the principal. Remember: The agent is an extension of the principal, an alter ego. Thus when an agent is acting within the authority granted by the principal, she can bind the principal to the deal.

The principal is bound contractually if the agent has either the *actual authority* (express or implied) to make a contract for the principal or has the *apparent authority* to do so.

If the agent can buy goods, manage real estate, or set up a branch office, she has the *implied authority* to make contracts to achieve these purposes. Almost every business transaction involves a contract, and the authority to conduct the principal's business usually carries with it the authority to make contracts assisting the business.

Apparent authority, unlike implied authority, arises out of actions or conduct of the principal that causes a third party to believe that the agent has the authority to make contracts for the principal. For example, a person dealing with a business over the telephone has the right to assume that the person answering the phone has the authority to transact normal business. Lawyers and judges sometimes say that an agent is "clothed" with apparent authority, that is, the principal has "dressed" the agent in such a manner as to lead others to rely on her authority. If the agent is given an office, a title, and a staff, third parties may reasonably believe the agent can bind her employer or principal. Indeed, any signals or other evidence of agency may create apparent authority (described earlier in this chapter as agency by estoppel).

Unknown to the third party, there may be a private order or memo to the agent that he is *not* to bind the principal, that the agent has no authority. Even so, if the third party relies on the appearance of authority, the principal is bound by the agent's contracts and is estopped (prevented) from denying the agent's authority.

Liability of the Principal for Torts of the Agent

DIRECT LIABILITY

A principal is directly responsible for his agent's torts under any of the following circumstances:

1. The principal gave the agent improper orders or instructions that caused the tort to occur.
2. The agent was improperly or negligently chosen or employed.
3. The principal failed properly to supervise or oversee the work when he had a duty to do so.

Examples: Direct Liability of the Principal

- An agent hired by the principal to drive the principal's bus has a record of drunken and negligent driving.
- A company car to be driven by an agent has defective brakes.
- An agent is given chemical pesticides with improper instructions for application to the fruit trees of a third person.

INDIRECT LIABILITY

This liability is founded on the common law doctrine of *respondeat superior:* "Let the superior respond." Because the principal chose the agent and held the agent out to the public as the transactor of the principal's business, that creates the public policy reason for holding the principal vicariously (indirectly) liable for the agent's misconduct.

The key requirement of indirect liability, *respondeat superior,* is that the agent act in the scope of her employment. The expression "scope of employment" is a legal phrase. An agent's conduct must meet four tests to create vicarious liability for the principal.

Hold the Principal Liable in Respondeat Superior if the Agent's Conduct:

- was of the kind the agent was hired to perform;
- occurred at an authorized place and time of employment;
- was motivated, at least in part, by service to the principal; and
- the methods chosen could have been anticipated by the principal.

If a night club bouncer evicts a drunken patron with such force as to cause death, the club owner is indirectly liable under the doctrine of *respondeat superior.* If, however, an elevator operator pulls a knife from his jacket and seeks to carve up a passenger, this tort would *not* be assigned to the building owner, the principal, under the doctrine of *respondeat superior* since the first, third, and fourth tests above are not met.

Another example: Suppose a campus security officer threatens to shoot a student. This tort would not be imputed to the university. (However, the negligent employment of the elevator operator or the security guard might give rise to direct tort responsibility.)

The principal is responsible for such torts as fraud and misrepresentation since they clearly meet the *respondeat superior tests.* Note that the principal's liability for fraud and misrepresentation is present even though no one, whether an agent or otherwise, has authority to misrepresent the product he is selling.

Torts of Independent Contractors

An independent contractor does not act under the supervision and control of the person who hired her. The contractor is chosen to accomplish a result by her own means. Consequently, the doctrine of *respondeat superior* does not apply to the torts of an independent contractor.

It is not always possible, however, to avoid liability by delegating work to an independent contractor. Under the law of torts, strict liability is imposed for certain "ultrahazardous activities," such as blasting and the transport of volatile chemicals or wild animals. Responsibility for mishaps arising from such activities cannot be delegated to an independent contractor.

Personal Liability of the Agent for the Principal's Contracts

DISCLOSED PRINCIPAL

If a third party knows, or should know, that the agent is acting for a principal *and* if the third party knows the identity of this principal, the principal is a *disclosed principal.*

The fact of the agency and the identity of the principal are usually disclosed in any contract with a third party. If the contract is between Priam, the principal, and Theo, the third party, then Agnes, the agent who negotiates the contract and signs Priam's name, is obviously the agent. Nevertheless, some word of agency should be used when Agnes signs—such words as *by* or *for* or *agent for*, or, if Agnes signs in her employment capacity, *president, sales manager,* or *secretary.* These words bind the principal, and the agent, who is acting within her authority, is not personally responsible.

Even if a principal is disclosed, however, the agent may have personal liability if, in fact, he had no authority. Obviously, if agent A merely claims to act for principal P, but P has not given her authority or clothed her with any appearance of authority, A is on her own and is bound by the contract, not P. Agent A may be personally liable for fraud.

However, if A, the agent, habitually acts for P and has the apparent authority to do so, but in fact P has either not given authority or has withdrawn it, *both* A and P may be liable to the third party. If the third party sues P and recovers, P may in turn recover from A, who had no authority in fact. In all cases where an agent discloses a principal, the agent is deemed to make an implied warranty that he has the authority to make a contract for that principal.

PARTIALLY DISCLOSED PRINCIPAL

This case involves a third party who knows that the agent is acting for a principal but does not know the identity of the principal. This *partially disclosed principal* situation occurs when a principal wishes privacy or seeks for financial reasons to conceal his identity. For example, a wealthy developer, seeking to accumulate a large commercial tract of land from a number of small landowners, may send his agent to obtain contracts with these owners. The fact of the agency is disclosed but not the name or identity of the principal. In such a situation the agent is liable on the contract. If the principal's identity can be determined and the agent cannot satisfy the contract, the principal may be liable on the contract also.

UNDISCLOSED PRINCIPAL

If neither the fact of agency nor the identity of the principal is disclosed (*undisclosed principal*), the agent is liable on the contract since the third party was led to believe the agent was the real party on the contract. The agent may recover from the undisclosed principal; if the third party learns of the agency, she, too, may recover directly from the principal, not just the agent.

Tort Liability of Agents

An agent who commits a tort, whether acting within the scope of his employment or not, is personally liable for the tort. If the agent is acting within the scope of employment, both he and the principal are simultaneously liable for the tort. In cases of such *joint and several liability*, the injured party may sue the principal, the agent, or both. Of course, the victim may not have a double recovery. The agent, the party who actually committed the tort, is liable to reimburse the principal for the latter's loss to third parties because of the agent's tort.

Example: Joint and Several Liability

Charlie Careless, a truck driver for the XYZ Hauling Co., while hauling a load of goods for the company, negligently runs over a child riding her bicycle. Both the principal (XYZ Hauling Co.) and the agent (Charlie Careless) are liable to the child for the tort. Technically, Charlie is liable to XYZ Hauling Co. for any judgment obtained by the child or her parents. (In practice, the principal's right to reimbursement is rarely invoked because the agent has too little money for it to be worthwhile.)

Liability for Crimes

If a principal directs, approves, or participates in a crime of her agent, the principal is criminally liable, as is the agent. An employer whose employees are violating criminal statutes in furtherance of their employment may be liable if the employer knows, *or should know*, of the criminal acts. Employees who violate pollution laws or antitrust laws create criminal liability both for themselves and for their employers if the employers fail adequately to supervise their job performance or negligently delegate work that the employees perform in a criminal manner.

TERMINATION OF AGENCY

By Acts of the Parties

The parties may terminate the agency by any act that would terminate a simple contract. If the agency was created for a specified time or for a specified purpose, it terminates upon the passage of that time or the accomplishment of that purpose. If no time is specified, the agency is terminated by the passage of a reasonable time.

The agency can also be terminated by mutual rescission, by revocation of authority by the principal, or by renunciation by the agent. Both revocation and renunciation are achieved by any communication, oral or written, manifesting withdrawal of consent. (Remember that agency is consensual; in the absence of a contractual obligation to continue the agency, the consent may be freely withdrawn by either party.)

To assure that there is no *lingering apparent authority*, the principal usually must give *actual notice* of termination (e.g., a telephone call, a certified letter) to third persons who previously dealt with the agent; for other third persons, the former agent's apparent authority may arise only if there was not even *constructive notice* of the termination.

Example of constructive notice: an announcement in a trade publication (newspaper or magazine read by people in that industry) that an agency had ceased.

Constructive notice serves as effective notice to these third persons regardless of whether they actually read the announcement or not.

By Operation of Law

The agency relation is terminated by any of the following:

1. The death or permanent incapacity of either the principal or the agent.
2. The bankruptcy of either party.
3. Frustration of the purpose of the agency. This frustration may occur because of the destruction of the subject matter (e.g., fire damage or loss to goods or property being bought or sold), changes in business conditions, or changes in the value of property being bought or sold.
4. Subsequent illegality of the business or of the business venture. This would occur, for example, if the business were prohibited, or if the agent were required to have a license that he could not reasonably obtain, or if the property were rezoned so as to prevent the legal operation of the business.
5. Impossibility of performance by either principal or agent. The test is the same as for terminating a contract because of impossibility (see Chapter 6).
6. Material breach of the agency contract by either principal or agent.

GENERAL PARTNERSHIPS

Comparison to the Other Main Types of Business Forms

There are three basic types of business organizations: sole proprietorships, corporations, and partnerships.

The *sole proprietorship* is the simplest form of business organization. The owner and her business are not distinct in the eyes of the law; that is, the owner is personally responsible for any debts she incurs on behalf of her business. The owner has *unlimited liability* for the debts and liabilities incurred by her business.

For the *corporation*, the business is treated as a separate entity from its owners. The owners of a corporation are the *shareholders*. Unlike a sole proprietor or a partner, under almost all circumstances the shareholders are not held personally liable for their corporation's debts or other legal liabilities. (Corporations are discussed in Chapter 10.)

In the *partnership*, two or more people are the owners of a business. By agreeing to establish and run a business for profit, these people have created a partnership. There are two main types of partnerships: *general partnership* and *limited partnership* (discussed below).

Introduction to Partnership Law

Partnerships are one of the oldest forms of business. Laws on partnerships can be found in Hammurabi's code as well as in early Hebrew and Roman texts. Although corporations, a more recent phenomenon, are the prevailing form among medium-sized and larger American businesses, and corporate law now involves a more extensive body of statutes and case law, the law of partnerships remains very important. Without knowledge of partnership law, a businessperson may be unable to decide intelligently what organizational form to use for a new, expanding, or recently acquired business.

Moreover, a businessperson will encounter partnerships in many of her personal and business activities and certainly should know something about their nature. For instance: How are partnerships created? What is their structure? How are they run, and who is responsible for their contracts, their debts, their torts?

A partnership consists of two or more co-owners of a business who expressly or implicitly agree to operate the business and who share in its profits or losses.

Creation of General Partnerships

Unlike corporations, a general partnership usually requires no special formalities in order to be created. All that is needed is a partnership agreement. Keep in mind, however, that this does not mean that the agreement must be in writing. Like most other contracts, the partnership agreement generally can be *express* or *implied,* with an express contract either written or oral. However, if a partnership agreement involves matters that fall under the Statute of Frauds, those matters must be in writing. For example, a partnership agreement authorizing a partner to transfer real estate must be in writing to be enforceable, at least with respect to the real estate concerns.

As a practical matter, a written document is usually the best way to assure that the partners, from the outset, understand the nature of the agreement and their responsibilities under the agreement. The existence of a partnership agreement, though, does not necessarily mean that the courts will treat the business as a partnership, especially if the so-called partners are not behaving as partners are expected to behave under the law.

BY EXPRESS AGREEMENT

Some typical provisions in an express partnership agreement include the following:

The partnership's name.

A general description of the partnership's business (i.e., what the partnership does).

A listing of the present partners.

A statement of the contributions made or to be made by the present partners.

A means of determining what constitutes partnership expenses rather than personal expenses.

A method for dividing profits and losses (if no method is provided, the law assumes that partners share profits and losses equally).

A statement of the general powers of the individual partners and the limitations on their authority.

A system for quickly managing routine matters while bringing more serious issues before a management committee or the full partnership.

Allocations of salaries and drawing accounts among partners.

Treatment of a partner's outside business interests (the partnership may want to limit any outside business activity by a partner that may compete with the partnership).

Conditions on an individual's withdrawal from the partnership.

Conditions on adding an individual to the partnership.

The partnership's term of duration.

The closing out or selling of the business upon the partnership's dissolution. Most of these provisions are discussed in greater detail below.

By Implied Agreement

If no express agreement (in writing or otherwise) exists between a set of individuals, a partnership may still exist between the individuals by *implied* agreement; that is, if a set of individuals behave like the co-owners of a business in relation to each other and in relation to the business, then they will be treated as partners in a partnership. This is so even if all of the individuals deny that they were partners.

The key factors that determine whether a set of individuals are indeed behaving like co-owners of a business are:

- whether the individuals *jointly owned* the business,
- whether the individuals *shared in the profits and losses* of the business, and
- whether the individuals had *equal management rights* in the business.

Generally, there must be some evidence of *all three factors*. For example, if Archie, Betty, and Chris jointly own property, contribute money to run a business on the property, decide how to conduct the business, and share the profits or losses from the business, a court probably would decide that they are all partners in a partnership.

Note, however, that installment payments on loans, interest payments, wages, rents, annuities, or money from the sale of business goodwill *do not* constitute profits. Thus, for example, if Archie and Betty own property together and receive rent from the leasing of the property to Dave, Archie and Betty will not be considered partners in their venture because one of the three crucial factors is missing: Archie and Betty are not sharing in the profits and losses of the business.

Furthermore, note that if Ernie borrows money from Frank for his business, and Frank agrees to structure repayment of the loan so that the payments are pegged to the profits of Ernie's business, Frank *is* sharing in the profits and losses of the business. This is so because his investment is conditioned on the financial well-being of Ernie's business. However, if Frank plays no active role in the operations of the business, Frank will not be found to have a role in the management of the business and thus will not be deemed Ernie's partner.

The *Uniform Partnership Act (UPA)*, adopted by every state but Louisiana, helps determine if a partnership exists in cases where no express partnership agreement has been reached. (It also fills in gaps in the agreement—matters that the partnership agreement does not cover.)

By Estoppel

A court may recognize that a general partnership exists by estoppel. In this case, a group of individuals never formed a partnership either expressly or impliedly. However, the law will treat a person as if he were a partner if:

- the person represents that he is a partner, or
- the person allows someone else to represent that he is a partner and does nothing to correct the misrepresentation.

The partnership to which the "partner" supposedly belonged may be fictitious, or it may be a real partnership, but one in which he is not actually a partner. (Either way, a partnership relationship does not exist between the supposed partners—it is only with respect to innocent third parties who reasonably believe there is such a partnership.)

The partnership by estoppel is created by courts for the benefit of innocent third parties that reasonably relied on false indications that there was a partnership. For example, Walter Weasel needs money so he goes to Big Bank. Walter tells the bank that he is partners with Ritchie Rich. The Bank, familiar with Ritchie's good reputation and extreme wealth, relies on that representation in granting Walter a loan. If Ritchie knew of Walter's falsehood but did nothing, the Bank will be allowed (by estoppel) to treat Ritchie as if he really were Walter's partner, collecting from Ritchie any money owed by Walter. Ritchie is estopped (prevented) from denying that a partnership exists.

Of course, Ritchie can seek to recover from Walter the money he had to pay to Big Bank. This is because the "partnership by estoppel" is only created for the benefit of innocent third parties (like Big Bank). Since Ritchie owes no duty (as a partner) to Walter, Ritchie can sue Walter for the money he had to pay Big Bank.

Rights and Duties of Partners

PARTNERSHIP VOTING AND DECISION MAKING

Each partner has both a right and a duty to help manage the partnership (UPA § 18). Ordinary business decisions are voted on by the partners. Unless the partnership agreement provides otherwise, each partner has one vote. Of course, an agreement by the partners to weigh votes differently is perfectly proper.

In some voting schemes, the weight of a partner's vote will depend on how much the partner contributed to the partnership. For example, Archie, Betty, and Charlie decide to form a partnership. Archie contributes $50,000 cash, Betty contributes a $100,000 office building, and Charlie contributes $150,000 worth of office equipment and supplies. The partners may decide that Charlie will have three votes, Betty two, and Archie only one.

Remember, however, that if the partners do not agree ahead of time on some kind of voting scheme, the law will treat each partner equally, granting each one vote.

Ordinary business decisions will usually require a simple majority vote. Because a decision cannot be made if the vote results in a tie, the partners should agree ahead of time on a method for resolving tie votes.

Certain very important business decisions will require the unanimous consent of all partners. Some of these include:

Amending the partnership agreement.

Changing the essential nature of a partnership's business.

Altering the capital contributions of partners (changing the capital structure).

Adding an entirely new line of business.

Admitting new partners.

Admitting partnership liability on a debt and agreeing to have a court judgment entered against the partnership on that debt (this is known as "confessing judgment").

Submitting the partnership to an arbitration proceeding as an alternative form of dispute resolution.

Transferring the partnership's goodwill.

Placing partnership assets in a trust or assignment for the benefit of creditors.

Conveying or mortgaging property (unless that is the usual business of the partnership).

Any act that would make it impossible to continue the operation of the partnership's business.

PARTNERS' RIGHTS AND DUTIES

Under the UPA, partners have certain rights and responsibilities. These include:

1. Each partner must work only for the benefit of the partnership, except for activities that do not compete with the partnership or infringe on the partnership's time. For example, a partner in a real estate business who works Monday through Friday *can* on the weekends add to his personal income by teaching windsurfing.
2. Partners are not generally paid a salary for partnership work. They are compensated in the form of partnership profits. Partners are also entitled to reimbursement for any partnership expenses or liabilities they personally incur.
3. Partners will generally receive a fixed salary for their services in winding up the affairs of a dissolved partnership (see "Dissolution" section below).
4. Each partner may examine and make copies of some or all of the partnership's records. Normally, partnership records are kept at the partnership's main place of business.
5. Each partner has a duty to produce, and a right to receive, complete information on all aspects of the partnership's business (e.g., financial records).
6. Partners are entitled to an *accounting* of partnership assets, liabilities, and profits whenever partners are excluded from the business or its records, whenever profits or other benefits have been wrongfully withheld or diverted, or whenever else such accounting would be just and reasonable.
7. Each partner has a *property interest* in the partnership, which is equal to (1) a return of her capital contributions upon dissolution of the partnership, and (2) a proportionate share of partnership profits. Each partner can assign, or creditors can attach, this property interest without dissolving the partnership itself.
8. Partners are *tenants in partnership* of all partnership property. This means a number of things: (1) the property may only be used for partnership purposes; (2) each partner has full possessory rights over the property; (3) none of the partners can assign, have attached, sell, or in any way transfer partnership property (including equipment, real estate, or office supplies); and (4) when a partner dies, his rights in partnership property pass to the surviving partners and *not* to the deceased partner's heirs. The heirs *do* have a right to the *value* of the deceased partner's property interest (see #7 immediately above).

PARTNER AS AGENT AND FIDUCIARY

Each partner is an agent for the other partner(s). As such, he or she owes the other(s) a high, fiduciary duty of care similar to that required in any principal/agent relationship. A partner must act in good faith for the benefit of the partnership.

Authority of a Partner to Bind Other Partners

There are four basic ways in which a partner may bind the partnership to a contract with a third party:

1. The partner has express actual authority stemming from the partnership agreement.
2. The partner has implied actual authority based on the partnership's business or the law of partnerships.
3. The partner has apparent authority as reasonably interpreted by the third party with whom he is dealing.
4. The partner's contract with a third party is ratified after the fact by the other partners.

Categories (2) and (3) (implied and apparent authority) are explained in the following sections.

IMPLIED ACTUAL AUTHORITY

Whether a partner was acting under implied actual authority requires review of various criteria, based mainly on the nature of the business and industry customs (if any). If the partner's activities were reasonably necessary to conduct ordinary partnership business, and if the partnership agreement did not prohibit such actions, then the partner's power to carry on such actions is implied.

For example, in most partnerships a partner can hire and fire employees, pay and collect partnership debts with partnership funds, and acquire personal property needed to conduct the business (e.g., inventory and equipment). Often, a partner has the partnership power to borrow money, settle claims, and receive notices on behalf of the partnership. The exact nature of these powers depends on the circumstances.

APPARENT AUTHORITY

The agency concept of apparent authority also applies to partnerships. Remember that the key to understanding apparent authority is to determine whether, under the circumstances, the third party was reasonable in his or her belief that the partner was authorized to act in the partnership's name. Apparent authority is particularly important concerning partnerships because, in the eyes of third parties, a partner is a co-owner of a business. As such, a partner will appear authorized to do much more than a mere employee.

Note that all four approaches (express actual, implied actual, apparent, and ratified authority) will bind a partnership to a contract with a third party. However, under express actual authority, implied actual authority, and ratification, a partner who enters into a contract with a third party can seek compensation from the partnership for any money he personally expended in a transaction with a third party. A partner with apparent, but not actual or ratified, authority not only has no rights against his fellow partner(s), but also may have to indemnify the partnership for binding it to an unauthorized transaction.

Liabilities of Partners to Third Parties

Because of their broad powers as the co-owners of a business, partners can bind the entire partnership to admissions or other statements made during the course of ordinary partnership business. Moreover, once a partner learns of facts relevant to running the partnership or its business, these facts are imputed to the partnership as a whole. Finally, because partners are principals for their employees *and for each other*, they are civilly liable under *respondeat superior* for torts or breaches of trust committed by an employee or partner acting within the scope of her authority. Note, however, that *respondeat superior* does not apply in criminal law. Thus, a partner will not be held criminally liable for a partner's crimes.

In cases of liability for torts or breaches of trust, the plaintiff may sue all of the partners together or any one or more of them separately (there is *joint and several liability*). However, for an alleged breach of contract, the plaintiff must sue all of the partners jointly (act simultaneously against all partners because they are jointly, but not individually, liable).

Partnership as a Distinct Entity Versus a Mere Aggregate

For a few limited purposes, partnerships are treated as entities; in these cases partnerships, like corporations, have a legal existence distinct from their individual owners (the partners). The following are some of the instances in which partnerships are considered distinct entities:

- In the case of bankruptcy, liquidation proceedings may be brought in the name of the partnership. This would effectively limit the liquidation to exclusively partnership assets and liabilities and would not include the nonpartnership assets and liabilities of individual partners.
- Judgments against the partnership entity usually must be collected from partnership property before collection remedies are instigated against individual partners.
- In most states, the partnership can, in the partnership's own name, sue, be sued, enforce judgments, have accountings performed, and own property.

For most purposes, the law makes no distinction between the partnership (as a legal entity) and its owners/partners. The law usually treats the partnership as a mere collection (aggregate) of individual partners. For example, as noted above, partners cannot generally disclaim personal liability for the partnership's acts or omissions. Furthermore, under federal income tax laws, the partnership, unlike the corporation, is *not* separately taxed. The individual partners are taxed on their shares of the profits but the partnership itself pays no "partnership income tax."

Termination of Partnerships

Partnerships are terminated upon their dissolution and liquidation (winding up).

DISSOLUTION

Dissolution is a change in the partners' relationship caused when one partner ceases, generally because of death or voluntary or involuntary withdrawal, to be associated with the partnership business (UPA § 29). There are three methods of dissolution: acts of the parties, operation of law, and court decree.

ACTS OF THE PARTIES

These acts serve to dissolve the partnership:

The partners agree to dissolve the partnership.

The partnership's term of duration expires (term of duration is usually provided for in the partnership agreement).

The partnership's purpose for being formed is completed (e.g., a partnership was formed to construct and sell an office building, and now the building has been built and sold).

A partner withdraws voluntarily from the partnership.

A partner is expelled by the partnership.

A new partner is admitted to the partnership (which will not only dissolve the existing partnership but create a new one).

If the partnership is *at will*, there is no set term of duration provided for by the partnership agreement. In such a case, a partner's expulsion or good faith withdrawal leaves neither the departing partner nor the remaining partners liable for breach of the partnership agreement. If a term of duration *is* specifically provided for, expulsion or withdrawal before the end of the term of duration is a breach if not done for good cause.

Whether or not a term of duration is provided for, *departing partners remain liable for partnership obligations existing at the time of their departure.* That is, no partner can cancel existing partnership obligations by dissolution. Of course, the remaining partners and any partnership creditor may agree not to hold the departing partner liable for the debts to that creditor.

A departing partner who fails to inform the remaining partners of her withdrawal may continue to be bound as a partner and held liable for future partnership obligations.

A new partner will be held liable only for partnership debts incurred after he joined the partnership.

Finally, note that a partner may assign his partnership interest or allow it to be attached *without* dissolving the partnership. The assignee or attaching party may acquire rights to profits or other rights, but not the right to get involved in the partnership at an operational or managerial level (UPA §§ 27, 28).

OPERATION OF LAW

This form of dissolution arises when:
- It would be unlawful to continue the partnership business or to conduct such business with one of the partners (illegality).
- The partnership or a partner has become bankrupt (*most* such cases serve as a dissolution).
- A partner has died.

A dead partner's share of partnership obligations passes to her estate. Thus, death will not eliminate that partner's liabilities. However, creditors for other debts will have their claims satisfied by the dead partner's estate *before* the estate pays claims from partnership creditors.

COURT DECREE

A court decree dissolving a partnership can be applied for by a partner or a third person. The *partner's grounds* for dissolution are as follows:
- A partner is insane or otherwise incapable of participating in the management of the partnership.
- A partner has acted improperly, either by breaching the partnership agreement or by doing something else that seriously harms the partnership's business or renders its continuation impracticable.
- The partnership's business can be operated only at a loss.
- Other circumstances, such as strong personal conflicts between partners, make dissolution equitable.

The *third person's grounds* for dissolving the partnership are more limited: if the third person is a partner's assignee or is the recipient of a judicial order attaching a partner's interests, then the third person may obtain a dissolution decree for a partnership (1) at will, (2) whose term of duration has expired, or (3) whose purpose for formation has been completed.

No matter which of the ways a partnership is dissolved, *notice of the dissolution* must be given to third persons to ensure that the partnership is not held accountable for future obligations. Of course, there is no duty to notify persons who did not know about the partnership. Likewise, in the case of a partner's withdrawal, there is no duty to notify anyone who did not know that the withdrawing partner was a partner.

Partnership creditors must receive *actual notice* (by mail, telephone, or the like). All others who knew about the partnership may be notified through *public notice* (e.g., a statement in the community newspaper).

LIQUIDATION

After the partnership is dissolved, it must be *liquidated.* The process of liquidation is commonly referred to as the "winding up" of the partnership. Under liquidation, the dissolved partnership retains authority to complete unfinished business and to do whatever else is needed to terminate the partnership. Typically, this process of winding up involves:

1. collection, preservation, and sale or other liquidation of partnership assets (including the collection of money owed by third parties to the partnership),
2. paying or otherwise settling partnership debts, and
3. accounting to each partner for the value of his partnership interest.

The distribution of assets proceeds in this order:

1. Third-party debts are paid off.
2. Any loans made to the partnership by one of its partners are repaid.
3. The capital contribution of each partner is returned.
4. The remaining assets are distributed to the partners in accordance with the scheme for dividing profits provided for in the partnership agreement. If the partnership agreement does not provide such a scheme, the remaining assets are divided equally among the partners.

NONBANKRUPTCY CREDITORS' PRIORITIES IN LOOKING FOR
PAYMENT FROM THE ASSETS OF:

A Dissolving Partnership	An Individual Partner
Higher priority: the partnership's creditors	*Higher priority:* the individual partners' creditors
Lower priority: the individual partners' creditors	*Lower priority:* the partnership's creditors

Only after the individual and partnership creditors are paid may partners seek contribution from another partner (payment of that partner's partnership obligations). Generally, a partner's personal creditors have no claim against the personal property of other partners.

LIMITED PARTNERSHIPS

Special laws on limited partnerships have existed since the Middle Ages, and the first limited partnership statutes in the United States were enacted during the early nineteenth century. A *limited partnership (LP)* is unlike a general partnership in that an LP has two distinct types of partners—general and limited. A *general partner* in an LP has essentially the same rights and responsibilities as a partner in a general partnership (discussed previously in this chapter). A limited partner, however, does not. A *limited partner* contributes capital to the partnership and receives a special share of the LP's profits. Unlike a general partner, the limited partner does not participate in the management of the partnership and is not held personally liable for partnership obligations and liabilities beyond the amount of her capital contribution.

A limited partnership must have at least one general partner and one limited partner. Ordinarily, there is no specified maximum number of limited partners.

A limited partnership must conform to state statutory requirements, including filing an LP certificate with the state. In this respect, as well as the limited liability of limited partners, the LP is similar to corporations. Almost all of the states have adopted a form of either the Revised Uniform Limited Partnership Act of 1976 (RULPA) or its 1985 amended version.

Limited partnerships can conduct almost any business that could be carried on by a general partnership. Exceptions include banking, insurance, and most professional partnerships, such as law firms.

Statutory Requirements

The LP certificate registered with the state must include the following information:

LP's name.

LP's location.

Name and address of its agents for service of process.

Names and addresses of its general partners.

Term of duration.

The 1976 RULPA (but not the 1985 amended RULPA) requires the following additional information:

A description of the LP's business.

Names and addresses of limited partners.

Cash amount or description and value of initial and subsequent (if any) contributions by each partner.

A description of all partners' rights to receive distributions, including return on contributions.

The method (if any) for withdrawing or changing partners and continuing the business.

Because limited partners are free from any liability beyond what they have contributed to the LP, statutory requirements must be carefully followed. If an LP fails to follow the proper filing procedures, third persons dealing with the partnership may have no way of knowing that the partnership is an LP. If this occurs, the third party will usually be permitted to treat the limited partners as if they were general partners. Thus, improper filing could subject a "limited" partner to unlimited liability. An LP doing business in more than one state should take care to follow the proper filing requirements in all of the states in which it operates.

The Limited Partner's Role

A limited partner is not automatically exempt from personal liability. His exemption from personal liability depends on his abstinence from any role in management, except for a few "safe harbor" activities listed in the RULPA, especially the 1985 version (e.g., the limited partner may consult with the LP's general partners, act as a contractor or surety for the LP, and propose and vote on fundamental changes to the LP).

The following factors are considered in determining whether a limited partner will be exempt from personal liability:

1. Under the law before the RULPA, the limited partner's contribution to the partnership had to be in the form of money or property, not services. The more liberal RULPA allows the limited partner's contribution to be in the form of money, property, services, a promissory note, or some other obligation.

2. The limited partner's name must not be included in the partnership name. Such inclusion would run the risk that third parties might think the limited partner is actually a general partner.

3. The limited partner must not represent or allow others to represent that she is anything but a limited partner.
4. The limited partner must withdraw from the LP, or at least renounce any future profits, upon learning that the partnership certificate is significantly defective (e.g., if the certificate contains material false statements).

If any of the above requirements are violated, the limited partner may be subject to personal liability. The limited partner will usually be protected, however, if the creditor seeking to hold the limited partner liable could not have had a reasonable belief that the limited partner was, in fact, a general partner. The limited partner is also protected if he engages in managerial activities within the partnership, but the creditor is unaware of the limited partner's involvement.

Unlike a general partner, a limited partner *does not* have the right to bind the partnership (e.g., in contracts with third parties). However, other than basic management tasks, the limited partner does have almost all of the other rights held by general partners.

Termination and Distribution of the Limited Partnership's Assets

Dissolution and winding up occur for the same reasons and by the same methods for an LP as for a GP. However, unlike in a GP, a limited partner's withdrawal, expulsion, or death does not automatically dissolve the partnership.

The order in distributing a dissolved LP's assets is dramatically different between the old Uniform Limited Partnerships Act (ULPA) and the RULPA. Under the ULPA, limited partners are elevated above the level of general partners. The ULPA priorities are:

Partnership creditors (including limited partners if they made loans to the partnership but *excluding* general partners who made loans to the partnership).
Limited partners' profit shares.
Limited partners' capital contributions.
General partners' loans to the LP.
General partners' profit shares.
General partners' capital contributions.

Under the RULPA, the limited partners and general partners are treated equally. The RULPA priorities are:

Partnership creditors (including both limited and general partners).
Accrued profit shares (of all partners).
Capital contributions (of all partners).
Any remaining assets (to all partners according to the LP's profit-distribution scheme).

Pros and Cons of Limited Partnerships

Pros: Tax laws sometimes make an LP more profitable than a corporation, which is subject to "double taxation" (discussed in Chapter 10). Also, in some instances, a group of individuals in the process of forming a GP may find that some of the members do not want to play a role in management or do not want to assume unlimited liability. In such cases, a limited partnership is in order.

Cons: The LP is not as effective as a corporation in shielding "owners" from personal liability. Moreover, LP agreements and certificates are subject to greater formalities than articles of incorporation, which can be very broadly drafted.

FRANCHISES

A *franchise* is a contractual arrangement in which the owner *(franchisor)* of a trademark, trade name, copyright, patent, trade secret, or some form of business operation, process, or system permits others *(franchisees)* to use that property, operation, process, or system in furnishing goods or services. Usually, the franchisee conducts a business in accordance with conditions and procedures prescribed by the franchisor, who in turn advertises, advises, perhaps lends capital, and otherwise assists the franchisees.

Types of Franchises

There are three main types of franchises:
1. Distribution system franchises (a manufacturer licenses dealers to sell products).
   Example: many gasoline or automobile dealerships.
2. Business format system franchises (the franchisees conduct a particular type of business under the franchisor's trade name and customarily follow the franchisor's standard method of operation).
   Example: fast-food franchises.
3. Manufacturing or processing arrangements (the franchisor provides its franchisees with the ingredients or formula for making a product and then marketing it in accordance with the franchisor's standards).
   Example: soft drink bottling franchises.

The Franchise Agreement

The franchise agreement, almost always prepared by the franchisor, is usually a very lengthy document covering many aspects of the prospective franchisor-franchisee relationship. It ordinarily contains, among other things, provisions on:
1. The franchisee's initial payment to the franchisor for receiving the franchise, as well as the continuing payments (royalties) throughout the term of the franchise. (Royalties are generally based on a percentage of the franchisee's gross sales, not his or her profits; thus, a franchisee will still owe the franchisor money even if his or her business is unprofitable.)
2. The franchisor's control over, or specifications about, business territory, structure, advertising, purchases, operations, inspections of the business premises, and audits of the franchisee's financial records.
3. The duration of the franchise, any renewal periods, and the franchisor's grounds for termination (usually numerous).

Benefits of Franchising

Some advantages to franchisors are:
1. Franchisees together provide much capital.
2. Franchisees provide a set distribution network.
3. Franchisees absorb much of the risk of losses.
Some advantages to franchisees are:
1. They can start a business despite limited capital and experience.
2. They take advantage of the existing goodwill associated with a trade name or product.

115

3. They can rely on the franchisor's business expertise.
4. They usually are assured access to supplies and prices based on volume buying.

Statutes and Case Law on Franchising

Franchisors tend to have more bargaining power than do the franchisees, particularly once the franchisee has joined a system and sunk its money into a franchised business. Many states have thus passed laws that require franchisors to register with the state and to provide certain information to a potential franchisee. The Federal Trade Commission mandates disclosure of rather detailed information about the franchisor and its business. Some states even regulate the substantive law of franchising, forbidding the franchisor from taking certain actions. The most common provisions (also adopted by case law in some states) require that franchisors act in good faith and that they have "good cause" (a fair reason) for terminating a franchise. In recent years, there have been numerous Congressional proposals to adopt a pro-franchisee national law on franchising. (Two federal laws already seek to protect the franchisees in particular fields—retail gasoline dealerships and automobile dealerships. Many states also have such specific franchise laws covering certain industries.)

QUESTIONS

Identify each of the following:

actual authority
actual notice
agency
agent
apparent authority
at-will partnership
commingling
constructive notice
corporation
creation of agency
direct liability
disclosed principal
dissolution
distribution of assets
duties
estoppel, agency by
express agencies
fiduciary
franchise

franchisee
franchisor
general partnership
implied agencies
independent contractor
indirect liability
joint and several
  liability
limited partnership
lingering apparent
  authority
liquidation (winding
  up)
partially disclosed
  principal
partnership
partnership by estoppel
partnership property
  interest

principal
ratification
respondeat superior
Revised Uniform
  Limited Partnership
  Act (RULPA)
scope of employment
shareholders
sole proprietorship
tenants in partnership
termination of agency
ultrahazardous
  activities
undisclosed principal
Uniform Partnership
  Act (UPA)
vicarious liability

Answer these Review Questions:

1. Is the agency relationship always created by contract?
2. May an agent pursue her own goals while acting for a principal?
3. What does it mean to be "clothed" with apparent authority?
4. Discuss the difference between a principal's direct and indirect liability for his agent's torts.
5. When may the hirer of an independent contractor be held liable for the torts of the independent contractor?
6. What are the three basic types of business organizations?

7. To what three factors do courts look for evidence of an implied partnership?
8. What acts generally require the partners' unanimous consent?
9. What are the three methods of partnership dissolution?
10. Choose the *false* statement: A partnership will dissolve if (a) a current partner dies, (b) a new partner is admitted into the partnership, (c) a partner decides she no longer wants to be a part of the partnership, (d) the partnership suffers a net loss in any given accounting period.

Apply Your Knowledge:

1. Why do corporations need agency law in order to function?
2. What type of obligation cannot be delegated to an agent?
3. Jim Johnson, a janitor at the Tiptop Trade Teepee in Topeka, Kansas, ordered 750 cartons of paper products from the LMN Toilet Supply Company. When the merchandise arrived, Tiptop paid the invoice. Three months later, Johnson ordered 750 more cartons from LMN. This time, when the merchandise arrived, Tiptop refused to pay and instead informed LMN of an internal Tiptop memorandum sent to Johnson that forbid him to order supplies. Who prevails?
4. Seedy Apartments employed Melvin Malefactor as a painter for the interior of its apartments. Unknown to Seedy, Melvin had been convicted of assault three years ago and of indecent exposure 15 years ago. Seedy had checked Melvin's references and found that he was an excellent painter on his last two jobs. While painting a Seedy apartment, Melvin raped a tenant. Is Seedy liable in tort?
5. Crud Corporation operates a large manufacturing plant. Minnie Manager, the plant supervisor, has caused sulfuric acid from the manufacturing processes to be dumped into a nearby river for years. Is Crud (a) criminally liable for this violation of the environmental laws, and (b) liable in tort to downstream property owners whose wells have been contaminated by the acid?
   Problems 6–9 refer to the following fact scenario:
   - There are six partners in a limited partnership (LP).
   - The general partners are A, B, C, and D.
   - The limited partners are E and F.
   - Under the partnership agreement, each general partner contributed $2,500 and is entitled to 15 percent of the profits of the partnership.
   - Under the partnership agreement, each limited partner contributed $20,000 and is entitled to 20 percent of the profits of the partnership.
   - On January 1, C assigns his interest in money receivable from the LP to Ms. C.
   - On February 1, E sells her partnership interest to Bank E.
   - On March 1, G is added to the LP as a new general partner; G makes no capital contribution.
   - On April 1, D dies.
   - Last year, the LP's accrued profits were $60,000, which have not been divided among the partners.
   - The LP has made no profits this year.
   - The assets and liabilities of the LP are as follows:
     * from January 1 to February 14,
         assets = $95,000, no liabilities
     * February 15 and thereafter,
         assets = $95,000, a judgment liability = $20,000
6. When was the LP dissolved?
7. Discuss other changes in the partnership concerning Ms. C, Bank E, and G.

8. Which partners are responsible for the judgment liability?
9. How is the money to be distributed? Answer under both the RULPA and the ULPA.
10. Charley Chef is a great cook, but he knows little about running a business. Marty Manager doesn't know spaghetti ricotta from terra cotta, but he is a very capable accountant and has served as manager of two restaurants in the past. Both have money to contribute to a possible business, and both would like to retain some control over the business. Which business form should be adopted? (a) A sole proprietorship by Charley, (b) a sole proprietorship by Marty, (c) a general partnership between Charley and Marty, (d) a limited partnership, with Marty as the general partner.
11. Leo and Gerald are partners in a limited partnership grocery store. Leo is the limited partner and Gerald is the general partner. Both Leo and Gerald contributed $50,000 in capital to the limited partnership.
    (a) Leo enters into a contract with Sally Supplier for $200,000 worth of goods. Sally is not familiar with the partnership, but is told by Leo that it is a general partnership. Relying on his representation and on Leo's good credit and reputation, Sally sells the partnership the goods on credit. Later, the partnership is unable to pay Sally any of the money owed. Which of these four statements is *true?*
       Leo can only be held liable for $50,000.
       Gerald can only be held liable for $50,000.
       The partnership can only be held liable for $100,000.
       Leo can be held liable for over $50,000.
    (b) Suppose Sally's dealings are with Gerald. Unbeknownst to Sally, Leo has taken on an active role in managing the affairs of the partnership. Later, the partnership is unable to pay Sally any of the money owed. Under the RULPA, can Leo be held liable for more than his $50,000 contribution?
12. Bob Baker has the time and expertise to put into a new bakery, but he has little money with which to do it. His friend, Mary Moneybags, has a substantial sum of money to invest, but she has no interest in the day-to-day operations of a business. What business form should be adopted?
13. Lonnie Loner wants to control a business completely, knows nobody else with whom he wishes to work, and dislikes formalities, paperwork, and (especially) lawyers. What business form should he adopt?

ANSWERS

Answers to Review Questions:

1. No. The agency relationship is consensual. The contractual requirement of consideration is not necessary to form an agency.
2. The principal's interests must always come first. The agent thus would be opening herself to a charge of conflict of interest. The agent should advise the principal in advance and obtain the principal's approval before pursuing these personal goals.
3. "Clothed" expresses the outward appearance of agency authority that a person with apparent authority has. He is not a real agent, yet those who reasonably believe him to be an agent may succeed in holding the supposed principal accountable for the apparent agent's actions.
4. Direct liability arises from personal participation in the tort; the principal herself is negligent, such as in choosing the agent or in supervising the agent. Indirect (vicarious) liability means that under the legal doctrine of *respondeat superior* the agent's negligence is imputed to the principal; the principal is an-

swerable for the agent's tort as if the principal committed it. (In effect, under *respondeat superior* the principal and the agent are the same—the latter's torts are also the former's.)

5. When strict liability is imposed because the work involves ultrahazardous activities. Also, when the hirer is directly responsible for the contractor's tort, such as when he negligently chooses or instructs the independent contractor.

6. Sole proprietorships, corporations, and partnerships.

7. Joint ownership, equal management rights, and the sharing of profits and losses.

8. Changing a partnership agreement or the essential nature of a partnership's business, adding a new business or new partners, confessing judgment, transferring goodwill, conveying or mortgaging most property, and altering capital contributions are the main such powers.

9. Acts of parties, operation of law, and court decree.

10. (d).

Answers to "Apply Your Knowledge":

1. A corporation is a legal "person," but it is not a real, flesh-and-blood individual. With no arms and legs of its own, the corporation must rely upon agents to do its business.

2. Obligations that are *personal* in nature, that require a particular person's skills or trust, cannot be delegated to an agent. These personal tasks are not merely clerical, administrative, or mechanical.

3. LMN. Tiptop's prior payment for an order placed by Johnson "clothed" Johnson with apparent authority. The private memorandum was not provided to LMN until after the order was shipped and thus should only serve to negate any potential *future* apparent authority.

4. Yes, insofar as Seedy was negligent in hiring Melvin. If Seedy should have checked police records or taken other precautions that would have revealed Melvin's criminal background, and if Melvin's record would have alerted a potential employer that Melvin was not suitable for this job, then Seedy's hiring of Melvin was negligent. If, however, checking the references was a sufficient inquiry, then Seedy did not breach a duty of care in hiring Melvin.

5. (a) Crud is liable for criminal acts committed by its plant supervisor in furtherance of her employment if the company knows or should know of these actions. The corporation has a duty to supervise the employee, and it seems that failure to do so may have permitted the wrongdoing. (b) Minnie has acted within the scope of her authority as plant supervisor, and thus her principal, Crud, is responsible for the tort. The four tests of "scope of employment," for *respondeat superior* to exist, are all met. Disposing of the acid is likely one of the tasks the supervisor is expected to handle; while her methods may not have been approved by Crud, certainly they could have been anticipated (and, one assumes, prevented).

6. On March 1, when G is added to the LP (a new LP is thereby formed); and on April 1, when D dies (terminating the new LP).

7. Ms. C can collect the profits due C; she just cannot participate as a general partner. If there is no agreement to the contrary, E may transfer her entire limited partnership interest and status to Bank E without dissolving the partnership. G may be added as a new general partner with the other general partners' permission.

8. G is not personally responsible for a debt incurred before his admission, except for an amount no greater than his capital contribution, which is nothing.

All of the other partners are responsible, with even the limited partners liable for the amounts of their capital contributions.

9. Under both the RULPA and the ULPA, the liability of $20,000 is paid, and $75,000 in assets remain.

   The following holds true, regardless of whether the law is the old or the new partnership act: C will receive nothing from the winding up because he assigned his interest to Ms. C; E will receive nothing from the winding up because she sold her partnership interest to Bank E; D will receive nothing personally from the winding up because he is dead, but his estate will receive whatever D was entitled to receive as a general partner (profits and D's capital contribution).

   Because there are no remaining creditors, the next priority under the *RULPA* is to pay the $60,000 in accrued profits. A, B, Ms. C, and D's estate each are entitled to 15 percent, and E and F each get 20 percent. The remaining $15,000 is distributed *pro rata* according to the partners' contributions. Thus F and Bank E each get 40 percent of the $15,000 (each had contributed 40 percent of the total $50,000 in contributions), while A, B, Ms. C, and D's estate each get 5 percent (each of these general partners, or the general partner from whom they acquired the interest, had contributed 5 percent of the total $50,000 in contributions). G receives nothing because he made no capital contribution.

   Under the *ULPA*, the $75,000 is first distributed to limited partners, with F and Bank E each receiving $32,000 (for each, a 20 percent share—$12,000—of the $60,000 in accrued profits, and then each getting back its $20,000 capital contribution). Assignee Ms. C, D's estate, and general partners A and B each receive one-fourth of the remaining $11,000; each is entitled to $9,000 in accrued profits—15 percent of $60,000—but because there is a total of only $11,000 to distribute, each of the four gets the proper proportion (one-fourth) of that. Nothing remains, so there is no return of any part of the general partners' capital contributions. Again, G, who had no accrued profits (he was not a partner then), receives nothing.

10. (c) Marty has too much of an interest in management, as does Charley, to be a *limited* partner.

11. (a) Leo can be held liable for over $50,000. Leo's actions removed the limits on his liability; he may be treated like a general partner. As a general partner, Gerald can be held liable personally—thus, for more than his $50,000 contribution. Likewise, if the partnership has any assets (e.g., accrued profits), the creditor can collect from those assets, not simply from the $100,000 in capital contributions. (b) No.

12. A general partnership seems inappropriate because of the disparity in wealth and interests of Bob and Mary. A limited partnership seems suitable, with Bob as the general partner and Mary as the limited partner. Bob's contribution could come in the form of property other than money (e.g., rent-free use of his house as a business location), or—under the RULPA—it could even be services or a promissory note.

   Whether to form a corporation instead of an LP depends upon the probable tax consequences and how concerned Bob is about his potential personal liability for partnership debts. Unless Mary's stock is nonvoting, however, Bob would probably be a minority shareholder, with true control of the company in the wealthier Mary's hands.

13. Sole proprietorship.

Chapter 10

Corporations

NATURE OF A CORPORATION

A *corporation* is an artificial being, or entity, entirely separate from the people who own and operate it. This separation gives the corporation a life of its own and the same accountability under the law as a natural person.

A corporation would continue to exist even if all the shareholders, directors, officers, and employees of the corporation were to die simultaneously. Stock ownership would pass to heirs of the deceased shareholders; these new shareholders would name new directors and hire new officers and employees.

Contrary to popular opinion, the typical corporation is quite small. Over 99.5 percent of all corporations have less than 20 shareholders.

COMPARISON WITH OTHER BUSINESS FORMS

COMPARISON OF SOLE PROPRIETORSHIPS, PARTNERSHIPS, AND CORPORATIONS

Item	Sole Proprietorship	Partnership	Corporation
Creation	Few, if any, requirements (easiest to organize)	By agreement of partners (generally should be written, but can be implied; limited partnerships, though, must complete and file a statutory form)	By statutory authorization (must meet state requirements to receive a state charter)
Formality required	Little	Some (more for limited partnerships)	The most
Governmental regulation of the business structure	Almost none	Little, except for limited or other special partnerships	The most
Owners	The proprietor	The partners	The stockholders

Item	Sole Proprietorship	Partnership	Corporation
Transfer of an owner's interests	By sale of business, inheritance, or other lawful means chosen by proprietor	Buyer can receive some but not all rights of a partner unless remaining partners agree; limited partner's interest is freely transferable	In most cases, stock is freely transferable
Legal entity separate from owners?	No	Generally no, but most states recognize the partnership as a legal entity for a few purposes, such as owning property in the firm's name	Yes, for almost all purposes
Agency	If business has employees (agents), proprietor is principal	Except for limited partners, each partner is both a principal and an agent of the other partner(s)	Officers are the corporation's agents; stockholders and directors are not
Liability of individual owners for business debts or actions	Unlimited	Unlimited except that in a limited partnership the limited partners usually can lose only their investments	Limited; stockholders generally can lose only their investments
Use of business funds to pay personal debts	Generally permitted	Usually prohibited	Prohibited
Profits	Solely the proprietor's	Shared equally by partners, unless partnership agreement states otherwise	Profits are retained by corporation or distributed pro rata to stockholders as dividends
Management	The proprietor	General partners—equal votes unless expressly stated otherwise in partnership agreement; limited partners have no direct management rights	Management distinct from owners; officers are appointed by directors, who are elected by stockholders

Item	Sole Proprietorship	Partnership	Corporation
Changes in business formation documents	Need not file with the state	Need not file with the state unless a limited partnership	Must file with the state and perhaps must obtain state permission (which is usually a mere formality)
Organizational fee, annual licensing fee, and annual reporting requirements?	No	Generally no	Yes
Requirements for doing business in other states	Usually none	Usually none, but limited partnerships must file copies of a completed statutory form	Generally must register to do business and obtain state certificate of authority
Ability to raise capital	Often difficult	May be difficult without adding new partners, to which all general partners must agree	Comparatively easy; may just issue (and sell) additional stock
Income taxes	Profits part of personal income; no separate tax for the proprietorship	Each partner's share of profits (whether distributed or not) is part of his personal income; no separate tax on the partnership	"Double taxation"—corporation pays income tax on net profits (no deductions for dividends); dividends then become part of each stockholder's personal income and thus are taxed again
Termination	By sale, insolvency, or voluntary cessation of business; or by death or incapacity of proprietor	By terms of partnership agreement; by subsequent agreement of partners; by death, incapacity, or withdrawal of one or more partners; or by sale, insolvency, or voluntary cessation of business	Can have perpetual existence, as provided by statute or articles of incorporation; can continue despite death, incapacity, or withdrawal of officers, directors, or stockholders

Item	Sole Proprietorship	Partnership	Corporation
Size of business	Can be substantial, but tends to be small	Can be substantial, but tends to be small	Varies from small to the largest business entities in existence: although most corporations are not large, the biggest, most significant businesses are or become corporations

ADVANTAGES AND DISADVANTAGES OF THE TWO MAJOR BUSINESS FORMS

General Partnership's Advantages Over the Corporation

Formation:	Easier
Organizational costs:	Usually less
Taxes:	(a) No "double taxation" (b) No tax on exempt interest (e.g., from municipal bonds) partner receives from partnership (c) Share of business operating losses more easily and immediately deducted from a partner's personal income (d) In many states, no state income tax on the partnership itself (e) No social security tax for partners (disadvantage: may have a self-employment tax)
Owners' voice in management:	A more direct role
Multistate operations:	Few legal formalities
Governmental regulation:	Generally less
Flexibility of decision making:	Generally greater

General Partnership's Disadvantages

Taxes:	(a) Partners required to pay tax on undistributed income (b) Missing many other tax advantages of a corporation
Number of owners:	As a practical matter, there are limits
Ability to raise capital without loosening control:	Usually more difficult; unless changed to a limited partnership, cannot raise capital by increasing number of owners without affecting actual or potential control of business
Duration:	Depends on good relationships of partners; withdrawal or death of a single partner can unhinge the entire partnership business
Owners' liability for entity:	Unlimited

General Partnership's Disadvantages (*cont.*)

Owners' liability for other owners' acts:	Often unlimited
Ability to transfer ownership interest:	Usually more difficult

Corporation's Advantages Over the General Partnership

Taxes:	(a) No personal tax on undistributed profits (b) Favorable tax treatment of some expenses or benefits (c) Employee stock option purchase plans are available (d) For corporations with only a few stockholders, Subchapter S status may be available: this permits the favorable tax treatment that a partnership sometimes has (no double taxation, immediate deductibility on personal income for business losses), while allowing corporate form in other respects
Number of owners:	Unlimited
Ability to raise capital without loosening control:	For medium or larger corporations, generally easier and can obtain larger amounts; use of nonvoting or preferred stock, can raise capital and increase number of "owners" without affecting control of business
Duration:	Can be perpetual; not structurally dependent on individual owner's good relationships or health
Owners' liability for entity:	Limited (however, lenders or other parties contracting with a small corporation often require that the corporation's stockholders personally guarantee any debts)
Owners' liability for other owners' actions:	Usually none
Ability to transfer ownership interest:	Generally easier

Corporation's Disadvantages

Formation:	More complicated
Organizational costs:	Usually more
Taxes:	(a) "Double taxation": corporate tax on the corporation's income (no deduction for dividends) plus a personal tax on the stockholder's income (including dividends) (b) Exempt interest distributed by corporation is fully taxed income for stockholders (c) Subject to state income tax (deductible on federal income tax) (d) Missing some of the tax advantages of a partnership
Owners' voice in management:	May be little or none

Corporation's Disadvantages (*cont.*)

Multistate operations:	Generally must register to do business in each state and also make other filings
Governmental regulation:	Generally more
Flexibility of decision making:	Generally less

For businesses owned by more than one person, the major types of organizations are partnerships and corporations. The decision of which organizational form to use depends on many factors, such as costs, relationships among owners, desirability of linking ownership and direct management, need to limit potential individual liability, raising of capital, size of the business, and (often most important) tax consequences.

A general partnership should require fewer legal formalities and afford a more direct tie between ownership and management. However, individual liability is unlimited, and duration is less assured and more dependent on continued good relations among all owners.

A corporation can increase ownership and (usually) capital without drastically affecting management; the duration is more definite (can be perpetual); and ownership interests are more easily transferred. Disadvantages for corporations include "double taxation," greater formal requirements and costs, and greater potential for separation of owners from management.

BACKGROUND OF CORPORATIONS

Although the imperial government of Rome suppressed private societies and associations of every kind, it permitted individuals to form *collegia*—nonprofit membership clubs for such diverse purposes as education, fire control, and burial of members. In the late Middle Ages and early modern period (the twelfth through the sixteenth centuries) the Roman model was expanded in France and Germany to permit merchants to form trading societies and craft guilds for business purposes.

In the late 1500s the English government began to grant monopolies to individuals or groups of individuals, for trading and revenue purposes, with the Crown receiving a share of the monopoly profits. Colonization of the New World was undertaken by such monopolies, which, when granted a charter for the colonization and development of a specified territory, operated as the government of that territory under the general supervision of the king. Trading ventures such as the *Massachusetts Bay Company*, *Hudson's Bay Company*, and the *East India Company* were established for exploration and development of the New World and other foreign lands.

During the colonization period corporate charters were granted to private individuals by special acts of the colonial legislatures. When the United States became a nation, corporations were created by a grant of charter from any of the individual states, first by legislative enactment, and later by special state agencies or commissions created for this purpose. In all states, corporations are created by a state corporation commission, although the management of corporations is left to internal controls within the corporate structure.

Most states now follow, to some degree, the Model Business Corporation Act (MBCA), which was first proposed in 1950 and since has been frequently amended (including a completely overhauled Revised Model Business Corporation Act (RMBCA) in 1984). Still, the state corporation commission is little more than the issuer of the corporate charter at the beginning of the corporate life. In practice, the state rarely takes any interest in the actual corporate function; nevertheless, a corporation must be a good citizen. It may be punished for its crimes, sued for its torts, and held accountable for its contracts. At all times it must be operated for the benefit of its shareholders, who are its owners.

CORPORATE ATTRIBUTES

A Legal Person

For most legal purposes a corporation is a person. Like any citizen, it can sue and be sued, make contracts, own property, and perform other personal acts. Moreover, it can be charged with almost any crime, except crimes that are only punished by imprisonment. For most purposes, a corporation is entitled to the protection afforded citizens under the Bill of Rights, except the Fifth Amendment's right against self-incrimination.

Creation by Statute

A corporation is created by filing—in compliance with state law—articles of incorporation. The evidence of a state-corporation contract is the corporation's granted charter (the accepted articles of incorporation). State statutes provide that, as a condition on the grant of a charter, the state later may modify the terms of that charter.

Limited Liability of Shareholders

Since a corporation is a legal entity separate from its shareholders, it, and not the shareholders, is liable for its debts. However, the courts may hold shareholders liable for corporate debts if the corporate name is used as a false front behind which the owners or operators commit fraud. This "piercing the corporate veil" occurs if two conditions are present: (1) a fraudulent purpose, and (2) operation of the corporate business as though the corporation does not exist.

Thus, the corporate veil may be pierced if someone creates a corporation and uses a corporate name, but holds no corporate meetings, keeps few corporate books or records, and generally disregards the corporation, while fraudulently permitting or causing others to believe that she is, in fact, personally responsible for the corporation's business and debts.

Perpetual Existence

Modern corporations are usually granted *perpetual existence* as a routine charter provision, although corporate existence may be for a limited period.

FORMATION OF THE CORPORATION

The Promoter

A *promoter* is the person who conceives of, organizes, and begins the corporation.

The corporation is the promoter's "brain child." The promoter finds others who are willing to participate in the development and exploitation of the idea.

Although not an agent of the corporation to be created, the promoter occupies a fiduciary relationship regarding the proposed corporation and its investors and creditors. A fiduciary relationship is a position of trust in which the fiduciary (the promoter) has a very high duty of fairness and honesty. This trust relationship requires that the promoter make full disclosure of any anticipated personal gain, the nature of the business, its prospects, and the promoter's plans for the business.

While forming the corporation, the promoter may incur costs, make contracts, and do other acts in furtherance of the corporation. Since the promoter is not an agent, the corporation is not automatically responsible or liable for these obligations and contracts; however, it *may* ratify (i.e., adopt or accept) them, provided that there is full and open disclosure by the promoter to the corporation. The promoter remains obligated on these contracts unless released by the other party to the contract or unless the corporation is substituted for him by a novation (see Chapter 5).

Obtaining the Charter

The people wishing to form a corporation (the *incorporators*) apply to the state corporation commission for a charter by filing with the commission a copy of a proposed charter. Although this charter is usually prepared by an attorney, that is not required. (A detailed discussion of the nature and content of the charter follows later in this chapter.)

A requested charter is reviewed by the commission; and if the state corporation law is met, the charter and a certificate of incorporation will be issued by the appropriate state official.

The certificate of incorporation *is the state's official authorization for the corporation to begin business.*

First Organizational Meeting

After receiving a certificate of incorporation, the incorporators call a meeting of the interim board of directors named in the charter. At this meeting, bylaws are adopted, officers are elected, and other necessary business is transacted. *Once stock is issued and sold, the shareholders meet and elect the regular board of directors.*

TYPES OF CORPORATIONS

Profit or Nonprofit

Business law primarily is concerned with corporations organized for profit. However, nonprofit, or charitable, corporations are of great importance, even in the business world, because of the important tax benefits and concessions given to such corporations and because of the importance of permitting these charitable groups to own property, form contracts, and otherwise engage in business without individual members having personal liability for business matters. Such corporations may be stock corporations, or *membership corporations* (owned by their members without issuing stock).

Domestic, Foreign, or Alien

A corporation is said to be *domestic* in the state of its incorporation, the state of its "birth." In all other states it is a *foreign corporation*. For example, in Delaware, a corporation incorporated in Delaware is a domestic corporation; in all other states it is foreign.

Corporations formed in foreign countries are called *alien corporations*.

Close Corporations

A *close corporation* is a stock corporation whose shares are held by relatively few people, frequently members of a family. In many states, a close corporation may be operated like a partnership, sometimes with no board of directors, or with other informalities not permitted in general stock corporations.

In exchange for permitting such loose organization, those states limit the number of stockholders. Most states also permit restrictions on stock transfer by a provision in the charter, or by an agreement among the shareholders.

S Corporations (formerly "Subchapter S" of the Internal Revenue Code)

S corporations are organized to minimize the effect of federal income taxes on small businesses, principally by doing away with corporate "double taxation." This double taxation, as explained earlier in this chapter, is taxation applied first to the corporation's income, then again to the individual shareholder's dividend income.

The S corporation does not pay a corporate income tax on earnings. The shareholders pay individual income tax on the entire corporate income, whether or not any of that income was actually paid out to them.

S corporations must meet a number of requirements. The main restrictions are: they cannot have more than 35 shareholders; all shareholders must own the same class of stock; and no shareholder can be a corporation, partnership, or other non-natural person. There are proposals to make the S corporation a more widely available option (by allowing more shareholders, different classes of stock, etc.).

Limited Liability Companies

Because S corporations have so many restrictions, the *limited liability company (LLC)* is an alternative. A 1988 IRS ruling that, for tax purposes, LLCs are to be treated like partnerships has led most states to authorize LLCs. Unlike the S corporation, the LLC has no restrictions on the number of owners, the class of stock, the owning of subsidiaries, and the like; and unlike general or limited partnerships, the LLC permits investors to *manage* the business yet not be personally liable for the business debts. Thus the LLC is a partnership-corporation hybrid. The corporate shield protects against personal liability, but LLC "members" are like partners in that, to avoid tax treatment as if the LLC were a corporation, two of these three partnership characteristics must be present: (1) a member's death or decision to pull out dissolves the LLC, (2) transfer of a membership requires the other members' approval, and (3) the LLC is managed by all of the members rather than elected managers or directors. However, LLC law is in its infancy, so many legal issues are still unsettled.

Professional Corporations

Professional corporations are created by lawyers, doctors, accountants, architects, engineers, and other professionals in order to gain corporate advantages for traditional partnership or proprietorship activities. These corporations, organized under state law enacted in conformity with Internal Revenue Code requirements, are generally identified by abbreviations: P.A. (Professional Association), P.C. (Professional Corporation), or S.C. (Service Corporation).

Professional corporations receive the tax benefits of a corporation without the double taxation.

Most states leave the individual professional within the corporation free from personal liability for the professional negligence of another member of the organization, unless the individual was supervising the negligent member. However, as in any other form of business, members are individually liable in tort for their own professional negligence. This contrasts with partnership law, in which each partner is responsible for the torts of the other partners within the scope of the partnership venture.

NATURE AND CONTENT OF THE CHARTER; BYLAWS

The Charter

The *charter* (sometimes called the *articles of incorporation*, or *articles*) is the state's grant of corporate existence. It is the birth certificate of the corporation. This formal document, executed by the state through its corporation commission, is the source of a corporation's authority, and is a public document.

Although the charter may contain any number of provisions, modern charters tend to cover only the minimum provisions required by law. *The charter document is more or less a form; however, the required coverage may vary from state to state.*

The following information is usually required in the charter:
- Incorporators.
- Corporate name.

- Corporate address and resident agent's name and address.
- Duration.
- Purpose.
- Capital structure.
- Internal organization.

INCORPORATORS

The incorporators are the people who apply for the charter. Their only function is to sign the incorporating documents. By so doing, they acquire no special legal liability. Generally, the only requirement is that an incorporator be old enough to make a contract (at least 18 years old). Usually, there must be at least three incorporators. Many states do *not* require that these incorporators be residents of the state.

NAME

Any name may be chosen for the corporation provided that: (1) the name indicates that the entity is a corporation by including one of these words, or an abbreviation: Company (in most states), Corporation, Incorporated, or Limited; and (2) the name is not the same as, or misleadingly similar to, the name of any other domestic corporation, or a foreign or alien corporation doing business in the state.

In addition, many states limit the use of certain words closely associated with particular types of businesses or industries. For example, a manufacturing concern would not be allowed to include in its name a word such as *insured, finance,* or *fiduciary.*

CORPORATE ADDRESS AND REGISTERED AGENT'S NAME AND ADDRESS

The corporate address is the principal address of the corporation in the state of its incorporation.

The registered agent is a person or another corporation authorized to receive service of process and other legal documents. The requirement that a legal agent be named is important, because a person having business with a corporation, or interested in bringing suit against it, must be able to find the corporation to hold it accountable for its actions.

DURATION

The duration may be perpetual or limited to a stated period of time.

PURPOSE

Modern statutes permit a corporation to be organized for any lawful purpose, and the charter may contain merely a broad statement such as "organized for any legal purpose." Usually, however, the charter states the specific purpose for which the corporation is being formed (for example, "to operate a restaurant business) followed by very broad grants of power and usually a statement of purpose to do any other legal act.

Charters that fail to contain a "for any legal purpose" provision are nevertheless granted such broad powers except those that conflict with express charter restrictions on certain powers or rights.

CAPITAL STRUCTURE

Requirements concerning charter statements about capital vary from state to state. Generally, state incorporation statutes require information about the number of shares of stock that the corporation has authority to issue, the par value, and other matters concerning both equity and capital.

INTERNAL ORGANIZATION

State statutory requirements about organization are quite minimal: Usually the only requirements are a statement of the number of directors and the names and addresses of those who will serve as an interim board until the shareholders meet and name the first board.

Other organizational and day-to-day matters are usually left for the bylaws.

OTHER PROVISIONS

The charter may include other provisions, not inconsistent with law, defining, limiting, or regulating the powers of the corporation, its directors, or its shareholders. Some provisions commonly included are a restriction on the transferability of stock (e.g., for a close or S corporation), a requirement that shareholders need greater than a majority vote to approve certain actions, a cumulative voting mechanism to enhance minority shareholder representation, and a preemptive rights clause.

Bylaws

Generally, the charter should be a lean, sparse document, and the bylaws should be more detailed. The reason is that charter amendments must be approved by the state as well as the shareholders. Bylaws are generally adopted by the directors and may or may not require approval by the shareholders.

Bylaws contain specific provisions for the organization and operation of the corporation, such as election and operation of the board of directors, voting requirements for shareholders, and the quorum and places for meetings.

The bylaws may not contain a provision contrary to, or inconsistent with, the charter.

CORPORATE POWERS AND LIMITATIONS

Powers

Modern corporations are granted very broad powers; in most states they can perform any act that is not illegal. Thus, for most purposes, a corporation has all of the rights of a natural person.

The MBCA and RMBCA list a number of general powers for a corporation, including the power:

- to sue and be sued;
- to make and amend bylaws, consistent with the articles of incorporation and with law;
- to purchase, lease, and otherwise acquire real and personal property;
- to sell or dispose of its property;
- to purchase, own, hold, vote, or pledge stock;
- to make contracts and guarantees, incur liabilities, and issue notes and bonds;
- to lend money and invest and reinvest its funds;
- to be a promoter, partner, member, associate, or manager of a joint venture or partnership;
- to conduct its business and exercise the powers granted by law within or outside the state; and
- to do any lawful act that furthers the corporation's business.

Limitations on Powers

Powers are, however, sometimes limited by statute, by the corporation's charter, by the bylaws, or by a resolution or other action of the board of directors.

By Statute

A number of statutory limitations may be placed on the power of corporations. For example, statutes frequently limit a corporation's power to make a gift.

By Charter, Bylaws, or Action of the Directors

Further restrictions on corporate power can be placed in the charter or bylaws. These may include limits on the borrowing power of officers, on pensions or salaries, on the purchase of real estate, and on the sale of assets.

Other limits may be established from time to time by resolution or other specific action of the board of directors.

REGULATION OF FOREIGN CORPORATIONS

If a corporation wishes to "do business" in a state other than the one in which it was incorporated, it must register in that other state as a foreign corporation. Although registration may be a mere formality, the corporation must pay a fee, sometimes post a bond, and always designate a registered agent in that state to receive service of process and other legal papers.

The out-of-state corporation, having subjected itself to the laws of the state in which it seeks to do business, is vulnerable to the expense and difficulty of suit in a more remote or inconvenient location. Penalties for failure to qualify or register can be severe, such as: loss of the privilege of using state courts to file a lawsuit; a fine for every day of failure to register while doing business; and personal liability of officers, directors, and agents for actions in the foreign state.

The key phrase in determining whether out-of-state registration is necessary—doing business.

Doing business—It is generally held that a foreign corporation is doing business within a state if it maintains sufficient contacts or ties within a state on a continuous or regular basis or otherwise so as to make it fair and equitable that the corporation be accountable in the foreign state.

(See the discussion of personal jurisdiction in Chapter 1.)

Not doing business—Under the federal constitution, a state cannot restrict or regulate interstate commerce. Therefore a state cannot require registration for a foreign corporation doing an *interstate* business, that is, coming through on its way to another state.

CORPORATE OVERVIEW

The Corporate Structure

The *shareholders* own the corporation. They elect a board of *directors*, who oversee the management of the corporation. The directors, in turn, name and employ the *officers*, who are responsible for the day-to-day operation of the business.

Officers

Directors

Shareholders

Corporate Objectives

Theoretically, the modern corporation has the power to accomplish any lawful purpose. However, corporate powers must be exercised in the interests of the shareholders. The trustees of the corporation (the board of directors) have wide discretion to determine precisely the best way to funnel corporate powers into shareholder gain. Corporate profits will result in shareholder gain; corporate losses become shareholder losses.

Gain or loss is not necessarily measured only in financial terms. A good corporate image created by conformity with environmental laws, charitable acts, and good neighbor policies within the larger community may foster profits and serve the shareholder. In contrast, a corporation that pollutes the air and water and neglects its employees may inhibit profits and harm its shareholders.

A corporation cannot act for the profit and benefit of others to the neglect of its shareholders. In other words, while the community at large, or certain charities, or the company's workforce, may benefit by corporate action, all such benefit must somehow contribute to the ultimate good of the corporation and therefore of the shareholders.

SHAREHOLDERS

Shareholder Functions

ELECTION OF DIRECTORS

Although shareholders own the corporation, they do not have the right to directly manage it.

The primary rights of the shareholder are to attend meetings of the shareholders, to elect directors, and to vote on other fundamental matters affecting the corporation that, by statute or charter, require a shareholder vote. Other than these three rights, a shareholder cannot interfere with the directors or with their management of the corporation, even though the shareholder may own a majority, or even all, of the outstanding shares.

AMENDMENT OF THE CHARTER

At common law, a corporate charter was considered a contract between the state and the corporation, and between the corporation and the shareholders. Change of the contract therefore required both state approval and unanimous shareholder approval.

Under modern corporate law a change can be accomplished by a less than unanimous shareholder vote. The percentage of shares required for approval of a charter amendment varies among the states and in accordance with the nature of the proposed amendment. Generally, minor changes, such as dropping the word *The* from the corporate name or changing the registered agent, do not require *any* shareholder approval and can be done by the directors. However, drastic changes in the nature of the corporate business, or changes affecting the value of the stock or voting rights may, depending on the applicable state statute, require approval of:

1. a majority of the shares present and voting, or
2. two thirds of the shares outstanding and entitled to vote, or
3. a majority of the outstanding shares entitled to vote.

(An *outstanding share* is a share owned by anyone other than the corporation itself.)

Change must be proposed by the board of directors; shareholders cannot propose a change. Certain changes may specifically require that dissenting shareholders be given the right to sell their stock to the corporation at its appraised value.

MERGER AND CONSOLIDATION

In a *merger*, corporation A buys all of the stock of B; A continues to exist, but B will either dissolve or continue as a subsidiary of A. In a *consolidation*, corporation C (which generally would be created for this specific purpose) buys the stock of A and B. Each old corporation, A or B, either dissolves or continues as a subsidiary of C.

In a merger, approval is required in all cases by the shareholders of B, the merged corporation. Approval also is required by the shareholders of A, the continuing corporation, unless that corporation (1) already owns most of the stock of the merged corporation, or (2) is so much larger than the merged corporation that the acquisition of the smaller corporation will have no effect on the business of the survivor or on the value of its stock.

<u>Example: Merger</u>

If corporation A, with assets in excess of $50 million, merges with corporation B, with assets of $100,000, approval by the shareholders of A would not be required. The shareholders of B, however, must approve.

In most states, two thirds of the outstanding shares eligible to vote must approve a merger or consolidation.

SALE OF ASSETS

Sale of substantially all of the assets of a corporation, other than in the regular course of business, requires shareholder approval. As with consolidations and mergers, most states require that two thirds of the shares outstanding and eligible to vote approve such a sale. The meaning of the phrase "substantially all" varies from case to case, but the principal test is whether the sale affects the corporate business to the extent that the nature of the shareholders' investment has changed.

> *Shareholder approval not required:* The corporation owns five fertilizer plants; two are sold and the proceeds are used to repair and remodel the remaining three.
>
> *Shareholder approval required:* Two of the five fertilizer plants are sold, and the proceeds are used to invest in facilities and technology for the manufacture of ice cream.

Prudent business practice dictates that the shareholders' approval be obtained in any doubtful or borderline case.

Shareholder Meetings

Shareholders carry out their functions at annual, and sometimes additional special, shareholder meetings.

NOTICE OF MEETINGS

Notice of both the annual meeting and of special meetings must be given to the shareholders of record, that is, shareholders whose names appear on the share transfer books of the corporation at the time of notice. The notice for special meetings must state the purpose of the meeting, such as a charter amendment or the sale of all or substantially all of the corporate assets.

Failure to give notice will void any shareholder action unless the shareholders waive their objection by attending the meeting without objection or by signing a written waiver.

CONDUCT OF THE MEETING

For the meeting to be official, a *quorum* (usually defined by state law as a majority of shares outstanding) must be present in person or by proxy. The president or chairman of the board usually presides, and minutes (a record of the meeting) are kept by the secretary of the corporation. Many states, by statute, permit shareholder action without a meeting, provided that all (in some states, a majority) of the shareholders give their consent in writing to the actions taken.

VOTING

Most matters are decided by a majority of the votes cast. In the election of directors, each share has one vote for each director. This mode of director election is usually referred to as *straight voting*. If, for example, seven directors are to be elected, the holder of 100 shares may cast up to 100 votes for each of seven nominees.

Cumulative Voting

In most states, cumulative voting is permitted by law, or by special provision in the charter. For the example just given, in cumulative voting the holder of 100 shares has a potential of 700 votes and may distribute them among seven nominees as the shareholder chooses. If this shareholder accumulates these votes and casts all 700 in favor of a single nominee, this nominee may very well be elected when there are, for example, a total of 1,000 shares present and voting.

By cumulative voting, a minority shareholder may be assured of some representation on the board of directors and a voice (albeit a minority voice) in management.

Proxies

A *proxy* means that a shareholder has named an agent (a proxy) to vote her shares. Several shareholders may join forces, name a single proxy, and control the corporation. A proxy may be revoked at any time.

Voting Trusts

Most states permit shareholders to transfer the right to vote their shares to a voting trustee for the limited purpose of electing directors and for voting on other matters. Alternatively, shareholders may enter into a contract creating a voting agreement or stock-pooling agreement whereby they combine forces in order to gain a voice or exercise control. Such *voting trusts*, voting agreements, or stock-pooling arrangements are governed by the law of contracts unless state statute imposes a special restriction or limitation.

Shareholder Rights

APPRAISAL RIGHTS (SOMETIMES CALLED "DISSENTERS' RIGHTS")

Most states give dissenters (shareholders that object to certain corporate actions that may diminish the value of their stock) the right to force the corporation to buy their stock at its fair value.

Dissenters' rights usually are provided for following two kinds of majority action: (1) consolidation or merger of the corporation, and (2) sale or transfer of substantially all of the corporate assets in other than the usual course of business. These rights also may be available when a charter amendment adversely affects stock values or shareholder rights.

The "fair value" of a dissenter's stock may have to be determined by appraisal if it cannot otherwise be determined. The appraisal procedure varies from state to state. If the stock is traded on a recognized securities exchange, the fair value is readily ascertainable. Otherwise, statutes provide for a judicial determination, or for the appointment of two appraisers, one by the corporation and one by the dissenter, and for the two appraisers to name another one if they cannot agree.

The dissenting shareholder must follow a strict procedure in order to use this appraisal right: The shareholder must file a written objection to the proposed action, must vote against the proposal (or in some states, abstain from voting), and must make a written demand for appraisal and buy-out within some specified time.

RIGHT TO SHARE IN DIVIDENDS

Dividends are the portion of corporate profits distributed to the shareholders. The decision to pay dividends is within the business judgment of the board of directors. In the absence of an agreement to the contrary, however, holders of a particular class of stock have the right to share in a dividend on an equal basis with other holders of the same class.

RIGHT TO APPROVE GIFTS; OTHER MATTERS

Since the assets of the corporation belong to the shareholders, these assets cannot be given away without shareholder approval.

Most states' statutes have special procedures for shareholder approval of charitable gifts to be paid from corporate profits. Furthermore, bonuses, stock option plans, and incentive plans not tied into contract payments for specific work performed may require shareholder approval since such payments may be judicially construed as gifts.

Conflict of interest questions involving members of the board of directors may be resolved by the shareholders. Indemnification of directors and officers, as well as all other matters pertaining to benefits and potential benefits to the corporate managers, may be subject to stockholder approval.

Prudent corporate management favors obtaining shareholder approval for major, fundamental decisions affecting the corporation.

RIGHT OF INSPECTION

Statutes in practically all states permit shareholders to inspect corporate books and records. However, this right of inspection may be limited with respect to the nature of the records sought, depending on the number (or percentage) of shares making the request and, in some states, the purpose of the request.

As a general rule, any shareholder (even one with a single share out of 100,000 shares outstanding) may inspect and copy the annual reports, minutes of the shareholders' meetings, the bylaws, the charter, and the list of shareholders' names and addresses. In addition, some percentage, frequently the holders of 5 percent or 10 percent of the outstanding stock (along with or through their attorneys and accountants), may inspect and copy all books and records, including books of account.

Whether the broad right of inspection accorded the holders of some specified percentage of stock will be permitted without showing good cause varies from state to state. Some courts, arguing that the corporate property belongs to the shareholders, and that the state does not closely police the corporate business, permit unlimited inspection unless the corporation can demonstrate an improper motive, such as proof that these shareholders are "fronting" for a competitor or seeking to discover trade secrets. Other states take a contrary view: Unless a proper purpose or motive is shown by the shareholders, inspection is not permitted.

PREEMPTIVE RIGHTS

Existing shareholders may have the *right to preempt*, or come ahead of, other purchasers of stock to protect their percentage interest in and control of the corporation. Thus, if 100 shares of common stock are outstanding, the owner of 20 of these shares has a one-fifth interest in the corporation. If the corporation were to sell 100 additional shares, the ownership of 20 shares would be diluted to a one-tenth interest. However, with a right to preempt, the owner would have the ability to maintain his one-fifth interest (by purchasing 20 of the additional 100 shares).

In most states, in the absence of a charter provision granting preemptive rights, shareholders do not have these rights.

Shareholders' Lawsuits

DERIVATIVE SUITS

Derivative suits are suits brought by one or more shareholders on behalf of the corporation and for its benefit. Because these suits are not for the benefit of the suing party, any recovery belongs to the corporation. If the suit is successful, the corporation must pay the stockholder's reasonable attorney's fees. A shareholder who loses the suit, on the other hand, may be required to reimburse the defendant's expenses, including attorney's fees.

Derivative suits usually are brought against individual officers or directors for waste or conflict of interest. There are certain strict requirements: (1) the shareholder must first demand that the directors bring the suit (demand may be excused if the shareholder can show that it would have been futile), and (2) that demand must be refused. Some states and the Federal Rules of Civil Procedure also require that the shareholder notify other shareholders of the intent to bring a derivative suit to give them an opportunity to ratify the allegedly wrongful action.

INDIVIDUAL SUITS

A shareholder may sue the corporation individually to protect that shareholder's personal rights or property in the corporation.

Shareholders' Liabilities

Basically, the only loss that a shareholder may sustain is his investment in the corporation's stock. This limitation on liability for stock ownership is one of the primary reasons for the existence of the corporate form. However, if the shareholders themselves disregard the corporate entity, and use the corporate form for fraudulent purposes, the "corporate veil" may be pierced and the shareholders may be personally responsible for corporate obligations.

BOARD OF DIRECTORS

Term

Directors are elected to a term of office, generally one or more years; they tend to serve until the next shareholders' meeting at which successor directors are elected.

The MBCA and RMBCA provide that one or more directors can be removed by the shareholders "with or without cause" unless the charter permits removal only for cause. The common law and some statutes differ from the Model Acts by permitting removal only for cause. *Cause* includes conflicts of interest or other violations of fiduciary functions, violation of the charter or bylaws, or other illegal actions.

Fiduciary Function

The board of directors is chosen by the shareholders to manage the corporation. In this management function the directors are neither employees nor agents of the shareholders; rather, they occupy a position of trust to the shareholders. This trust relation is legally described as a *fiduciary*—a position of loyalty to the corporate interest and well-being, superior to the director's self-interest or desire for personal gain.

In general, this fiduciary relationship also applies to the officers of the corporation.

Four important aspects of the fiduciary relationship are:

1. **Duty of loyalty.** This fiduciary function requires an uncompromising duty of loyalty by the directors and officers to the corporation and to its shareholders. Above all, the corporate manager must make full disclosure of any personal interest in any matter involving the corporation or its business, and in any doubtful case should refrain from voting upon, or taking any action regarding, any such matter. Corporate loans, bonuses, and gifts to directors and offi-

cers are assumed to be a conflict of interest and should have prior shareholder approval.

2. **No personal use of corporate opportunity.** Directors or officers violate their fiduciary duty if they personally take advantage of a business opportunity that should have been reserved for the corporation.

<u>Example:</u> <u>Corporate</u> <u>Opportunity</u>

A director or officer of a corporation owning and operating timber acreage cannot personally purchase other timber lands for private gain without first disclosing her personal objective and giving the corporation an opportunity to make the purchase, instead.

3. **No personal use of corporate assets.** A director or officer cannot use corporate property or personnel to conduct personal business. Moreover, directors and officers cannot divulge company secrets or technology.

4. **Restrictions on transactions in shares.** Directors and officers cannot deal in corporate stock if they receive such stock at an unfair price or on advantageous terms. Moreover, federal statutes require certain disclosures of insider transactions.

Business Judgment Rule

Both directors and officers of the corporation must govern its affairs with reasonably good judgment.

The phrase "reasonably good judgment" is somewhat difficult to define, but is intended to describe a standard of care lower than that applicable to a sharp, well-trained, prudent businessperson but higher than that of a casual, disinterested outsider. Three standards are generally applied to director or officer actions to determine compliance with the *business judgment rule:*

1. Exercise of due care—the decision must be based upon sufficient information.
2. Good faith.
3. Reasonable belief that the action is in the corporate interest.

If these standards are met, directors and officers will not be liable for bad business decisions. The law seeks to grant directors and officers the freedom to act in what they believe is the best interest of the corporation without having to worry about being second guessed by a court. A court is understandably reluctant to substitute its wisdom or judgment for that of a director—after all, directors are chosen by the shareholders, and presumably they are familiar with the business and its goals. However, a court may be compelled to substitute its judgment for that of a director who, in effect, forfeits responsibility by breach of the fiduciary or loyalty duties.

Number and Qualifications of Directors

Generally, the bylaws determine the number and qualifications of directors.

There can be any number of directors, but to avoid tie votes the number should be odd. The board should be a size that functions well as a committee, although many large corporations, banks, and other widely held corporate entities have boards of 25 directors or more.

In most states, any person who can make a simple contract can be a director. A director is generally not required to own stock.

Compensation of Directors

Most state statutes permit directors to set their own reasonable compensation. Extraordinary compensation must be approved by the shareholders.

Meetings of the Board

As a fiduciary, the director can act only in person; she cannot delegate duties or attend board meetings by proxy.

A director can act only as a member of the board, not individually. Meetings are held at the times and places designated in the bylaws or at special times and places as indicated in the notices of meetings. It is important that each director attend board of directors meetings, that minutes be kept of such meetings, and that the directors' votes be recorded. Failure to attend meetings or to use business judgment are acts of negligence that may create personal liability to shareholders who sustain financial losses as a result of such negligence.

The bylaws usually establish the number of directors required for the transaction of business. A majority of the members is ordinarily designated as a quorum.

Most state statutes permit action without a meeting, by telephone conference or other informal procedures, provided that all the directors consent in writing.

Committees

Although board members cannot delegate their individual duties as directors, *committees* of board members may be designated to perform a number of board type activities under the general supervision of the whole board. The executive committee, the finance committee, the audit committee, and the like may meet on a daily or weekly basis to attend to management affairs. Such committees keep agendas and minutes of business transacted for the information and, when appropriate, ratification of the entire board.

Decisions Regarding Earnings

The decision whether to declare dividends or to reinvest profits is for the board of directors, acting within the business judgment rule. In the absence of proof of negligence or bad faith, all such decisions are immune from shareholder attack.

OFFICERS

The *officers* are hired by the board of directors. Designation of the various offices and the duties of each office are set forth in the bylaws. Generally, the officers are the president, one or more vice presidents, the secretary, and the treasurer.

President

The *president* usually serves as the chief executive officer (CEO) of the corporation. He also may be a member of the board of directors and preside at meetings of the board and of the shareholders. Frequently, all or some of these functions are performed by a chairman of the board, as determined in the bylaws.

Vice President

The *vice president* usually fills the office of president in the absence of the latter. In most corporations, vice presidents are given responsibility for various line activities—manufacturing, sales, administration, for instance. Sometimes executive or senior vice presidents are designated to supervise one or more vice presidents to relieve undue burdens that may otherwise fall on the president. Quite often, at least one vice president is a member of the board of directors.

Secretary

The *secretary* is in charge of the corporate books and records. This includes responsibility for keeping the minutes, giving notices, and affixing the corporate seal. (The seal attests to (witnesses) the corporate validity of action and the authority of the individual signing the document on behalf of the corporation.) Because of the need for knowledge of corporate functions and director and officer duties, many corporations, especially large ones, require that the secretary be an attorney. Other than responsibility for books and records, the secretary generally exercises *no* executive functions (e.g., negotiating contracts).

Treasurer

The *treasurer* is responsible for managing the corporation's funds. The treasurer can bind the corporation by issuing checks, indorsing negotiable instruments, and otherwise collecting or disbursing money, but he performs no other executive functions.

OTHER EMPLOYEES

The corporation's other employees are hired by the officers and given such duties at such pay as is within the authority of the officers. The bylaws may designate specific duties for one or more employees.

The law of agency governs the authority of these corporate agents. See Chapter 9 on both the corporation's liability for its agent's actions and the agent's personal liability for her actions in furtherance of corporate business.

END OF THE CORPORATE LIFE

Although most corporations have perpetual existence, the life of the corporation may end in either nonjudicial or judicial *dissolution*. After dissolution, the corporation must (1) wind up its affairs, and (2) liquidate its assets.

Nonjudicial Dissolution

Shareholder approval is usually required for *nonjudicial dissolution*, although an act of the state legislature, or expiration of the period of existence stated in the charter (if a period is stated) will result in nonjudicial dissolution without shareholder action. Voluntary dissolution is achieved by (1) passage of a resolution by the board of directors and (2) approval of the directors' resolution by a majority of the shares entitled to be voted at a shareholders' meeting called for that purpose.

Judicial Dissolution

There are three methods of *judicial dissolution:*

1. The shareholders may petition for judicial dissolution upon their claim that the directors are hopelessly deadlocked, or that the shareholders themselves are deadlocked with regard to election of directors or to some other matter requiring shareholder approval, or that the directors are operating the corporation in an illegal or fraudulent manner.
2. Creditors may implement court action if (a) the corporation cannot pay its debts in the usual course of business *and* a creditor has obtained a judgment against the corporation that the corporation cannot satisfy, or (b) the corporation has stated in writing that it cannot pay the claim of a creditor.
3. The state itself may request judicial dissolution if the corporation fails to file its annual report with the secretary of state, fails to pay its annual franchise tax, abuses its corporate authority, or fails to maintain a registered agent in the state.

In the case of failure to file an annual report or pay the annual franchise tax, the secretary of state usually dissolves the corporation by *administrative action*. After giving the corporation notice and after a specified period of time (usually with publication of the proposed dissolution), the secretary dissolves the corporation by signing a certificate of dissolution. Many, if not most, small and insignificant corporations allowed to languish without conducting any business are dissolved by administrative action in this manner and without penalty.

Winding Up and Liquidation

After dissolution, the board of directors *liquidates* (sells) the assets of the corporation and distributes the proceeds, first to creditors, second to preferred shareholders (if any), and finally to common shareholders.

Summing Up

For most legal purposes a corporation is a person.

A corporation is created by statutes and granted a charter by the state. This charter, prepared by the incorporators, is officially approved and certified by the state corporation commission. The corporation is usually granted perpetual existence.

A corporation, and not its shareholders, is liable for its debts. An exception is "piercing the corporate veil."

Business law is generally concerned with profit corporations; however, nonprofit corporations are also important, because of (1) tax considera-

---

tions and (2) protection of their members from personal liability in the course of corporate business.

A corporation is domestic in the state of its creation, and foreign in all other states.

Corporations are subject to a corporate income tax. In addition, the shareholders are also taxed on distributions or dividends received from the corporation. This is known as double taxation.

S corporations and limited liability companies are exceptions; they do not pay a corporate income tax.

Under modern law corporations are granted very broad powers. These powers may be limited, however, by statute, by the corporation's charter or bylaws, or by a resolution or other action of the board of directors.

If a corporation is doing business in a state other than that of its incorporation, it must register in that state as a foreign corporation.

The phrase "doing business" means that the corporation maintains sufficient contacts in the foreign state on a continuous or regular basis as to make it accountable to that state for its actions.

The corporate structure consists of shareholders, the owners of the corporation; directors, elected by the shareholders to oversee its management; and officers, named by the directors to operate it.

Although the corporation must be operated for the benefit of its shareholders, good corporate operation considers also the larger community welfare and the public interest.

Although shareholders own the corporation, their ownership does not give them the right of direct management (a function of the board of directors). Shareholders have the right to elect directors, control major charter amendments, and approve mergers, consolidations, and the sale of substantially all the corporate assets.

Shareholder functions are exercised chiefly at annual or special meetings of shareholders. A quorum of shareholders must be present, in person or by proxy. In the election of directors, straight voting is generally required, although state law or the charter may permit cumulative voting.

In addition to the right to attend meetings and to vote on directors and other corporate business, shareholders have other rights: to appraisal if they dissent from corporate acts that may affect the value of their stock; to share in dividends; to approve corporate gifts; to inspect and copy the corporate books; and, if permitted by the charter, to preemptive stock purchase.

Shareholders may bring legal action against the corporation by derivative suits (suits for the corporate benefit and on its behalf) or by direct suit.

Directors are chosen by the shareholders to manage the corporation. They occupy a fiduciary (trust) relationship to the shareholders. This trust relationship requires an uncompromising duty of loyalty to the corporation, no personal use of corporate opportunity, no personal use of corporate assets, no unfair dealing in the corporation's stock, and the exercise of reasonably good judgment in managing corporate affairs.

The bylaws generally provide for the number and qualifications of directors. Most state statutes permit the directors to provide reasonable compensation for themselves. Directors must personally attend board meetings; they cannot attend by proxy.

Committees of board members may be appointed to supervise day-by-day functions, but these committees must report to the full board.

Declaration of dividends is subject to the discretion of the board, acting within the business judgment rule.

The officers are named and hired by the board of directors. The officers and their duties are prescribed by the bylaws.

Officers usually include the president, one or more vice presidents (generally with responsibility for line activities), a secretary (with responsibility for maintaining books and records), and a treasurer (with responsibility for management of corporate funds).

A corporation's life is ended by dissolution, followed by winding up and liquidation.

Dissolution can be done judicially (by court action) or nonjudicially (by shareholder action, expiration of charter period, or act of the state legislature). Administrative dissolution occurs by action of the secretary of state following the corporation's failure to report and pay the annual franchise tax to the state.

QUESTIONS

Identify each of the following:

alien corporation
appraisal rights
articles of incorporation
business judgment
   rule
bylaws
certificate of
   incorporation
charter
close corporation
committee
consolidation
corporation
cumulative voting
derivative suits

director
dissenters' rights
dissolution
dividends
domestic corporation
fiduciary
foreign corporation
incorporators
limited liability
   company
membership
   corporation
merger
officer
outstanding share

"pierce the corporate
   veil"
president
professional
   corporation
promoter
proxy
quorum
S corporation
secretary
shareholder
straight voting
treasurer
vice president
voting trust

Answer these Review Questions:

1. List some ways in which a corporation is treated as a person and some ways in which it is not treated as a person.
2. What is meant by corporate "double taxation"? Explain several ways in which double taxation may be avoided.
3. What is the meaning of the expression "pierce the corporate veil"? Is this a moral as well as a legal principle?
4. Why should the charter be a "lean" document?
5. What is meant by the phrase "misleadingly similar to" in establishing a corporate name?
6. Why is it necessary that a foreign corporation "do business" within a state in order to be subject to the registration requirements of that state?
7. Can a majority shareholder, acting alone, dismiss an officer of the corporation?
8. Why are the directors of a corporation having assets of over $100 million not

required to submit to their shareholders a proposed merger with a corporation having assets of less than $1 million?

9. What advice should be given to someone who strongly objects to the consolidation of a corporation in which he owns stock with another corporation?

10. How can you determine the necessity of attending a special meeting of shareholders?

11. Do shareholders have the right to compel the board to declare a dividend?

12. What is one relatively effective and inexpensive way to cause a corporation to be dissolved?

Apply Your Knowledge:

1. Doctors Hacksaw, Smith, and Spurgeon operate a general medical practice as a professional corporation, known as HSS, P.C. While performing a tonsillectomy on one Samuels, Hacksaw is allegedly negligent, and as a result, Samuels is left partly paralyzed. Each of the doctors is quite wealthy, but the corporation is without substantial assets. Advise Samuels as to whether he can expect to win a case against each of the doctors as individuals.

2. In 1980, Soper and his two adult sons, Sam and Steve, created a corporation, Soper and Sons Electrical Company. During the first year or so, they maintained corporate bank accounts, had the name printed on trucks and stationery, and held annual stockholders' meetings. After the elder Soper died in 1985, Sam and Steve forgot about the corporation and failed to hold meetings and otherwise follow the corporate formalities. In 1992, Sam's allegedly negligent electrical wiring caused a disastrous fire at a local elementary school, in which several children and school personnel were injured.

   Are there legal theories under which Steve and Sam can be personally liable to the injured parties?

3. You own about 1 percent of the outstanding stock of XY Corporation. A number of shareholders believe that the management is paying a grossly exorbitant salary to Ms. X, secretary to the president of the company and believed to be his mistress. Ms. X and the president are known to take trips to Europe and other places on "corporate business" and at corporate expense. What course of action should be considered to protect your rights as a shareholder?

4. The vice president of corporation AB, a jewelry company, attends an auction at the direction of the corporation. She is directed to bid up to $100,000 for the Omega diamond. The bidding reaches $125,000, and the vice president then buys the diamond for her own account for $126,000. Is this action proper?

5. MM corporation has received an order of the state department of health to cease the discharge of acid into the waters of the state. The board of directors has before it the proposal of a management team to spend over $50 million for capital equipment that will correct the discharge. The company has operated at a loss for the past two years. Director Q and a majority of the board vote against the proposal. Later the corporation is fined $1 million for acid discharge, and shareholders ultimately bring a derivative suit against Q, claiming violation of the business judgment rule. What will be the result?

ANSWERS

Answers to Review Questions:

1. A corporation has all of the constitutional rights of a person, except protection from self-incrimination, provided for in the Fifth Amendment to the Constitution. This protection against self-incrimination has been construed to be "a human protection," and the courts have refused to extend it to a corporate entity. Other constitutional rights, such as the protection of property

rights, extend to the corporation. A corporation cannot commit a crime if the only punishment for that crime is a jail sentence. Bear in mind, however, that the mere fact that a corporation may be guilty of a crime or liable for a tort does not protect the corporate employee, agent, or officer; these individuals may also be guilty of the crime or liable for the tort, along with their corporate employer.

2. "Double taxation" is taxation on the corporation's profits and further taxation on these profits when they are distributed to shareholders. The S corporation and the limited liability company provide a direct way of dealing with this problem. Professional corporations permit professionals such as doctors, lawyers, and accountants to incorporate without double taxation and receive a number of tax benefits through corporate planning. In a small "mom and pop" corporation, the principals, who are usually the shareholders, may pay themselves reasonable salaries, expense monies that are not taxed to the corporation.

3. "Piercing the corporate veil" has a moral aspect in that the shareholders are not directly responsible for corporate losses unless the corporate form is abused: The corporation is operated as a "front" for a fraudulent purpose, and the corporate business is operated as though the corporation does not exist.

4. The charter is more difficult to amend or change than bylaws or other documents. Approval of the state corporation commission may be required, as well as that of the shareholders and directors.

5. Members of the public should not be misled by the name into believing that they are dealing with some other corporate entity. Many corporations spend vast sums establishing an identity or a reputation for excellence; it would not be fair to permit a new enterprise to adopt a similar name and thus benefit from the older company's established identity or reputation.

6. A state cannot interfere with interstate commerce; hence it is necessary that the state have legitimate control over foreign corporate activity in order to prohibit it or police it in some manner. The state has legitimate interests of its own citizens to protect. If a corporation's business is not interstate (and subject to federal control), but is performed on a continuous and regular basis within the state, it becomes accountable to the state.

7. A shareholder—even the owner of all of the outstanding stock—cannot directly dismiss an officer or other employee. The shareholder can only elect a board of directors that will consider the shareholder's wishes regarding corporate management, including the hiring and firing of officers.

8. The purchase of such a disproportionately small business would not affect the nature of the business of the larger corporation or the value of its stock. Shareholder approval is therefore not necessary.

9. He must file a written objection to the proposed consolidation, attend the shareholders' meeting in person or by proxy, vote "no," and promptly demand a buy-out of his shares. If the stock is traded on a national exchange, the value will have been set by the board of directors as of some previously specified date. If the stock is not traded, the shareholder will proceed to have "fair value" determined by the appraisal routine.

10. You are entitled to a notice of the meeting, which will set out its purpose and matters to be voted upon.

11. Declaration of a dividend is usually regarded as a question for the board, not the shareholders. Of course, the decision is subject to the business judgment rule.

12. If the corporation fails to file an annual report with the state or fails to pay its annual franchise tax, the state may cause it to forfeit its charter by administrative action.

Answers to "Apply Your Knowledge":

1. The creation of a professional corporation does not protect the individual doctor from professional torts. Hacksaw is personally responsible. Unless Smith or Spurgeon were personally involved with the tonsillectomy, most states would not hold them responsible for Hacksaw's tort (although if the doctors had held themselves out as general partners each would be liable for the torts of the others). A few courts might hold both Smith and Spurgeon responsible for Hacksaw's negligence on the theory that professional corporations do not alter the old partnership obligations of the members to each other.

2. This question has broad implications beyond the subject matter of this chapter. However, one obvious problem, that of "piercing the corporate veil," is covered in the current chapter. The veil would not be pierced in the absence of a showing of a fraudulent purpose; hence this theory is not adequate to reach the individual stockholders or principals. However, in Chapter 9 (Agency) we dealt with the personal responsibility of employee agents for their torts while undertaking company business. Under agency law, Sam and Steve may well be liable if they, or others acting under their supervision, personally committed the tort.

3. So far, you have only hearsay and suspicion as a basis for objection to improper payments and corporate expenditures for Ms. X. Assuming that your state permits shareholders to freely inspect the corporate books but that some minimum percentage of shares is required (e.g., 5 percent) in order to make demand, you should join with other shareholders in order to develop the required percentage.

   If inspection rights are obtained without litigation (filing a petition in court), you should inspect the corporate expense records, probably with an attorney or an accountant. If waste or impropriety is discovered, you may consider a derivative suit. This, of course, will be preceded by a demand on the directors to take action to stop the waste and to force the president to account for the misappropriation of funds. State law should be checked to determine whether other shareholders must be notified of the wrongdoing and planned lawsuit.

4. The question is one of corporate opportunity. Has the vice president seized for herself an opportunity belonging to the corporation? Probably not: she had no authority to exceed $100,000. To have purchased the stone for a price in excess of that amount for the corporation would have violated the terms of her employment. She was impliedly authorized, therefore, to act for her own account and for her own opportunity.

5. The shareholders would probably lose their suit against Q. If he acted in the reasonable belief that his negative vote was in the corporate interest, if he acted in good faith, and exercised due care, he acted properly. We are not told of his other options; we do not know what other competent advice he may have received. We do not know the history of the violations or the reasonableness of the corporation's course of action.

Chapter 11

Debtors and Creditors

HISTORY

In the past, people who did not pay their debts to creditors were severely punished. Depending upon the time and place, debtors have been sent to prison, used as slaves, tortured, and even put to death. Often the debtor's relatives also were punished.

Now the debtor is protected. Creditors complain that debtors receive too much protection under bankruptcy and consumer protection laws.

CREDITORS' RIGHTS: COLLECTION OF DEBTS

There are ten major methods by which a creditor may collect debts:

First, a creditor may place a *lien* upon the debtor's property. A lien is an encumbrance on the debtor's property; it limits the property's transfer and sometimes its use. The types of liens include a *mechanic's lien,* an *artisan's lien,* and a *hotelkeeper's lien.* A mechanic's lien placed on real estate allows the creditor (lienholder) to force a sale of the property to satisfy the debt. An artisan's lien and hotelkeeper's lien allow a creditor to hold personal property until a debt for services, repairs, improvements, or care is paid.

Another action that may be taken by creditors is to obtain a *prejudgment attachment.* This is a court order allowing the property to be taken into custody before a judgment is entered. It protects the creditor by keeping the property from being either wasted or removed before completion of the lawsuit. There are Fourteenth Amendment due process limits on this type of action (see Chapter 2 on the Constitution).

The creditor also may take a *security interest* in the debtor's property. If the debtor does not pay the debt as promised, the creditor may use the collateral (personal property or fixtures) as a substitute for all or part of the debt.

Recovery of the debt before or during the course of a *bulk transfer* occurs when a business sells a large portion of its materials, supplies, merchandise, or other inventory outside of the normal course of business. Creditors are given notice at least ten days before the transfer so that they may protect their interests. Bulk transfers are governed under UCC Article 6.

A creditor may proceed against property fraudulently conveyed to a third party. A *fraudulent conveyance* is a transfer of property to a third party (e.g., a friend, relative, favored supplier, or customer) in order to avoid paying the creditor.

A creditor may also seek payment from a surety or guarantor who has agreed to be liable for a person's debt. A surety is primarily liable, allowing the creditor an immediate remedy. A guarantor is *secondarily* liable; he or she is liable only after the creditor has attempted to collect from the debtor. A suretyship does not have to be in writing, but all guaranty agreements must be in a written document.

Guaranty agreements are either general (applying to all creditors) or special (applying only to a specific creditor). Special guaranty agreements are usually not assignable.

Examples of suretyship contracts are performance bonds covering the costs of a party's failure to meet the terms of a contract (construction of a building), and fidelity bonds, which protect against losses from employee theft or other dishonest acts. Both types of bonds cover costs or losses only up to a stated maximum amount.

Both sureties and guarantors may raise any claim or defense that the debtor may have raised except infancy, bankruptcy, and in some cases the statute of limitations. Other defenses may be that the debtor has already paid the debt or that the debtor's obligation was materially changed without permission of the surety or guarantor. Most sureties and guarantors may collect reimbursement from the debtor in a right called *subrogation*.

A creditor may foreclose on real property if the loan is secured by the real property, such as a mortgage agreement. Although some states allow the mortgagee (creditor) to take immediate possession of the real property, most states require a judicial sale. Under a judicial sale, proper notice must be given to the mortgagor (debtor), and then the sheriff or other court official takes control of the property and sells it. Proceeds of the sale are applied first to cover the costs of the sale, second to the creditor, and third, if any proceeds remain, to the debtor. If the sale does not cover the entire debt, most states permit a deficiency judgment to be issued so that the creditor can collect from other property owned by the debtor. A mortgagor has the right, known as equity of redemption, to recover or keep his or her home by paying the debt and any interest and foreclosure costs in full.

A judgment creditor may obtain a *writ of execution* or *garnishment*. A writ of execution is a court order allowing a sheriff or other court official to seize and sell a debtor's nonexempt property (see Debtors' Rights, below). Under garnishment, third parties holding property or owing money to the debtor, such as banks or employers, may be required to send that property to the creditor.

When there are two or more creditors, they may accept a *composition, extension agreement*, or an *assignment to a trustee*. In a composition agreement, each creditor agrees to receive a percentage of the amount owed. An extension agreement allows the debtor more time to pay the debt. Under either circumstance, if the debtor complies, he or she is released from the obligation (discharged). An assignment to a trustee involves transferring some or most of the debtor's property to a trustee. The trustee then sells the property for cash and distributes the proceeds to the creditors using a *pro rata* (proportionate) share. Creditors accepting these payments also must discharge the remainder of the debt.

DEBTORS' RIGHTS AND CONSUMER PROTECTION

Both state and federal laws provide certain protection to debtors: exemption statutes, limits on garnishments, consumer protection statutes, and lender liability.

State law exempts certain types of property from being seized and sold to satisfy debts. The *homestead exemption* allows a debtor to retain a specific amount of equity (ownership interest) in his home in order to protect his family and find another home.

Example: Homestead Exemption

X has a home with a $50,000 mortgage and Y has a judgment against X for $25,000. If the state homestead exemption is $10,000 and the house sells for $75,000, then X gets $10,000, the mortgagee gets $50,000, and Y can only take the remaining $15,000. In most states, the balance remaining on the debt may be collected from other nonexempt property owned by the debtor.

Personal property, up to a specified dollar amount, is also covered under exemption statutes. This includes household furnishings, clothes, personal possessions, automobiles, livestock, pets, and veterans' pensions.

Garnishments are regulated under the federal Consumer Protection Act (Truth-in-Lending Act), which limits garnishment to the lower of either 25 percent of weekly disposable earnings or the amount by which a week's disposable earnings (net income after federal and state income tax and social security tax) exceeds 30 times the federal minimum hourly wage. States are allowed to substitute a larger exemption and some permit judges to set a higher exemption rate to prevent undue hardship.

Numerous federal consumer protection statutes apply to the debtor/creditor relationship.

The *Truth-in-Lending Act* (1968) requires a lender or seller to disclose the credit terms, including finance charges, on all transactions whereby the creditor, in the ordinary course of business, makes a loan or extends a credit amount under $25,000. The proceeds must concern real or personal property used for personal, family, household, or agricultural purposes.

The *Fair Credit Billing Act* (a 1974 amendment to the Truth-in-Lending Act) requires prompt posting of all payments and a notice of prospective finance charges on new purchases. This act prohibits credit card issuers from forbidding merchants to offer cash discounts and provides procedures for disputes about credit card statements, billings, and purchases.

The *Fair Debt Collection Practices Act* (1977) prohibits certain abusive practices by debt collectors.

The *Fair Credit Reporting Act* (a 1970 addition to the Truth-in-Lending Act) provides debtors access to their credit reports and sets forth procedures for correcting errors or otherwise protecting a consumer's credit reputation.

The *Equal Credit Opportunity Act* (1976) prohibits discrimination in the extending of credit.

Credit card rules in the Truth-in-Lending Act limit the liability of a cardholder whose card is lost or stolen to $50 per card, provided the creditor is notified about the loss or theft. The rules also prohibit billing a consumer for unauthorized charges such as those made on a card never accepted by that consumer.

States have their own laws and regulations, which may set maximum interest rates (usury laws) or otherwise protect consumers who have been extended credit. The *Uniform Consumer Credit Code (UCCC)*, adopted by ten states, establishes maximum interest rates that may be charged and requires full disclosure to buyers on credit. The UCCC provides for criminal and civil penalties against creditors who do not follow these rules. The UCCC attempts to systemize the law and forbids multiple agreements used to obtain higher interest rates; balloon payments more than double the average payment; assignment of a debtor's wages; and, in most cases, judgments for money (deficiency judgments) beyond that received from repossessing the goods that were purchased on credit.

Lenders may be sued by consumers for damages resulting from misconduct while extending or revoking credit, foreclosing on security, administering a loan, refusing to make a loan, or even making a loan that the debtor now claims he should not have received! The lender's liability may include breach of contract, fraud, excessive control (e.g., interfering with the debtor's contracts with others), negligence, economic duress, breach of fiduciary duties, and fault based upon the consumer protection statutes, securities or tax laws, and the Racketeer Influenced and Corrupt Organization Act (RICO).

BANKRUPTCY AND REORGANIZATION

Bankruptcy is a method for settling debts of individuals or business entities that are unable to pay their debts as they become due. A bankruptcy serves to relieve (discharge) the debtor for all or most of his debts once the bankruptcy proceeding is properly completed.

Bankruptcy proceedings are supervised by federal bankruptcy courts. Appeals are filed either in a U.S. District Court or to a bankruptcy appellate panel. The bankruptcy appellate panel consists of bankruptcy judges from within that federal circuit.

The important issues in bankruptcy are governed by *federal law* as stated in the Bankruptcy Code and interpreted in federal court opinions. However, some matters of state law may arise in a bankruptcy proceeding. For example, a federal bankruptcy court may have to decide if orders about legal fees and costs associated with a divorce are part of a debtor's obligation to pay alimony or child support. If they are, the debts cannot be discharged via bankruptcy.

Chapters 7, 11, and 13 of the Bankruptcy Code

The Bankruptcy Code provides three main alternatives for proceedings: Chapter 7 (Liquidation), Chapter 11 (Business Reorganization), and Chapter 13 (Adjustment of an Individual's Debts). A fourth type, available under Chapter 9, allows for the adjustment of a municipal corporation's debts and is authorized by the state where the municipal corporation (city, county, and so on) is located. (Family farming business reorganizations are governed by Chapter 12 of the Bankruptcy Code.)

A debtor may file a voluntary petition for bankruptcy under any of these alternatives. Creditors may initiate an involuntary petition only under Chapter 7 or Chapter 11. A filing of any type of bankruptcy petition creates an estate consisting of all of the debtor's property.

In a Chapter 7 case, the court appoints a trustee to take charge of the estate. The trustee sells the debtor's nonexempt property and then distributes the proceeds to the creditors in order of their priorities under the law. For example, taxes are usually paid before creditors are paid.

A Chapter 7 bankruptcy discharges all debts, including judgments, that the debtor had before the bankruptcy court order granting the discharge. This prevents most creditors from trying to collect their debts after the bankruptcy proceedings are over. (Even during the proceedings there tends to be a stay or halt to creditors' *independent* collection of the petitioner's debts.)

Chapter 7 discharges cover only individuals, not corporations or partnerships. Corporations and partnerships are still technically liable for their debts if in the future they acquire assets. The effect of this lack of discharge is to prevent the entity from reforming after a Chapter 7 liquidation.

Railroads, banks, savings and loan associations, credit unions, insurance companies, and other financial institutions are regulated by administrative agencies and are not covered under the Bankruptcy Code. They are not allowed to file bankruptcy. However, railroads may file for reorganization under Chapter 11.

Chapter 11 bankruptcy proceedings allow ongoing businesses to restructure their debts using a reorganization plan. A court-appointed trustee or examiner conducts an investigation, files reports to the court, and either submits the reorganization plan covering all aspects of the business operation (including assets and debts) or recommends that the business convert to a Chapter 7 liquidation. The plan must be accepted by the bankruptcy judge and, for each "class" of creditor (e.g., suppliers, employees, lenders), by a portion of the creditors representing at least two-thirds of the dollar value for that group's total claims and more than one half of the total number of claimants. Each creditor must receive at least as much as he or she would be entitled to under a Chapter 7 liquidation.

Chapter 13 adjusts the debts of an individual. This alternative is only available to individuals with regular sources of income, unsecured debts not exceeding $100,000, and secured debts of $350,000 or less. A payment plan is set up that allows the debtor to pay about one fourth of his or her disposable income, depending upon the level of income and family responsibilities, to a court-appointed trustee who, in turn, pays the creditors. The payment plan must begin within 30 days after the petition is filed and continues for up to five years. Upon completion of the plan, a Chapter 13 discharge is granted. Under Chapter 13, payments to creditors must also be at least the same amount as the creditors would receive under a Chapter 7 liquidation. The debtor or the bankruptcy court may convert the case into a Chapter 7 proceeding at any time.

Procedure

FILINGS AND EXEMPTIONS

A debtor must file with the court a statement of income and expenses together with a list of assets, creditors, and exempt property. The list of creditors must include addresses and the amount owed to each creditor. Property that is exempt under bankruptcy proceedings includes the following:

Equity in a home and burial plot up to $7,500.

Interest in one motor vehicle up to $1,200.

Trade or business items up to $750.

Prescribed health aids.

Unmatured life insurance policies excluding credit life insurance.

Federal and state benefits such as social security, local public assistance, veterans', disability, and unemployment benefits.

Interest in jewelry not to exceed $500.

Alimony and child support, as reasonably necessary for the debtor.

Certain pensions, stock bonuses, and annuities.

An interest in household furnishings or goods, clothes, books, appliances, pets or other items of a personal, family, or household nature (up to $200 for each item, with the total not to exceed $4,000).

Wrongful death benefits, life insurance benefits to a dependent beneficiary, personal injury payments not to exceed $7,500, and restitution payments to victims of crime.

Any other property worth altogether no more than $400, plus up to $3,750 of the unused portion of the $7,500 homestead exemption in item 1 of this list.

SECURED TRANSACTIONS

Creditors having liens or security interests in the debtor's property may sell or otherwise dispose of the property in order to collect the debt. If the property sells for more than what is owed, the balance is included in the debtor's estate. If the property sells for less, the creditor becomes an unsecured, general creditor for the remaining amount.

THE TRUSTEE'S ROLE IN BANKRUPTCY

The *trustee*, appointed by the court, receives title to all of the debtor's property and is responsible for collecting and liquidating the assets as well as deciding claims. The trustee may sue, accept, or reject executory contracts, revoke unperfected property transfers, and void preferential or fraudulent transfers.

The trustee pays costs, claims, or other expenses for the debtor's estate in the following order:
1. Costs of administering, collecting, and maintaining the estate, including attorney's fees.
2. Claims arising in the ordinary course of business, after the petition was filed but before the trustee was appointed or an order of relief was made.
3. Claims up to $2,000 per employee for wages earned within 90 days before the bankruptcy petition was filed.
4. Claims up to $2,000 per employee for contributions to employee benefit plans arising from services rendered within 180 days before the bankruptcy petition was filed.
5. Claims up to $900 for deposits with the debtor that were for consumer purchases or leases of property or services, if the property or service has not been provided.
6. Taxes and penalties due in the three years before the bankruptcy petition was filed.
7. Claims of general creditors and any claims that exceed the money or time limits in categories 3, 4, or 5 above.

NONDISCHARGEABLE DEBTS, DENIAL OF OVERALL DISCHARGE, AND LIMITS OF DISCHARGE

There are five types of debts that are too important to be discharged by bankruptcy:
1. Alimony.
2. Child support.
3. Fines and penalties by some governments.
4. Taxes owed for the three years before bankruptcy.
5. Student loans received within seven years of bankruptcy.

The main reason for not discharging a debt may be the misconduct of the debtor. Debts that are nondischargeable are:
- intentional tort claims;
- judgments based on drunk driving;
- claims to money or property obtained by fraud, false pretense, embezzlement, or misuse of funds;
- criminal restitution obligations;
- claims not listed in the bankruptcy petition;
- debts exceeding $500 for luxury goods or services purchased within 40 days of the bankruptcy filing and certain cash advances exceeding $1,000 made within 20 days of the filing; and
- claims denied a discharge in a prior bankruptcy action.
  Overall bankruptcy discharge may be denied in the following cases:
- The debtor (1) waived his or her right to a discharge; (2) destroyed, concealed, or transferred the property and/or records in order to hinder or defraud a creditor; (3) unjustifiably failed to maintain adequate financial records; (4) inadequately explained a supposed loss of assets; (5) committed a bankruptcy

scam or other such crime; or (6) refused to obey a bankruptcy court order to answer questions or appear at scheduled meetings or hearings.
- A bankruptcy court granted the debtor a discharge within six years of the current filing (except when the prior bankruptcy was a good faith Chapter 13 plan paying at least 70 percent of unsecured claims).
- A prior bankruptcy petition was dismissed within 180 days of the present petition.
- A consumer debtor's Chapter 7 discharge would be a "substantial abuse" of the system.

When an overall discharge is denied, the debtor's nonexempt assets are still distributed to the creditors and the debtor remains liable for the unpaid debts.

Discharge does not affect the liability of a co-debtor, surety, or guarantor. Also, if within one year after a discharge, evidence arises that a debtor committed fraud or lied during the bankruptcy proceedings, the discharge may be revoked by the bankruptcy court.

Debtors may agree to pay a dischargeable debt. That is a reaffirmation agreement. It must be in writing and contain a statement to the effect that the debtor knows of his or her right to cancel the reaffirmation before the discharge occurs or within 60 days of the reaffirmation agreement, whichever period is longer. The reaffirmation agreement must be filed in the bankruptcy court and include the affidavit by the debtor's attorney stating that the affirmation would not impose an undue hardship on the debtor or her dependents and that the agreement was made voluntarily. If the debtor was not represented by an attorney, the agreement usually requires special approval by the bankruptcy court. (Once the debt is discharged, a debtor may, without a reaffirmation agreement, volunteer to repay that debt; but these promised payments cannot be required.)

SECURED TRANSACTIONS

A *secured transaction* is any transaction in which a debtor gives a creditor a security interest in personal property or fixtures.

Introduction

Secured transactions are governed by UCC Article 9. In a typical case, a debtor has borrowed money from a creditor. As protection against nonpayment of the debt, the creditor requires the debtor to provide *collateral*, which is a security interest in the debtor's personal property. If the debtor fails to make payment on the debt, the creditor may use the collateral as a payment substitute or as another method to collect the debt.

Generally, security interests are given in the actual property for which the credit is received, such as an automobile. Secured credit allows a consumer or business to make large-scale purchases while assuring lenders that, if the debtor defaults, they can recover some or all of the money lent by taking or selling the secured property.

PLEDGE

A *pledge* is the oldest and simplest type of secured transaction. The creditor takes actual physical possession of the property and, if the debtor defaults, the creditor sells or uses the collateral to satisfy the debt. This collateral may be in the form of tangible assets, such as jewelry or machinery, or may be an intangible asset, such as stock.

Example: Pledge

Xavier Extravagant owes a credit card company $600. He borrows the money from Paula Pawnbroker and as collateral leaves Paula jewelry worth $800.

One obvious problem with a pledge is that the debtor will not or cannot give up possession of the property. In fact, a pledge contradicts the purpose of many credit transactions, which is to help the debtor purchase *and use* the property.

SECURITY INTERESTS

Because of problems with the pledge, the law allows the use of security devices that do not require transfer of possession of the property. These devices include chattel mortgages, trust receipts, and assignments of accounts receivable. These devices are all called *security interests*.

COLLATERAL

Article 9 of the UCC states the following types of property may be used as collateral: goods, including inventory and equipment; documents proving rights such as commercial paper, securities, bills of lading, receipts; accounts receivable; and most other personal property or fixtures. Specifically excluded are items such as real estate, mortgages, insurance, deposit accounts, landlord's or mechanic's liens, and claims arising from lawsuits.

After-acquired property (personal property the debtor acquired after the security agreement was executed) may be collateral for consumer goods, unless they are *accessions* (physically added to existing collateral). The limit, though, is that the property had to have been acquired within ten days after the security agreement was executed. Collateral even may be used to secure future credit.

Requirements for an Effective Security Interest Attachment

The security interest must be attached to the secured property (the collateral) in order to be effective between the parties to a secured transaction. The three requirements of an attachment are: (1) a written agreement sets forth the security interest, describes the collateral, and is signed by the debtor; (2) value is given by the secured party (creditor) to the debtor; and (3) the debtor has rights in the collateral. "Value" arises from commitments to extend credit, from consideration sufficient for a contract, or from pre-existing consideration. No written agreement is necessary when the secured party obtains possession of the collateral.

PERFECTION

To make the security interest effective against third parties, it must be perfected. *Perfection* gives the secured creditor priority over other parties seeking to attach or use the collateral. For example, if C perfects a security interest in D's equipment, most third-party creditors will not be permitted to seize and sell the equipment in order to satisfy D's debts to them.

The method of obtaining perfection depends upon the type of collateral. The three methods are possession, attachment, and the filing of a financing statement.

1. Possession is the method of perfection for pledges and is required for negotiable instruments or other documents such as stocks and bonds, except for purely intangible collateral such as (a) paper showing rights to accounts receivable or (b) chattel paper that provides both a monetary interest and security interest in, or lease of, specific goods.

2. Automatic perfection (perfection by attachment) usually involves a purchase money security interest (PMSI) in consumer goods other than fixtures or motor vehicles. UCC § 9-107 defines a PMSI as a security interest that is (a) held by the seller of the collateral in order to secure all or part of the sales price, or (b) held by a person lending money or otherwise giving value that the debtor uses to acquire or use the collateral. Automatic perfection thus eliminates the need to file financing statements for consumer goods PMSIs.

   (The other typical instance of automatic perfection involves assignments of accounts or contract rights that alone do not amount to a significant portion of the debtor's outstanding accounts or contract rights.)

3. The most common method of obtaining perfection is to *file a financing statement*. The financing statement must include the debtor's signature, the addresses of the debtor and secured party, and a description of the collateral. Filing at a state or local government office is necessary if perfection is to be obtained unless: (a) possession is the required method for perfection (e.g., negotiable instruments); (b) the secured party, in fact, possesses the collateral; or (c) there is automatic perfection (e.g., consumer goods PMSIs).

It is the responsibility of the secured party to file the financing statement. Section 9-401(1) of the UCC provides three alternatives on where financing statements should be filed. Each state has chosen one of these alternatives, with about half adopting some form of the second:

1. A central filing with a state office, except where local filings are required for timber, minerals, and some fixture collateral.
2. Local filings for farm or consumer goods, timber, minerals, and some fixtures, and central filings for other collateral.
3. Same as 2, above, but sometimes requiring a local filing in addition to the central filing requirements (e.g., the county where the debtor lives, or where the collateral is located). This additional filing is necessary if the debtor has a place of business in just one county or has no in-state place of business but lives in the state.

If a person is in doubt as to whether or not he should file a financing statement, he should file it just to be safe. If a person does not know where to file, the financing statement should be filed in every possible county or state.

The financing statement is not a substitute for a security agreement; the former provides only enough information to give other parties notice of a security interest. To obtain further information, the debtor or secured party may have to be contacted directly.

A proper filing will be good for five years unless a shorter maturity date is indicated. Continuations may be filed to extend the statement for an additional five years. The number of extensions is unlimited and the debtor's signature is not required.

Rights and Duties of Secured Parties and Debtors

WHAT IS DEFAULT?

Default on a debt is not defined in UCC Article 9, but usually is defined in the security agreement. The typical default is a failure to make timely payments on the loan. Another type of default occurs when a security interest's collateral is, despite a warranty of exclusivity, also used as collateral for other security interests.

RIGHTS AND DUTIES BEFORE DEFAULT

Before default, the parties have certain rights or duties unless specified differently in the security agreement.

The secured party (1) may release or assign all or part of the collateral; (2) may file an extension or amendment of a financing statement (the latter requires the debtor's signature); and (3) if in possession of the collateral, must use reasonable care to preserve it.

The debtor (1) may periodically request and receive from the secured party a written statement of the current amount due on the debt, and perhaps a full listing of the collateral; (2) bears the risk of loss or damage to the collateral; and (3) must pay for all reasonable expenses incurred in taking care of the collateral.

RIGHTS AND DUTIES AFTER DEFAULT

Upon default by a debtor, the secured party may sue on the underlying obligation, enforce the security interest directly, or both (UCC § 9-501(1)). Under UCC § 9-503, the secured party has the right to take possession of the collateral unless prohibited by the security agreement itself. A court order is not required; however, taking possession must not lead to a breach of the peace. The secured party still has to exercise reasonable care over any collateral it now possesses.

As an alternative to direct possession, the secured party may require the defaulting debtor to assemble the collateral at a place designated by the secured party, or the secured party may choose not to remove the collateral but to make it unusable to the debtor and dispose of it on the debtor's premises.

SPECIAL PROVISIONS IF THE SECURED PARTY CHOOSES TO KEEP THE COLLATERAL

The secured party may decide to keep the collateral in order to satisfy the debtor's obligation. If over 60 percent of the price (or the loan for collateral) of consumer goods has been paid by the debtor, the secured party may not retain the goods without the debtor's signed approval. In cases involving payments of 60 percent or less, the secured party must notify the debtor of her decision to keep the collateral unless a signed statement from the debtor already allows retention.

For collateral other than consumer goods, the secured party must notify other parties who have given written notice of an interest in the collateral. If the debtor or other secured party within 21 days objects to the secured party's retention of the goods, a sale must take place. Otherwise, the secured party may keep the collateral (UCC § 9-505).

SALE OF COLLATERAL

The secured party may choose to sell the collateral or may be forced to conduct a sale under UCC § 9-505. The disposition of the collateral must be *commercially reasonable*. Commercially reasonable means that the property is sold in the same manner as done in a recognized market for that type of property, that the sale conforms to practices of merchants selling that type of property, *or* that the sale garners the current market price.

The debtor has the right to redeem the property by paying the full amount of the debt plus any additional expenses incurred by the secured party. In addition, a second secured party may pay the creditor the amount owed by the debtor in order to secure its collateral. The purchaser takes the collateral free and clear of all claims by the debtor or by secured parties.

The proceeds of a sale of collateral are distributed in the following order:
- reasonable expenses related to possessing, preserving, and selling the collateral, including attorney's fees;
- the debt owed to the secured party; and
- claims of other secured parties who have given written notice of an interest in the collateral.

Any leftover proceeds go to the debtor. If the sale of the collateral does not cover the entire amount of the debt, the secured party usually has the right to collect the balance by other means unless barred by consumer protection statutes or by the security agreement.

TERMINATION STATEMENT

A termination statement may be required by the debtor after his obligation has been satisfied. For financing statements concerning *consumer goods*, a termination statement is mandatory even if not required by the former debtor. Termination statements are to be filed wherever the financing statement was originally filed. Failure to file subjects the secured party to fines and also liability to the debtor for any resulting losses.

Priority of Creditors

The major purpose of the secured transaction is to ensure that the secured party can use the collateral to collect the debt before other creditors may do so. One creditor has priority over another creditor even though they may both have a security interest in the same collateral. The following table shows the major priority controversies and their usual outcomes.

GENERAL RULES

Opposing Creditors		Priority Creditor
Perfected security holder	Another perfected security holder	The first to perfect (UCC § 9-312(5))
Perfected security holder	Unperfected security holder	The perfected security holder, regardless of whose security interest arose first (UCC § 9-312(5))
Unperfected security holder	Another unperfected security holder	The first party whose security interest attached (UCC § 9-312(5))
Unperfected security holder	Unsecured creditor or unlevied judgment creditor	The unperfected security holder (UCC § 9-301)

PMSI and Crop Exceptions to "First to Perfect" Rule

Perfected PMSI in inventory	Earlier perfected non-PMSI	PMSI (and also as to PMSI cash proceeds if notice was given to non-PMSI on or before debtor takes possession) (UCC § 9-312(3))
Perfected PMSI in noninventory collateral	Earlier perfected non-PMSI in the same collateral	PMSI, if perfected within ten days after debtor obtains possession (UCC § 9-312(4))
Perfected security interest in crops	Earlier perfected interest in crops that secures obligations due over six months before crops began	Later perfected security interest if, within three months before planting, new value was given to enable debtor to grow crop (UCC § 9-312(2))

Opposing Creditors		Priority Creditor
Lien Creditors		
Lien creditor	Unperfected or later perfected security holder	Lien creditor, except if PMSI is perfected before or within ten days after debtor possesses the collateral (UCC § 9-301(1), (2))
Lien creditor	Perfected security holder	Lien creditor, but subject to the perfected security interest inasmuch as (1) it secures advances the secured party made before or within 45 days after the lien creditor obtained the lien, or (2) it secures advances made without knowledge of the lien (UCC § 9-301(4))

Other Exceptions to "First to Perfect" Rule: Purchasers of the Debtor's Collateral and Trustees in Bankruptcy*

Purchaser of negotiable instruments, documents of title, and/or securities	Earlier perfected security holder	The purchaser (UCC § 9-309)
Purchaser of chattel paper	Earlier perfected security holder	The purchaser, if gave new value, took possession in the ordinary course of business and had no actual knowledge of the security interest (last requirement unnecessary when chattel paper claimed as proceeds of inventory) (UCC § 9-308)
Purchaser of goods in the ordinary course of business	Earlier perfected security holder for a security interest created by the goods seller	The purchaser, even if purchaser knows of the security interest (UCC § 9-307(1))
Purchaser of consumer goods	Earlier PMSI or other security interest perfected without filing a financing statement	The purchaser, if gave value, had no knowledge of the security interest, and used the goods for personal, family, or household purposes (UCC § 9-307(2))
Trustee in bankruptcy	Earlier perfected security holder	Trustee, if the perfected security holder's security interest was given for antecedent debt no more than four months before bankruptcy petition was filed

*Of course, a purchaser or trustee may not, in fact, be a creditor. Nonetheless, priority disputes often arise between purchasers (or trustees) and creditors.

Opposing Creditors		Priority Creditor
Fixtures to Real Estate and Accessions to Personal Property		
Perfected security holder in a fixture	Conflicting real estate claimant (e.g., mortgagee)	First to file, except that PMSIs filed within ten days of affixation (when the goods became a fixture) always have priority (UCC § 9-313)
Unperfected security holder in a fixture	Conflicting real estate claimant	Conflicting real estate claimant (UCC § 9-313(7))
Security holder in an accession	Security holder in the chattel to which the accession is added	Generally, the security holder in the accession, whether perfected or unperfected, if security interest attached to accession before the accession was added to the chattel (UCC § 9-314(1))

Summing Up

Creditors have several methods for collecting debts. The major methods are liens (mechanic's and artisan's), prejudgment attachments (which require strict statutory and constitutional compliance), use of security interests, the preventing or setting aside of bulk transfers or fraudulent conveyances, payment from sureties or guarantors, mortgage foreclosures on real property, writ of execution, garnishment, composition or extension agreements, and assignments to a trustee.

Protection for debtors is provided by certain federal and state laws. State law exempts some property from seizure to satisfy debts. After the proceeds on the sale of a home have paid the mortgage, most states exempt a specific amount of the remaining proceeds. This exemption is called the *homestead exemption.* For personal property, state law tends to exempt up to a specified dollar value for items such as household furnishings, clothes, personal possessions, motor vehicles, livestock, pets, and veterans' benefits.

The federal Consumer Credit Protection Act (known as the Truth-in-Lending Act) limits the amount of a garnishment to 25 percent of disposable earnings or even less in the case of low-income wage earners. State law may further limit garnishment depending upon the individual's needs. Numerous federal and state statutes regulate creditor practices, prohibit abuses, provide dispute-resolution mechanisms, or otherwise protect debtors.

The test for bankruptcy is whether or not a debtor can pay his debts. Bankruptcy is governed by federal law, with a system of U.S. Bankruptcy Courts.

The Bankruptcy Code has three main alternatives: Chapter 7 (Liquidation), Chapter 11 (Business Reorganization), and Chapter 13 (Adjustment of an Individual's Debts). Petitions for bankruptcy may be voluntary—filed by the debtor—for all three chapters, or involuntary—filed by creditors—for Chapters 7 and 11.

Chapter 7 is the traditional "straight" bankruptcy. Certain regulated businesses cannot file such a bankruptcy. Chapter 11 involves a reorganization of business debts, with a plan requiring the approval of the bankruptcy judge and most creditors. Chapter 13 permits individuals with a regular source of income, and debts not exceeding a statutory amount, to seek court approval of a payment plan lasting up to five years.

The Bankruptcy Code exempts certain property, or amounts of property, from being used to satisfy creditors' claims.

A court-appointed trustee administers the debtor's property (the estate) and distributes the debtor's nonexempt property according to the priority of claims outlined in the Bankruptcy Code.

The Bankruptcy Code prohibits the discharge of certain debts and also allows the judge to deny discharges because of a debtor's misconduct. Discharges do not remove the liability of co-debtors, sureties, or guarantors, and a debtor may, in writing, reaffirm a discharged debt.

Secured transactions are governed by UCC Article 9. A security interest may be taken in almost any type of personal property. To make the security interest effective between the debtor and the creditor, it must "attach" to the secured property (the collateral). Attachment requires (1) a written agreement stating a security interest, describing the collateral, and signed by the debtor; (2) value from the secured party to the debtor; and (3) rights of the debtor in the collateral.

To keep the security interest from third parties, it must be "perfected" by possession, attachment, or the filing of a financing statement. The proper method depends on the type of collateral, with the financing statement being the most common method.

Parties to a security agreement have numerous rights or duties with respect to the collateral, financing statements, and debt information. Upon default of a debtor's obligations, the secured party may sue on the underlying obligations or enforce the security interest directly.

In some cases, the secured party may keep the collateral as satisfaction of the debtor's obligation. In all defaults, the secured party may sell the collateral by any commercially reasonable method. The debtor also has the right to redeem until the time of sale. Proceeds from a sale are distributed first to cover expenses, then to pay, in order, (1) the secured debt, (2) other secured parties, and (3) if any money is left, the debtor.

Once the debt has been paid off, the debtor may require that the secured party file a termination statement that serves as proof that the debtor's obligations were satisfied. For consumer goods, a filing is mandatory.

The order in which creditors are paid follows an established system of priorities. The first to perfect a security interest normally takes precedence.

QUESTIONS

Identify each of the following:

attachment
bankruptcy
bulk transfer
collateral
default
discharge
equity of redemption
financing statement
foreclosure
fraudulent conveyance

garnishment
guarantor
homestead exemption
judicial sale
lender liability
lien
mortgage
perfection
pledge

prejudgment
  attachment
reaffirmation agreement
secured transaction
security interest
subrogation
surety
trustee
writ of execution

Answer these Review Questions:

1. Name ten lawful methods for collecting debts.
2. Name five or more types of personal property that may be at least partially exempted from debt collection enforcement.
3. (a) Name at least four federal statutes that regulate creditor practices, prohibit abuses, provide dispute-resolution mechanisms, or otherwise protect debtors.
   (b) Would you include the UCCC in your list?
4. Which federal or state law governs bankruptcy proceedings?
5. Under the Bankruptcy Code, what is the bankruptcy test?
6. Name three main chapters of the Bankruptcy Code, the type of relief provided, and the party that may ask for that type of relief.
7. Name at least four types of property totally exempt from being liquidated or otherwise disposed of to help pay claims against a bankrupt debtor.
8. Name at least four types of debts that cannot be discharged under bankruptcy and the other main reason for not discharging a debt.
9. Does a bankruptcy discharge affect the liability of a co-debtor, surety, or guarantor?
10. What is the simplest type of secured transaction?
11. Name four types of property that can be subject to a security interest (used as collateral).
12. (a) What are the requirements of an attachment?
    (b) What does an attachment accomplish?
13. (a) What are the three methods for making a security interest "perfect"?
    (b) What does perfection accomplish?
14. Upon default, what may a security party (creditor) do with the collateral?
15. What is the general rule governing priority between two conflicting security holders?

Apply Your Knowledge:

1. Sure-Thing Surety has entered into suretyships with the following debtors. In each case, the creditor is Wanda Wealthy.
   (a) Deon Debtor owes $20,000 on a loan. Payments are in default. Deon is only 15 years old.
   (b) Delilah Delinquent purchased a number of items on credit. Wanda demands payment. Delilah says a check is in the mail.
   (c) Ollie Obligor persuaded Wanda to extend the duration of his loan, in return for Ollie's agreeing to pay a higher interest rate. Ollie now defaults.

       (d) Carmina Committed goes bankrupt. She receives a discharge of her debt to Wanda.

          (i) For each case, given the facts, can Wanda collect payment from Sure-Thing Surety?

          (ii) What additional two defenses might be raised if Sure-Thing were a guarantor and not a surety?

2. Henry Homeowner owes $50,000 on a mortgage for a house. The house is owned solely by Henry and lived in by his entire family. Henry also owes $5,000 to unsecured creditor A and $3,000, perfectly secured by his sailboat, to creditor B. Henry is in default on all three debts. The house would sell for $69,000 with costs of the sale being $2,000. The state homestead exemption is $9,000.

       (a) If the mortgagee conducts a foreclosure sale, what will happen to the sales proceeds?

       (b) If Henry files bankruptcy, what will happen to the boat and the home, and how will the proceeds be distributed?

3. Betty's Boutique (BB) has filed a Chapter 7 liquidation. BB's creditors are as follows:

    Corporation A: $7,000 claim for business deliveries (in the normal course of business) between the time of filing the bankruptcy petition and appointment of a trustee. Ms. B and Mr. C: Paid deposits of $400 and $1,900, respectively, for purchases of consumer goods not yet provided. State D: Unpaid taxes of $10,000 for the past 2 years. Workers E, F, G: Wages in the amount of $500, $2,000 and $3,000, respectively, owed for last two months' work as BB's employees. Secured Creditor H: $5,000 owed on car loan with perfected security interest in the car. Unsecured Creditors J and K: $8,000 owed to each.

       (a) Assume the proceeds, after costs, from the sale of BB's car are $3,000. Assume that the liquidated value of the estate is $37,800 with costs of administration, collection, and maintenance being $5,000. State the distribution of remaining proceeds to each creditor.

       (b) If BB proposes a Chapter 11 reorganization, name one creditor whose single refusal would make the plan disallowed. How much must the creditor receive under the reorganization plan?

4. Dottie Debtor purchased an automobile on credit. May her creditor take priority over a previously perfected security holder who took a security interest in Dottie's present and after-acquired motor vehicle?

5. A lends money to B. As collateral, A takes possession of stocks and promissory notes owed to B. Later, B receives a business loan from C, with a security interest (and properly filed financing statement) specifying a security interest in B's stocks, promissory notes, and other documents. Who has priority as to the stocks and promissory notes, A or C?

6. (a) Derek Debtor is lent money by Bob Bucks, who takes an unperfected security interest in a number of items, including a word processor Derek has owned for three years. If Telly's Type Shop (TTS) obtains a lien for repairs on Derek's word processor, who has priority, Derek or TTS?

       (b) What if Bob now perfects his security interest?

7. Joe lends money to Kay and receives a signed agreement stating a security interest and describing the collateral (Kay's accounts receivable). Kay already has a judgment against her in favor of A. She also already owes money to B, although there is no collateral or security interest. After Joe lends money to Kay and takes her security interest, C also lends money to Kay and gets her to sign a security agreement almost identical to the one she signed for Joe. C follows up by filing, in the correct location, a financing statement containing

Kay's signature, the full names and addresses of Kay and Joe, and a description of Kay's accounts receivable.

In each of the following, who has priority?

(a) Joe or A (b) Joe or B (c) Joe or C

8. (a) Mary has a perfected security interest in Nancy's inventory of 100 widgets. Nancy regularly sells widgets, and soon sells eight widgets to Opal. Opal knows about Mary's security interest, but knows nothing that would indicate the sale to her violates that security interest. If Nancy defaults, can Mary enforce her security interest against the eight widgets sold to Opal?

(b) Assume that the widgets are consumer goods. Further assume that Mary has a PMSI perfected by attachment, but not filed. If Nancy is not ordinarily in the business of selling widgets, can Walter, a widget purchaser, be free of Mary's security interest?

ANSWERS

Answers to Review Questions:

1. Ten lawful methods for collecting debts are by: lien (mechanic's, artisan's, or hotelkeeper's), prejudgment attachment, use of security interests, preventing or setting aside bulk transfers or fraudulent conveyances, payment from sureties or guarantors, mortgage foreclosure, writ of execution, garnishment, composition or extension agreement, and assignment to a trustee.

2. Personal property at least partially exempted from debt collection enforcement are: homes, household furnishings, clothes, personal possessions, livestock, pets, and veterans' pensions.

3. (a) The federal statutes are: The Consumer Credit Protection Act (Truth-in-Lending Act), the Fair Credit Billing Act and Fair Credit Reporting Act (both part of the Truth-in-Lending Act), the Fair Debt Collection Practices Act, and the Equal Credit Opportunity Act. (b) No, the Uniform Consumer Credit Code (UCCC) is not a federal statute, but has been passed in some states.

4. Federal.

5. The debtor cannot pay his debt obligations as they become due.

6. Chapter 7, Liquidation (straight bankruptcy), voluntary or involuntary; Chapter 11, Reorganization of a Business, voluntary or involuntary; Chapter 13, Readjustment of an Individual's Debts, voluntary by debtors.

7. Exempt property includes criminal restitution payments, child support, alimony, prescribed health aids, unmatured life insurance policies, pensions and annuities, and federal and state benefits such as social security, disability, and unemployment benefits.

8. Nondischargeable debts include alimony, child support, some government fines and penalties, taxes owed for the three years prior to bankruptcy, and student loans received within seven years of bankruptcy. The main policy reason for a nondischarge is the debtor's misconduct.

9. No, the co-debtor, surety, or guarantor may still be liable.

10. A pledge is the simplest type of security transaction wherein the creditor takes possession of the collateral.

11. Almost any type of personal property can be subject to a security interest, such as goods, including equipment and inventory; documents proving rights, such as commercial paper, securities, bills of lading, and accounts receivable; and after-acquired property.

12. (a) Requirements for attachment are: (1) written agreement sets forth a security interest, describes the collateral, and is signed by the debtor; (2) value passes from the secured party to the debtor; and (3) the debtor has rights in

the collateral. (b) An attachment makes the security interest effective between the secured party and the debtor.

13. (a) Three methods for making a security interest perfect are possession, attachment, and filing of a financing statement. (b) Perfection makes the security interest effective against most third parties.

14. Upon default, a secured creditor may either (1) take the collateral in satisfaction of the debtor's obligation, or (2) sell the collateral and apply the proceeds toward payment of the debtor's obligation.

15. The general rule is that the first to perfect has priority.

Answers to "Apply Your Knowledge":

1. (a) Yes. Deon's infancy (15 years old) is not a defense for Sure-Thing. (b) Maybe. If Delilah really mailed the check, the claim would be reduced or eliminated by the amount of the payment. (c) No. Ollie's obligations were materially altered (changed interest rate to higher rate and lengthened term of loan) without consent of Sure-Thing.

   (d) (i) Yes. Carmina's bankruptcy is not a defense for Sure-Thing. (ii) Guaranty agreements must be in writing, and the creditor must first attempt to get paid from the debtor. Neither is necessary for a suretyship.

2. (a) First, $2,000 to pay foreclosure costs; second, $50,000 to mortgagee; third, remainder to Henry. If creditors A or B had acquired a judgment or some other right to the remaining proceeds, they would receive any remaining proceeds after Henry's homestead exemption.

   (b) The boat and home will be liquidated. Proceeds from the home are first applied to the costs of the sale and second to the mortgagee. The remaining would be applied to Harry's homestead exemption.

   Proceeds from the boat sale will go first to sales costs and then to B. If there is a remaining balance due to B, B will become an unsecured creditor for the remainder of the estate. If there are remaining proceeds, they will go to the estate.

   In summation, the mortgagee and house sales costs will be paid in full. Of the remaining $17,000, either $9,000 (state) or $7,500 (federal) will be kept by Henry. The rest goes to the estate for distribution according to the priority of the claims. As an unsecured creditor, A is at the bottom of the priority list and B is in the same position because of the deficiency after the sale of the boat.

3. (a) Proceed in order of priority:
   1. Costs of $5,000 for administering the estate.
   2. Corporation A: $7,000.
   3. Workers E, F, and G: $500, $2,000 and $2,000, respectively. Worker G becomes a general creditor for his remaining $1,000.
   4. Ms. B and Mr. C: $400 and $900, respectively. (Mr. C also becomes a general creditor for his remaining $1,000.)
   5. State D: $10,000.
      General creditors and amounts of claim would be as follows:
      C, $1,000; G, $1,000; H, $2,000 (H was owed $5,000, but got $3,000 as a secured creditor from the sale of the car); J, $8,000; K, $8,000 (TOTAL $20,000).
      The balance remaining to general creditors is $10,000 after priority claims (Categories 1–5, above). $10,000 remaining/$20,000 total claim = 50 percent. Each general creditor will be given one half of his claim.

   (b) Worker E. At least $500.

4. Yes, if the creditor perfects his security interest before or within ten days after Dottie, the debtor, takes possession of the automobile.

5. A. Here possession generally constitutes perfection. For stocks and promissory notes, possession is the only means of perfection. C cannot perfect since A retains possession. Even if C could perfect, A perfected first, so A wins under the general "first to perfect" rule.

6. (a) TTS. Lien creditors take priority over unperfected security holders except for PMSIs. Because Derek owned the word processor for three years, his loan from Bob did not enable Derek to purchase the word processor (so not a PMSI). (b) Bob has priority, at least inasmuch as his security interest concerns a loan made before or within 45 days of Telly's lien.

7. (a) Joe. Unperfected security holders have priority over unlevied judgment creditors. (b) Joe. Unperfected security holders have priority over unsecured creditors. (c) C. Unperfected security holders lose to subsequent perfected security holders (UCC § 9-312(5)).

8. (a) No. UCC § 9-307(1) provides that a purchaser of goods in the ordinary course of business takes priority over a perfected security interest holder. (b) Yes. Walter's ownership would not be subject to Mary's PMSI if Walter gave value to Nancy and did not know about Mary's security interest, and used the widgets for personal, family, or household purposes (UCC § 9-307(2)). If Mary files a financing statement, even though not needed to perfect a PMSI in consumer goods, that would prevent this type of outcome. Walter could not then take the eight widgets free and clear of Mary's security interest.

Chapter 12

Property

PROPERTY AS A LEGAL CONCEPT

In law, property is a collection of rights and interests, centered around the idea of ownership and use. There are two main types of property: (1) *real property*, which is land and the buildings, trees, or other items attached to, grown upon, or built on the land; and (2) *personal property*, which is essentially all other property besides real property. Personal property generally is property without a permanent location.

The law of contracts strongly influences property law. Unless a contract solely involves services, it probably has property (goods, land, and so on) as its subject matter. In fact, a contract itself may be a form of property; the contractual rights owned by the contracting parties usually are transferable. For example, a negotiable instrument is a special type of contract *and* property. Under the broad definition of property as a "bundle of rights," property is anything capable of ownership, whether individually, by a group, or for the benefit of others.

PERSONAL PROPERTY

Tangible and Intangible

Personal property can be tangible or intangible. *Tangible personal property* is subject to physical possession. It can include almost anything that takes up space and is movable (nonmovables would be real estate or fixtures).

Intangible personal property consists of rights in something that lacks physical substance. Examples include contracts, stocks, bonds, computer software (programs), employment, utility services (telephone, electricity, etc.), and intellectual property (copyrights, patents, and trademarks). Documents or other materials related to intangible personal property are really just evidence of the property, *not* the property itself. Thus, a written agreement, stock certificate, employment card, or copyright certificate is proof of a property interest, but the rights under these documents are the actual property. These rights are intangible—they cannot be physically possessed. One cannot control a portion of IBM with only a ten-share interest in that company, nor can one simply pick up job tenure and put it in one's pocket, nor can one *physically possess* the exclusive right to publish a book. The rights of stock ownership, employment, and copyright are real, but intangible.

Fixtures

Fixtures consist of personal property that has become attached to real property. Since the fixture is connected to a house, or other real property, the fixture is usually treated as part of that real property. Once personal property has become so much a part of the real property that it is difficult, costly, or impossible to remove, the personal property is considered a fixture. Often, the main question is whether an item's value is actually related to the surrounding real property; the more closely the two are connected, the more likely the item (be it a backyard swing, a washing machine, or a chandelier) is a fixture.

When parties do not have an agreement, courts often look to the parties' apparent intent to have (or not have) a fixture. This "intent test" looks at: (1) the item's purpose, (2) the way in which it was attached, and (3) its customary treatment (is it viewed as a fixture?).

A tenant may place *trade fixtures* on rented real estate for use in the tenant's business. Unlike other fixtures, the trade fixture remains personal property. However, if removal causes damages, the tenant must reimburse the landlord. If removal would cause severe damage, the trade fixture may have to stay.

Acquiring Title (Ownership)

GIFTS

A *gift* is a voluntary transfer of property from its owner (*donor*) to another person (*donee*) without any compensation for the donor. When the donee is a minor and the property is held in trust (described later in this chapter), the Uniform Gifts to Minors Act often outlines the custodian's (trustee's) duties and the minor's rights.

ELEMENTS OF A GIFT

The three elements of a gift are as follows:
1. donative intent (language or circumstances indicate that the owner intended to give away the property);
2. delivery (the property was actually or symbolically [e.g., keys to an automobile] placed in the donee's hands, with the owner giving up control);
3. acceptance by the donee (usually presumed).

EXCLUSIONS
1. Since delivery is essential, there are no "executory" gifts.
2. When there is absence of consideration, a mere promise to give something is unenforceable.

TYPES OF GIFTS

The three categories of gifts are *inter vivos*, *causa mortis*, and *testamentary*.

Gifts inter vivos are made during the donor's lifetime, when she is not facing imminent death. The three elements are those listed above.

Gifts causa mortis are a type of conditional gift, which places a precondition on permanent retention of the item. When the donor, believing that his death is imminent, gives property with the intent that the donee keep it after the donor's death, that is a gift *causa mortis*. The property must be returned to the donor if (1) the donor recovers, or dies from a different cause than contemplated by the parties; (2) the donee dies before the donor; or (3) the donor revokes the gift.

A *testamentary gift* is stated in a will. It serves to transfer property when the donor dies. (There is no actual gift until after death.) Because wills are changeable until death, the effect is to make testamentary gifts also changeable.

ACCESSION

Accession is an addition to the value of personal property, by labor, materials, or natural process (e.g., growing fruit).

Examples: Accession

1. Adding an air conditioner to a car.
2. Turning an uncut diamond into a finished gem.

The property owner has a right to the increased value. Typically, he has paid for or performed the accession.

If ownership is at issue, these rules control:

1. When accessions are performed in bad faith (e.g., without the owner's consent, such as by a thief), the original property's rightful owner is entitled to the accession.
2. When accessions are performed in good faith, the more the accession increases the value of the property, the more appropriate it becomes to place title with the person responsible for the accession. If the original owner keeps the property, he must compensate the improver for the accession. If the improver gets the property, he must pay the original owner for its pre-accession value.

Example: Accession Performed in Good Faith

Bobby Booby, thinking that a beat-up chair in his late Aunt Esmerelda's house was left to him, does extensive work to refinish it. A chair formerly valued at $20 is now worth about $100. Actually, the chair was left to cousin Kate.

Bobby probably will be allowed to keep the chair, after giving Kate $20 for what it was originally worth. If, instead, Kate takes the chair, Bobby should be compensated for the accession.

CONFUSION

When the personal property of different owners is combined (commingled), there is *confusion of goods;* the various owners' properties can no longer be distinguished. For collective warehouses, silos, storage tanks, and the like, confusion is avoided by maintaining thorough records showing how much of a fungible good (e.g., a particular grade of oil or grain) is held by each owner.

If the confusion was the intentional or otherwise wrongful act of one of the owners, then title to property rests exclusively with the innocent owner(s). On the other hand, all owners share equally if the confusion occurred by the owners' consent or agreement, through an accident or honest mistake, or by an act of God or a third party. The only way for one owner to obtain more than an equal share (or, perhaps for insurance purposes, to show a disproportionate share of loss) is to produce records that adequately support such a claim.

POSSESSION

When personal property is lost, mislaid, or abandoned, or clearly had no prior owner, a person may obtain title simply by taking possession of it.

Property is *lost* when it is accidentally left somewhere by its owner, who cannot find it but does not intend to give up ownership. The finder of lost property is a *gratuitous bailee* for the true owner, with title against all other persons but the true owner. (A gratuitous bailee has a right of possession, but the owner retains superior title interests. This bailee usually must take measures, but only those reasonable under the circumstances, to protect the property and locate the owner. Bailments are discussed later in this chapter.) If the property is found by a *tres-*

passer or by an *employee at work,* then the owner of the premises on which the item was found, not the finder, acts as bailee.

Property is *mislaid* when it is intentionally put somewhere, but then forgotten. In most states, the owner of the premises, not the finder, becomes the gratuitous bailee with good title against everyone but the true owner.

Property is *abandoned* when the owner discards it without intending to reclaim it. Title passes to the first person who takes possession of the property and intends to keep it. However, valuable items are presumably mislaid, not abandoned.

According to the *treasure trove rule* followed in most states, a nontrespassing finder has title to money or other treasure buried so long ago that it is unlikely a prior owner will return. (Otherwise, the landowner usually has the rightful claim.) More important are the *estray statutes* found in most states. They provide the procedures (including publication of notice) whereby the finder/holder of lost or mislaid property may claim full title to it if it is not reclaimed by the true owner within the statutory period.

OPERATION OF LAW

Federal, state, and local laws provide for transfer of property title via intestate succession or escheat (see the discussion of wills, later in this chapter), via bankruptcy or execution on judgments (see Chapter 11), or via lawsuits for conversion (see torts, Chapter 3). Except in certain limited instances (e.g., a UCC "bona fide purchaser" of goods; see Chapter 7), even innocent third persons cannot obtain title to stolen property; the thief never obtained title, which remains with the true owner.

CREATION

Gaining title by invention, art, or other intellectual endeavor is called *creation* and is considered in the next section.

INTELLECTUAL PROPERTY

A special form of *created* property is known as *intellectual property.* This protects—gives ownership over—not ideas, but tangible *expressions of ideas.* The basic types of intellectual property are patents, copyrights, trademarks, and trade names.

PATENTS

A *patent* is the 17-year exclusive right to make, use, and sell a new and useful process, machine, manufacture, or other composition. (Design patents, concerning the *appearance* of a manufactured article, are for 14 years.) To be patented, something must be novel, useful, and nonobvious.

Patent law is exclusively federal. The U.S. Patent Office searches prior patents to determine whether a proposed patent conflicts with a previously issued or pending patent.

Patents cannot be renewed. Once a patent lapses, the invention enters the public domain; this means that anyone can make, use, or sell it without obtaining a license from the inventor. However, a person can combine or add to unpatented or lapsed works in such a way as to create a new, patented invention.

COPYRIGHTS

A *copyright* is the exclusive right to print, reproduce, sell, and exhibit written material, musical compositions, art works, photographs, movies, television programs, data systems, and other creations placed in a tangible, preserved medium of expression.

Copyright law is almost exclusively governed by federal statutes. A copyright lasts for the life of the creator, plus 50 years. Copyrights predating the revised federal copyright law (effective January 1, 1978) do not have that time frame, but may last for as long as 75 years.

Unlike the situation for patents, the exclusivity of copyrights (as to use, and so on) is subject to a number of exceptions. The most important one is *fair use*. This exception includes, among other things, limited reproduction for classroom purposes. To determine whether the use is fair, these four factors are considered: (1) purpose and nature of the use (e.g., nonprofit or educational versus commercial); (2) proportion and importance of the part used in comparison to the work as a whole; (3) the nature of the work; and (4) the use's effect on the value of the work, including its potential market.

TRADEMARKS AND OTHER TRADE SYMBOLS

A *trademark* is a distinctive symbol, word, letter, number, picture, or combination thereof adopted and used by a merchant or manufacturer to identify her goods.

The law of trademarks and other trade symbols includes both federal and state statutes and cases. It is meant to keep businesses from cashing in on the goodwill and reputation of a competitor's products or services. It helps to prevent or punish the fraudulent marketing of goods or services as being those of another, presumably more reputable, business. Obviously, if unchecked, such unfair competition deceives the public and steals trade from honest businesspersons.

The owner or user of a trademark may seek to register it in the U.S. Patent and Trademark Office. If approved, a registration lasts ten years from the first use and can be renewed for any number of additional ten-year periods. Infringement of the registered trademark may be enjoined (ordered stopped by a court) and damages awarded.

Immoral, deceptive, confusing, or merely descriptive "marks" are not protected. To be protected, a trade symbol (1) must not lapse from disuse and (2) must remain associated with the business or its products and services (and not become a generic term). Some former trade names now in common public use (becoming generic, and thus no longer protected) are aspirin, cellophane, and thermos.

Besides trademarks, other types of trade symbols include *service marks* (similar to trademarks, but referring to services rather than goods) and *trade names*, which may act as trademarks or service marks, but serve mainly to designate the business entity itself. Although trade names cannot be federally registered, infringement is still subject to injunction and damages.

TRADE SECRETS

Employees owe their employers a duty not to disclose trade secrets. The duty remains even after the job is gone. The law usually permits people to change jobs and join a competitor, but they cannot turn over *trade secrets*—any formula, process, customer list, or method of operation used in the production of goods or services, meant to be held in the employee's confidence, and needed by the employee to perform her job.

BAILMENTS

A *bailment* involves a transfer of personal possession, but not title. The *bailor* (owner) transfers possession to the *bailee.*

The requirements for a bailment are as follows:
1. Bailor retains title.
2. Bailee obtains possession:
   (a) delivery by bailor,
   (b) acceptance by bailee.
3. Possession is for a specific purpose.
4. Possession is temporary; property ultimately goes back to bailor or bailor's designee.

The bailor also has duties. He must deliver to the bailee property safe and fit for the bailment's purpose, must defend against any third party's wrongful claim to title in the property, and must tell the bailee about property defects of which the bailor has or should have knowledge.

Types of Bailments

Bailments usually are express or implied agreements, but they can be imposed by operation of law (a *constructive bailment*). The three general types of bailments are (1) bailments solely benefiting the bailor; (2) bailments solely benefiting the bailee; and (3) bailments beneficial to both parties.

BAILMENT TO BENEFIT SOLELY THE BAILOR (A GRATUITOUS BAILMENT)

Example: Billie Jo Bailor leaves her cat with Bailey Bailee while Bailor is on vacation; Bailee is to take care of the cat, with no compensation expected or received.

This bailment is really a favor performed by the bailee. Thus the bailee usually owes *just a slight degree of care*; only gross negligence will leave him responsible for damages to, or loss of, the bailed property.

Constructive bailments usually fall into this category. The constructive bailee has found lost or stolen property, has received a misdelivery, or has otherwise had the property "thrust upon her." Once the constructive bailee takes control of the property, she is held to the standard of care (that is, slight care) associated with a gratuitous bailment.

BAILMENT TO BENEFIT SOLELY THE BAILEE

Example: Bobo Bailor lends his car to Biff Bailee, with Bailor neither expecting nor receiving compensation for the "loan."

Because in this situation the bailor is doing the bailee a favor, with the bailee providing nothing in return to the bailor, it seems only fair to hold the bailee to *a duty of great (extraordinary) care.* Unless he was exceedingly careful, the bailee may be held accountable for damages to, or loss of, the bailed property.

BAILMENT OF MUTUAL BENEFIT

Example: Goods are left with a moving company entrusted to packing and storing them. The bailor pays for the bailee company's services.

Here the bailee owes *a duty of ordinary care.* In effect, she is held to the "reasonable person" standard found in the tort law of negligence.

Note that parking lot bailments involve transfer of the keys of the vehicle and physical control of it. If a person parks the car and retains the keys, she has merely rented parking space. There is no bailment because delivery and acceptance of possession are lacking.

REASONABLENESS TEST

Some courts consider who the bailment benefits and whether the bailee is compensated as simply two important factors in determining the duty of care. For these courts, the question is simple: Given all of the circumstances, what was reasonable care? The overall effect of this reasonableness approach usually does not differ from that of a "benefit of the bailment" test. For instance, most judges and juries will hold that the degree of care reasonable when the bailee is simply doing a favor for someone is lower than when the bailee is compensated for his services.

Limits on the Bailee's Liability

Express, written bailments can expand or (more typically) limit the bailee's potential liability. For bailees bearing a special, public interest (e.g., parking garages, hotels), liability limits may be forbidden by state statute or municipal ordinance; even if not prohibited, limits must be reasonable, and most states require that they be clearly expressed before the bailment begins.

Bailment Termination and the Return of Property

Bailments are terminated by performance, time, destruction of bailed property, acts of the parties, or operation of law.

Performance arises when the bailment's purpose has been fulfilled or when the agreed-upon duties of bailor and bailee have otherwise been completed.

Time terminates the bailment when the period expressly provided or implicitly agreed to by the parties has lapsed.

Destruction of bailed property can occur through a third party or by an act of God (e.g., a hurricane). It also arises when the bailed property is no longer appropriate for the bailment's purpose.

Acts of the parties include (1) the parties' subsequent agreement to terminate; (2) either party's decision to terminate a bailment that is for the sole benefit of one party or has an indefinite duration; and (3) the "innocent" party's choice to terminate and, if applicable, to seek damages, because the other party has materially breached the bailment agreement (e.g., the bailee used the property in a way not agreed to by the bailor).

Operation of law concerns the bailee's death, incompetence, insolvency, or other such event that renders performance impossible.

Upon termination, the bailee must return the bailed property to the bailor *unless:*

1. it was lost, stolen, or destroyed through no fault of the bailee;
2. it was delivered to someone with a better claim to it than the bailor has;
3. it was taken by legal process (e.g., attachment); or
4. the bailee has an unpaid lien on it.

Most states have statutes permitting a *bailee's lien* on the bailed property if the bailee has not been paid for services performed on the property. After notice, the property is sold to pay off the lien (see discussion of liens in Chapter 11). Usually the lien is solely possessory (if the bailee gives up possession, the lien ends) and cannot be used for work done on credit.

The Common Carrier as a Special Type of Bailee

A *common carrier* holds itself out to the public as available for transporting goods or passengers. It may be regulated by state agencies or, if an interstate carrier, by federal agencies such as the Interstate Commerce Commission.

Passenger carriers are not insurers of their passengers' safety (hence not strictly liable) but they are usually *held to a high duty of care,* more than just avoiding ordinary negligence.

Common carriers of goods are a special type of bailee *held strictly liable* for property damaged, lost, or taken while in its possession *unless* the damage, loss, or taking resulted from:

Negligent acts, such as improper packing by the shipper (who sends the goods via the carrier). The common carrier remains liable if the resulting problem should have been obvious to it.

Governmental acts, such as attachment or confiscation pursuant to legal proceedings.

An act of God (a natural catastrophe, such as a tornado, earthquake, or hurricane).

An act of a "public enemy," a term that includes nations, groups, and individuals seeking the violent overthrow of the government.

The inherent nature of the property, such that the shipper should have made special carrying arrangements. The non-negligent carrier is thus not responsible if, for example, perishable goods spoil.

Most states permit liability limits except for gross negligence. For interstate commerce, federal law applies. That law and UCC § 7-309(2) allow limits if the shipper can obtain a higher amount of liability by paying increased rates.

Once transportation is completed, the common carrier is considered a warehouse for goods still in its possession. Thus, strict liability is replaced by a *duty of ordinary care* (a negligence standard) when (1) the goods are unloaded and placed in a storehouse or (2) the consignee (the person to whom the shipment was sent) has had reasonable time to inspect and take possession of the goods. (Some states require that the consignee receive notice of the goods' arrival.)

REAL PROPERTY

Real property interests center around ownership, use, and possession.

Acquisition of Title

Ownership (title) may be acquired in many ways.

VOLUNTARY TITLE TRANSFER BY DEED

The official transfer, by sale or gift, happens when the grantor delivers to the grantee a *deed*, which customarily includes

- the grantor's name and signature and the grantee's name;
- consideration paid, if applicable;
- "words of conveyance," stating the parties' intent to convey;
- a precise, formal description of the property;
- any exceptions or reservations, such as easements or profits (both described later in this section);

- quantity (acreage); and
- covenants or other warranties.

General warranty deeds include all of the usual covenants associated with sales of land, such as guarantees of good title and of quiet enjoyment (possession without disturbance). The grantor warrants title against defects or drawbacks arising before or during her ownership.

Special warranty deeds include the general warranty's covenants, but warrant only against defects or drawbacks arising after the grantor acquired the property.

Deeds (whether general warranty or special warranty) usually warrant the grantor's "good and merchantable title." If disputes over title arise later, the grantor may be subject to a breach of title lawsuit.

A *quitclaim deed*, however, contains no warranty of title; it simply transfers all of the grantor's rights in the property, whatever those rights may be. Unless the grantor's actions were fraudulent, she is not liable to the grantee even if it turns out that the grantor had no title at all and hence did not give title to the grantee.

Recording the deed in the local records office is not needed to transfer title. However, recording provides notice to others, and in many states establishes priority over unrecorded deeds involving the same property.

Factors Involved in Real Property Sales: The sale of real property generally involves the following:

1. Contract of sale, which must be in writing to be enforceable (Statute of Frauds).
2. Title search, generally performed to determine if the grantor has a marketable title.
3. Mortgage(s), when money is borrowed to purchase the property.
4. At closing, delivery of the deed to the buyer, who pays the purchase price. The money may then be disbursed to, among others, the broker or agent (if any), the title company (if applicable), the seller's mortgagee (if money is still owed), and the seller.

Mortgages: Mortgages are a type of security transaction involving real property. The mortgage is a document and an interest in land provided by the *mortgagor* (debtor) to the *mortgagee* (creditor). The debtor's real property is described and given as security for the loan the mortgagee made to the mortgagor.

Two alternatives to the mortgage are the *installment land contract* and the *deed of trust.* For the installment land contract, the seller retains a security interest until the total purchase price is paid. The buyer possesses the property with forfeiture conditions (such as for default in payments) stated in the contract. For the deed of trust, the property is transmitted to a third person (the trustee), who holds it in trust as security for the debt. The debtor retains possessory and other property rights. Foreclosure is generally along the same lines as for mortgages, but the trustee, not the sheriff, may conduct the public sale.

INVOLUNTARY TITLE TRANSFER BY OPERATION OF LAW

Involuntary title transfer may occur through a *foreclosure sale* (because of an unpaid mortgage or a mechanic's lien) or a *judgment sale* (because of an unpaid judgment, leading to a writ of execution). For more, see Chapter 11. Also, the federal government, the states, and some other governmental entities have the power to take privately owned real property for the public benefit. This is *eminent domain*, and the Fifth Amendment to the U.S. Constitution requires that the owner be compensated, generally at the property's fair market value before the taking occurred. Lastly, there is *adverse possession* when a trespasser occupies property continuously, exclusively, openly, and without the owner's permission for the period of time required by state statute (it varies from about five to 20 years). The owner's title thereby passes to the trespasser. Some states require that the trespasser had at least some claim of title beforehand, and most states consider whether or not the occupier paid taxes on the property. Neither government land nor land occupied by permission of the owner can be acquired by adverse possession.

Transfer By Inheritance: *Title to real property may be transferred either through a will or general state inheritance laws.*

Rights Associated with Land Ownership

The following rights accompany land ownership:

1. **Surface rights**—the exclusive right to occupy the land's surface.
2. **Subterranean rights**—the exclusive right to oil, minerals, and other substances beneath the land's surface, as well as reasonable use of subsurface waters. This last right is often treated as a riparian right (see number 8, below).
3. **Air rights**—the exclusive right to the air above the land, to that height over which control is reasonable. (Obviously, without zoning restrictions, a landowner cannot prevent airplanes from flying over her property at a safe altitude.)
4. **Right to fixtures** on the land (e.g., a shed or a patio).
5. **Right to trees, crops, or other vegetation** on the land.
6. **Right to lateral and subjacent support**—neighbors may not excavate or otherwise change their own land to such an extent that the owner's lands or buildings are damaged.
7. **Right to be free of public or private nuisances,** such as pollution, noxious odors, excessive noise, or other interference with enjoyment of the land. (If governmental actions make the land uninhabitable, the owner may seek *inverse condemnation,* an order that the government take the property by eminent domain and compensate the owner.)
8. **Riparian rights**—reasonable use of a natural waterway within her property. (Title to navigable streams extends only to their low water mark, with the federal government owning the rest.)

These rights do not entitle landowners to interfere with other landowners' rights. For example, despite his riparian rights, a landowner has a duty not to pollute or divert a waterway passing through his property.

Restrictions on Land-Use Rights

GOVERNMENTAL CONTROLS

An owner's right to use her land is now subject to many governmental controls, including zoning and building codes.

Zoning is legislative action, usually at the city or county level. It regulates the use of property, including the types of construction permitted within different zoning districts.

Like other administrative rulings, zoning decisions are subject to court review but are very rarely overturned unless they were clearly arbitrary or otherwise violated due process.

Unlike eminent domain, zoning changes generally do not afford landowners an opportunity to receive compensation from the government. Typically, to qualify for compensation, some or part of the land must actually be taken, not merely adversely affected by land-use regulation.

PRIVATE RESTRICTIONS

Private restrictions that do not violate public policy may be placed in deeds, subdivision plans, or the like. Such restrictions are usually upheld if they benefit the landowners as a whole. Examples include limits on the size and design of houses or other buildings, and prohibitions of commercial establishments.

Possessory Interests

There are three main types of possessory interests in real property:

1. **Fee simple estate.** The highest form of ownership and possession, fee simple estate includes all rights in the land. Owners in fee simple may pass to others rights in the land without giving up absolute ownership.

Besides *fee simple absolute* (FSA), there are *fee simple determinable* (FSD; ownership automatically ends if a specified action occurs) and *fee simple subject to a condition subsequent* (FSSCS; ownership is subject to a grantor's right of repossession if a specified action occurs). In either case, ownership and possession are absolute until and unless the specified action occurs.

Example of FSA: Land is granted to X, with no conditions and no possibility of reversion.

Example of FSD: Land is granted to a university "so long as the land is used for educational purposes." If the educational purpose ceases, the land automatically reverts back to the grantor or his heirs.

Example of FSSCS: Land is granted to a museum, but "if a painting by Andy Warhol is ever exhibited on the premises, the grantor or his heirs may re-enter." If a Warhol is shown, it is up to the grantor or his heirs whether or not to have the land revert.

2. **Life estate.** In life estate, a person's possessory interest in land is the duration of one or more human lives as specified in the granting contract. Usually the estate is for the life of the grantee (the person receiving the life estate). When the life tenant dies, the land either reverts to the grantor or her heirs (a reversionary interest) or the remaining estate, called a "remainder," passes to another party, the "remainderman," named in the granting contract.

Life tenants may generally do anything with their property, including leasing or transferring it, that will not cause permanent damage to it. Of course, if A has a life estate for the life of B, she cannot give to C a fee simple estate or any other estate that exceeds the lifetime of B. (A cannot transfer more than she herself holds.)

3. **Leasehold.** Both fee simple estates and life estates are labeled "freeholds." In both cases, the estates are of uncertain duration. A leasehold, however, generally has a set term. Unlike freeholds, the leasehold's property owner is distinct from its occupant, because a leasehold grants only possession, not title. (Leases are discussed later in this chapter.)

Nonpossessory Interests

Three nonpossessory interests are *profits*, *licenses*, and *easements*.

Profits are rights to obtain a possessory interest in some aspect of another's land, such as crops, timber, or minerals. An easement usually accompanies the profit, so that the profit holder can enter the land to remove the crop, mineral, or whatever.

For *licenses,* the owner permits someone to use his land, generally for a limited, specific purpose (e.g., to camp, hunt, hike, or fish). The license is subject to revocation at any time.

Easements are created either by agreement (express) or by operation of law (implied). The easement gives to its holder a limited right to use, or forbid the use of, another person's land for a specific purpose. Most easements are *affirmative*— granting the use of a person's property to another party (e.g., a farmer's driving on a neighbor's private road to get to a second parcel of land that he owns). However, easements can also be *negative*—restricting a property owner's use of her own property, the "servient" estate, because such a use would affect an adjoining, "dominant" estate (e.g., servient estate S cannot build in such a way as to deprive dominant estate D of access to sunlight). (The effect of negative easements is similar to that of *restrictive covenants.* The latter are express provisions, usually placed in deeds, that attempt to restrict the transfer or use of property.)

Deeds transferring title, or documents accompanying deeds, are the usual means of creating express easements. One main type of express easement is the *appurtenant easement*, which concerns adjoining land. The dominant estate holds a negative or affirmative easement over the neighboring, servient estate. Appurtenant easements, intended for holders of particular property, "run with the land." Thus, when the dominant estate is transferred, the appurtenant easement also passes to the new owner.

The other main type of express easement, an *easement in gross*, is for a specific purpose. No adjoining, dominant estate exists. At common law, this "personal" easement could not be transferred. However, most states now allow such transfers, especially for easements necessary for commerce or other public purposes. A utility company's right to run lines on private property is an easement in gross.

Three types of easements not expressed in a document are:

1. **Implied easements,** which, like implied contracts, are based on the parties' presumed intent.

2. **Easements by prescription,** resulting from actual, open, continual, and nonpermissive easement use of another's land for the statutory period of time needed to establish adverse possession. (Like adverse possession, prescriptive rights typically cannot be acquired in public lands.)

3. **Easements by necessity,** arising if a land conveyance makes such an easement necessary for the use and enjoyment of granted or retained land. If Omar Owner transfers some land to Beulah Buyer, and Beulah's tract has no access to a public road except through Omar's retained land, there is an easement by necessity through Omar's land.

Tenant/Landlord Relationship

The owner of real property may be a *landlord,* having put possession in the hands of a *tenant.*

THE LEASE

The rental agreement, a *lease*, is between the lessor (owner) and lessee (tenant). Although leases should be in writing, most states permit short-term leases (one year or less) to be oral or simply implied. The Statue of Frauds, however, bars enforcement of an unacknowledged, unwritten lease covering more than one year. Also, federal, state, and local fair housing laws bar discrimination based upon race, color, religion, national origin, sex, handicap, or familial status.

Leaseholds are nonownership, possessory interests in realty. There are four main types:

1. **Estate for years.** Tenancy is for a definite period of time, and usually ends on or by a date stated in the lease, although termination may occur because of the parties' mutual agreement, a condition stated in the lease, operation of law (e.g., bankruptcy), or merger (lessee acquires fee simple title to the property).

2. **Periodic tenancy.** Tenancy is for a definite period of time, often month to month, that automatically renews until a contrary notice is given by the lessor or lessee (usually one rental period in advance).

3. **Tenancy at will.** Either party may end the tenancy at any time, although most states require a termination notice.

4. **Tenancy at sufferance.** In this situation, the tenancy has continued after the lease expired, with most states holding that this leasehold implicitly becomes a periodic tenancy.

COVENANTS

Most written lease agreements contain *covenants*—statements about the parties' rights and duties. Covenants customarily cover security deposits, rent (e.g., requiring payment in advance), lease assignments or subleases (whether, and in what circumstances, they are permitted), and restrictions on use of the premises (e.g., as solely a retail store, no manufacturing allowed). There generally are *implied* covenants that (1) the landlord has the right to transfer possession to the tenant; (2) the tenant will not cause "waste," that is, damage the property beyond normal wear and tear; (3) the landlord grants "quiet enjoyment," that is, will not disturb a lawful tenant's use and enjoyment of the premises; and (4) the property is livable—in good repair (warranty of habitability).

TERMINATION OF THE LEASE

Before its term has run, a lease may be terminated because of:

1. Tenant's breach of covenants. The landlord must generally serve notice and follow other statutory provisions before evicting a breaching tenant.

2. Constructive eviction. When a landlord significantly impairs the tenant's ability to enjoy the premises, the tenant may terminate the lease. (The law considers the landlord's conduct to be, in effect, an eviction.) Other breaches of covenant by the landlord usually permit the tenant just to collect damages, not terminate the lease.

3. Frustration of the lease's purpose due to zoning changes, eminent domain, or the like. Also, if a mortgage predates a lease, its foreclosure ends the lease.

A tenant's unilateral abandonment of the premises does not terminate the lease. He remains liable for the remaining rent, while the landlord has a duty to try to get a new tenant (mitigate damages).

MAINTENANCE OF RENTED PROPERTY

The common law left maintenance completely up to the tenant. Now, though, statutes, case law, and leases themselves may place maintenance responsibility on the landlord, tenant, or both. Obviously, landlords are in charge of common areas (facilities used by all tenants, such as parking lots, halls, and shared electric and plumbing systems).

Tort Liability for Real Property

A landowner may be liable in tort for a visitor's personal injuries resulting from property conditions.

The traditional approach is to label the visitor an *invitee* (e.g., someone entering the premises to engage in business, such as shop or make repairs), a *licensee* (e.g., a social guest or household member), or a *trespasser.* The property owner's duty to invitees extends beyond the issuance of warnings to the exercise of reasonable care in protecting invitees against all dangerous conditions they are unlikely to discover; his duty to licensees is to warn them of known, dangerous conditions they are unlikely to discover; his duty to trespassers is merely not to injure them intentionally, simply for trespassing. When the landowner knows or should know that children, attracted by a swimming pool or some other feature or artificial condition, are likely to trespass, he generally has a higher duty of care (the "attractive nuisance" doctrine).

Most states no longer look only at the status of the injured party. Instead, the test of due care is the overall reasonableness of the landowner's acts or omissions, considering all of the circumstances. Therefore, status as an invitee, a licensee, or a trespasser is only one consideration out of many.

Other important principles of liability are:

1. Tenants, as occupants of the premises, have the primary potential liability to injured persons.
2. *Recreational use statutes,* found in most states, remove from the landowner any duty to make safe, or to post warnings on, real property being used without charge for recreation.
3. Case law and statutes increasingly have held landlords responsible under fitness warranties customarily involved in land sales. Thus, a landlord may be responsible to third parties injured because of the landlord's failure to (a) repair defects as required by the lease; (b) reveal known defects to the tenant; and (c) keep the premises in compliance with the local building code.
4. A lease may provide that the landlord is not liable for injury to anyone on the premises. However, courts often find these exculpatory clauses to be unfair, and thus refuse to enforce them (e.g., the landlord knew or should have known about an extremely dangerous defect in a stairway, while the injured person had no such actual or constructive knowledge).

JOINT OWNERSHIP OF PROPERTY

Both personal and real property may have more than one owner.

A *joint tenancy* occurs when equal interests in property are conveyed by a document expressly stating that parties acquire the property as joint tenants. Four "unities" are necessary to make a joint tenancy: the owners must all have received their interests in the property (1) at the same time (unity of time), (2) from the same source (unity of title), (3) in equal interests (unity of interest), and (4) with each owner having a right to possess the whole (unity of possession).

Because joint tenants have a *right of survivorship*, the property rights of a dead tenant pass equally to the surviving joint tenants. A joint tenancy position cannot pass by inheritance (it goes to the surviving joint tenants, not the deceased joint tenant's heirs). It also cannot be transferred by one of the joint tenants; such a transfer destroys the unity of time and converts the new tenants' ownership to that of a tenancy in common (see below) for the new owner as well as the remaining original owner(s).

A *tenancy by the entirety,* which only a married couple can create, is similar to a joint tenancy in that there are four unities and a right to survivorship. Unlike a joint tenancy, though, the unilateral actions of one tenant-by-the-entirety (e.g., an attempt to transfer his or her interest to a third party) cannot turn this tenancy into a tenancy in common. Only death, divorce, or agreement by both spouses terminates this tenancy. Many states, including all community property states, no longer recognize this tenancy.

A *tenancy in common* requires only one of the four unities: unity of possession. There is no right of survivorship; a deceased common tenant's heirs receive his interest in the tenancy. If the type of co-ownership is unspecified or otherwise unclear, a conveyance to two or more persons is treated as creating a tenancy in common.

Lastly, some southwestern and western states (and, to a certain extent, Wisconsin) follow a system known as *community property*. Almost all property acquired by the husband or wife during the marriage, except for gifts or inheritances, is owned equally by both spouses. Property acquired before marriage is not included, unless it becomes so commingled with community property that it can no longer be traced.

A special form of real property, the *condominium*, features sole ownership of individual office or apartment units, with joint ownership (by all the sole owners) of the land and common areas. The owners' management participation and their shares of expenses are governed by state law and terms of the condominium agreement. Condominium owners typically have the right to free and equal use of the common areas, and to transfer their units subject only to lawful restrictions in the condominium agreement.

COMPARISON OF MAJOR PROPERTY ARRANGEMENTS

The following table shows the comparative characteristics of the major arrangements governing property.

Property Arrangement	Transfers Title (T) or Possession (P)	A Right to Use (RU) and a Right to Assign (RA) Possession or Use*	Consideration Necessary to be Enforceable	Right to Sell/Keep Property to Pay Owner's Debts**
Bailment	T – No P – Yes	RU – Rarely RA – No (but may create a subbailment)	No (can be gratuitous)	If permitted by statute
Lease	T – No P – Usually Yes	RU – Yes RA – Usually Yes unless lease specifically prohibits it	Yes	No**
Sale (see Chapter 7)	T – Yes P – Yes	RU – Yes RA – Yes	Yes	Already completely has the property

*Such right would be by the person that acquired this property interest (i.e., the bailee, lessee, buyer, or secured creditor)

**Tenant cannot "convert" a leasehold to fee simple even if landlord owes tenant money

Property Arrangement	Transfers Title (T) or Possession (P)	A Right to Use (RU) and a Right to Assign (RA) Possession or Use*	Consideration Necessary to be Enforceable	Right to Sell/Keep Property to Pay Owner's Debts**
Security Interest (see Chapter 11)	T – No P – Usually No (except for pledges)	RU – Usually No RA – Usually No	"Value" must be given	Yes

*Such right would be by the person that acquired this property interest (i.e., the bailee, lessee, buyer, or secured creditor)

**Tenant cannot "convert" a leasehold to fee simple even if landlord owes tenant money

ESTATES, TRUSTS, AND WILLS

Estates

A person's real and personal property is her *estate*. When the person dies, the estate passes to others by trust, will, or state statute.

Trusts

To establish a *trust*, one party (the *settlor*—also sometimes called the donor, creator, or trustor) transfers property to another party (the *trustee*), who administers it for the benefit of a third party (the *beneficiary*). People can create a trust while still alive, or provide for one through a will.

REQUIREMENTS FOR CREATION OF AN EXPRESS TRUST*
1. Capacity of settlor to make a contract or will.
2. Intention to create a trust.
3. Adherence to any formal, statutory requirements.
4. Conveyance to trustee of specific property that settlor has right to convey.
5. Clearly identified beneficiary.
6. Trust not violative of law or other public policy.

Two types of implied trusts are imposed by law to remedy unjust situations: (1) *constructive trusts*, used to require the return of wrongly obtained property (a trust meant to correct fraud or other misconduct) and (2) *resulting trusts*, making a person who received property she was not intended to receive a trustee for the intended beneficiary (a trust meant to correct mistakes).

*The usual types of express trust.

Wills

A *will* is an instrument, executed by a *testator* (male) or *testatrix* (female) with the formalities required by statute, stating how that person's estate is to be distributed after death. It may also specify guardians of the person or property of minors or others for whom the testator/testatrix acts as guardian.

Most states require that a will be (1) in writing, (2) made by someone who is an adult and of sound mind, and (3) signed by the testator/testatrix in the presence of two or three witnesses, who also sign in the presence of each other.

To amend a will, the testator/testatrix completes a *codicil*, which must meet the same formalities of procedure as a will itself. Although a will can be revoked by the testator's or testatrix's simply destroying it, the clearest expression of revocation, rather than worrying about possible unrevoked copies, is to execute a new will that specifically revokes all previous wills.

Wills are submitted and approved by a court according to the process known as *probate*. An *executor* (sometimes referred to as a personal representative) is usually named in the will itself; if not, the probate court names an administrator, usually a close relative or friend of the decedent. The executor or administrator takes inventory of the estate, settles debts and taxes, oversees sales or other liquidation of assets, and (if there is a will) distributes the estate in accordance with the decedent's intentions as expressed in the will.

Intestate Succession by State Statute

To die *intestate* is to die without leaving a valid will. Distribution of the estate is then governed by intestate succession laws. Each state has its own such law, specifying the order in which the estate is divided among surviving relatives. Only if there are no surviving relatives does the estate pass over (*escheat*) to the state.

INSURANCE

Insurance is a special contract intended to transfer and allocate risks from the insured (person taking out the policy) to an insurance company (insurer). The insurer issues an insurance policy covering a possible loss. For the insurance agreement to be enforced, it must meet the usual requirements of a contract and the insured person must have an insurable interest in the subject matter (e.g., property, health, life) that is being insured.

An *insurable interest* is a legal or equitable interest in the subject matter. For property (real or personal) insurance, the insurable interest is usually ownership; for life insurance, it may be the insured's own life, or that of his or her spouse, children, parents, business partners, debtors, and other shareholders or key personnel.

Insurable losses are accidents that occur by chance. If the loss is an intentional act or from normal wear and tear, then the loss is not insurable.

There are many types of insurance, such as term life, whole life, health, and disability. Property insurance covers automobiles (personal or business), homes, fire, and theft. Liability insurance covers damages that are the insured's legal responsibility to pay to a third party. Liability insurance is often found in property insurance policies. Workers' compensation is a special type of liability insurance where the employee is paid by the employer's (insured) insurance policy.

Businesses generally have commercial liability policies. They also may have interruption insurance, which covers losses due to equipment downtime or other covered risks that may stop a business from its normal operation. An insurance policy may include a coinsurance provision. Under this provision, the insured business agrees to carry other insurance for a portion of the property's value. If the second policy is not in force, there would be a *pro rata* reduction in the amount paid for the loss.

The insurer usually must give permission before a property or liability insurance policy can be assigned to a third party. As for policy interpretation, uncertainties are interpreted most strongly against the insurer. Insurers must act in good faith. Failure to do so (e.g., denying a legitimate claim) may lead to liability for compensatory and punitive damages.

An insurer "stands in the shoes" of the insured by way of *subrogation.* The insurer may seek reimbursement from a third party whose intentional or negligent act caused the loss. There is no subrogation right against a third party who causes the death of someone covered by life insurance.

Insurance policies may be canceled by either party upon giving required notice (normally in writing). Most policies contain a grace period that allows for delinquent payments or to prevent a lapse in coverage. Other than failure to pay premiums, a policy also loses enforceability if (1) important contractual sections, such as those on notice of loss and on proof of loss, are ignored; (2) the policy was procured by fraud; (3) there is no insurable interest; or (4) certain acts are illegal or otherwise violate public policy.

COMPUTERS

The most serious legal problem created by computers is their encroachment upon the individual's right to privacy. Through the use of national and world-wide networks, computers have provided numerous businesses and governments with the means to gain a large amount of information about many individuals.

In 1974, Congress passed a Privacy Act restricting the types of computerized records that the government may maintain and its uses of those records. This act also gives the individual access to the information and the right to copy, challenge, and correct what they find in these records. In many cases, information may not be released unless the individual concerned is notified.

The Computer Security Act of 1987 and the Computer Matching and Privacy Protection Act of 1988 also protect the public against the release of U.S. government computer data. The Counterfeit Access Device and Privacy Protection Act of 1984 (with 1986 amendments) prohibits the unauthorized use of computers to obtain certain restricted information and banned dealing in U.S. government computer passwords.

Two other federal acts involving electronic data systems are the Electronic Funds Transfer Act (1978), which governs bank transactions (discussed in Chapter 8), and the Fair Credit Reporting Act (1970) (introduced in Chapter 11), which has these provisions:

1. Credit information may be shared only in these permitted cases:
   (a) credit, insurance, and employment applications;
   (b) relevant business transactions (those involving the person whose credit now matters);

(c) governmental license applications; and

(d) sharing consented to by the person concerned or ordered by a court.

2. The use of out-of-date negative information is prohibited. Generally, this includes general data older than seven years, bankruptcies older than 14 years, and specially prepared investigative reports from more than three months earlier. There is no time limit on information used in deciding applications for life insurance policies worth at least $50,000 or jobs paying at least $20,000.

3. Governmental use of information is limited.

4. Credit-reporting agencies are required to:

(a) follow reasonable procedures for assuring maximum accuracy; and

(b) disclose to a requesting consumer the information in his file (except for medical information or the sources of information) and the identities of those who have received credit information.

5. Those who order an investigative report must inform the consumer and, if rejection is caused by a credit report, tell the consumer the reasons and the name of the reporting agency.

6. Consumers may dispute the information on file, force a reinvestigation, and even include a statement (no more than 100 words) in the file, with copies going to businesses that received the disputed information.

7. Violations of the act are punishable by fines or even jail, with civil actions open to persons who can prove financial damages.

In addition to privacy concerns, there are also intellectual property problems. The Computer Software Act was passed by Congress in 1980. It clarified the law by expressly providing that computer programs can be copyrighted. A copyright, though, only prohibits copying. There is no violation if another person independently develops the same or similar software. Also, certain limited uses of copyrighted materials are permitted, particularly for those who have purchased software. This is why software producers usually market their programs through licenses, not outright sales.

A patent, on the other hand, grants in effect a monopoly. Thus, many commentators believe that computer software will not be adequately protected until Congress expressly states that it can be patented.

An important example of intellectual property piracy concerning computer technology involves semiconductor chips, whose design and manufacture may involve large sums of labor and money. In 1984, Congress enacted the Semiconductor Chip Protection Act (SCPA), which provides a ten-year copyright protection for the masks used in producing semiconductor chips. SCPA treatment of infringements includes injunctions, disgorging (taking) of the wrongdoer's profits, and statutory damages up to $250,000.

QUESTIONS

Identify each of the following:

abandoned property	community property	easement by necessity
accession	condominium	easement by
adverse possession	confusion	prescription
air rights	constructive bailment	easement in gross
appurtenant easement	copyright	eminent domain
bailee	deed	escheat
bailment	donee	estate
bailor	donor	estate for years
codicil	easement (affirmative	estray statutes
common carriers	or negative)	exculpatory clause

executor
fee simple determinable
fee simple estate
fee simple subject to a
    condition subsequent
fixture
general warranty deed
gift
gift *causa mortis*
gift *inter vivos*
gratuitous bailment
insurable interest
intangible personal
    property
intellectual property
intestate
joint tenancy
landlord
lease
leasehold

license
life estate
lost property
mislaid property
mortgage
patent
periodic tenancy
personal property
probate
profit
quitclaim deed
real property
recreational use statutes
restrictive covenant
right of survivorship
right to lateral and
    subjacent support
riparian rights
special warranty deed
subrogation

subterranean rights
surface rights
tangible personal
    property
tenancy at sufferance
tenancy at will
tenancy by the entirety
tenancy in common
tenant
testamentary gift
testator/testatrix
trade fixture
trademark
trade secret
treasure trove rule
trust
will
zoning

Answer these Review Questions:

1. Name at least five forms of intangible personal property.
2. What are the three basic elements of a gift?
3. What are the four requirements for a bailment?
4. Name four types of bailments and the bailee's duty of care for each.
5. (a) For each of the three main types of intellectual property that can be registered, state its duration (assume the property was created after 1978), two examples (or its definition), and the degree to which the law is federal (not state).
   (b) Name two elements needed to show the existence of a trade secret.
6. If your state follows the community property system, where in the United States do you live?
7. Is it necessary to record a deed? If not, why do it?
8. (a) Name two examples of voluntary transfer of real property, and name the document that must be delivered in order to make such transfers.
   (b) Name three types of deeds.
   (c) Name four methods of involuntary transfer of real property.
9. Name eight rights associated with land ownership.
10. Name three possessory and three nonpossessory interests in real property.
11. (a) What are the four main types of leaseholds?
    (b) Name four implied covenants.
12. In most states, what is the test of the landowner's due care toward visitors?
13. Name three general requirements for a will to be effective.
14. What insurable interest can a person have in (a) life insurance; (b) property insurance?
15. *True or False*: Workers' compensation law does not generally involve questions about fault.
16. Can computer programs be (a) copyrighted or (b) patented?

Apply Your Knowledge:

1. Darryl Dentist leases an office from Laura Landlady. He has hung several abstract paintings on the walls, and has strongly bolted and attached his dental

equipment to the walls and to plumbing and electric outlets. Now that his lease is expiring, Darryl wants to take all of this property to a new location. Laura claims that he cannot do that; the paintings and equipment are not his. Discuss.

2. Joe suffers a heart attack. Believing he hears the "flapping wings of the Angel of Death," he gives his prized sports trophies to Herb. Joe recovers. When he asks for the trophies back, Herb says, "Sorry, Joe, they're mine now."
   (a) Can Joe get the trophies back?
   (b) What if Joe recovers, thinks about asking for the return of the trophies, and then dies in a car accident?

3. While you are in a restaurant, you find a diamond-studded hat under your chair. Is it now yours? Discuss.

4. A shipper's goods are damaged during transit by a common carrier. No one can show why. Who will probably be liable?

5. (a) Husband Horace and wife Wilma own property P as tenants by the entirety. Without telling Wilma, Horace transfers his interest in P to Otherwoman. Horace dies. Wilma then dies, with her will leaving each of her heirs an equal interest in P. How much of P do the heirs own, and how much does Otherwoman own? What type of tenancy now exists?
   (b) Same questions as (a), but assume that husband and wife held P as joint tenants.

6. A fee simple owner conveys a life estate to Lisa, with the remainder to Robert. Lisa wants to lease her interest. May she do so?

7. Kelly Kiddie passes through Nellie Neighbor's yard every school day in order to catch the bus, and to return home after getting off the bus. This use continues for several years, during the school year. When Kelly's parents sell their house, the new owners start to use Kelly's former pathway to walk to and from a local store. Nellie asks them to stop. If she goes to court, who will win?

8. (a) Ichabod Insured has a liability insurance policy covering all negligent acts by employees. One of his employees behaves negligently, and Ichabod is sued. The insurer refuses to provide Ichabod with a defense because it believes that the employee was not meant to be covered by the policy. Ichabod wants to file a claim against the insurer for bad faith. Discuss.
   (b) Assume that the insurer pays on the policy. Is subrogation possible? If so, against whom?

ANSWERS

Answers to Review Questions:

1. Contracts, stocks, bonds, computer software (programs), employment, utility service, and intellectual property.

2. Donative intent, delivery, and acceptance.

3. Bailor keeps title, bailee obtains possession (delivery and acceptance), possession is for a specific purpose, possession is to be temporary.

4. (a) Bailment solely for bailor's benefit (gratuitous bailment)—slight. (b) Bailment solely for bailee's benefit—great. (c) Mutual benefit bailment—ordinary. (d) Constructive bailment—usually slight.

5. (a) Patents—17 years (design patents, 14 years). Examples: a new type of mechanical process, a new industrial cleaning formula; exclusively federal.
   Copyright—creator's life plus 50 years; examples: a song, a novel; almost exclusively federal.
   Trademarks—no set term—ten-year registrations can be renewed any num-

ber of times; any distinctive mark used by a business to identify its goods; little preempted—state law plays an important role.

(b) Formula, process, or method to produce goods or services that is (1) meant to be held in employees' confidence, and (2) needed by employees to perform their jobs.

6. Probably in the Southwest or the West.

7. No. To provide notice to others and to establish priority over unrecorded deeds to the same property.

8. (a) Gift and sale; deed. (b) General warranty, special warranty, and quitclaim. (c) Foreclosure sale, judgment sale, eminent domain, and adverse possession.

9. Subterranean, surface, air, riparian, and lateral support rights; the right to fixtures; the right to trees, crops, or other vegetation; the right to be free of nuisances.

10. Possessory: fee simple estate, life estate, and leasehold. Nonpossessory: easement, profit, and license.

11. (a) Estate for years, periodic tenancy, tenancy at will, tenancy at sufferance. (b) Landlord has right to transfer possession, tenant will not cause "waste," landlord warrants habitability, and landlord grants quiet enjoyment.

12. Reasonable care given all facts and circumstances, including but not limited to the visitor's status as invitee, licensee, or trespasser.

13. In writing, by a competent adult, and signed by the testator or testatrix in the presence of two or three witnesses (who also sign, as witnesses).

14. (a) The insured's own life or that of his or her spouse, parent, child, debtor, partner, or other shareholder in a close corporation, and (for business entities) lives of key personnel. (b) Usually ownership, but can be any legal, economic interest existing when the loss occurs.

15. True.

16. (a) Yes. (b) Generally no.

Answers to "Apply Your Knowledge":

1. Laura evidently claims that the various properties are fixtures. However, if the dental equipment is a fixture, it is obviously a trade fixture. Thus Darryl can take it, although he will have to reimburse Laura for any costs or damages associated with detaching the equipment. The paintings probably are not fixtures. Only if they were attached in such a way as to make removal difficult and costly, or only if other circumstances indicate they were intended to remain on the premises, will Darryl be barred from taking them.

   If the paintings are fixtures, Darryl may claim that they are subject to the trade fixture exception. However, unless the paintings are actually pictures of bicuspids or otherwise oriented toward dentistry, a court may well hold that they are not crucial to Darryl's business. Even if they are trade fixtures, removing them might be, on balance, too costly to be permitted.

2. (a) Yes. First, a gift *causa mortis* is freely revocable. Second, Joe recovered, so the trophies revert to him anyway. (b) It does not matter. Even though merely thinking about asking for return would not constitute revocation, Joe's recovery automatically rescinds the gift. To be effective, the death must be of the type contemplated; the car accident certainly is not.

3. It appears unlikely that the hat was abandoned because valuable items are presumably mislaid. In most states, the restaurant owner would become a gratuitous bailee. After following the mandates of the estray statute (found in most states) and otherwise reasonably attempting to locate the owner, the hat would become the restaurant's. However, if the property were deemed to

have been lost rather than mislaid, or if there were a specific statutory provision on this point, you the finder, might get the hat (after attempts to locate the owner have failed).

4. The common carrier. Usually a strict liability standard is applied, with the carrier having the burden of proving an exception to liability.

5. (a) Heirs—all; Otherwoman—none. The present tenancy could be joint or in common, depending on how the will sets it up. (b) Heirs—half; Otherwoman—half. Unlike situation (a), the transfer to Otherwoman is effective, although it does convert the tenancy to one in common (no longer joint).

6. Yes. However, because Lisa can rent out the land only for as long as she is alive, prospective tenants should be informed of that fact, including the possibility that Robert may suddenly become their new landlord. Depending on landlord/tenant law, the rental agreement may have to make the lease subject to early termination upon a condition subsequent: Lisa's demise.

7. Probably Nellie. The question appears to be whether the new owners have an appurtenant easement. Kelly's use, if it constituted an easement, was probably an easement in gross—to Kelly personally, for purposes of catching and leaving a school bus. As such, it would not pass on to the new owners. There are no facts that show that the owners have to use the pathway (easement by necessity), or that the previous use was long or frequent enough (note that the pathway was used only when school was in session) to constitute an easement by prescription.

   Actually the judge may well decide that Kelly's use was merely a license, not transferable and, in any case, freely revocable by Nellie.

8. (a) Presumably the insured prepared the policy. Unless it can point to language in the policy supporting its interpretation, the insurer will be bound by these facts: (1) the policy appears to cover all employees, and (2) any ambiguities should be resolved in favor of the insured (the non-preparer of the policy). A claim for bad faith could succeed if Ichabod shows the usual elements necessary to receive punitive damages, including willful or incredibly reckless acts by the defendant and resulting harm to the plaintiff. (b) The only person we know about is the employee. Unless barred by the policy itself, or by a separate policy between that particular employee and the insurer, or by virtue of public policy, the insurer might proceed against the employee. Note, however, that if the employee had a right to indemnity from his employer, the insurer's claim would be self-defeating.

Chapter 13

Business Regulation

SECURITIES

We now look at the shareholder's role as an investor. First, let us examine the various sources of corporate financing, and then we will investigate these three topics—issuance, trading, and the regulation of corporate securities.

Corporate Financial Structure

Sources of Corporate Funds—Debt, Equity, Retained Earnings

The corporation may raise money by borrowing. The board of directors usually decides whether or not to borrow money. The board typically does not need the shareholders' approval to make this decision. When the corporation borrows money, it issues a security to the lender as proof of the loan. The corporation becomes a debtor, and the holder of the security becomes a creditor. These are known as debt securities.

A corporation may borrow for a short-term, which means it will repay the loan (debt) in less than a year. There are two main types of *debt securities:* notes and bonds.

NOTES

The corporation's *notes* are controlled by the provisions in Article 3 of the Uniform Commercial Code (see Chapter 8). If secured, the notes are governed by UCC Article 9 (see Chapter 11).

BONDS

Bonds are written promises to pay a fixed sum of money at a set date. A bond also promises to pay a specified interest at stated intervals. Bonds may be secured (backed) by a debtor's property. Bonds may be *debentures*, which are not secured.

If the corporation can pay back (redeem) the bond early, before its set date, then it is a *callable bond*. A bond that may be converted by the creditor into another form of corporate security is a *convertible bond*.

An *indenture* is a contract stating the terms under which debt securities are issued. For example, for secured bonds, the indenture may describe not only the collateral, but the conditions of default (e.g., non-payment). For debentures, the indenture may seek to protect the debenture holder by restricting the corporation's other borrowing as well as its declaration of dividends.

A corporation may generate funds by selling shares of stock called *equity securities.* Equity financing may open up participation in corporate ownership to additional investors. Corporations usually attempt to maintain a fair balance between debt and equity.

There are two classes of equity stock: *common shares* and *preferred shares.*

COMMON SHARES

Holders of common shares participate in management control and have a threefold interest in the corporation: (1) to vote for directors and on other fundamental matters, (2) to participate in the distribution of dividends, and (3) to share in the distribution of net assets after the dissolution and liquidation of the corporation.

PREFERRED SHARES

Preferred stock may be cumulative or noncumulative, participating or nonparticipating (explained below).

ADVANTAGES OF OWNING PREFERRED SHARES

Preferred shareholders are "preferred" to common shareholders in two respects:

1. **In the distribution of dividends.** If the directors determine that dividends are to be paid, holders of preferred shares may receive a specific percentage share of the dividend before the common stockholders are paid.

   If the preferred stock is *noncumulative,* the preferred shareholders lose their dividend rights for years in which no dividend was declared. If the preferred stock is *cumulative,* unpaid dividends accumulate for years of nonpayment, and these accumulated dividends, plus current ones, are paid before common shareholders receive any dividend. *Participating preferred stockholders* (as opposed to *nonparticipating*) may also share in the dividend to common stock on a *pro rata* basis.

2. **In the distribution upon liquidation.** The preferred shareholders may also be owners of part of the equity. Upon liquidation and dissolution, after the payment of debt to the creditors, the preferred stockholders may receive the first distribution of the net assets, before payment to the common stockholders, provided that this is stated in the articles of incorporation. Otherwise, the preferred shareholders participate pro rata with the holders of common stock upon liquidation.

TWO OTHER ASPECTS OF PREFERRED SHARES: RIGHTS OF THE CORPORATION, IF PROVIDED UNDER THE ARTICLES OF INCORPORATION

1. **Redemption**—the corporation's right to purchase (redeem) preferred shares, even over the objection of their owners.

2. **Conversion**—the corporation's converting preferred stock into common stock or from one class of preferred stock to another.

Generally, preferred shareholders have no voting rights. However, the articles of incorporation may give them such rights or may permit them to vote for directors in the event that the corporation fails to pay dividends.

CLASSIFICATION OF SHARES

Authorized shares—the number of shares that the articles of incorporation permit a corporation to issue.

Issued shares—shares, within the authorized number, that have actually been sold to shareholders.

Outstanding shares—issued shares that have not been repurchased by the corporation.

Treasury shares—issued shares repurchased by the corporation.

Canceled shares—shares repurchased by the corporation and then canceled. Such shares cease to exist.

STOCK OPTIONS, RETAINED EARNINGS, AND DIVIDENDS

Stock options grant their holders the right to purchase stock, at such time and price as are specified in the option. Stock options may be granted to employees, directors, and officers as incentive payments and to purchasers of other classes of securities as an added inducement to buy.

Retained earnings are earnings and profits of the corporation that are not paid out to shareholders as dividends, but are kept within the corporation to be invested or put back into the corporate enterprise.

A distribution of cash or stock is usually called a *dividend*. Distribution of corporate assets (shares are not such assets), while also a dividend, is generally referred to as a *distribution*. The expectation of a dividend or distribution is one of the basic reasons for an investor to purchase the shares of the corporation.

The decision to declare a dividend is within the business judgment of the board of directors. The dividend may take the form of cash, other property or assets, or stock. Real estate, merchandise, or other tangibles may be distributed to the shareholders.

RESTRICTIONS ON DIVIDENDS

If a corporation has borrowed large sums of money, creditors may have restricted its ability to declare dividends. Moreover, all states prohibit the payment of a dividend or other distribution if such payment would render the corporation unable to pay its debts as they become due in the ordinary course of business.

PRESENT VERSUS FUTURE CONSIDERATION

Stock may be paid for in cash, by check, with tangible or intangible property, or by services previously rendered. In most states, contracts for future services or benefits or for promissory notes are not good consideration for shares. The trend, however, may be to permit such future consideration.

PAR AND NO-PAR SHARES

A *par share* has a specific dollar amount indicated on the share certificate. The par value may be any amount chosen by the board. This value may or may not reflect the actual value of the share. The par value must be set out in the articles of incorporation. The corporation must receive, as a minimum, the par-value price for each share it sells.

No-par shares are issued for any amount that the board assigns to such shares.

TREASURY SHARES AND DISCOUNT SHARES

Treasury shares may be reissued for an amount equal to their fair market value even though this amount may be less than the par or stated value.

Discount shares are shares issued for less than par value or stated value. A shareholder who purchases shares at discount from the corporation is liable to (owes) the corporation for the amount of the discount.

SHARE SUBSCRIPTIONS

A *subscription* is a promise to buy shares at a specified price. This usually takes place before a business becomes incorporated. Since the promoters require assurance that enough equity funds will be raised to support the business, it is important that subscribers be bound to their promises to purchase stock that the corporation, once formed, will issue. The promoters, *and relying third parties*, may enforce the subscription.

ISSUANCE OF SHARES

A *share* in a corporation is a fractional interest in the ownership of the corporation. The share interest may be physically represented by a share certificate (a stock certificate), or it may be "uncertificated" under general state corporate law or under the provisions of the Model Business Corporation Act.

TRANSFER OF SECURITIES

At the state level, UCC Article 8 governs the transfer and registration of investment securities. Share certificates, bonds, debentures, and corporate notes are covered by its provisions. Even if a certified security (certificate) meets the requirements of Article 3 (Negotiable Instruments), it is governed by Article 8.

Securities certificates are either in *registered form* (registered with the issuer, usually the corporation, in a specific name) or in *blank* (payable to the holder). A registered certificate is transferred by delivery plus indorsement or by delivery plus the execution of a stock power (or assignment). If a share certificate is transferred without designating a transferee by name, the certificate is a *street certificate* and may be further transferred by delivery only, without indorsement.

Restrictions on transfer are permitted, but should be conspicuously noted on the certificate or, for uncertificated securities, in the initial transaction statement. Restrictions often serve to maintain voting controls, preserve S corporation or close corporation status, and remain exempt from federal or state securities laws requiring registration of public offerings.

Securities Regulation

Statutory regulation of securities operates within three broad categories:
1. The Securities Act of 1933.
2. The Securities Exchange Act of 1934.
3. Securities regulation within the various states.

The Securities Act of 1933

The Securities Act of 1933 is a federal "consumer protection law" for investors. It requires that the public be given complete and full disclosure about *new* securities being offered for sale. This act, as well as the other federal securities laws, is administered by the Securities Exchange Commission (SEC), established in 1934.

Congressional investigation during the early 1930s into the 1929 stock market crash led to the passage of the Act, which is intended to (1) assure the investor an opportunity to make informed decisions, and (2) protect honest businesses seeking funds through public investment.

The Securities Act defines *security* not only as a note, stock, bond, debenture, or evidence of indebtedness, but also as an "investment contract," or a "fractional undivided interest in oil, gas, or other mineral rights, or, in general, any interest or instrument commonly known as a 'security'." This broad definition is designed to prevent circumvention of the law by the form of the document. For instance, the Supreme Court has broadly interpreted "investment contract" to include most investments of money in a commonly held enterprise when the investor's expectations, or hopes, for a profit stem not from his own efforts but those of a promoter or third party.

SECURITIES EXEMPT BY STATUTE

Section 3(a) of the Securities Act exempts a number of securities:

1. Any security issued or guaranteed by the United States, by any state, by any political subdivision of any state, or by a public instrumentality of any state. Municipal bonds and industrial revenue bonds, as well as "authority" bonds and securities, are thus exempt.
2. Short-term commercial paper, that is, paper having a maturity date at time of issue not exceeding nine months.
3. Securities issued by an organization operated exclusively for religious, educational, benevolent, fraternal, charitable, or reformatory purposes, and not for profit.
4. Securities of domestic banks, savings and loan associations, building and loan associations, cooperative banks, and the like.
5. Securities whose issuance is regulated by the Interstate Commerce Commission.
6. Securities issued by a receiver or trustee in bankruptcy.
7. Any insurance or endowment policy or annuity contract issued by a regulated insurance company.
8. Securities issued for conversion or exchange with existing shares of a security holder where no commission or other payment is paid or given directly or indirectly.
9. Securities issued for local (intrastate) investment only. This exemption applies to issues for the local financing of local industry or business. To qualify for the exemption, the offering must be made solely to investors in a single state by a resident doing business within that state. In-state purchasers cannot buy for the purpose of reselling to persons outside the state.

Registration is the heart of the 1933 Act.

REGISTRATION STATEMENT

The *registration statement*, filed with the SEC, contains all relevant information about the securities to be offered, the issuer and the business involved, and plans for the use of the dollar proceeds of the issuance. The registration statement makes the party writing it (chief executive officer, financial officer, board of directors) responsible for errors in the statement. The statement becomes effective on the twentieth day after its filing with the SEC, although this date may be advanced by the SEC.

STATUTORY PROSPECTUS

The statutory prospectus is derived from the registration statement and is used to aid the potential investor in making an informed decision about the security. The statutory prospectus is a comprehensive and detailed booklet about the security, its issuers, the use of funds to be generated, the terms of payback to the investors if minimum financing is not obtained, the prospects of a successful business, financial statements, and other matters.

COMMUNICATION WITH INVESTORS

Before the filing date there should be no communication with the public or potential investors concerning the planned offering of the security. However, SEC Rule 135 permits the publication of a limited, informational notice beforehand, called a *tombstone advertisement*.

After the filing date, but before the approval date, the securities may be offered orally but not sold. Also, preliminary prospectuses (*red herring prospectuses*) must accompany any written offer when securities are not yet available for sale. They contain a mandatory red-ink warning on the cover that the registration is incomplete.

After the effective date, the securities, accompanied by the final prospectus, may be freely offered to investors.

EXEMPTED TRANSACTIONS

Section 4 of the Securities Act exempts (1) transactions by an issuer that are private offerings (meaning, offerings to no more than a total of 25 offerees, although the number of actual buyers may be far fewer) and (2) transactions by any person other than an issuer or an underwriter. Brokers' and dealers' transactions are exempt from this Act to the extent that their transactions are not those of an underwriter (part of the plan of distribution).

REGULATION A (SMALL PUBLIC OFFERING)

This regulation permits a simplified and limited registration for public offerings of up to $1.5 million of securities in any 12-month period. The issuer must notify the SEC at least ten days before the initial date of offering, furnish general information about the issuer, the nature of the securities, the purpose of the issue, and a description of any arrangement to return investors' funds if the financial objectives are not met. The issuer must also distribute to potential investors an offering circular, containing essentially the same information as the notification to the SEC.

REGULATIONS B AND C

Regulation B covers oil and gas securities. Regulation C deals with general registration requirements, registration by foreign governments, and other rules.

REGULATION D (PRIVATE SALES OFFERINGS)

This regulation is intended to simplify offerings to informed, sophisticated investors and to accredited investors such as banks, insurance companies, and investment companies. Several SEC rules, requiring SEC notification of an offering, are issued under this regulation.

Rule 504 covers securities offerings in an amount up to $1 million (no more than $500,000 of which can be without registration under a state's securities laws) within a 12-month period. There is no limit on the number of purchasers, but the offering may not be publicly promoted—nor may the securities be resold—unless in compliance with state blue sky law (see below) requiring presale delivery of disclosure documents.

Rule 505 covers securities offerings in an amount up to $5 million within a 12-month period. There is no limit on the number of accredited purchasers, with up to 35 unaccredited purchasers permitted so long as they receive an offering circular. No public promotion is allowed, and resale is restricted.

Rule 506 provisions are like those of Rule 505 except that the total dollar amount and time period are both unlimited and, in return for such greater freedom, the issuer cannot offer securities to the unaccredited investors (again, up to 35) unless it reasonably believes they have sufficient experience to evaluate the risks.

CIVIL LIABILITY UNDER SECTIONS 11 AND 12

Under Section 11, one can be made to pay damages or, perhaps, rescind the transaction, for:

1. Selling an unregistered security required to have been registered.
2. Selling a registered security without providing a statutory prospectus.
3. Offering securities for sale before the filing (or approval) of a registration statement.
4. Including a false statement in the registration statement.
5. Omitting a material fact from the registration statement. Non-issuer defendants (e.g., accountants, corporate directors and officers, the underwriter) may defend themselves by proving their own *reasonable due diligence* concerning failures in the registration.

Section 12 imposes broad liability for any person offering or selling a security by means of an oral statement or a prospectus containing a false statement of a material fact or an omission of a material fact. The seller may defend on the grounds of lack of knowledge about the falsity or omission.

CRIMINAL LIABILITY

Willful violation of the Securities Act or of SEC rules pursuant to the Act can be punished by fines and up to five years' imprisonment.

The Securities Exchange Act of 1934

The Securities Exchange Act of 1934 is a federal statute concerned with *existing* securities in the marketplace. There are four major goals:
1. To regulate the securities market and securities exchanges.
2. To make available to persons who buy and sell securities information relating to the issuers of such securities.
3. To prevent fraud in trading securities.
4. To prevent the use of insider information for the private gain of a privileged few, to the detriment of outsiders.

REGISTRATION AND REPORTS

The Act requires that all stock exchanges, over-the-counter brokers, and dealers register with the SEC. Any security that is to be traded on an exchange must be registered with both the SEC and the exchange. If an issuer has gross assets in excess of $1 million and at least 500 stockholders, securities traded in the over-the-counter market must be registered with the SEC.

Registration requires disclosure of financial and organizational information concerning the business; terms governing outstanding securities; names of underwriters and security holders with at least 10 percent of any class of registered security; and balance sheets and profit and loss statements for each of the three prior fiscal years.

A corporation must file three types of reports with the SEC: an annual report (10-K), a quarterly report (10-Q), and—for significant changes during the interim—a monthly report (8-K).

STATEMENT BY 5 PERCENT SHAREHOLDERS

Section 13(d) of the Act requires owners of more than 5 percent of any class of registered security to file a notification statement with the commission, the issuer, and each exchange on which the security is listed. The purpose is to inform potential investors of a possible attempt to take over corporate management.

INSIDER TRANSACTIONS AND FRAUD

An *insider* is a director, officer, or owner of 10 percent or more of the corporate stock of an issuer listed on a national stock exchange. Section 16(b) of the

Securities Exchange Act prohibits an insider from engaging in "short-swing" trading based on inside information not available to the public. The Securities Exchange Act provides that any profit gained by the insider within any period of less than six months shall be recoverable by the issuer.

The term "insider" includes not only top management and controlling shareholders, but also may include (1) any employee or consultant with access to special information, (2) close relatives and friends of directors and officers, (3) brokers and dealers, and (4) "tippees" who receive confidential, inside information on subjects significantly affecting the value of the corporation's securities.

Persons convicted of insider trading face up to $1 million in fines ($2.5 million for corporations), prison sentences up to ten years, and civil penalties that, in effect, could require payments of four times the profits gained or losses avoided.

SEC Rule 10b-5 permits the SEC and private parties to sue those who have knowingly engaged in fraud and thereby gained an unfair advantage in buying or selling securities.

State Securities Regulation (Blue Sky Laws)

Many states regulated the intrastate sale of securities long before the 1933 Securities Act. Since these statutes were enacted to protect unsophisticated investors from dishonest securities salespersons who peddled everything, even "the blue sky," these state statutes are sometimes referred to as *blue sky laws*.

Every state has a blue sky law. These laws tend to regulate securities only issued or traded at the state or local level and otherwise too small to be reached by federal law.

Liability of Accountants

Lawyers and accountants, acting as employees in or consultants for a corporation, are an integral part of the corporate team having responsibilities for finance and securities. In addition, both attorneys and accountants are subject to professional *malpractice suits* based in tort law. They both have professional codes governing their behavior, and have extraordinary liability exposure in some instances under statutory law.

Liability Under the Securities Laws

Section 11 of the Securities Act of 1933 imposes *civil liability* upon issuers of new securities for misstatements or omissions of material fact in registration statements. This section specifically includes accountants and financial officers within its coverage. A complaint against an accountant or financial officer under Section 11 is sufficient if it alleges that the investor purchased the security pursuant to a registration statement containing a materially defective financial statement certified by the accountant or financial officer, and that as a result of the material defect, the plaintiff suffered damages. Reliance by the plaintiff is not required; the accountant may defend on the grounds of due diligence (lack of negligence).

The Securities Exchange Act of 1934 imposes civil liability on accountants who furnish false or misleading statements in documents filed with the SEC. A purchaser who relied on false or misleading information provided by an accountant may sue the accountant, who may assert as a defense that he acted in good faith.

The Securities Act provides for *criminal liability* in that a participating accountant can be punished by fines and imprisonment for up to five years. Violations of the Securities Exchange Act can lead to very steep fines and imprisonment for up to ten years. State securities laws include similar criminal sanctions.

TAXES

Governments levy many kinds of *taxes*. State and local governments tax property, basing the tax on the assessed value of a residence, commercial real estate, or personal property. Another type of tax is on transactions, such as federal tariffs on imported goods and general state or local retail sales taxes. The latter is an especially important source of revenue for many states.

Governments also tax licenses and may impose excise taxes on the sale of particular products (e.g., tobacco, alcoholic beverages, and gasoline). It is usually only people with high incomes or substantial levels of wealth who may be subject to inheritance taxes, estate taxes, or gift taxes. (An *estate tax* is assessed against a dead person's property before it is passed on to the heirs, while an *inheritance tax* is levied against the heirs based upon the value of what they have received as an inheritance. The *gift tax,* paid by the donor, is often intended to keep people from avoiding any estate taxes by giving property away while still alive—gift amounts above a certain yearly limit may be taxed.)

Income taxes are levied by the federal government, most states, and some local governments. This tax is on personal income, the income of businesses, and, sometimes, the income of estates and trusts. *Personal income taxes* reach the incomes of individuals and families, while *corporate income taxes* apply to corporate earnings. Special taxes, based on income, include the social security contributions made by both employees and employers, as well as the other *payroll taxes* employers may have to pay to fund unemployment compensation, workers' compensation, and other programs.

A *proportional income tax* applies the same tax rate for all amounts of taxable income. The federal government, and most states, has a *progressive income tax*, instead. Here, the tax rate increases as taxable income increases. Thus, for example, a person with $10,000 in taxable income may pay a tax of 15 percent on that income ($1,500), while a person with a taxable income of $50,000 may pay at a rate of 15 percent on the first $25,000, but at a higher rate (e.g., 28 percent) on the income above that level. Under a progressive system, the taxpayer has a *marginal tax rate* that is the rate applied on her income made "at the margin"—her last dollars earned. This rate can be referred to as one's "tax bracket." (If Ted Taxpayer is taxed on $100,000 of income, and the first $20,000 is taxed at 15 percent, the next $30,000 is taxed at 20 percent, the next $40,000 is taxed at 25 percent and above that is taxed at 30 percent, then his marginal tax rate is 30 percent; someone with taxable income of $70,000 would have a marginal tax rate of 25 percent, and someone at $25,000 a rate of 20 percent.)

To determine one's income tax, a person takes his or her total annual income (salary, wages, dividends, interest, rent, royalties, or almost any other earnings received, not including most gifts, loans, alimony, or government benefits). Certain business expenses, moving costs, and other expenses may be subtracted from this *gross income* to produce an *adjusted gross income;* then, one may exempt a certain amount of income based on the number of dependents (e.g., minor children) one has. In addition, deductions from the adjusted gross income may be taken for certain expenditures such as home mortgage interest, charitable contributions, state and local property or income taxes, and medical or other expenses above a certain percentage of one's adjusted gross income. The result is one's *taxable income.* The tax rate, proportional or progressive, is levied against only the taxable income. Some taxpayers are eligible for tax credits—subtracted from the amount of tax due—for such expenses as child care. (A credit is worth more than a deduction because a $500 credit means that the taxpayer pays $500 less in taxes, while a $500 deduction means simply that the taxable income is reduced by $500—at a 28 percent tax rate (tax bracket), that simply means $140 less in taxes (28 percent ¥ $500).

Failure to pay taxes, or paying less than is owed, can lead to substantial penalties. If failure to pay or an incorrectly low payment is deemed intentional, not merely a mistake, it is a crime subject to severe penalties, including jail.

ANTITRUST LAW

The common law generally has tried to maintain open competition in a free marketplace. However, during America's industrial revolution, big new business powers such as trusts or other monopolies emerged. Because state legislatures and the courts were unable to control these powers, a body of *federal antitrust law* was designed to advance free competition while at the same time regulating the activities of businesses engaged in interstate commerce. The four main antitrust statutes are the Sherman Antitrust Act, the Clayton Act, the Robinson-Patman Act, and the Federal Trade Commission Act.

Sherman Act

The *Sherman Act* (1890) outlaws contracts and conspiracies "in restraint of trade," as well as monopolization or attempted monopolization. Taking into account all circumstances, the courts apply a "rule of reason" test. Thus, in practice the Sherman Act is subjective and relatively lenient, requiring *actual* adverse impact on competition before finding a violation, and subjecting the violator to criminal penalties and civil suits.

There are some automatic (*per se*) violations: price fixing, group boycotts, certain territorial limitations or market divisions, production quotas, and some tying arrangements (requiring one product's purchase in return for a contract involving another product). But, under the rule of reason, most unintended, reasonable restraints of trade are not prohibited if they are connected to a legitimate business goal. Monopolies resulting from luck, business skills, or patented products, therefore, do not violate antitrust laws.

Clayton Act

The *Clayton Act* (1914) is much stricter on alleged monopolistic activities than the Sherman Act because violations require only a probable adverse impact on competition. These illegal activities can be enjoined:
- Exclusive dealing and *tying arrangements* for the sale of commodities when such contracts tend to reduce competition or create monopolies.
- Interlocking directorships, in which the same individual serves as director of two or more companies, with each company having: (1) capital, surplus, and undivided profits of more than $10 million (adjusted for post-1990 inflation); and (2) competing activities that account for at least 4 percent of one company's

total sales and—for each company—more than $1 million in sales and 2 percent of total revenue.
- Monopolistic mergers. The three types are:
  1. **Horizontal**—the merged entities operated the same type of business at the same level (e.g., both were car manufacturers). This is usually illegal if it substantially lessens competition.
  2. **Vertical**—the merged entities operated the same type of business, but at different levels (e.g., a car manufacturer merges with a dealership). This is generally permitted.
  3. **Conglomerate**—the merged entities are in different businesses, geographic areas, or both. This is very likely permitted.

Robinson-Patman Act

The *Robinson-Patman Act* (1936) forbids sellers engaged in interstate commerce to charge different prices for the same good if that may significantly lessen competition or tend to create monopolies. Different prices are permitted if they result from disparities in costs (e.g., shipping expenses), an honest attempt to meet competition in a certain geographical area, or varying market conditions. Buyers may also be penalized for requesting or knowingly receiving an illegal price.

Federal Trade Commission Act

The *Federal Trade Commission Act* (1914) outlaws "unfair or deceptive" business practices or methods of competition. The Federal Trade Commission (FTC) investigates possible violations and considers several factors: whether the alleged violation (1) is against public policy; (2) is immoral, oppressive, unscrupulous, or otherwise unethical; and (3) causes considerable harm to consumers. The FTC enforces the act via:

Advisory opinions (on the legality of a contemplated business venture).

Consent decrees (in return for the business ceasing a certain activity, the FTC agrees to refrain from imposing a penalty).

Cease and desist orders (telling businesses to stop breaking certain laws).

Extreme measures (e.g., selling off a business' assets or ordering that it be dissolved).

The FTC and the U.S. Justice Department are primarily responsible for enforcing the federal antitrust laws, and both have issued enforcement policy guidelines. The FTC's function is very controversial; businesses often resent FTC trade regulation rules and enforcement, but consumer groups often criticize the FTC as too lenient on business. (Of course, FTC actions may be reviewed and, in effect, overturned by Congress or the federal courts.)

Exemptions from Antitrust Laws

Government officials, farm cooperatives, fishermen, export associations, insurance companies, and labor unions usually are exempt from antitrust laws. In addition, professional baseball has an overall exemption.

ENVIRONMENTAL LAW

In the past 30 years, Congress and state legislatures have enacted laws in response to increased pollution of air, water, and land. To complement these new laws, both court accessibility and the number of remedies have grown dramatically. Many statutes have expanded both the types of lawsuits, as well as potential plaintiffs, for private actions against businesses allegedly in violation of federal or state environmental laws. Typical penalties include injunctions, damage awards, fines, and, sometimes, jail sentences.

The Environmental Protection Agency (EPA) was created in 1970. It sets national pollution standards and enforces federal environmental laws, such as the Federal Water Pollution Control Act of 1965 (FWPCA) and, with the Federal Aviation Administration, the Noise Control Acts of 1970 and 1972. Besides FWPCA and the noise laws, other important federal statutes are:

The *National Environmental Policy Act* of 1969 (NEPA). NEPA established the Council of Environmental Quality to supervise and report yearly on the state of the nation's natural resources. The council also studies conservation plans and programs impacting the environment and suggests legislation.

NEPA demands an *environmental impact statement* (EIS) on any activity that may significantly affect environmental quality and that involves federal funds, licensing, approval, or monitoring. The EIS requirement has a particularly strong impact on power plant activities and transportation facilities. A federal agency usually prepares the EIS, but contacts concerned businesses when doing so.

The *Clean Water Act* of 1972 (CWA). It establishes deadlines for cleaning up the nation's waterways. The EPA may declare *water quality criteria* (amount of pollutants permitted in a certain water body) and *effluent limitations* (amount of pollutants released from a given source). A permit system instructs permit holders about what pollutants they may discharge and in what amounts. Permit holders must note their discharges and provide summaries to the authorities.

The *Clean Air Act* of 1963 (CAA). It delegates air pollution control responsibilities to the states, although the EPA sets standards and intervenes when needed. Under a 1977 amendment, states may issue permits for prohibited pollutant emissions, as long as certain prerequisites are satisfied. A 1990 amendment announced several current goals, such as stricter emission limits for cars and tougher emission standards at coal-burning plants and other producers of acid rain.

The *Resource Conservation and Recovery Act* (RCRA). Enacted in 1976, RCRA requires that handlers of hazardous waste meet certain designated standards.

The *Federal Environmental Pesticide Control Act* of 1972 (FEPCA). FEPCA outlaws the improper use of pesticides and controls the content and labeling of pesticides in interstate commerce or manufacturing.

The *Endangered Species Act* (1963). This act authorizes the Secretary of the Interior to shelter certain plants as well as wildlife and their habitats from extinction. A committee reviews whether particular projects can be exempted from its coverage.

The *Oil Pollution Act* (1990). It broadens the maximum liability of individuals responsible for oil spills and creates a fund to pay for clean-up efforts when the perpetrator is unknown or has already paid the maximum limit.

EMPLOYMENT AND LABOR LAW

Employment Law

The states and the federal government have many statutes concerning employment. For instance, all states have workers' compensation statutes, and many states have minimum wage and maximum hour laws that approximate federal statutes and cover employees not protected by federal laws. In addition, sometimes state laws cause analogous federal laws to be developed (e.g., following a great deal of state legislation prohibiting the use of lie-detector tests, Congress enacted the *Employee Polygraph Protection Act*). The purpose of employment legislation is to protect the health and safety of workers, provide workers with a base level of economic support, and preserve a workplace free from discrimination and disruptive labor/management wars.

HEALTH AND SAFETY LEGISLATION

Every state has a *workers' compensation statute* mandating that employees give up the right to sue their employers for accidental death, injury, disease, or illness arising out of or during the course of their employment. In return, the employer must pay an employee financial benefits when such incidents occur, regardless of who, if anyone, was at fault. The compensation is defined in, and limited by, a statutory schedule of benefits.

The most important federal statute on health and safety in the workplace is the *Occupational Safety and Health Act* (1970). It requires employment settings to be "free from recognized safety hazards" that could cause death or serious injury. The act establishes a federal agency, the Occupational Safety and Health Administration (OSHA), to ensure that both employers and employees comply with health and safety standards. OSHA conducts inspections and investigations; employers must keep comprehensive records on employees' illnesses and accidental deaths or injuries.

FAIR LABOR STANDARDS ACT

The *Fair Labor Standards Act* (FLSA) was enacted in 1938. The FLSA establishes a minimum wage and a 40-hour work week, requires "time and a half" (150 percent of normal wage rate) for overtime work, and restricts the employment of minors. Professionals, executives, and administrative or outside salespersons are not covered by FLSA. Many states, in effect, have their own FLSA applying to some employees not protected under federal laws.

INCOME PROTECTION
For Workers Discharged Without Cause

Under a joint federal/state program, employers pay taxes into unemployment insurance pools. If workers in such covered groups are fired through no fault of their own, they can collect unemployment benefits. To qualify, discharged workers must have worked for at least a minimum time period or earned at least a minimum level of wages. These qualifications, as well as the length and amount of benefits, vary from state to state. The unemployed individual must at all times be willing to accept new employment.

Another protection is the federal *Worker Adjustment and Retraining Notification Act* (WARN) that took effect in 1989. This act requires large businesses to give workers at least 60 days' notice before a plant closing or mass layoff.

For Disabled or Retired Workers

The two most important federal statutes on retirement benefits are the *Social Security Act of 1935* (SSA) and the *Employment Retirement Income Security Act of 1974* (ERISA).

The Federal Insurance Contributions Act (FICA) mandates that employers withhold a specified percentage of each employee's salary and contribute a matching amount. From this pool of money, the SSA provides compensation when job incomes decline or cease because of death, disability, or retirement.

ERISA sets standards for the funding of private pensions. Also, the Department of Labor and the Internal Revenue Service both make ERISA regulations. Statutory or regulatory violations are a basis for prosecuting or suing individuals that allegedly mismanaged pensions or defrauded pension holders.

PROTECTION AGAINST DISCRIMINATION

The Doctrine of Abusive (Wrongful) Discharge

At common law, a worker without an employment contract was called an *at-will employee:* the employee could quit at any time, for any reason, and the employer could fire him at any time for any reason. However, federal and state statutes have now limited the scope of the *at-will doctrine.* For example, most at-will employees cannot be fired because of their race, sex, or religion. Cases also have undermined the at-will doctrine by disallowing terminations that the courts decide violate public policy (e.g., firing an employee because she reported the employer's criminal activity).

Title VII

Although cases on wrongful discharge have risen in importance, federal statutes still play the leading role in resolving employment disputes. The most important statute on discriminatory employment practices, Title VII of the 1964 Civil Rights Act, outlaws discrimination in hiring, firing, promotion, compensation, or any other aspect of employment, because of an individual's race, color, religion, sex, or national origin. Title VII also prohibits any employment discrimination against someone because he protested a Title VII violation or participated in a Title VII proceeding.

Title VII does not apply to businesses with fewer than 15 employees. Moreover, courts recognize a reason to discriminate—a *bona fide occupational qualification*—when religion, sex, or national origin are, in effect, a job requirement (e.g., a Baptist church may interview only Baptist ministers for the job of parish pastor).

The *Equal Employment Opportunity Commission* (EEOC) has the power to enforce Title VII and other federal statutes, such as the Equal Pay Act. Complaints may be filed by individuals, state human rights commissions, or the EEOC itself, and appeals may be taken to the courts. Since required procedures before the EEOC are very complicated, it is important that all covered employers maintain accurate records, even when not currently involved in a dispute.

Title VII not only bans expressly discriminatory practices and actions, but it also prohibits discrimination under the judicially created doctrines of *disparate treatment, adverse impact,* and *pattern or practice.*

Disparate Treatment: To win under disparate treatment, the plaintiff must demonstrate what appears to be discrimination on its face (e.g., she interviewed for a job, she was qualified for that job, she was not hired, and the employer continued to search for a new employee). The burden then shifts to the defendant employer to show that there were genuine, nondiscriminatory reasons for its actions. Finally, if the defendant puts forth such reasons, the burden shifts back to the plaintiff to show that these reasons were only a pretense (that the defendant, in fact, practiced discrimination).

Adverse Impact: Under this theory, plaintiffs must show that the allegedly discriminatory employment practice (e.g., tests), while neutral on its face, has an unequal, negative impact on one or more classes of individuals covered by Title VII. The defendant employer must then establish that the practice is a "business necessity," and therefore legitimate (e.g., a test can predict how a potential employee would perform on the job). Then, it is up to the plaintiff to show that there are other methods, with less harm to a protected group, that the employer could use to achieve the same goal.

Pattern or Practice: Sometimes plaintiffs can use statistics to show that there is a much greater percentage of protected group members in the labor market as a whole as compared to the defendant employer's business. This fact may support a Title VII claim by suggesting a widespread *pattern or practice of discrimination.* However, a defendant employer is permitted to provide any evidence in his defense refuting such a discrimination claim.

Sexual Harassment and Quotas: There are two types of sexual harassment, both of which violate Title VII: (1) *quid pro quo* (requiring an employee to engage in sexual activity in order to keep her job, obtain a promotion, or the like); and (2) *work environment* (sexual behavior and atmosphere that create an intimidating or offensive work environment).

Affirmative action programs have been designed to hire and promote larger numbers of women and minorities in the work force because these groups traditionally have been under-represented. These programs are required for employers receiving federal funds, holding federal licenses, or, in some cases, operating under a court order finding prior discriminatory practices by that employer. Many affirmative action programs are voluntary. However, *quotas* can subject employers to claims of "reverse discrimination." Quotas are policies *mandating* that *certain percentages* of minorities or women be hired or promoted, even if that means better qualified persons are turned away. Passed over persons (e.g., white males) may argue that a quota is illegal race or sex discrimination that violates Title VII.

Other Laws

Besides Title VII, several other statutes prohibit discrimination in specific areas of employment:

The *Equal Pay Act* (1963), an amendment to FLSA, outlaws differences in pay between the sexes for employees performing essentially the same work.

What if the jobs are quite different but are, arguably, worth essentially the same? The wage differential between two employees working for the same employer, one performing a traditional male job (e.g., construction worker) and the other performing a traditional female job (e.g., a nurse), does not violate the Equal Pay Act (or Title VII) since the jobs are not substantially "equal" (same ability, effort, responsibility, and working conditions). This "comparable worth" argument continues to be fought, mainly at the state and local levels, and particularly as a policy matter for large corporate or government employers worried about payscale fairness.

The *Age Discrimination in Employment Act* (ADEA) was enacted in 1967. It prohibits job discrimination against people age 40 and older. Employers must have a minimum of 20 employees to be covered by ADEA.

The *Americans with Disabilities Act* (ADA) was passed in 1990, and applies to virtually the same number of employers as does Title VII. ADA outlaws employment discrimination against qualified individuals with mental or physical impairments, so long as they can perform the job with "reasonable accommodation" by the employer (e.g., modified work schedules, making facilities accessible, job retraining or restructuring). Employers are *not* required to accommodate—and thus hire—disabled individuals when that would result in an "undue hardship" for the employer (e.g., great expense). Furthermore, as with Title VII, if an employer can show that his hiring practice is justified as a "business necessity," then his refusal to hire disabled individuals will not constitute a violation of ADA. (A variety of so-called disabilities are not covered by ADA, such as illegal drug use, various sexual behaviors, and compulsive gambling.)

The *Pregnancy Discrimination Act* (1978) amended Title VII to command that employers treat pregnancy and childbirth just as they treat any other medical condition similarly affecting an employee's work performance.

Section 1981 of the Civil Rights Act of 1866 prohibits discrimination on the basis of race, color, and sometimes national origin in the creation and execution of employment contracts, as well as in all other private contract areas. Unlike Title VII, small businesses are not exempted and a jury trial is available.

Civil Rights Law amendments, passed in 1991, enable Title VII or ADA plaintiffs claiming discrimination based on disability, religion, or sex, to receive punitive damages, although such damages are capped (between $30,000 and $300,000) depending on the size of the employer. These amendments reduce some of the discrepancies between the treatment of racial discrimination under Section 1981 and the treatment of other forms of discrimination under Title VII.

Most states have laws similar to Title VII, ADEA, and, to a lesser extent, ADA. Also, some states or cities go beyond federal law and, for instance, prohibit employment discrimination based on marital status or sexual orientation. These state and local laws apply to governmental bodies and small businesses often exempted by federal employment laws.

Labor Law

Until 1932, American unions had few recognized rights. Injunctions against union activities often were granted since such activities were regarded as conspiracies in restraint of trade. However, in the 1930s, a substantial body of federal *labor relations law* emerged. The *Norris-LaGuardia Act* (1932) revoked the power of federal courts to issue injunctions in peaceful labor disputes and announced a federal policy that employees are free to form unions.

NATIONAL LABOR RELATIONS ACT

A comprehensive statute, the *National Labor Relations Act of 1935* (NLRA, also known as the *Wagner Act*), created the National Labor Relations Board (NLRB). Section 7 of the Act proclaims a federally protected right to create unions and participate in collective bargaining. Section 8 outlaws certain *unfair labor practices* by *employers*: (1) interference with rights to unionize and to bargain collectively; (2) control of, or contribution to, unions; (3) discrimination against employees because of their union activities or because they filed charges with or testified before the NLRB; and (4) refusal to negotiate in good faith with the employees' elected representatives (the union).

Employers cannot prevent all union activities on company property. In addition, although employers may relocate a business for economic reasons, employers may not move a business solely for the purpose of busting a union.

An amendment to the NLRA, the *Taft-Hartley Act* (1947), states that *unions* must not commit these unfair labor practices: (1) refuse to bargain collectively with an employer; (2) mandate that an employer pay for work not done; (3) charge extreme or discriminatory fees or dues; (4) impede employees' choice of a union; (5) discriminate against particular employees; (6) conduct secondary boycotts against businesses besides the primary one in the labor dispute (except against a business that has allied itself with the primary one for a common purpose, or to inform the public through narrow methods that the secondary business has connections with the main employer); and (7) strike or boycott to force an employer to recognize a union without NLRB precertification.

Taft-Hartley protects "employer free speech" insofar as it is merely an opinion or argument, not a threat. The Act also prohibits employers from only hiring union members; and it prohibits the "closed shop" (which had forced all employees, before being hired, to become and remain union members as long as they were employees). Taft-Hartley permits states to outlaw "union shops," which require that new employees become union members within a certain period after they start work. (Twenty-one states have such *right-to-work laws.*)

Another NLRA amendment, the *Landrum-Griffin Act* (1959), forbids "hot cargo" contracts, in which the employer consents to not using or purchasing goods from a certain business. Also, the act provides for federal regulation of union internal activities, including NLRB monitoring of union officer elections (which must use secret ballots and be scheduled periodically). The Act further requires that union officers be bonded and answerable for union property and funds, and that they permit the participation of union members at meetings.

THE ROLE OF THE NATIONAL LABOR RELATIONS BOARD

The NLRA and subsequent amendments are designed to *advance good-faith bargaining* between employer and union. Both sides must negotiate, but the NLRB cannot mandate an agreement. Instead, the NLRB investigates and tries to correct unfair labor practices. Threats, unnecessary interference with union solicitation of employees, and campaign statements found to be misrepresentations are all Section 8 unfair labor practices.

The NLRB decides disputes over what is an appropriate bargaining unit (managers, government workers, and independent contractors are not covered by the NLRA). In addition to union officer elections, the NLRB monitors elections where employees select a union to represent them and elections in which unrepresented employees decide if they want a union (certification) or represented employees choose whether to remove a union (decertification). A certified union has the sole right to bargain on behalf of the employees it represents, and the employees may not enter into separate agreements with the employer.

STRIKES

U.S. labor law recognizes a right to strike. After a strike is settled, the employer must rehire all of the striking employees if the strike involved an *employer* unfair labor practice (no rehire requirement for strikes over purely economic issues).

Strikes generally are allowed except when they: (1) are violent; (2) violate a collective bargaining agreement; (3) are not called by the designated union ("wildcat strikes"); (4) involve physical occupation of the employer's property ("sitdown strikes"); (5) concern government employees (e.g., police, air traffic controllers) and are outlawed because of their harm to the public; or (6) violate a court-ordered "cooling off" period of further negotiation.

Employers may use *lockouts* to combat strikes. Thus, when one union bargains throughout an industry by striking against one or more employers, the employers not struck may employ a *defensive* lockout mechanism to preclude members of the striking union from coming on to the firm's property. Sometimes, in anticipation of a strike, *offensive* lockouts are permitted.

INTERNATIONAL BUSINESS LAW

International Law and U.S. Law

Courts usually recognize another nation's sovereign immunity; however, the *Foreign Sovereign Immunities Act* (1976) states that another country is not protected from suits in the United States for its business activities pursued in this country.

Trade and Immigration

All countries regulate trade. The *Export Administration Act* (1979, amended 1985) requires export licenses and places controls on the outflow of goods and technical data. The *Export Trading Company Act* (1982) promotes exports and enables applicants to seek antitrust immunity for their export activities. Two other acts give tax exemptions on the export income of American sales corporations and shared foreign sales corporations. The *Foreign Corrupt Practices Act* (1977) outlaws bribery or attempted bribery of foreign officials to get special treatment and also mandates accounting standards and controls so as to avoid the hiding of improper payments.

There are several economic "unions" of nations, such as the European Community, that encourage trade by providing a large geographical area where similar trade rules apply. Most nations have agreed to the *General Agreement on Tariffs and Trade* (GATT). Through its regular meetings ("rounds"), GATT has reduced tariffs and has provided methods for reducing trade wars. Furthermore, the *United Nations Convention on Contracts for the International Sale of Goods* (CISG) adapts many principles from UCC Article 2 and it controls most international sales of goods unless the parties' contract excludes CISG provisions.

The *Immigration Reform and Control Act of 1986* (IRCA) is designed to dissuade illegal aliens from entering the United States by eliminating employment possibilities. Employers with actual knowledge that an employee is unauthorized to work in the United States may be penalized. They are shielded if they complied with IRCA requirements to verify each new employee's status as a U.S. citizen or legal alien authorized to work in this country.

Nationalization

Nationalization involves changing a private (typically foreign) business into a government-owned business. It is illegal confiscation if done without a proper goal or without just compensation. However, effective remedies for confiscation often are impossible, with insurance the only method of recovering losses.

International Dispute Resolution

There is no guaranteed technique for resolving international disputes peacefully. For example, the effectiveness of a U.N. agency, the International Court of Justice, depends on the agreement and cooperation of the countries involved. Nations may refuse to enforce a court judgment. Therefore, businesses often prefer arbitration to a national court or international tribunal.

International business contracts increasingly include clauses that require arbitration and state where it will occur and what substantive law will apply. The United Nations and many nations' courts tend to enforce contracts' arbitration clauses and arbitrators' decisions.

QUESTIONS

Identify each of the following:

abusive discharge
adjusted gross income
adverse impact
affirmative action
Americans with
    Disabilities Act
"at-will" doctrine
authorized share
bonds
callable bond
canceled share
Clayton Act
Clean Air Act
Clean Water Act
closed shop
comparable worth
convertible bond
cumulative share
debenture
debt security
deductions
disparate treatment
distribution

dividend
environmental impact
    statement
Equal Pay Act
equity security
FLSA
Fair Credit Billing Act
Fair Credit Reporting
    Act
Federal Trade
    Commission Act
GATT
indenture
insider
issued shares
lockout
malpractice suit
marginal tax rate
NLRA
nationalization
noncumulative
no-par shares
outstanding shares

par share
"pattern or practice"
payroll tax
preferred share
progressive income tax
quotas
retained earnings
right-to-work laws
Robinson-Patman Act
rule of reason
Section 1981
sexual harassment
Sherman Act
street certificate
subscription
Taft-Hartley Act
taxable income
Title VII
tombstone ad
treasury share
tying arrangement
UCCC
unfair labor practice

Answer these Review Questions:

1. What are some advantages and disadvantages of raising funds for a corporation through equity financing versus debt financing?
2. What is the main difference between a bond and a debenture?
3. In what three ways do common shareholders have an interest in the corporation?
4. Is the term "insider" limited to a defined group?
5. What rationale underlies various exemptions to the federal securities laws based on private offerings or on the size of offerings?
6. Name several types of taxes.
7. Name the four major statutes comprising the body of federal antitrust law.
8. What is the name of the antitrust law doctrine that holds that most accidental and reasonable restraints of trade are not prohibited if connected to a legitimate business goal?
9. Name three activities declared unlawful by the Clayton Act.
10. Under what circumstances are different prices permitted under the Robinson-Patman Act?
11. (a) What are three factors that the FTC considers in determining whether business practices are unfair or deceptive?
    (b) What may the FTC do to enforce the antitrust laws?

12. Name at least six environmental statutes.
13. *True or false:* Workers' compensation law generally does not consider fault.
14. What does the Fair Labor Standards Act accomplish?
15. (a) What is the most important statute on discriminatory employment practices?
    (b) Does this statute apply to all businesses?
16. Name the three judicially created theories under which Title VII prohibits discrimination.
17. What are the two types of sexual harassment?
18. *True or false:* Both affirmative action programs and quotas violate Title VII.
19. What valid excuse may an employer give for refusing to hire a disabled person?
20. Name (a) at least three unfair labor practices by employers and (b) at least four by unions.
21. Name the main goals of the National Labor Relations Board.
22. What is the difference between closed shops and union shops?
23. What has GATT accomplished?
24. Will an employer be punished under the Immigration Reform and Control Act of 1986 (IRCA), even if he honestly does not know that his employee is an illegal alien?

Apply Your Knowledge:

1. Finn is the owner of a large, unincorporated country estate on which is located an established golf course. Approximately 100 people regularly play golf on the course, paying annual dues for the privilege.

   Finn needs to raise $1 million to build a clubhouse and put the course in first-class condition. She proposes to create a corporation and issue $1 million of $10-par-value capital stock.
   (a) Each of the 100 present members signs a stock subscription agreement for 1,000 shares of stock, and Finn enters into contracts with builders and developers for the work. Finn defaults on these contracts, and the contractors bring suit on the subscription agreement. What should be the result?
   (b) Suppose that Finn wishes to form a corporation in Ohio (where the golf course is situated) and to sell the capital stock ($1 million worth) to the present members, all residents of Ohio. Discuss the liability of Jones, CPA, for errors in Finn's financial statements that overstate the value of her estate in the amount of $300,000.
2. Why should accountants receive special attention for civil and criminal liability under the securities laws?
3. I-Want-Everything (IWE) is a company that controls 80 percent of the market in retail sales of tires. IWE wants to take over (1) Lousy Sales (LS), which controls 7 percent of tire retail sales; (2) Mid-Sized Manufacturers (MSM), which has no retail sales but manufactures approximately 30 percent of all tires; and (3) Some-of-Everything Company (SOEC), which has about 1 percent each of retail tire sales and tire manufacturing, and runs a hamburger joint so customers can eat while they wait for their tires. Which merger is most likely to be permitted? Which is least likely?
4. You are the chief executive for a nationwide, Fortune 500 company. A little firm in the Midwest continually undersells your company's product, P. Can you lower P's price in response, doing so only in the Midwest?
5. You are in charge of a construction project that uses federal funds and will necessitate discharges into waterways and the atmosphere.
   (a) What three documents should you develop or obtain?

(b) If you fail to do so, what are the possible consequences?

6. Corky Creep fires Fanny Fritz, age 50, because he "just doesn't like that dame." What legal actions may Fanny bring (a) without any specific employment statute to rely upon; and (b) with respect to federal statutes?

7. An executive at Heavy-Handed, Inc. tells employees that unionization may lead to higher costs and force shutdown of factories, resulting in unemployment for many workers. Is that statement a violation of labor laws?

8. Big Business has two groups of unionized workers on strike. Union A's workers are protesting the discharge of their union president from her job with Big Business. Union A claims, and an NLRB administrative law judge ultimately agrees, that the discharge stemmed from the president's union activities. Union B's workers simply want better wages. Big Business has replaced the striking workers. When the strikes are settled, must it rehire the strikers from Union A or Union B?

ANSWERS

Answers to Review Questions:

1. Equity financing need not be repaid, but the new equity investors acquire some right to control (run) the corporation. On both issues (repayment and control), the debt securities are opposite to those of equity shareholders.

2. A bond is secured and a debenture is unsecured.

3. Voting for directors and on other fundamental matters, receiving a dividend, and sharing in any distribution of net corporate assets after dissolution and liquidation.

4. No. It extends to any person with inside information giving him an unfair advantage over ordinary investors.

5. Because the main purpose of the securities laws is to protect the investing public, that goal is less urgent when the investor needs less protection—he is already a sophisticated person with many means already at his disposal.

6. Tariffs and property, personal income, corporate income, excise, license, inheritance, estate, gifts, sales, and payroll taxes.

7. The Sherman Antitrust Act, the Clayton Act, the Robinson-Patman Act, and the Federal Trade Commission Act.

8. The rule of reason.

9. Exclusive dealing and tying arrangements for the sale of commodities; interlocking directorships; and monopolistic mergers.

10. When the seller can show that price differentials result from disparities in costs, from a good-faith attempt to meet competition, or from varying market conditions.

11. (a) Whether the practice (1) is against public policy; (2) is immoral, oppressive, unscrupulous, or otherwise unethical; and (3) causes considerable harm to consumers. (b) Advisory opinions, consent decrees, cease and desist orders, and extreme measures such as ordering divestiture or dissolution.

12. Nine environmental laws are the National Environmental Policy Act, Federal Water Pollution Control Act, Clean Water Act, Clean Air Act, Resource Conservation and Recovery Act, Federal Environmental Pesticide Control Act, Noise Control Act(s), Endangered Species Act, and Oil Pollution Act.

13. True.

14. It (1) establishes a minimum wage, (2) requires "time-and-a-half" for overtime work, and (3) restricts employment of minors.

15. (a) Title VII. (b) No. Title VII does not apply to businesses that have fewer than 15 employees.

16. Disparate treatment, adverse impact, and pattern of practice.

17. *Quid pro quo* and work environment.
18. False. In general, affirmative action programs do not violate Title VII, while quotas do.
19. Undue hardship or "business necessity."
20. (a) Employers—(1) preventing unionization and collective bargaining; (2) control of, or contribution to, unions; (3) discrimination against employees because of their union activities or because they pursued an action under the NLRA; (4) unwillingness to negotiate in good faith with the elected representatives of the union. (b) Unions—(1) refusing to bargain collectively with an employer; (2) mandating that an employer pay for work not done; (3) charging extreme or discriminatory fees or dues; (4) impeding employees' choice of a union; (5) discriminating against particular employees; (6) conducting secondary boycotts against businesses besides the primary one in the labor dispute (except against a business that has allied itself with the primary one for a common purpose, or to inform the public through narrow methods that the secondary business has connections with the main employer); (7) striking or boycotting to force an employer to recognize a union without NLRB precertification.
21. To oversee enforcement and refinement of the NLRA; to investigate and decide complaints; to supervise union elections, as well as certification and decertification elections; to advance good-faith bargaining between employers and unions.
22. Closed shops are illegal. They coerce all employees, prior to being hired, to become and remain union members throughout the course of their employment. Union shops are only illegal in states with "right-to-work" laws. They do not force an employee to join a union before being hired, but do require that the employee become a member within a certain time after employment begins.
23. GATT has reduced tariffs and has provided methods for reducing trade wars.
24. No, if he complied with IRCA requirements that he seek to verify each new employee's citizenship or legal alien status.

Answers to "Apply Your Knowledge":

1. (a) Persons relying on the subscription agreement can win lawsuits against subscribers who had not paid the agreed-upon subscription price. If the contractors knew of the subscription agreement, presumably they relied upon it. (b) Jones would be liable to Ohio authorities under the state blue sky law, to golf course members (purchasers of the shares) with whom he had contact, and to other investors (regardless of whether he dealt with them) who relied upon the erroneous financial statements.
2. As the compilers and preparers of financial data, accountants are in a unique position to mislead or deceive (intentionally or carelessly) not only regulators but also issuers and their officers, as well as the investing public.
3. The LS acquisition would be a horizontal merger since they are both in the same business; the MSM merger would be a vertical merger because they operate at different levels in the same business; and SOEC is a mixture of both a horizontal and vertical merger, as well as, in part, a conglomerate since SOEC operates a completely different business (the hamburger joint) from what IWE does. LS is the least likely merger to be permitted (since it would remove much of IWE's competition in the market). The MSM merger most likely will be permitted. An argument also can be made to approve the SOEC merger because, although involving some horizontal elements, the acquisition likely would have the smallest probable adverse effect on competition.
4. The resulting price differential probably will not violate the Robinson-Patman Act if it is simply a good-faith effort to meet the competition's price

on product P. Robinson-Patman is not designed for this case but for preventing firms from dropping their prices on goods in order to eliminate competition and create a monopoly for themselves.

5. (a) An environmental impact statement, a Clean Water Act permit, and a Clean Air Act (1977 amendment) state permit. (b) Failure to obtain these documents may bring the project to a halt as well as lead to lawsuits and penalties such as fines, injunctions, and even imprisonment.

6. (a) In many states, Fanny must still point to a specific breach of contract. Otherwise, as an "at-will" employee, she can be fired without cause. Some states, however, might consider this to be an abusive discharge, wrongly based on her age, sex, or appearance or on other illegitimate reasons. (b) Fanny could sue for damages and, if she chooses, reinstatement. The statutes that she might invoke include Title VII and ADEA.

7. Probably not. Under Taft-Hartley, employers have a right to free speech. Unless the statement was accompanied by something else (and the tone could be important, too), the executive's statement usually would be seen as simply an opinion regarding the potential problems of unionization, not threat of retaliation.

8. Yes as to union A, whose strike was about an unfair labor practice. No as to union B, whose strike was over economic issues.

GLOSSARY

ABANDONMENT — surrendering control of property with the intention to give up all claims to it. This is a voluntary act; losing property is involuntary. When used in regard to duty, abandonment means repudiation (denial).

ABATEMENT OF NUISANCE — removal or cessation of that which is causing a nuisance. Also, a suit seeking to terminate a nuisance.

AB INITIO (Latin) — "from the beginning."

ABUSE OF DISCRETION — failure to exercise reasonable, legal discretion. Referring to errors of law and plainly erroneous conclusions of fact, this is a standard that usually must be met in order to overturn decisions of administrative agencies and trial courts.

ABUSE OF PROCESS — the use of a court process (e.g., attachment, injunction) for a purpose for which it was not intended.

ABUSIVE (WRONGFUL) DISCHARGE — a modification of the common law doctrine that at-will employees (those without a set term of employment) may be terminated for any reason. This tort occurs if a firing violates a clear mandate of public policy.

ACCELERATION CLAUSE — for a mortgage or promissory note payable in installments, a provision that default in payment of a single installment makes the debt immediately payable.

ACCEPTANCE — 1. for contracts: an assent to an offer in accordance with its terms. 2. for commercial paper: the drawee's signed agreement to pay a draft upon presentment.

ACCEPTOR — the person accepting a draft and thus agreeing to be primarily responsible for its payment. *See also drawee.*

ACCESSION — an addition to personal property by labor or materials. The property owner generally has the right to increased value, although compensation may be required for an accession added in good faith by another person.

ACCOMMODATION PAPER — a negotiable instrument in which an accommodation party has, in effect, agreed, usually without consideration, to share liability or potential liability on the instrument with another, accommodated party.

ACCORD AND SATISFACTION — an agreement by the parties to a contract to substitute a new performance in place of, and in satisfaction of, an existing obligation.

ACCOUNT — 1. for goods sold or leased or services rendered, a right to payment not evinced by an instrument or chattel paper. 2. the concept of the individualized funds maintained by banks for each particular customer.

ACCOUNT DEBTOR — a person obligated to pay on an account, contract right, chattel paper, or other intangible property right.

ACCOUNTING — equitable proceeding/remedy (e.g., in partnership law) whereby the court directs an investigation of all potentially relevant transactions and all records to ascertain the rights and responsibilities (e.g., amounts owed and owing) of the parties.

ACCOUNT STATED — an agreement on the final amount due between parties.

ACCREDITED INVESTORS — banks, insurance companies, and knowledgeable persons who may receive private sales offerings of securities under Regulation D of the Securities and Exchange Commission.

ACCRETION — 1. the gradual, natural accumulation of land (sediment) by, and next to, a river or other body of water; 2. method by which a party on whose, or next to whose, real property this sediment (alluvium) accumulates, obtains title over the accumulation.

ACT OF GOD — a natural event (e.g., hurricane, tidal wave) operating beyond the control of a party to a contract and excusing his performance; also, a tort defense, a type of superseding (intervening) cause.

ACT OF STATE DOCTRINE — the judicial doctrine that courts should refrain from inquiring into the validity of a foreign nation's actions within its own territory.

ACTUAL AUTHORITY — the express or implied authority of an agent to act for a principal.

ACTUS REUS (Latin) — "a wrongful act"; if it is combined with *mens rea* ("guilty mind"), the person is deemed to be criminally liable.

ADHESION CONTRACT — a form of unconscionable contract, between a merchant and consumer, in which the superior party presses a printed form contract upon the other.

ADJUDICATION — hearing or otherwise reviewing the claims of litigants and then rendering a judgment; an exercise of judicial power, just as legislation is an exercise of legislative power.

ADMINISTRATIVE AGENCY — a governmental body (e.g., a board, a commission) created by the federal, state, or local government in order to implement and administer particular legislation.

ADMINISTRATIVE LAW — rules, regulations, orders, and decisions issued by administrative agencies. Generally, the term encompasses that body of law created and enforced by the agencies and, on occasion, reviewed by courts of law.

ADMINISTRATIVE PROCESS — procedures governing an agency's exercise of administrative power, as well as a private party's right to advance rule-making proposals, present quasi-judicial claims or defenses, and otherwise take part in administrative proceedings.

ADMINISTRATOR — the person named by a probate court to administer the decedent's estate. (Generally, either there is no will or the will did not designate an executor.)

ADVERSE POSSESSION — ownership of real property acquired by openly, continuously, and exclusively occupying the property without the owner's permission and over a period of time established by state statute (varies from about five to 20 years). Some states require that the adverse possessor have had some claim of title beforehand. Governmental property cannot be acquired by adverse possession.

AFFECTATION DOCTRINE — doctrine whereby courts refuse to probe Congressional motives and uphold regulatory legislation enacted under the commerce clause, if the regulated activity affects, even in a minor way, interstate commerce.

AFFIDAVIT — a voluntary, written statement of facts sworn to under penalty of perjury, usually before a notary public or another person authorized to administer oaths.

AFFIRMATIVE DEFENSE — a defense based not merely on denying the facts asserted by the plaintiff, but also on asserting additional facts or legal theories on the defendant's behalf. Generally, the defendant has the burden of proving his affirmative defenses.

AGENCY — a legal relationship whereby one person acts for another.

AGENT — a person authorized to act for another (principal).

AGREEMENT — a meeting of the minds; the bargain reached by the parties.

AIR RIGHTS — the exclusive rights of a landowner to the air above her land, to that height over which control is reasonable.

ALIEN CORPORATION — a corporation formed under the laws of a foreign country.

ALIENATION — voluntary, absolute transfer of title to, and possession of, real property from one person to another; owners in fee simple have a right to alienate.

ALLEGATION — an assertion of a claimed fact, particularly in a pleading.

ALLONGE — a paper physically attached to, and made a part of, a negotiable instrument; this paper generally contains one or more indorsements.

ALTER EGO (Latin) — "other self"; a person (e.g., an agent) who is legally the same as, and interchangeable with, another (e.g., the principal).

ALTERATION — *See material alteration.*

AMENDED PLEADING — a changed pleading, with added, altered, or removed allegations or legal arguments, that replaces a previous pleading of the same type (e.g., an amended complaint takes the place of the original complaint).

AMICUS CURIAE **BRIEF** (Latin) — "friend of the court" brief, filed by a nonparty interested in the law that an appellate court may decide and develop in a particular case.

ANSWER — the defendant's response to the complaint; the answer usually admits or denies each of the various allegations in the compliant, and may include affirmative defenses.

ANTICIPATORY BREACH — a contract breach occurring if one party clearly states or implies that he cannot or will not perform the contract, even though the time of performance has not yet arrived.

ANTITRUST LAW — statutory, regulatory, and case law, the most important being federal, designed to prevent and correct unreasonable restraints on trade.

APPARENT AUTHORITY — authority created by estoppel, that is, through conduct of a principal that causes a third party to believe that the agent has the authority to make contracts for the principal.

APPEAL — a request that a higher court review the decision of a lower court.

APPEARANCE — coming into court, whether in person or via a pleading; performed by the appearing party or the attorney.

APPELLANT — the party that appeals a court decision.

APPELLATE JURISDICTION — the power of a court to hear appeals from other courts' decisions.

APPELLEE — the party against whom an appeal is filed.

APPRAISAL RIGHTS — the rights of shareholders (who object to certain corporate actions that may diminish the value of their stock) to compel the corporation to purchase their stock for its appraised value; sometimes called "dissenters' rights."

APPROPRIATION — taking an item of tangible, personal property for one's own or using it for one's own interests. If wrongful, appropriation is a tort (e.g., conversion).

APPURTENANT EASEMENT — an easement that is attached (appurtenant) to a parcel of real estate (the dominant estate) and "runs with the land" (passes to successive owners of the dominant estate). The dominant estate holds a negative or affirmative easement in the adjoining servient estate. *See also easement.*

ARBITRARY — without rational basis, given the facts or law; such arbitrariness often must be proven to overturn decisions by juries, trial courts, or administrative bodies.

ARBITRATION — an out-of-court procedure in which a dispute is presented to one or more persons (arbitrators), whose decision is binding on the parties.

ARBITRATION CLAUSE — a provision in a contract for arbitration if a dispute develops between the contracting parties. Such a clause either makes arbitration mandatory or permits either party to choose arbitration in lieu of a lawsuit.

ARGUMENTS — statements (written or oral) to the court setting forth the opposing parties' positions on the facts and law. The oral arguments by the attorneys at the conclusion of a trial are called the "summation."

ARSON — the act of willfully setting fire to and burning a building.

ARTICLES OF INCORPORATION — a formal document that creates a corporation; a charter.

ARTICLES OF PARTNERSHIP — the written agreement by which a partnership is formed and its terms of operation stated; often called simply the "partnership agreement."

ARTISAN'S LIEN — a possessory lien held by a person who has added value to (repaired or improved) another person's personal property. The lienholder retains as security the repaired or improved property to ensure payment for her service.

"AS IS" — a disclaimer of warranty by asserting that goods are sold "as is," without warranty.

ASSAULT — the intentional tort (or crime) of unjustifiably arousing in another individual the apprehension of immediate harmful or offensive contact (battery).

ASSAULT AND BATTERY — the compound crime or tort of (a) assault (e.g., threat) and (b) carrying out the threatened harmful or offensive contact (battery).

ASSIGN — to transfer legal rights from one party to another.

ASSIGNEE — the party to whom an assignment is made.

ASSIGNMENT — the transfer of legal rights from one party to another.

ASSIGNMENT FOR THE BENEFIT OF CREDITORS — *See assignment to a trustee.*

ASSIGNMENT TO A TRUSTEE — an arrangement whereby (a) the debtor transfers to a trustee the title to some or most of the debtor's property, (b) the trustee sells or otherwise disposes of the property for cash and distributes the proceeds *pro rata* among the debtor's creditors, and (c) any creditor accepting such payment discharges the entire debt owed to him.

ASSIGNOR — the party making an assignment.

ASSUMPTION OF RISK — the tort defense that a plaintiff who knowingly and voluntarily faces a dangerous situation may not recover for an injury arising out of the known risks inherent to that situation.

ATTACHMENT — court-ordered seizure of a debtor's property for payment of money owed to a creditor; may be accomplished before judgment (with property under the sheriff's control until a judgment is entered), in order to prevent depletion of assets pending the completion of a lawsuit.

ATTEMPT — the crime of intending to do a specific criminal act and in addition to that intent, taking action beyond mere preparation.

ATTORNEY — a representative or agent.

ATTORNEY AT LAW — a legal representative; a person, trained in law, employed to represent others in lawsuits and other legal matters.

ATTORNEY/CLIENT PRIVILEGE — privilege whereby disclosure of confidential communications solely between the attorney and the client cannot be compelled; the privilege can be waived by the client.

ATTORNEY IN FACT — a person named as a representative or agent in a power of attorney.

AT-WILL EMPLOYEE — an employee without a set term for employment (i.e., she can quit at any time, for any reason).

AT-WILL EMPLOYMENT DOCTRINE — the common law principle that an at-will employee can be fired at any time, for any reason; now qualified by modern anti-discrimination statutes and the doctrine of abusive (wrongful) discharge.

AUTHORIZED STOCK — the number of shares (common or preferred) that the charter permits the corporation to issue.

AVULSION — sudden changing of course of a stream or river. Landowners retain the property lines as existed before the change; thus, distinct from property changes caused by accretion.

BAD FAITH — purposely misleading another person or otherwise acting dishonestly or with ill will; willfully failing to act in accordance with statutory or contractual obligations. *Compare good faith.*

BAIL — money or other security given to insure the appearance of a criminal defendant in all proceedings in her case; in return, the arrested person is freed ("out on bail") pending trial.

BAILMENT — the transfer of possession, care, or control of a chattel from one person (the bailor) to another (the bailee) for a limited time for a special purpose.

BANK DRAFT — a check drawn by a bank either on its own funds within the bank or on funds it has on deposit at another bank.

BANKRUPTCY FRAUD — a business crime and tort (fraud) involving the filing of false claims by creditors or debtors, fraudulent transfer or concealment of assets, or obtaining credit with the specific intent to avoid paying debts.

BANKRUPTCY PROCEEDING — a legal procedure for settling the debts of individuals or business entities unable to pay debts as they become due.

BATTERY — the intentional tort (or crime) of unjustifiable contact with someone else's body or anything connected to the body.

BEARER — the person in possession of bearer paper.

BEARER PAPER — a negotiable instrument payable to "cash," indorsed in blank, or otherwise payable to "bearer," so that it can be negotiated merely by delivery (change in possession).

BENEFICIARY — one who benefits from the actions of another; a person for whose benefit a trust, a will, a contractual promise, or an insurance policy is made. *See also creditor, donee, and incidental beneficiary.*

BEQUEST — a gift of personal property through a will (verb form: bequeath). *See also devise.*

BILATERAL CONTRACT — a contract created by an exchange of promises.

BILL OF ATTAINDER — legislation intended to single out an individual or punish him without benefit of trial; forbidden by the U.S. Constitution, Article I, Sections 9 and 10.

BILL OF EXCHANGE — a form of negotiable instrument, commonly called a draft. *See also draft.*

BILL OF LADING — document evincing receipt of goods for shipment, issued by a person engaged in the business of transporting goods.

BILL OF RIGHTS — the first ten amendments to the U.S. Constitution, all ratified in 1791.

BILL OF SALE — a written document by which one person assigns or transfers her right or interest in goods and chattels to another.

BINDER — a written, temporary insurance policy until a formal policy is issued or the insurer decides not to issue insurance and notifies the insured that the binder is terminated.

BLANKET POLICY — insurance covering 1. property at more than one location or 2. two or more types of property.

BLANK (GENERAL) INDORSEMENT — indorsement of a negotiable instrument by a holder whose indorsement lacks any accompanying instruction and does not indicate (e.g., by indorsing "Pay to the order of X") that any other indorser is necessary; thus the instrument is bearer paper, freely negotiable merely through delivery (change in possession).

BLUE LAWS — laws that prohibit the making of certain contracts or the operation of certain businesses on Sundays.

BLUE SKY LAWS — state laws regulating the intrastate issuance and sale of securities.

BOARD OF DIRECTORS — group, elected by shareholders, to oversee the management of the corporation.

BONA FIDE (Latin) — "in good faith"; genuine.

BOND — a secured, long-term corporate debt security.

BOOK VALUE — the value of capital stock as calculated by the excess of assets over liabilities.

BREACH — nonperformance of a contract or part of a contract.

BREACH OF DUTY — failure to perform a legal duty owed to another person.

BRIBERY — illegal payments to governmental officials or other persons for the purpose of receiving information, favorable treatment, or other assistance that the briber either is not entitled to receive or cannot lawfully receive by this method (e.g., kickbacks, pay-offs).

BRIEF — a written argument supported by citations of court decisions, statutes, or other authorities.

BROKER — in securities law, a person who buys and sells stock as the agent for a customer but who does not hold stocks in inventory. *Compare dealer.*

BULK TRANSFER — a transfer made outside the ordinary course of the transferor's business and involving a substantial part of his equipment, supplies, or inventory. UCC Article 6 governs most bulk transfers.

BURDEN OF PROOF — 1. the degree of proof necessary for a criminal conviction or for a successful civil suit. In a civil case, the plaintiff has a "preponderance of the evidence" burden of proof; her version of the facts must be considered, by the judge or jury, to be, at the very least, slightly more credible than the defendant's. In a criminal case, the prosecution must prove its case "beyond a reasonable doubt." 2. a party's obligation, when asserting a fact, to come forward with evidence supporting that fact.

BURGLARY (breaking and entering) — unlawful entry into a building with the intent to commit a felony (e.g., larceny).

BUSINESS JUDGMENT RULE — the legal rule requiring that directors and officers govern corporate affairs with reasonably good judgment.

BUY AND SELL AGREEMENT — a contract, particularly appropriate for partnerships or closely held corporations, whereby the remaining owners of the entity are to buy the interest of a withdrawing or deceased owner.

BYLAWS — a comprehensive set of rules providing for the organization and operation of a corporation. *Compare charter.*

C & F — "cost and freight"—the lump sum price of the goods includes the cost of shipping and freight, but not insurance.

CANCELED STOCK — stock that was issued but has been repurchased by the corporation and canceled.

CAPACITY — a legally defined level of mental ability sufficient to reach an agreement. *See also insanity.*

CAPITAL; CAPITAL ASSETS — the total assets of a business; the owners' equity in a business.

CAPITAL STOCK — the class of shares that represent the owners' equity in the corporate business.

CARRIER — person or business entity receiving consideration (e.g., money) for transporting passengers or goods. *See also common carrier.*

CASE LAW — decisions of the courts, together with the rationale; the whole law as declared by the courts through cases decided before them.

CASHIER'S CHECK — a check drawn by a bank upon itself.

CAUSATION IN FACT — the relationship between an act or omission and an event (including alleged damages to the plaintiff) that would not otherwise have happened; that is, the plaintiff's harm would not have occurred but for the defendant's wrongful conduct. *Compare proximate cause.*

CAUSE OF ACTION — facts that indicate the right to seek a remedy in a judicial proceeding. Requirements are the existence of a right and a violation of that right.

CAVEAT EMPTOR (Latin) — "Let the buyer beware."

CAVEAT VENDITOR (Latin) — "Let the seller beware."

CERTIFICATE OF DEPOSIT — a type of negotiable instrument, issued by a financial institution as an acknowledgment that the institution has received the deposit of a specified sum of money; the institution promises to pay the depositor the sum of money deposited, plus interest at a stated rate, at a specified time in the future.

CERTIFICATE OF INCORPORATION — the state's official authorization for a corporation to begin to do business.

CERTIFICATE OF STOCK — physical evidence of share ownership in a corporation.

CERTIFICATED SECURITY — a security for which a certificate has been issued.

CERTIFIED CHECK — a check the drawee has marked as "accepted" and thus has certified that there is money in the drawer's account to cover the check. Certification guarantees payment and therefore enhances the check's negotiability.

CERTIFIED (CERTIFICATED) STOCK — a security (stock) for which a certificate has been issued.

CERTIORARI, WRIT OF — an appellate court's order that a lower court send to it for review the records of a case. The appellant requests the writ, and a grant or denial of the request is within the discretion of the higher court. (A denial of the writ means that the appeal is denied.)

CHARTER — a formal document that creates a corporation; articles of incorporation.

CHATTEL — a movable piece of property; an article of personal property.

CHATTEL PAPER — a document showing both a monetary obligation and a security interest in, or lease of, specific goods (UCC § 9-105(1)(b)).

CHECK — a special type of draft in which the drawee is always a bank and the instrument is payable on demand. *See also cashier's, certified, stale, and traveler's check.*

CHECKS AND BALANCES — the arrangement whereby powers of each government branch (legislative, executive, judiciary) check or balance powers of the other branches.

C.I.F. — "cost, insurance, freight"—the lump sum price of the goods includes the cost of insuring and shipping the goods.

CIRCUMSTANTIAL EVIDENCE — indirect evidence; circumstances or other secondary facts by which connected, principal facts may be inferred.

CITATION — 1. a reference indicating where a relied upon legal authority (e.g., court decision, statute) can be found. 2. an order for a criminal defendant to appear in court and/or answer charges; often used in minor cases (e.g., alleged traffic violations); analogous to a summons in a civil case.

CIVIL ACTION — legal proceeding to enforce a private, civil right or remedy, as distinguished from a criminal prosecution.

CIVIL (CODE) LAW — law based on the Roman Code of Justinian; the basis of the legal system of most European and Latin American nations.

CIVIL LAW — non-criminal law.

CLASS ACTION — a lawsuit in which a group of similarly situated persons, perhaps large in number, are represented by a few persons; the class is usually a plaintiff, but a defendant class is possible.

CLEARINGHOUSE — an association of banks or other payors that exchanges drafts (e.g., checks) drawn on association members, determines balances, and otherwise clears (settles) these drafts.

CLOSE CORPORATION — a stock corporation whose shares are held by a relatively few persons, frequently members of a single family.

CLOSED SHOP — an employment arrangement, outlawed by the Taft-Hartley Act (1947), requiring employees to belong to a union before being hired and to remain members throughout their employment.

CLOSELY HELD CORPORATION — a corporation the stock of which is not freely circulated.

CLOUD ON TITLE — an outstanding claim or other evidence on record that, if true, would adversely affect the title or other interests of the presumed owner of real property. A quiet title action may be brought by the presumed owner against the claimant(s) who have thus clouded the owner's title.

CODE — 1. Civil Law: a collection of laws into a single, organic whole; 2. common law: a collection of currently effective statutes enacted by legislative bodies, including Congress and state legislatures.

CODICIL — a change in, or addition to, a will, executed in the same formal manner as the will itself.

COLLATERAL — an interest in property given by a debtor to his creditor in order for the latter to secure payment of the debt. If the debt is paid, the creditor's interest in the property (collateral) generally ceases; if the debt is not paid, the creditor usually may sell or use the collateral to collect all or part of the debt.

COLLATERAL ESTOPPEL — doctrine that issues decided in one lawsuit are conclusively resolved for other lawsuits between the same parties.

COLLECTIVE BARGAINING — negotiation between the employer's and employees' representatives.

COMAKER — a person who joins one or more other persons, also called comakers, in the making of a negotiable instrument; the person thus becomes primarily liable (jointly and severally) with the other comakers for the instrument's payment.

COMITY — the recognition (deference, judicial restraint) that one nation gives to another nation's laws and judicial decrees.

COMMERCE CLAUSE — the authority granted to Congress by Article I, Section 8, of the U.S. Constitution to regulate foreign and interstate commerce.

COMMERCIAL LAW — the entire body of substantive law applicable to the rights and duties of persons engaged in commerce or mercantile pursuits.

COMMERCIAL PAPER — in its broadest sense, documents used to facilitate the exchange of money or credit.

COMMINGLING — mixing the money or goods of another with one's own.

COMMON CARRIER — a carrier that presents itself to the public as available (for hire) for transporting goods or passengers; it is subject to regulation as a public utility.

COMMON LAW — law as developed and pronounced by the courts in deciding cases (case law), based on the common law of England and judicial precedent.

COMMON STOCK — the class of shares that participate in the management of a corporation and also own the corporate equity.

COMMUNITY PROPERTY — a system of joint ownership in some western and southwestern states whereby almost all property acquired by the husband or wife during the marriage, except for gifts or inheritances, is owned equally by both spouses.

COMPARABLE WORTH DOCTRINE — a legal principle (not generally applied under existing federal law) that, if two different jobs (one held mainly by men, the other by women) are essentially worth the same, there should not be a wage disparity or other difference in treatment between such comparably worthwhile jobs.

COMPARATIVE NEGLIGENCE — a legal principle applied when the negligence of the plaintiff and the negligence of the defendant are concurrent causes of the plaintiff's damages; any damages awarded to the plaintiff are reduced by an amount proportionate to the degree of her fault. This rule for negligence cases has replaced the rule of contributory negligence in almost all states. *See also contributory negligence.*

COMPENSATORY DAMAGES — the sum of money needed to compensate an injured party by making him "whole."

COMPLAINANT — 1. a plaintiff; a person who files a complaint. 2. in criminal cases, a person who instigates a prosecution by making charges of criminal conduct.

COMPLAINT — the initial pleading in a lawsuit, sometimes called a declaration, petition or bill of complaint; it includes a statement of facts, the legal basis of the suit (case of action), and a request for one or more remedies.

COMPOSITION AND/OR EXTENSION AGREEMENT — an arrangement whereby a debtor and her creditors agree that each creditor will receive a certain percentage (less than 100 percent) of the amount owed (the composition) and/or extend the payment period (the extension); the debtor's full compliance discharges the entire debt.

COMPOUNDING A CRIME — the crime of accepting money or something else of value in return for not reporting or prosecuting another crime.

COMPUTER CRIME — a crime committed by using a computer (e.g., to steal information, embezzle, or defraud).

CONCURRENT JURISDICTION — the simultaneous authority of two or more different courts (e.g., federal and state) to hear and decide a case.

CONDITION — in the law of contracts, a fundamental requirement that must be met by one party before the other party has an obligation under a contract. *See also express and implied condition.*

CONDITION CONCURRENT — a condition to be performed by both contracting parties simultaneously.

CONDITION PRECEDENT — a condition that must be complied with, or occur, before the other contracting party becomes obligated.

CONDITION SUBSEQUENT — a condition the occurrence of which removes the obligation of one or both of the parties to the contract.

CONDITIONAL INDORSEMENT — an indorsement in which the indorser places a present or subsequent condition (other than failure of prior parties to pay) that must be met before the indorser is liable on the instrument.

CONDOMINIUM — a form of real property featuring sole ownership of individual office or apartment units, with joint ownership (by all the sole owners) of the land and common areas.

CONFESSION OF JUDGMENT — an admission of liability made by a creditor in the name of his debtor without the formality of the usual adversarial court hearing; instruments frequently contain such admissions, which are to take effect if the debtor fails to pay in accordance with the terms of the instrument.

CONFISCATION — governmental seizure of private property or business without a proper purpose or just compensation; in international law, nationalization may be confiscation. *Compare expropriation.*

CONFLICT OF INTEREST — in agency law, an act of divided loyalty whereby the agent acts for herself rather than for the principal.

CONFLICT OF LAWS — a body of law concerning the determination of which law should be applied to the facts of a particular case when the laws of more than one state or nation may be applicable.

CONFUSION — commingling of two or more owners' personal property so that each owner's property or property interest (e.g., a precise amount of fungible goods) can no longer be determined or distinguished from the property as a whole.

CONGLOMERATE MERGER — a merger between two or more business entities that are different industries; not a horizontal or vertical merger.

CONSENT — the defense, to all torts and a few crimes, that the plaintiff agreed voluntarily to submit to the defendant's actions or proposals.

CONSENT DECREE — a judgment in which the parties, having agreed on the disposition of a case, have their agreement approved and recorded by the court.

CONSEQUENTIAL DAMAGES — damages that include lost profits and other indirect injury caused by a faulty performance or other breach of a contract if the principles of foreseeability and certainty are met.

CONSIDERATION — something of value that is given in exchange for a promise or an act; one of the requirements for a valid contract.

CONSIGNEE — the party receiving goods on consignment.

CONSIGNMENT — a delivery of goods, title remaining in the seller, for the buyer to sell. Risk of loss passes to the buyer.

CONSIGNOR — the party delivering goods on consignment.

CONSOLIDATION — combining two corporations by a procedure under which a third corporation purchases the stock of both corporations.

CONSPIRACY — an agreement between, or any combination of, two or more persons to commit an unlawful act.

CONSTITUTION — a nation's or state's supreme set of laws, outlining the basic organization, powers, and responsibilities of the government and guaranteeing certain specified rights to the people.

CONSTRUCTIVE — the legal character or nature of a thing regardless of its actual character or nature.

CONSTRUCTIVE BAILMENT — a bailment imposed by law rather than agreement; for example, a person who finds lost property or receives misdelivered property may be a constructive bailee.

CONSTRUCTIVE EVICTION — such material impairment by a landlord of the tenant's ability to enjoy the leased premises as to give the tenant a right to terminate the lease.

CONSTRUCTIVE NOTICE — knowledge of a fact presumed or imputed by law, such as by recording an instrument, filing a document in court, or placing a legal advertisement in a newspaper or trade journal. Such "knowledge" is regardless of actual knowledge, which may never have been present or may have become forgotten.

CONSTRUCTIVE TRUST — a trust imposed by law against a person who wrongfully obtained or retains property; this trust is intended to correct fraud or other misconduct.

CONTINGENT FEE — a charge permitted in some civil cases (e.g., negligence lawsuits) whereby the attorney's fee is dependent on successful outcome of the case; generally, the fee is a percentage of the client's recovery.

CONTRACT — a legally enforceable agreement, express or implied. *See also adhesion, bilateral, destination, executed, executory, express, implied, investment, option, output, quasi, requirements, shipment, unconscionable, unenforceable, unilateral, void and voidable contract.*

CONTRIBUTION — the right of a defendant liable for a loss to obtain a sharing of expenses (e.g., payments to the plaintiff) by other persons also responsible for that loss.

CONTRIBUTORY NEGLIGENCE — an absolute defense to negligence by the defendant because the plaintiff's own negligence contributed to his injuries; replaced by the doctrine of comparative negligence in almost all states.

CONVERSION — an intentional tort (or crime) involving unauthorized, unjustified exercise of control over another's personal property.

CONVERTIBLE BOND — a bond that may be converted by its holder into other securities of a corporation, such as preferred or common stock.

CONVERTIBLE STOCK — stock that the corporation may convert from one class (preferred) into another class (common).

CONVEYANCE — 1. an instrument (e.g., a deed) by which title or other interests in real property are transferred from one person to another. 2. any transfer of property or interests in property.

COOPERATIVE — an association of individuals formed to carry out a common productive enterprise, the profits being shared in accordance with the capital or labor contributed by each individual or otherwise going to the members without gain to the cooperative itself; cooperatives may be for consumers, workers, labor unions, marketing or business purchasing, financial institutions, farmers, insurers, or others.

COPYRIGHT — the exclusive right to print, sell, and exhibit written material, musical compositions, art works, photographs, movies, television programs, data systems, and other creations placed in a tangible, preserved medium of expression.

CORPORATE CRIME — a crime committed by and thus chargeable to a corporation because of activities of its officers or other employees.

CORPORATE OPPORTUNITY — a business opportunity available to a corporation; an officer or director who takes personal advantage of a corporate opportunity violates her duty to the corporation.

CORPORATION — 1. an artificial being created by operation of law, with an existence distinct from the individuals (shareholders) who are its "owners." *See also alien, close, closely held, de facto, de jure, domestic, federal, foreign, membership, parent, private, professional, public, quasi-public, and S corporation.* 2. a word that indicates a business is incorporated.

COSTS — in litigation, an award to the winning party for expenses incurred (but usually excluding attorney's fees), to be paid by the losing party.

COUNTERCLAIM — a "reverse" complaint: one by the defendant against the plaintiff; sometimes called a "cross-complaint."

COURSE OF DEALING — the customary method of doing business between two parties; it is a requirement of the Uniform Commercial Code that the course of dealing of the parties be a factor in determining their contractual intent.

COURSE OF PERFORMANCE — the conduct between the parties in the implementation of a contract. This conduct is useful in determining the meaning of the contract and the intent of the parties.

COURT — a unit of the judiciary; a governmental body intended to apply the law to controversies brought before it and to administer justice.

COVENANT — an agreement or promise to do or not to do something; an express or implied promise incidental to a deed or contract.

COVENANT OF (FOR) QUIET ENJOYMENT — a grantor's, landlord's, or other landowner's express or implied promise that the grantee or tenant will neither be evicted nor be disturbed in his use and enjoyment of real property (e.g., by hostile claimants of title).

Covenant Running with the Land — a covenant that concerns the land itself and binds (or benefits) all subsequent owners of that land.

Cover — to seek a substitute performance of a contract; when seller S breaches, "covering" permits buyer B to purchase goods which conform to the S-B agreement and charge S for any portion of the substituted goods' price exceeding the S-B agreement price.

Cramdown — confirmation of a bankruptcy reorganization plan over the objections of one or more class of creditors.

Creditor Beneficiary — a person, not a party to a contract, who claims that she is owed the performance of the contract.

Crime — a public wrong, committed with intent or, in a few cases, by negligence, for which the law provides punishment or compensation to society.

Crimes *Per Se* — certain crimes that either presuppose or do not require criminal intent so that the act alone constitutes a crime.

Criminal Fraud — fraudulent conduct that is a crime (e.g., larceny by fraud, filing false tax returns).

Criminal Law — a body of substantive law governing and defining crimes and punishments for crimes.

Cross-Claim — a claim filed against one or more parties on the same side of a lawsuit as is the claimant (e.g., by one defendant against another defendant).

Cross-Complaint — *See counterclaim.*

Cumulative Preferred Stock — preferred stock that receives dividends accumulated for years in which no dividends were declared or paid.

Cumulative Voting — in the election of directors, a voting procedure whereby a shareholder may accumulate her votes and distribute them among the candidates as she wishes. *Compare straight voting.*

Cure — seller's right, under UCC § 2-508, to correct a defective performance rather than be liable for breach of contract.

Curtesy — *See dowry.*

Custody — concerning personal property, immediate charge and control of the property. Custody is not synonymous with possession or ownership; a person can have custody without owning or possessing.

Customer — Under UCC Article 4, any person or entity (including another bank) having an account with a bank or for whom a bank has agreed to collect on instruments.

Damages — in general, compensation designed to make an injured party "whole"; in the law of contracts, the compensation due to the nonbreaching party to recover any financial loss or injury caused by a breach of contract. *See also compensatory, consequential, direct, exemplary, incidental, indirect, liquidated, nominal, punitive, and special damages.*

D/B/A — "doing business as."

Dealer — in securities law, a person engaged in the business of buying and selling securities for his account as a principal. *Compare broker.*

Debenture — an unsecured, long-term corporate debt security.

Debt Security — a security issued as evidence of a corporate debt.

Deceit — *See fraud.*

Declaration — *See complaint.*

Decree — a judgment, particularly in an equity court.

Deed — a document by which title to property (usually real property) is transferred. *See also general warranty, quitclaim, and special warranty deed.*

Deed of Trust — a document similar to a mortgage; when a debtor's purchase of real property is financed (i.e., he obtains a loan), a deed of trust conveys title to, but not possession of, the real property to a trustee (someone other than the debtor or creditor), who holds title as security for the debt.

De Facto Corporation — a corporation that has not been properly formed, even though the incorporators may have made a good faith effort to do so. *Compare de jure corporation.*

Defamation — a tort; a false communication, oral (slander) or written or otherwise recorded (libel), by the defendant to a third person that harms the plaintiff's reputation.

Default — failure to perform a duty as promised in a contract, negotiable instrument, deed, loan or other transaction.

Default Judgment — judgment for the plaintiff because the defendant failed to respond to a summons or appear at trial. (Plaintiff's failure to appear may result in dismissal of the case.)

DEFENDANT — the person against whom a criminal prosecution or civil action is filed.

DEFICIENCY JUDGMENT — a judgment against the debtor (mortgagor) for the remaining amount if a creditor (mortgagee) is still owed money on a secured debt (mortgage) after the collateral (mortgaged property) has been sold and the proceeds applied toward payment of the debt.

DEFRAUD — to deprive a person of his rights or property by use of deceit (fraud, misrepresentation).

DE JURE **CORPORATION** — a corporation formed in accordance with all the requirements of the law. *Compare de facto corporation.*

DEL CREDERE **AGENCY** — an agency in which the agent holds harmless the principal against the default of those with whom contracts are made.

DELEGATED AUTHORITY — in administrative law, powers delegated by the legislature to administrative agencies.

DELEGATION — transfer of duties under a contract from one person to another.

DELIVERY — the actual or constructive (implied or inferred) transfer of goods or of an instrument from one person to another.

DEMAND — a request by one person that another person perform an act (e.g., pay an instrument), the performance of which the first person is entitled to receive.

DEMAND PAPER — an instrument payable on demand; a negotiable instrument that either (a) expressly states it is payable on demand, presentation, or sight, or (b) does not state a time for payment.

DE MINIMIS — part of the Latin phrase *de minimis non curat lex*, "the law does not concern itself with trifles"; thus, trifling, of no importance and of no legal consequence.

DEMURRER — a motion to dismiss; an initial pleading by the defendant alleging that the complaint fails to state a cause of action.

DE NOVO (Latin) — "new"; a new proceeding without regard to prior legal actions.

DEPOSITION — pretrial discovery involving sworn testimony by a party or any other witness, usually recorded and transcribed by a court reporter or notary public; testimony; ordinarily taken in response to oral questions from the parties' attorneys.

DERIVATIVE SUIT — a suit brought by one or more shareholders on behalf of the corporation and for its benefit, claiming waste of corporate assets by directors or corporate principals.

DESTINATION CONTRACT — a contract that passes the risk of loss to the buyer when the goods are delivered to the specified destination.

DETRIMENT — in the law of contracts, forbearance serving as consideration or value.

DEVISE — to bequeath property, usually real property, by a will.

DICTA — short for the Latin words *obiter dicta*, "statements in passing"; statements in a judicial opinion that are unnecessary for the decision of the case; dicta are not binding, nor do they carry the force of precedent, as do arguments intrinsic to a judicial holding (singular form: dictum).

DIRECT DAMAGES — damages immediately and directly caused by breach of contract.

DIRECT LIABILITY — direct responsibility of a principal for torts committed by her agent under certain circumstances.

DIRECTED VERDICT — a judge's decision that one side has not presented evidence sufficient to support a verdict in its favor; thus the court renders a judgment in favor of the other party immediately before jury deliberations begin.

DIRECTOR — a person elected by the shareholders to oversee the management of a corporation.

DISAFFIRMANCE — cancellation or rejection of a contract made by a person during her minority upon reaching the age of majority or within a reasonable time thereafter.

DISCHARGE — 1. the termination or completion of a contract. 2. in commercial paper, the removal of parties' liability on an instrument, usually by payment. 3. the release of an employee from his employment. 4. in bankruptcy law, the release of a debtor from his debts.

DISCLAIMER — 1. a denial of warranty. 2. in negotiable instruments law, an indorsement phrase (most frequently, "without recourse") that places subsequent holders on notice that the indorser will not be liable if the instrument is not paid.

DISCLOSED PRINCIPAL — a principal/agency relationship in which a third party knows, or should know, that the agent is acting for a principal, and the third party knows the identity of the principal. The agent thus has no personal responsibility.

DISCOUNT SHARES — shares issued for less than par or stated value; a shareholder who purchases shares at discount is liable to the corporation for the amount of the discount.

DISCOVERY — pretrial procedures by which the parties to a lawsuit obtain information from other parties and from potential witnesses.

DISHONOR — to refuse to pay (or accept for later payment) an instrument.

DISPARAGEMENT — trade libel; a business defamation that involves injurious falsehoods about a product or a competitor's reputation.

DISSENTERS' RIGHTS — *See appraisal rights.*

DISSOLUTION — 1. the termination of a corporation's existence. 2. a change of partners' relationship caused when one partner ceases, generally because of death or voluntary or involuntary withdrawal, to be associated with the partnership business.

DISTRIBUTORSHIP — a business arrangement in which a manufacturer licenses dealers to sell products.

DIVERSITY JURISDICTION — the authority of federal courts to hear a civil case based on state law if the case involves parties from different states and the amount in controversy is more than $50,000.

DIVESTITURE — compulsory sale or other removal, by a business entity, of assets acquired in violation of antitrust laws.

DIVIDEND — a distribution of cash or stock to the shareholders of a corporation.

DIVISION OF POWERS — the arrangement in which constitutions (e.g., the U.S. Constitution) give to each branch of government a different, major area of responsibility: legislative (law making), executive (law enforcement), judiciary (law interpretation).

DOCKET — in the court records of a case, a book or case jacket briefly stating all pleadings, hearings, and other actions in the case.

DOING BUSINESS — for a corporation, the maintenance of sufficient contacts in a foreign state, on a continuous and regular basis, to make it accountable to that state for its actions.

DOMESTIC CORPORATION — a corporation carrying on business in the state of its creation; in that state, it is "domestic."

DOMICILE — an individual's permanent legal residence; for corporations, the central office, where its primary functions are discharged, according to law.

DONATIVE INTENT — language or circumstances indicating that the owner intended to give away a particular property; a necessary element of a gift.

DONEE — the recipient of a gift.

DONEE BENEFICIARY — a person, not a party to a contract, who claims that the performance of the contract was a gift to him.

DONOR — the person who makes a gift.

DOUBLE JEOPARDY — prohibition in the U.S. Constitution, Fifth Amendment, against trying a person twice for the same crime.

DOWRY — property or something else of value given as additional consideration for the obligation of marriage; the promise to give dowry is subject to the Statute of Frauds. Dowry is that which is given to the wife; curtesy is given to the husband.

DRAFT — a three-party instrument in which the drawer orders the drawee to pay a certain sum of money to the payee, or another person specified by the payee, either on demand or at a particular time in the future.

DRAWEE — the person upon whom a draft is drawn by the drawer. The drawee, usually (always, when the draft is a check) a bank, is directed to pay the sum of money stated on the draft.

DRAWER — the person who draws (writes) a draft. The drawer directs the drawee to pay the sum of money stated on the draft.

DUE CARE — the standard of care a person owes to others in the law of torts; usually that degree of care that a reasonable person would exercise in the same situation. Also referred to as "duty of care."

DUE PROCESS — protection granted by the U.S. Constitution, Fifth and Fourteenth Amendments, against the government's depriving a person of "life, liberty, or property" without according that person fundamental procedural rights. (In some cases of "substantive due process," the deprivation is not permitted, no matter what procedure is followed.)

DURESS — coercion (force), either physical or mental, that deprives a person of free will to make a contract.

DUTY OF CARE — *See due care.*

EARNED SURPLUS — undistributed net profits or income of a corporation.

EARNEST (MONEY) — the payment of some part of the price of goods sold, or the delivery of some part of such goods, in order to bind the contract.

EASEMENT — a limited right to use (affirmative easement), or a prohibition of use of (negative easement), another person's land for a specific purpose.

EASEMENT BY NECESSITY — an implied easement that occurs when a land transfer makes an easement necessary to gain access to granted or retained land.

EASEMENT BY PRESCRIPTION — an easement acquired in essentially the same manner as title to land is gained through adverse possession: here, actual, open, continual, and nonpermissive easement use of another's land for the required statutory period of time.

EASEMENT IN GROSS — an express easement given for a specific purpose (e.g., for commerce or other public purposes such as placing utility lines). There is no adjoining dominant estate for this "personal easement" (i.e., not running with the land).

EIUSDEM GENERIS (Latin) — "of the same class or kind"; a rule of contract or statutory construction indicating that in a series of words or phrases each word or phrase lends meaning to other words and phrases in the series. *Compare noscitur a sociis.*

EJECTMENT — 1. a civil action to recover possession of real property. 2. a civil action to determine whether plaintiff or defendant has title to certain land.

EMANCIPATION — the act by which a minor is freed from the control of parent or guardian.

EMBEZZLEMENT — crime whereby a person lawfully possessing or having access to money or property belong to another, unlawfully uses that money or property for her own purposes.

EMINENT DOMAIN — the power of, and its exercise by, the government to buy, at fair market value, privately owned real property for the public benefit.

EMPLOYEE — one who agrees to perform work under the control and supervision of another.

EMPLOYMENT — a contractual relationship whereby one person agrees to perform work under the control and supervision of another; a master/servant relationship.

EMPLOYMENT LAW — law pertaining to the individual rights of employees and employers (e.g., as to hiring, firing, promotion).

ENABLING ACT — legislation by which an administrative agency is created and powers are delegated to it.

ENCUMBRANCE — a burden on either title to property or on the property itself (e.g., a mortgage, a lien). Also spelled as "incumbrance."

ENDORSEMENT — *See indorsement.*

ENJOIN — to issue an injunction.

ENTITY — a being, thing, or organization having a legal existence.

ENTRAPMENT — the defense that a criminal act was induced by a governmental agency, with criminal intent originating from that agency (e.g., police).

ENVIRONMENTAL IMPACT STATEMENT — a comprehensive statement on the ecological effects, possible alternatives, and so on, required by the National Environmental Policy Act (1969) for any action that may significantly affect environmental quality and that involves federal funds, approval, licensing, or supervision.

ENVIRONMENTAL LAW — statutory, regulatory, and case law, the most significant being federal, designed to protect and clean the environment.

EQUAL PROTECTION — a provision in the U.S. Constitution, Fourteenth Amendment, that no person may be denied "the equal protection of the laws"; generally requires that any differences in treatment be reasonable and related to a permissible, governmental purpose (the "rational basis" test), but for cases involving "suspect" classifications (e.g., by race or religion) or fundamental rights (e.g., voting, marriage) differential treatment must be as narrow as possible and also necessary to achieve a compelling governmental interest (the "strict scrutiny" test).

EQUITABLE SERVITUDE — a restriction on the use of land that is enforceable by the court.

EQUITY — historically, in England and the United States, a parallel and independent legal system based on principles of "fair play" or equity; now merged into the general court system with responsibility for (among other matters) family law, injunctions, and specific performance of contracts.

EQUITY OF REDEMPTION — the mortgagor's right, from the time of default until the foreclosure sale, to redeem (recover) the property by fully paying the debt, plus the foreclosure costs to date and any interest.

EQUITY SECURITIES — securities issued to generate funds to operate the corporate enterprise; shares of common and preferred stock.

ESCHEAT — the passage of property to the state when a person dies intestate (without a will) and without any surviving relatives (heirs).

ESCROW — placing a document, instrument, or funds in the hands of a third person, who holds the item or funds as a fiduciary, until the contract is performed or some other event occurs such that the escrow holder should then deliver the item or funds to the proper party (e.g., the grantee).

ESSENCE (OF THE) — an expression stating that a certain thing (generally time of performance) is a condition of the contract.

ESTATE — the sum total of a person's real and personal property.

ESTATE FOR YEARS — a tenancy (leasehold) for a definite period of time.

ESTOP — to be blocked by one's previous actions from asserting certain legal claims or defenses.

ESTOPPEL — a legal circumstance in which a person, by reason of his actions, cannot assert certain legal defenses or rights that are contrary to these actions. *See also waiver.*

ESTRAY STATUTES — state statutory procedures (including publication of notice) whereby the finder/holder of lost or mislaid property may claim title to it if it is not reclaimed by the owner within the statutory period.

ET AL. — Latin abbreviation meaning "and another" or "and others."

EVICTION — action by the landlord to expel a tenant from the leased premises; eviction may be actual or constructive. *See also constructive eviction.*

EVIDENCE — testimony, documents, and other relevant information presented at a trial, in accordance with the rules of evidence, so that the trier of fact (judge or jury) can determine the truth of facts at issue.

EXCLUSIVE JURISDICTION — the authority of only one type of court (e.g., state or federal) to decide a case.

EXCULPATORY CLAUSE — a provision in a contract excusing one or both parties from the legal consequences of her or their actions or negligence.

EXECUTED CONTRACT — a contract fully performed by both parties.

EXECUTOR — the person named in a will to administer the decedent's estate. Sometimes referred to as a "personal representative."

EXECUTORY CONTRACT — a contract that has not been fully performed by one or both parties.

EXEMPLARY DAMAGES — damages designed to make an example of the defendant. *See also punitive damages.*

EXEMPT SECURITY — a security not subject to the registration requirement of the Securities Act of 1933.

EXEMPTED TRANSACTION — a transaction in which the issuance of securities is not subject to the registration requirements of the Securities Act of 1933.

EXEMPTION — legal excuse from a duty imposed by law or from the operation of a law (e.g., property exempt from a bankruptcy proceeding).

EXHAUSTION OF REMEDIES — a doctrine whereby court appeals are not permitted until administrative remedies are exhausted; the appellants must use all available agency procedures before complaining to a court of law.

EX PARTE (Latin) — "on or from one side"; judicial proceeding requested by one party without notice to or attendance by an opposing party (e.g., a hearing to decide whether to impose a temporary restraining order).

EX POST FACTO **LAW** (Latin) — "from a thing done afterward"; a law making criminal a past action that was not defined as criminal when it occurred; forbidden by the U.S. Constitution, Article I, Sections 9 and 10.

EXPRESS CONDITION — a condition deliberately created by the parties at the time when the contract was made.

EXPRESS CONTRACT — a conscious, specific contract; it must be written or oral, or partly written and partly oral.

EXPROPRIATION — governmental seizure of private property or business for a proper public purpose and with the payment of just compensation. *Compare confiscation.*

EXTRADITE — to return an alleged criminal to the state in which his crime supposedly occurred, and where a trial should take place.

FACTOR — an agent (a) employed to sell goods for a principal, usually in the agent's own name, and (b) given possession of the goods for that purpose.

FAIR USE — an exception to the exclusivity of use generally given to copyrights; an example is limited reproduction, for classroom or other nonprofit purposes, of a small portion of a work in such a way as to have little effect on the market for the work.

FALSE ARREST — the intentional tort (or crime) involving detention of the plaintiff, without her permission, under the falsely asserted authority of the defendant.

FALSE IMPRISONMENT — the intentional tort (or crime) involving wrongful use of force, physical barriers, or threats of force to restrain the plaintiff's freedom of movement.

FAMILY LAW — the law of divorce, adoption, and other family matters, transferred from the ecclesiastical courts of England to the equity court in the time of King Henry VIII.

F.A.S. — "free alongside ship"—seller's risk and cost of transport until delivered next to the ship.

FEATHERBEDDING — an unfair labor practice, prohibited by the Taft-Hartley Act (1947), whereby employers pay for work not actually performed.

FEDERAL CORPORATION — a corporation organized under the laws of the United States for a federal purpose.

FEDERAL QUESTIONS JURISDICTION — a type of subject-matter jurisdiction; the authority of federal courts to hear and decide cases involving the U.S. Constitution, federal statutes, or treaties.

FEDERALISM — a form of government in which power is divided between a national government and state (provincial) governments.

FEE SIMPLE ABSOLUTE — the highest form of ownership and possession; a fee simple estate includes all rights in real property.

FEE SIMPLE DETERMINABLE — ownership of an estate that automatically ends if a specified action occurs.

FEE SIMPLE SUBJECT TO A CONDITION SUBSEQUENT — ownership of an estate that is subject to a grantor's right of repossession if a specified action occurs.

FELONY — a serious crime punishable by imprisonment; a crime placed by a state's criminal code in a class more serious than the other main class of crimes, misdemeanors.

FICTITIOUS PAYEE — a made-up payee whose account is actually controlled by a dishonest employee or other person, with the drawer/maker duped into drafting or making negotiable instruments payable to this fictitious person; under negotiable instruments law, negotiation is effective, and thus the drawer/maker may not have an effective defense against paying the instrument (except to those who actually duped him).

FIDUCIARY — a person occupying a position of trust in relationship to another.

FINANCING STATEMENT — a document filed to perfect a security interest.

FIRM OFFER — an irrevocable, signed, written offer by a merchant to sell or buy goods, stating that the offer will not be withdrawn for a specified period (not to exceed three months).

FITNESS, WARRANTY OF — an implied warranty that the specified goods are fit for the buyer's use or purpose.

FIXTURE — personal property that has become attached to real property (i.e., so incorporated into real property that it is difficult, costly, or impossible to remove); generally treated as part of the real property.

F.O.B. — "free on board"—risk and cost of loss pass to buyer at the designated point.

FORBEARANCE — refraining from acting when one has the right to act. In this sense, forbearance may be consideration.

FORCE MAJEURE — an occurrence that is beyond the control of a party to a contract and therefore excuses her performance (e.g., an act of God).

FORECLOSURE — the proceeding whereby a mortgagee takes title to, or forces the sale of, mortgaged property in order to satisfy the mortgagor's debt.

FOREIGN CORPORATION — a corporation carrying on business in any state other than the state of its creation; in all such states, it is "foreign."

FORGERY — 1. falsely making or materially altering a legal document (e.g., a negotiable instrument) in order to defraud another person or otherwise affect rights. 2. without authority, writing another person's name (signature) on a legal document as if that person has done so.

FRANCHISE — a contractual arrangement in which the owner (franchisor) of a trademark, trade name, copyright, patent, trade secret, or some form of business operation, process, or system permits others (franchisees) to use that property, operation, process, or system in furnishing goods or services.

FRAUD — an intentional tort (or crime) consisting of intentional misrepresentation of a material fact, made knowingly with intent to defraud, that is justifiably relied upon by the other party and causes injury to him. Also called "deceit" or "misrepresentation."

FRAUD AGAINST CONSUMERS — a crime (or tort: fraud) involving such activities as fraudulent solicitation in the mail, false advertising about products, and false labeling.

FRAUD IN THE EXECUTION — a fraud pertaining to the execution or signing of an instrument or a contract.

FRAUD IN THE INDUCEMENT — a fraud, pertaining to the value of goods to be sold or services to be obtained, thus inducing the execution of an instrument or a contract.

FRAUDULENT CONVEYANCE (TRANSFER) — a transfer of property or property rights made to defraud creditors. Such transfers may be challenged, and the creditor can reach (e.g., attach) the property by following the appropriate legal procedures.

FREEHOLD — 1. real property held for life or in fee (e.g., fee simple). 2. an estate of uncertain duration, as opposed to a leasehold.

FULL FAITH AND CREDIT CLAUSE — a provision in the U.S. Constitution, Article IV, Section 1, requiring that, once a court with jurisdiction has rendered a judgment, other states honor that decision insofar as it affects the rights and duties arising between the parties to the judgment.

FUNGIBLE GOODS — goods that, when mixed, cannot be separately identified, since each unit is basically like any other unit (e.g., grain, minerals, fruit).

GARNISHMENT — a procedure whereby a court orders a third party holding property of a debtor (e.g., an employer holding wages due, a bank holding a customer's account) to transfer some or all of that property to a judgment creditor (person with an unpaid judgment against the debtor).

GENERAL AGENT — one authorized to act for one's principal in all matters concerning a particular business.

GENERAL PARTNER — a partner who has power to manage partnership business and has unlimited liability for partnership debts.

GENERAL PARTNERSHIP — a partnership in which there are no limited partners, and each partner has managerial power and unlimited liability for partnership debts.

GENERAL WARRANTY DEED — a deed wherein the grantor warrants title against defects or encumbrances arising before or during his ownership, and also makes any other covenants typically included in conveyances.

GIFT — a transfer of title to goods without consideration; the three elements of an effective gift are donative intent by the donor, delivery (actual or constructive) to the donee, and acceptance by the donee.

GIFT *CAUSA MORTIS* — a conditional gift in which the donor, believing that her death is imminent, conveys property with the intent that the donee keep it after the donor's death; the gift is automatically revoked if the donor recovers.

GIFT *INTER VIVOS* — a gift made during the donor's lifetime, when he is not facing imminent death.

GOOD FAITH — 1. acting honestly, without knowledge of a legal defect; sincerely endeavoring to behave in accord with one's own agreements, ethical standards in the industry, and the law itself. Generally, the term denotes an honest intention to abstain from taking unfair advantage of another person. *Compare bad faith.* 2. in sales contracts, a UCC requirement that a merchant act with honesty and in accordance with reasonable commercial standards of fair dealing in the trade.

GOODWILL — the special favor or advantage enjoyed by a particular business because of its reputation for skill or judgment; hence, the capitalized value of the excess of estimated future profits over the rate of return on capital considered normal for that kind of business or industry.

GRAND JURY — a body of jurors (larger in number than a petit jury) that, under the guidance of a prosecutor, decides whether a person or persons should be charged with a crime (indicted).

GRANDFATHER CLAUSE — an exemption from a statute that, but for the exemption, would make certain acts or conditions illegal, provided that those acts or conditions took place before the statute was enacted.

GRANT — to bestow upon another person property, rights in property, an instrument, or some other right or privilege.

GRATUITOUS BAILMENT — a bailment to benefit solely the bailor, with no benefit passing to the bailee.

GROSS NEGLIGENCE — lack of even slight care; recklessness; extreme failure to comply with one's duty of care; conduct appreciably worse than ordinary negligence.

GUARANTEE(Y) — in contracts, a promise by one person to pay the debts of another.

GUARANTOR — generally, a person who has expressly or implicitly agreed to be liable for another person's debts if the creditor cannot collect directly from the debtor; one who makes a guaranty; in negotiable instruments law, an indorser who guarantees payment or collection on the instrument.

GUILT BEYOND A REASONABLE DOUBT — the burden of proof necessary for conviction of a crime.

HABEAS CORPUS, **WRIT OF** — judicial order that a government official produce a detained or imprisoned person in an action testing the legality of that detention or imprisonment.

HEARSAY — evidence heard or otherwise learned from someone other than the person testifying in court; the truth of the matter rests on the credibility of someone not a witness (hence, not subject to cross-examination).

HOLDER — a person who possesses a negotiable instrument issued, drawn, or indorsed to that person or his order or to bearer.

HOLDER IN DUE COURSE — a holder who takes a negotiable instrument (a) for value, (b) in good faith, and (c) without notice that is overdue, has been dishonored, or is subject to defenses or claims.

HOLDING COMPANY — a corporation that holds or owns the stock of another corporation or corporations.

HOLOGRAPHIC DEED OR WILL — an unwitnessed deed or will handwritten entirely by the grantor or testator, respectively; its validity depends upon state law.

HOMESTEAD EXEMPTION — a provision in the law of most states that, when a home (debtor's residence, not rental property) is sold to pay a judgment, a specific amount may be retained by the debtor, free of the judgment debt; mortgages are not subject to this exemption.

HONOR — to pay (or to accept for payment) an instrument.

HORIZONTAL MERGER — a merger in which the merged business entities operated the same type of business at the same level (e.g., both were manufacturers); if monopolistic, usually illegal under antitrust law.

HORIZONTAL PRIVITY — privity among persons at the same level of the chain of distribution or consumption.

HOT-CARGO CONTRACT — an unfair labor practice, prohibited by the Taft-Hartley Act (1947), whereby an employer agrees with employees not to purchase, use, or handle products from a specified business.

ILLUSORY PROMISE — a promise that appears to be real but in fact imposes no legal obligation upon the promisor.

IMPLIED CONDITION — a condition implied from the nature of the transaction but not expressly specified by the parties.

IMPLIED CONTRACT — a contract implied from the conduct of the parties; sometimes referred to as an "implied-in-fact contract."

IMPLIED PARTNERSHIP — a partnership implied from the conduct of the co-owners of a business.

IMPLIED PROMISE — a promise implied from conduct.

IMPLIED WARRANTY — a warranty implied by law, arising out of the buyer/seller relationship.

IMPOSSIBILITY — such absolute factual impossibility as will discharge a contract; alternatively, commercial impracticability.

IMPRACTICABILITY — commercial impracticability created by an unforeseen occurrence sufficient to discharge a contract (treated by some courts as impossibility).

IMPUTED NEGLIGENCE — negligence by another party for which one is held liable although she did not directly commit negligence. The negligence is imputed because of the relationship, privity, or other ties between the negligent party and the "imputed" one. A related term is "vicarious liability."

INCAPACITY — lack of mental capacity to make a contract.

INCIDENTAL BENEFICIARY — a person, not a party to a contract, who receives some slight or indirect benefit from the contractual promise.

INCIDENTAL DAMAGES — the damages paid to a person to reimburse the cost of his minimizing the damages to which the person is entitled.

INCUMBRANCE — *See encumbrance.*

INDEMNIFY — to hold harmless from, to guarantee against, loss or liability.

INDENTURE — a contract stating the terms under which long-term debt securities (both bonds and debentures) are issued.

INDEPENDENT CONTRACTOR — a person hired to undertake a contractually defined result without direct supervision (not an employee and usually not an agent).

INDICTMENT — a criminal charge (or charges) issued by a grand jury.

INDIRECT DAMAGES — damages not proximately caused by a breach of contract; remote damages.

INDORSEE — the person to whom a negotiable instrument is transferred by indorsement.

INDORSEMENT — the signature of the holder of a negotiable instrument, written on the instrument by or on behalf of the holder, with or without additional or qualifying words, so that title to the instrument and the holder's property interest in the instrument are transferred to a new holder. *See also blank, conditional, qualified, restrictive, and special indorsement.*

INFANCY — being a minor; in most states, under the age of 18.

INFORMATION — a criminal charge (or charges) issued by a magistrate, prosecutor, or police officer.

INFRINGEMENT — an intentional tort (or crime) involving violation of another person's intellectual property rights (e.g., patents, copyrights, trademarks).

INJUNCTION — a court order to do or to refrain from doing a specified act.

INNOCENT MISREPRESENTATION — misrepresentation of a material fact without intent to deceive.

IN PARI DELICTO (Latin) — "equally at fault."

IN REM JURISDICTION — the authority of a court to take action directly against the defendant's property; jurisdiction is thus based on the location of the property (i.e., the court is in the same state or county as is the property).

INSANITY — mental impairment sufficient as to prevent a person from appreciating the nature of an agreement or the consequences of her actions; a defense to crimes and intentional torts.

INSIDER — an owner of 10 percent or more of the corporate stock of an issuer listed on a national stock exchange, or a director or officer of such an issuer, as well as others, including employees, consultants and tippees, with inside information about corporate affairs.

INSOLVENCY — 1. inability to pay debts as they become due: this is the test for bankruptcy. 2. a financial state in which liabilities exceed assets.

INSTRUMENT — 1. a formal document or other writing that proves a legal relationship (e.g., a deed, will, lease, mortgage). 2. under the UCC, a negotiable instrument, security, or other writing demonstrating a right to payment and not itself a security agreement or lease.

INSURABLE INTEREST — a legal or equitable interest in the subject matter such that the insured benefits from its preservation or incurs a loss if it is destroyed or damaged.

INSURANCE — a contract whereby risks are transferred; the insurer issues a policy covering (paying compensation in the event of) certain occurrences (risks) that, if they occur, will result in a loss to the insured.

INTANGIBLE PERSONAL PROPERTY — property (rights in something) that lacks physical substance (e.g., stock, intellectual property).

INTELLECTUAL PROPERTY — protected expressions of scientific, artistic, or other creative, or commercial endeavors; a special type of intangible personal property, arising from the creative endeavors of the human mind, generally evinced by patents, copyrights, trademarks, or trade names.

INTENT — an express or implied desire to perform a particular act; a state of mind (to do the act) preceding or accompanying an act.

INTENTIONAL INFLICTION OF MENTAL (EMOTIONAL) DISTRESS — an intentional tort involving disturbance of the plaintiff's peace of mind by the defendant's outrageous conduct.

INTENTIONAL MISREPRESENTATION — *See fraud.*

INTENTIONAL TORT — a tort in which the tortfeasor expressly or implicitly intends to do the act(s) causing the injury.

INTER ALIA (Latin) — "among other things."

INTERFERENCE WITH CONTRACT — an intentional tort with three requirements: (a) a valid contract exists, (b) a third party knows about the contract, and (c) the third party intentionally (and unjustifiably) causes one of the contracting parties to breach the contract, or otherwise unjustifiably prevents performance of the contract.

INTERFERENCE WITH PROSPECTIVE ECONOMIC ADVANTAGE — an intentional tort with essentially the same three requirements as the tort of interference with contract, except that the interference affects a prospective contract or other economic arrangement, not an existing contract.

INTERLOCKING DIRECTORSHIP — a violation of antitrust laws whereby the same person serves as director of two or more competing companies, at least one of which has capital, surplus, and undivided profits altogether exceeding $1 million.

INTERNATIONAL LAW — law governing relations between nations; derived from custom, past court cases, treaties, texts, and all other sources used in national law.

INTERROGATORIES — a method of discovery: written questions, to be answered, in writing and under oath, by another party.

INTERVENING CAUSE — *See superseding (intervening) cause.*

INTESTACY SUCCESSION — the order in which an intestate's estate is divided among surviving relatives.

INTESTATE — to die without leaving a valid will; the term also is a noun, designating a person who so dies.

INTOXICATION — an impairment of the mind and will by alcohol or drugs so as to bring about contractual incapacity; if involuntary (occurring by force or mistake), it may be a defense to a crime or tort.

INVASION OF PRIVACY — an intentional tort involving interference with a person's right to be left alone.

INVESTMENT CONTRACT — a contract that may be a "security" if it requires an investment of money in a common enterprise with the expectation of profits from the efforts solely of others.

INVITEE — person entering real property at the express or implicit invitation of the owner/possessor, generally to engage in business (e.g., to shop, to make repairs).

INVOLUNTARY BANKRUPTCY — a proceeding initiated by one or more creditors against an insolvent debtor.

ISSUE — in negotiable instruments law, the first delivery of a negotiable instrument to a holder; to issue securities; a decedent's lineal descendants (e.g., children, grandchildren).

ISSUED SHARES — shares in a corporation that have been sold to shareholders.

ISSUER — a person who issues securities, and any other persons or entities acting under her control or as part of a plan of sale or distribution of the securities.

JOINT AND SEVERAL LIABILITY — liability in which all parties are concurrently liable, but each is also individually liable; a plaintiff has the option of suing one of them, some of them, or all of them (i.e., any combination).

JOINT LIABILITY — liability in which all parties are concurrently liable and all must be sued together.

JOINT TENANCY — joint ownership of property, established when the instrument conveying the property states that the parties acquire the property as joint tenants; the co-owners must have received their property interest at the same time, from the same source, in equal interests, and with each owner having the right to possess the whole.

Joint Tortfeasors — two or more persons who commit a wrong with a common intent.

Joint Venture — an association of two or more entities to carry on a single business enterprise for profit.

Judgment — a court's final decision on matters submitted to it; a pronouncement, holding, or decree by a court with competent jurisdiction.

Judgment Creditor — a creditor who has obtained a judgment against her debtor.

Judgment *Non Obstante Veredicto* (J.N.O.V.) — literally, a judgment notwithstanding the verdict; if, after the jury has rendered a verdict for one party, the judge finds that there is insufficient evidence to support the jury's decision, he enters a judgment for the other side.

Judgment Proof — having few, if any, assets that can be reached by a judgment creditor; thus, persons against whom money judgments are of no practical effect.

Judicial Review — a doctrine whereby courts, notably the federal courts (in particular, the U.S. Supreme Court), have the power to declare federal or state actions to be in violation of the constitution, or unconstitutional.

Judicial Sale — when the mortgagor is in default, the customary method of foreclosure on mortgaged property; after proper notice, the sheriff or other court official takes control of the property and sells it.

Jurisdiction — the power of a court to hear and decide the issues in a case and to bind the parties. *See also appellate, concurrent, diversity, exclusive, "federal questions," in rem, original, personal and subject-matter jurisdiction.*

Jurisprudence — the science or philosophy of law.

Jury — a body of persons charged with declaring the facts in a case and deciding (a) whether a criminal defendant is guilty, or (b) whether a civil defendant is liable; a petit jury usually has 12 members (jurors), although some states and the federal courts allow as few as six. *See also grand jury.*

Justice — the major goal of most legal systems; encompasses such ideals as impartiality, equity, and fairness.

Kite — to secure temporary use of money by negotiating or issuing worthless paper and then redeeming such paper with the proceeds of similar paper.

Labor Relations Law — statutory, administrative and case law, almost exclusively federal, dealing with labor/management relations.

Laches — an equity concept similar to statutes of limitations but with no stated period; serves to bar recovery for a claimant who waited too long to assert his rights.

Laissez-Faire — a political or legal doctrine favoring governmental restraint, if not outright abstention, from the regulation of business.

Land-Use Restrictions — governmental restrictions (e.g., zoning) on the use and disposition of real property.

Larceny — the crime of unlawfully taking personal property with the intent to deprive the owner of it.

Lateral Support, Right to — a right protecting a landowner by prohibiting her neighbors from excavating or otherwise changing their own land to such an extent that the landowner's land or buildings are damaged.

Law — that which a judge will decide concerning matters properly brought before him; in a broader sense, any rule that society will enforce.

Law Merchant — the English system of commercial law, once enforced in special merchant courts, now merged into the common law; part of it was the basis for negotiable instruments law.

Lawsuit — a broad, general term for an action or proceeding in a civil court.

Lease — a transfer of possession of property (real or personal), but not title (ownership), for a period of time for a consideration (e.g., rent).

Leasehold — a real property estate held by a tenant, under a lease, for a set term.

Legacy — personal property transferred (bequeathed) by will.

Legatee — the person to whom a legacy is given.

Lessee — the person to whom a lease is granted.

Lessor — the person who grants a lease to another.

Letter of Credit — any instrument by which a drawer requests a particular person or people in general to give the bearer or a named person money or something else of value and to look for recompense from the drawer. Unlike most notes and drafts, letters of credit have no standard format; they are governed by UCC Article 5.

LEVY — lawful seizure of property to obtain money owed.

LEX TALIONIS (Latin) — "the law of retaliation" (an eye for an eye).

LIBEL — written, photographic, or otherwise recorded defamation.

LICENSE — 1. freely revocable permission by a landowner to use his land for a limited, specific purpose (e.g., camping, hunting); persons given this right of use have a nonpossessory interest in the real property. 2. a revocable privilege granted by the government to do something (e.g., sell liquor, broadcast at a particular frequency) that would otherwise be illegal. 3. a contractual arrangement whereby a party receives (in effect, purchases or leases) another party's rights to manufacture, distribute, or sell goods or services.

LICENSEE — a person entering real property with the permission of the owner/possessor (e.g., a guest invited to a party).

LIEN — an encumbrance imposed on property to force payment of a debt; if the debt remains unpaid, the property (collateral) can be sold to satisfy the debt (lien). *See also artisan's lien and mechanic's lien.*

LIEN CREDITOR — a creditor who has a lien on the debtor's property.

LIFE ESTATE — a person's possessory interest in real property for the duration of one or more human lives as specified in the granting instrument.

LIFE ESTATE *PUR AUTRE VIE* — a life estate measured by the life of a person other than the grantee (person holding the estate).

LIMITED PARTNER — a partner without power to manage partnership business and with liability for partnership debts only up to the amount of her contribution to the business.

LIMITED PARTNERSHIP — a partnership conforming to state statutory requirements and having one or more general partners and one or more limited partners.

LIMITED WARRANTY — a warranty expressly limited as to duration or other effects.

LIQUIDATED DAMAGES — the damages for breach of contract that are specified in the contract; these damages will be upheld in court if reasonable.

LIQUIDATED DEBT — an undisputed debt for a known or ascertainable sum of money.

LIQUIDATION — 1. conversion of assets to cash, usually in order to pay creditors; the procedure followed before distribution in a Chapter 7 bankruptcy proceeding. 2. in partnership law, part of the "winding up" after dissolution; collection, preservation, and sale of partnership assets.

LITIGANTS — the parties to a lawsuit.

LIVING WILL — instrument making known an individual's wishes concerning life-sustaining medical treatments.

LOBBYING — attempting to influence legislation.

LOCKOUT — a management tactic whereby employees are prevented from entering the work premises, generally in order for management to obtain better terms. Defensive lockout (permitted)—when a single union bargains throughout an industry by striking one employer (or more), but not all employers, the struck employer responds by locking the workers out. Offensive lockout (sometimes allowed)—management keeps workers out in anticipation of a strike.

LONG-ARM STATUTE — a state law extending personal jurisdiction over out-of-state persons, including corporations, that do business in the state, own real property there, or have taken other relevant actions (e.g., committed an alleged tort, entered a contract) in a state.

LOST PROPERTY — personal property accidentally left somewhere; the owner does not intend to relinquish ownership.

L.S. — an abbreviation for *locus sigilli*, "place of the seal," that may serve as a seal.

MAILBOX ACCEPTANCE RULE — principle of contracts law that, unless the offer states otherwise, an acceptance using the same method of transmission as the offer is effective when the acceptance is sent (when the offeree places it in the mailbox or otherwise relinquishes control over it).

MAKER — a person or institution that issues a promissory note or certificate of deposit (i.e., promises to pay).

MALICIOUS INSTITUTION OF CIVIL PROCEEDINGS — the intentional tort of instigating civil proceedings against someone for an improper purpose and without good or probable cause, with those proceedings ending decisively in the defendant's favor.

MALICIOUS PROSECUTION — an intentional tort involving the same factors as malicious institution of civil proceedings, except that the improperly instituted proceedings are criminal, not civil.

MALPRACTICE SUIT — a lawsuit alleging failure to exercise the standard of care expected of someone in a particular profession (e.g., law, medicine, accounting), that is, negligence by a professional during the course of his/her professional employment.

MARGIN — the amount that must be paid in cash (not borrowed) to purchase securities.

MASTER — an employer. *Compare servant.*

MATERIAL ALTERATION — substantial change in one or more terms of an instrument that gives the instrument a different legal affect (e.g., changes the liability, duties, and/or rights of one or more parties to the instrument).

MATERIAL MISTAKE — a mistake that goes to the very heart of the engagement; significant.

MATURITY — the date when an obligation to pay a debt (e.g., a note, a draft) becomes due.

MAXIM — a legal principle; an equity principle of fair play.

MECHANIC'S LIEN — a statutory lien filed against a debtor's real property for materials or labor expended (but unpaid for) in repairing or improving that property.

MEDIATION — an alternative method of dispute resolution, preceding or in lieu of litigation, whereby a third party (mediator) tries to help the disputing parties to settle their case.

MEMBERSHIP CORPORATION — a corporation owned by its members, such as a church or other nonstock corporation.

MEMORANDUM — the written evidence required by the Statute of Frauds for certain kinds of contracts.

MENS REA (Latin) — "criminal intent"; usually a requirement for criminal liability.

MERCHANT — one who deals in goods or has knowledge or skill with regard to goods.

MERCHANTABILITY — fitness for the ordinary purposes for which goods of a specific class are sold.

MERGER — concerning businesses and antitrust law, the combination of two or more business entities. Specifically, in corporate law, the combining of two corporations by a procedure under which one acquires the stock of the other. *See also conglomerate merger, horizontal merger, and vertical merger.*

METES AND BOUNDS — a precise description of the territorial limits of a parcel of real property, including measured distances and angles.

MINOR — in most states, a person under the age of 18.

MISDEMEANOR — a crime placed by a state's criminal code in a class less serious than the other main class of crimes, felonies, with lessor punishment than is generally accorded a felony.

MISLAID PROPERTY — personal property intentionally put somewhere, but then forgotten; the owner does not intend to relinquish ownership. *Distinguished from lost property.*

MISREPRESENTATION — a false statement of fact.

MISTAKE OF FACT — in criminal law, ignorance of an important fact; this may negate *mens rea* and hence serve as a defense.

MISTAKE OF LAW — the criminal defense that a person honestly did not know that he was breaking the law and (a) the law was not published or otherwise made public, or (b) the person relied on an erroneous but official statement of the law; otherwise, ignorance of the law.

MITIGATION — the requirement that an injured party reduce her damages to a minimum.

MONOPOLY — exclusive or practically exclusive control of the supply or sale of a product or service by one business or organization.

MORALITY — the body of self-imposed rules of conduct generally perceived to be right.

MORTGAGE — a written agreement between a creditor (mortgagee) and debtor (mortgagor) whereby real property is given as security (mortgage) for a loan.

MORTGAGEE — the creditor who has a security interest in real property (a mortgage).

MORTGAGOR — the debtor who has given a security interest in real property (a mortgage).

MOTION — a request that a court take a specified action in a case; motions can concern numerous matters.

MOTION TO DISMISS — a motion contending that, even if the plaintiff's allegations are true, there is no legal basis for finding the defendant liable. *See also demurrer.*

MUTUAL MISTAKE — a mistake by both parties to an agreement concerning a fundamental fact.

MUTUAL RESCISSION — an agreement between the parties to a contract to terminate the contract.

MUTUALITY — the reciprocal obligations of the parties to a contract, in the absence of which there is no legally binding agreement.

NATIONALIZATION — the conversion of a private business into a government-owned business.

NECESSARIES — goods or services considered essential to sustain existence (e.g., food, shelter) or to maintain a person's station in life.

"NECESSARY AND PROPER" CLAUSE — a provision in the U.S. Constitution, Article I, Section 8, granting to Congress the authority to make laws "necessary and proper" for carrying out any of the government's enumerated powers under the Constitution; hence, Congress has implied powers under this clause.

NEGLIGENCE — failure to exercise the standard of care that a reasonable person would exercise in like circumstances. To succeed in court, the plaintiff must show (a) duty of care, (b) breach of that duty, (c) causation, and (d) damages.

NEGLIGENT MISREPRESENTATION — a tort involving essentially the same elements as fraud, except that negligence replaces *scienter* (knowledge of falsity, or reckless disregard of truth or falsity); it applies mainly to special situations involving negligent opinions by supposed experts (e.g., lawyers, title examiners, accountants).

NEGOTIABLE — capable of being transferred by indorsement or delivery so that the subsequent holder has all the rights that, and possibly more than, were held by the transferor, particularly the right to sue on the instrument in the holder's own name.

NEGOTIABLE INSTRUMENT — a type of commercial paper; specifically, a written, signed, unconditional promise or order to pay a certain sum of money to order or bearer either on demand or at a definite time.

NEGOTIATION — 1. contracts: the transaction of business; the usual setting for the formation of a contract. 2. negotiable instruments: the process by which both possession of and title to an instrument are transferred from one party to another, with the transferee becoming the holder.

NIMBLE DIVIDEND — a dividend to shareholders from current earnings, paid even though there are debts outstanding from previous years.

NOLO CONTENDERE (Latin) — "I will not contest it"; a pleading by an accused criminal that does not admit guilt but is equivalent to a plea of guilt for sentencing purposes.

NOMINAL DAMAGES — damages in the amount of $1 or some other token amount, awarded when the plaintiff has been legally wronged, but not actually injured.

NONCUMULATIVE PREFERRED STOCK — preferred stock that loses its dividend rights for years in which no dividend is declared or paid.

NO-PAR STOCK — stock for which no dollar amount is indicated on the share certificate; no-par stock is issued for any amount assigned by the board of directors.

NOSCITUR A SOCIIS (Latin) — "known by association"; a rule of statutory or contract construction meaning that words occurring together in a phrase are to be defined by their common relationship or their similarity of meaning. *Compare eiusdem generis.*

NOTE — *See promissory note.*

NOTICE — the formal presentation of information concerning matters of legal import. Notice is legally required in many situations (e.g., by service of process at the beginning of a lawsuit), regardless of whether the person receiving notice already has the information given in the notice.

NOVATION — an agreement among contracting parties and an outside third party that the third party will perform the duties (and receive the rights) of one of the original parties to the contract.

NOW — a negotiable order of withdrawal, treated the same as a check under the UCC; the federal Consumer Checking Account Equity Act (1980) permits savings and loan associations, mutual savings associations, credit unions, and banks to offer their savers NOW accounts.

NUDUM PACTUM (Latin) — "a naked promise"; a gratuitous promise for which there is no consideration; a promise to make a gift.

NUISANCE — the intentional tort (or crime) of substantially interfering with the plaintiff's right to use and enjoy his property (private nuisance) or with rights common to all (public nuisance).

OBLIGEE — a person to whom an obligation is owed.

OBLIGOR — a person who owes an obligation to another.

OFFER — a proposal made by one person to another and intended to create a contract if the other party expresses her assent.

OFFEREE — the person to whom an offer is made.

OFFERING CIRCULAR — information prepared by the issuer for distribution with a small public offering of securities under Regulation A of the Securities and Exchange Commission.

OFFEROR — the person making an offer.

OFFICER (CORPORATE) — a person named by the board of directors to operate the corporate business.

OPINION — the statement of reasons forming the basis for a court's judgment.

OPTION CONTRACT — a contract to keep an offer open for a specified time.

ORDER PAPER — a negotiable instrument payable to a specific person or to her order, so that it requires the proper indorsement(s) and delivery in order to be negotiated.

ORDINANCE — a law passed by a governmental body below the state level (i.e., city, county) and dealing with a local concern.

ORIGINAL JURISDICTION — the authority to hear a case after it has first been filed, including holding a trial and passing judgment on the law and facts.

OUTPUT CONTRACT — a contract whereby the seller (usually a manufacturer) agrees to sell all of his output or production of certain goods to a single, specific buyer.

OUTSTANDING SHARES — shares that have been issued, except those repurchased by the corporation after their original issuance.

OVERDRAFT — a check for more than the amount in the customer's account.

OVERDRAW — to make an overdraft.

P.A. — an abbreviation for "Professional Association," indicating a professional corporation (e.g., doctors, accountants).

PAR VALUE STOCK — stock for which a specified dollar amount is indicated on the share certificate; the par value must be set out in the charter.

PARENT CORPORATION — a corporation that owns all, or a majority of, the stock of another corporation.

PAROL — oral; in spoken words.

PAROL EVIDENCE — evidence concerning a written agreement that is not part of the writing.

PARTNERSHIP — the association of two or more persons who have expressly or implicitly agreed to carry on, as co-owners, a business for profit. *See also general partnership, implied partnership, and limited partnership.*

PARTNERSHIP AGREEMENT — *See articles of partnership.*

PARTNERSHIP AT WILL — a partnership with no set term of duration.

PARTNERSHIP BY ESTOPPEL — a partnership created by law because third parties were led to the reasonable belief that a partnership existed.

PAST CONSIDERATION — an action completed in the past and claimed as consideration for a present promise.

PATENT — the 17-year exclusive right, granted by the U.S. government, to make, use, and sell a new and useful design, process, machine, manufactured item, or other composition; a patentable invention must be novel, useful, and nonobvious.

PAWN — *See pledge.*

PAYEE — the party to whom a negotiable instrument is made payable.

PAYOR — a party (e.g., drawee) directed to make a payment, generally pursuant to a negotiable instrument.

P.C. — an abbreviation for "Professional Corporation."

PEREMPTORY CHALLENGE — *See voir dire.*

PERFECT TENDER RULE — the UCC rule that goods must be tendered strictly in conformity with the contract.

PERFECTION OF SECURITY INTEREST — a procedure whereby a secured party obtains priority over other parties that seek, or may seek, to attach or otherwise use the collateral.

PERFORMANCE — discharge of a contract by substantial completion or by the performance of all of the conditions (essentials) of the contract.

PERIODIC TENANCY — (lease) tenancy for a definite period of time, which automatically renews until a timely notice to the contrary is given by the lessor or lessee.

PERPETUAL EXISTENCE — for most modern corporations, the period of corporate existence.

PER SE (Latin) — "by itself"; this expression means "in and of itself," without looking (or having to look) to other persons or things.

PER SE VIOLATIONS — agreements among competitors that are automatic violations of antitrust laws (e.g., concerning price fixing, production quotas, and some boycotts or tying arrangements).

PERSONAL (LIMITED) DEFENSE — any defense not a "real" defense; generally, insufficient against holders in due course.

PERSONAL JURISDICTION — the authority of a court to bind the parties in a case.

PERSONAL PROPERTY — all property, tangible and intangible, except real property; generally, property without a permanent location or property that may be easily moved without damage to real estate.

PERSONAL REPRESENTATIVE — *See executor.*

PERSONAL SERVICE CONTRACT — a contract to perform services for another; generally cannot be transferred or delegated to another.

PETIT JURY — *See jury.*

PETITION — *See complaint.*

PETITIONER — the plaintiff; the term is often used in equity cases.

PIERCE THE CORPORATE VEIL — to disregard the corporate entity, and thus hold the shareholders liable for corporate actions; this is possible under circumstances involving fraud.

PLAINTIFF — the person who initiates a lawsuit.

PLAT — a chart or map, usually filed in the local court or records office, delineating parcels (boundaries) of real property.

PLEA BARGAIN — a deal between the criminal defendant and the prosecutor; typically, a trial is avoided as the defendant pleads guilty to a lesser charge; judges have the final authority over whether to approve these compromises.

PLEADINGS — the papers filed in court, with copies to other parties concerned, in preparation for bringing or defending a lawsuit before the court.

PLEDGE — the oldest and simplest type of secured transaction, whereby the debtor provides the creditor with physical possession of some of the debtor's property, which serves as collateral.

PLENARY POWER — authority not granted (expressly or implicitly) to the federal government, and thus reserved to the states and the people, by the U.S. Constitution, Tenth Amendment.

POLICE POWERS — state power to promote or protect public health, safety, morals, and general welfare.

POSITIVE LAW — the aggregate of legal rules specifically enacted or otherwise recognized by governments, as distinguished from natural law, moral principles, customs, or ideal law.

POSSIBILITY OF REVERTER — a grantor's future right to retake real property if a specified action occurs; the right a grantor has under a fee simple subject to a condition subsequent.

POSTDATE — to write on an instrument a date later than the one on which the instrument is actually executed.

POWER OF ATTORNEY — an instrument authorizing a specified person to act as agent or attorney for the person executing the instrument.

PRECEDENT — a prior judicial decision relied on as authority or guide for resolving later, similar cases.

PREEMPTION — federal law expressly or implicitly covers a subject so completely that the states are barred from making their own laws on this subject.

PREEMPTIVE RIGHT — the right of existing shareholders to preempt, or purchase first, before other purchasers of stock of the same class in order to protect their percentage interest in, or control of, the corporation.

PREFERENTIAL TRANSFER (PREFERENCE) — a transfer (of money or other property) that unfairly favors one creditor over others (i.e., the favored creditor gets more than he would under the bankruptcy laws); prohibited, and thus, overturned, if to pay a pre-existing debt and made during the 90-day period before the bankruptcy petition is filed.

PREFERRED STOCK — the class of shares that take precedence over common shares as to (a) distribution of dividends, and (b) distribution upon liquidation.

PREJUDGMENT ATTACHMENT — an attachment before a judgment, permitted if all statutory and constitutional (due process) requirements are met. *See also attachment.*

PREPONDERANCE OF THE EVIDENCE — the burden of proof necessary for civil liability.

PRESENTMENT — the giving of a draft or note to a party (e.g., a bank) that is asked to transfer to the bearer the sum stated in the instrument.

PRESENTMENT WARRANTY — a warranty imposed both on the person who obtains payment of a negotiable instrument and on all prior transferors; it warrants title, signature authorization, and lack of material alteration and is given to any person who, in good faith, pays or accepts the instrument.

PRIMA FACIE (Latin) — "on first face" or at first blush; creates a rebuttable presumption.

PRIMA FACIE **CASE** — a presumptively good case that shifts the burden of proof to the opposing party; a case strong enough to require a jury's consideration.

PRIMARY BENEFIT — under the holdings in some cases, the doctrine that an accountant is liable only to the party receiving the primary benefit of his services and not to all those to whom he could foresee injury because of his negligence.

PRIMARY PARTY — in negotiable instruments law, the maker or acceptor (the party primarily liable on the instrument).

PRINCIPAL — the person for whom an agent acts and from whom the agent derives authority.

PRIVATE CORPORATION — a corporation created for other than public or municipal purposes.

PRIVATE OFFERING — an offering of securities to a limited number of investors.

PRIVILEGE — an immunity existing under law and constituting a defense in most tort cases (e.g., the privilege of self-defense can defeat the tort of battery).

PRIVITY — in regard to contracts, the requirement that a person be one of the parties to a contract in order to have a legal interest in the contract. *See also horizontal and vertical privity.*

PROBABLE CAUSE — proper grounds for a search or arrest; reasonable grounds (something more than mere suspicion) to believe that a particular person committed a crime.

PROBATE — a court procedure by which a will is held to be valid or invalid; broadly, all matters concerning the administration of estates and guardianships.

PROCEDURAL LAW — the operating rules through which cases are presented, tried, and decided.

PROCESS, SERVICE OF — in accordance with statutory, procedural requirements, formal notification to a civil defendant that she is being sued.

PROFESSIONAL CORPORATION — a corporation created by a professional or professionals in order to gain corporate tax advantages for traditional partnership or proprietary activities.

PROFFER — to tender.

PROFIT — the right to obtain a possessory interest in some aspect of another's land (e.g., crops, timber, minerals).

PROMISEE — the person to whom a promise is made.

PROMISOR — the person who makes a promise.

PROMISSORY ESTOPPEL — such reliance on the promise of another to make a gift, or on some other gratuitous promise, that the promisor is bound by his promise notwithstanding the absence of consideration. *See also estoppel.*

PROMISSORY NOTE — a two-party negotiable instrument in which one person (the maker) makes an unconditional, written promise to pay another person (the payee), or a person specified by the payee, a certain sum of money either on demand or at a particular time in the future.

PROMOTER — a person who conceives of, organizes, and begins a corporation.

PROPERTY — a collection of rights and interests, generally associated with the concept of ownership; anything subject to use, possession, transfer, or ownership. The two main types are real property and personal property. *See also intangible personal, intellectual, personal, real, and tangible personal property.*

PRO RATA (Latin) — "in proportion"; division (e.g., of assets) according to the proportionate share held by each person.

PROSPECTUS — a statement or document describing securities to be offered or being offered; a statutory prospectus meeting the requirements of the Securities Act of 1933 must be prepared and submitted to the Securities and Exchange Commission before securities subject to the act may be advertised or offered.

PROXIMATE CAUSE — an essential element for almost all tort cases, consisting of causation in fact and foreseeability; a tort defense can thus be that the plaintiff's damages were not the natural and probable consequence of the defendant's acts (i.e., the damages were unforeseeable—too remote in time, distance, or chain of events).

PROXY — a limited power of attorney whereby a shareholder names a proxy (agent or representative) to vote her shares.

PUBLIC CORPORATION — a corporation formed to meet a governmental or public purpose.

PUBLIC LAW — the body of law dealing with the relationship between society (government) and individuals.

PUBLIC POLICY — concepts of prevailing morality used by courts to determine the legality or illegality of contracts.

PUBLIC UTILITY — a private corporation created for certain public purposes, and governmentally controlled as to services and prices charged (rates).

PUFFING — exaggerated statements of value that induce a party, usually a buyer, to enter into an agreement; usually not the basis of fraud or misrepresentation in the legal sense.

PUNITIVE DAMAGES — damages recovered in tort (not contract) cases to punish the defendant for outrageous and malicious conduct. *See also exemplary damages.*

PURCHASE MONEY SECURITY INTEREST — a security interest that is (a) held by the seller of the collateral in order to secure all or part of the sales price, or (b) held by a person lending money or otherwise giving value that the debtor uses to acquire or use the collateral (UCC § 9-107).

QUALIFIED INDORSEMENT — *See disclaimer, 2.*

QUANTUM MERUIT (Latin) — "as much as he earned"; the compensation permitted by law to the actor in a quasi contract.

QUASI (Latin) — "as if," "as if it were."

QUASI CONTRACT — a contract remedy created by operation of law to prevent unjust enrichment.

QUASI-PUBLIC CORPORATION — a privately owned corporation created for public purposes, such as a public utility.

QUID PRO QUO (Latin) — "something for something (else)"; the thing sought; consideration.

QUIET TITLE — *See cloud on title.*

QUITCLAIM DEED — a deed containing no warranty of title; it simply conveys all of the rights in the property that the grantor has, whatever those rights may or may not be.

QUORUM — for corporations: a majority of the outstanding shares of a corporation; the number of shareholders required to be present to conduct business at a shareholder's meeting.

RATIFICATION — a person's explicit or implicit approval or adoption of a prior act that did not bind her.

REAFFIRMATION AGREEMENT — a debtor's written, signed agreement, filed in bankruptcy court, in which the debtor reaffirms (again agrees to pay) a dischargeable or already discharged debt.

REAL (UNIVERSAL) DEFENSES — defenses to the enforcement of an instrument that are good against anyone, including holders in due course; examples are fraud in the execution (factum), forgery, discharge in bankruptcy, statute of limitations, material alteration, and defenses (e.g., duress, illegality) that render a contract void.

REAL PROPERTY — land, whatever is growing or built on land, and the rights associated with ownership and use thereof.

REASONABLE DOUBT — *See guilt beyond a reasonable doubt.*

"REASONABLE PERSON" STANDARD — a tort doctrine, used especially in negligence cases; the duty of care that a hypothetical, reasonable person would meet in the circumstances in question.

RECEIVER — a fiduciary (for all parties) appointed by the court to take charge of property involved in a lawsuit and to manage and dispose of it as the court orders.

RECIDIVISM — repeated criminal conduct.

RED HERRING PROSPECTUS — a preliminary prospectus, tentatively reviewed by the Securities and Exchange Commission, designated in red ink as such, and required to accompany a written offer of securities during the waiting period before the securities are formally offered for sale.

REDEMPTION — *See equity of redemption and statutory period of redemption.*

REDEMPTION RIGHT — the right of a corporation to redeem (purchase) preferred shares, even over the objection of their owners.

REFORMATION — an equity action used to revise a written contract so that it will state the actual agreement of the parties.

REGISTRATION STATEMENT — a statement filed by an issuer with the Securities and Exchange Commission under the Securities Act of 1933 and containing all relevant information about the securities to be offered for sale.

RELEASE — an agreement by one party to a contract excusing the other party from performance.

REMAINDER — an estate that commences upon the termination of a prior estate; for example, A gives B a life estate, with the remainder to C or C's heirs.

REMAINDERMAN — the person entitled to the remainder.

REMAND — to return a case, by order of an appellate court, to the trial court for further action.

REORGANIZATION — rearrangement of a business under Chapter 11 of the Bankruptcy Code.

REPLEVIN — a court proceeding instituted to recover personal property wrongfully held by another person.

REPOSSESSION — a creditor's taking possession of collateral after the debtor defaults (e.g., fails to make payments).

REPUDIATION — refusal to accept goods that have been tendered in accordance with a sales contract.

REQUESTS FOR ADMISSIONS — a method of discovery; written requests that another party admit particular facts or acknowledge the genuineness of certain documents.

REQUIREMENTS CONTRACT — a contract whereby the buyer agrees to purchase all of his requirements of certain goods from a single, specified seller.

RES (Latin) — "thing," "matter"; the subject of a legal action (e.g., the land involved in a quiet title action).

RESCIND — to cancel.

RESCISSION — cancellation.

RESIDENT AGENT — a person or other entity authorized to receive service of process and other official papers for a corporation.

RES IPSA LOQUITUR (Latin) — "the thing speaks for itself"; a principle in the law of torts excusing the requirement that a plaintiff prove the defendant negligent if, under certain conditions, the fact of the negligence is obvious.

RES JUDICATA — a doctrine prohibiting subsequent litigation between parties as to a dispute between those parties that has already been adjudicated (with final judgment entered and appeals either completed or not taken).

RESPONDEAT SUPERIOR (Latin) — "Let the superior respond"; liability of the principle for her agent's torts if committed while acting within the scope of the agent's authority.

RESPONDENT — a term for the defendant, often used in an equity case.

RESTITUTION — restoring the status quo; return of property; a tort or breach of contract remedy, such as for unjust enrichment; a criminal sentence requiring repayment of the victim.

RESTRAINT OF TRADE — in a contract, a provision unreasonably restricting a person from making a livelihood after the sale of that person's business or that person's leaving his employment; any number of business practices that may violate antitrust laws.

RESTRICTED SECURITY — a security that has been issued under an exempted transaction, with further transfer being subject to limitations.

RESTRICTIVE COVENANT — an express provision (e.g., placed in a deed) that attempts to restrict the transfer or use of property; also, a clause of an employment, partnership, or other agreement barring similar type of work (e.g., for a competitor) within a certain geographic area for a specified period of time after the contract ends.

RESTRICTIVE INDORSEMENT — an indorsement that (a) is conditional, (b) attempts to prohibit further transfer of the instrument, (c) includes the words "for collection," "for deposit only," "pay any bank," or a similar term, or (d) states that it is for the benefit or use of the indorser or another person.

RESULTING TRUST — a trust that results when the person receiving property was not intended to receive it; she is made a resulting trustee for the intended beneficiary. This type of trust is meant to correct a mistake.

RETALIATORY EVICTION — eviction or eviction proceedings initiated by a landlord because a tenant has complained or otherwise exercised contractual or statutory rights.

REVERSION — in effect, a remainder retained by the grantor of an estate; for example, A gives B a life estate, with reversion to A or his heirs.

RIGHT — a power, privilege, interest, or immunity; a legally enforceable demand or claim; that which, upon its violation, affords one a remedy at law or in equity.

RIGHT OF CONTRIBUTION — *See contribution.*

RIGHT OF REDEMPTION — *See statutory period of redemption.*

RIGHT TO LATERAL SUPPORT — *See lateral support, right to.*

RIGHT TO SURVIVORSHIP — *See survivorship, right of.*

RIGHT-TO-WORK LAW — a state statute prohibiting union shops; that is, in that state, union membership cannot be required for continued employment.

RIPARIAN RIGHTS — a landowner's rights (use, accretion, etc.) in a natural waterway within his property.

RISK — in insurance, a contingency, peril, or other area of potential exposure, which a policy may cover.

ROBBERY — larceny accomplished by using force or threats of force.

RULE — an established standard, guideline, principle, or doctrine; in administrative law, a regulation issued by a federal, state, or local administrative agency (or court) and governing procedure or conduct in a specific field.

RULE OF REASON — the antitrust doctrine whereby most unintentional, reasonable restraints of trade are lawful if tied to a valid business purpose considering all facts and circumstances.

S (FORMERLY SUBCHAPTER S) CORPORATION — a corporation to limit the effect of federal income taxes; taxes are not paid until corporate income has been distributed to shareholders.

SALE — a transfer of title to goods for a consideration or price.

SALE ON APPROVAL — a delivery in which title and risk of loss remain with the seller until the buyer inspects and approves the goods.

SATISFACTORY PERFORMANCE — a measure of performance that is a condition of a contract containing satisfaction as subjective in nature; not a condition if satisfaction is objectively tested.

SCIENTER (Latin) — "knowingly," "with guilty knowledge" (i.e., with the intent to deceive).

SCOPE OF EMPLOYMENT — conduct of an agent while engaging in the business of his principal such that, if the agent commits a tort, the principal and the agent will both be liable for the tort.

SEAL — a distinctive mark, wax impression, letters such as L.S. (*locus sigilli*), or the word "seal" itself, indicating an intention to sign a document with a seal.

SECONDARY BOYCOTT — a boycott against businesses other than the one involved in the primary labor dispute; like secondary picketing and secondary striking, usually an unfair labor practice.

SECURED PARTY — a secured creditor.

SECURED TRANSACTION — any transaction in which a creditor acquires a security interest in personal property or fixtures of the debtor; if the debtor fails to perform, the secured creditor can use the personal property or fixtures (known as collateral) as a substitute for, or as a means to collect, the debtor's performance (e.g., payment).

SECURITIES — any instrument or interest commonly known as a security and regulated by the Securities Act of 1933. These include the following: stocks, bonds, debentures, notes, or other instruments representing an interest or debt in a business or venture. *See also certificated, exempt, restricted, and uncertified security.*

SECURITY AGREEMENT — an agreement granting a security interest.

SECURITY INTEREST — an interest in a debtor's personal property (or fixtures) held by a creditor to ensure payment or other performance of an obligation.

SELF-DEFENSE — a defense to a criminal or tort liability that permits people to use a degree of force reasonably necessary to protect themselves (or others) from criminal acts.

SELF-PROVED WILL — instrument recognized in states following the Uniform Probate Code, eliminating certain formalities of proof.

SERVANT — an employee; subject to great control by the master (employer).

SERVICE MARK — a distinctive symbol, word, letter, number, picture, or combination of these, that is adopted and used by a business as a form of identification.

SERVICE OF PROCESS — *See process, service of.*

SETTLOR — *See trustor.*

SHARE (OF STOCK) — a proportionate ownership interest in a corporation or its equity. *See also stock.*

SHAREHOLDER — an owner of a share in a corporation through the ownership of its stock.

SHELTER RULE — a doctrine of negotiable instruments law whereby, in the chain of title after a holder in due course, all transferees have the status and benefits of a holder in due course, except transferees who (a) were parties to fraud or illegality affecting the instrument, or (b) as prior holders, had notice of a claim or defense to the instrument (UCC § 3-201 (1)).

SHIPMENT CONTRACT — a contract in which the seller pays delivery costs, and bears risk of loss, only until goods are delivered to the carrier; from there, the risk of loss passes to the buyer.

SHORT-SWING PROFITS — profits made by insiders by selling securities within six months after purchase.

SIGHT DRAFT — draft payable upon proper presentment.

SIGNATURE — in commercial law, any name, word, or mark used for the purpose of executing or authenticating a document.

SLANDER — oral defamation.

SOLE PROPRIETORSHIP — the simplest form of business, in which a sole owner and her business are not legally distinct entities; the owner is personally liable for business debts.

SOVEREIGN IMMUNITY — the doctrine under which a government (sovereign) may not be sued without its consent.

SPECIAL AGENT — a temporary agent for a single transaction or some other limited purpose.

SPECIAL DAMAGES — damages unique to the plaintiff in the situation or circumstance in question.

SPECIAL INDORSEMENT — an indorsement specifying the person to whom, or to whose order, an instrument is payable. *Compare blank (general) indorsement.*

SPECIAL WARRANTY DEED — similar to a general warranty deed, but warrants only against defects or encumbrances that arose after the person issuing this deed acquired the property.

SPECIFIC INTENT CRIMES — certain crimes (e.g., burglary, arson) requiring proof of an intent to commit that particular crime; otherwise, *mens rea* (criminal intent) can be transferred from the crime intended to the one that actually occurred.

SPECIFIC PERFORMANCE — a court order to a breaching party to perform his/her contract.

STALE CHECK — an uncertified check more than six months old.

STANDING (TO SUE) — a requirement that a person must have a sufficient stake in a dispute in order to sue. Plaintiffs must show that they have been either harmed or threatened with harm.

STARE DECISIS (Latin) — "Stand by the decision"; a requirement that a court follow its own and higher court precedents.

STATED CAPITAL — the amount of money received by a corporation upon issuance of its shares, except capital stock.

STATUTE — a law passed by the U.S. Congress or a state legislature.

STATUTE OF FRAUDS — a requirement that certain agreements be evidenced in writing, and are not provable in court if entirely oral; based on a 1677 statute of the English Parliament and on the Uniform Commercial Code.

STATUTE OF LIMITATIONS — a statute containing the period during which a lawsuit must be brought after a right to sue arises and after a person knows or should know of his/her right to sue.

STATUTORY PERIOD OF REDEMPTION — a brief, specified time after the foreclosure sale, in which the mortgagors are allowed by statute in most states to redeem (recover) the mortgaged property; the mortgagor must pay all of the amounts necessary to redeem under pre-sale equity of redemption, and also (in most states) the non-refundable expenses incurred in the foreclosure sale.

STOCK — a share; also, the physical evidence of share ownership, the share certificate; also, the aggregate of corporate shares. *See also authorized, canceled, capital, certified, common, convertible, cumulative preferred, noncumulative preferred, no-par, par value, preferred, and treasury stock.*

STOCK CERTIFICATE — *See certificate of stock.*

STOCK OPTION — a right to purchase stock at a time and price specified in the option.

STOCK SUBSCRIPTION — a promise to buy shares of a stock at a specified price.

STOCK WARRANT — a certificate sold to the public and entitling the owner to buy a specified amount of stock at a specified time and price.

STOP-PAYMENT ORDER — an order by a depositor directing his bank not to honor a specified check.

STRAIGHT BANKRUPTCY — a Chapter 7 bankruptcy proceeding.

STRAIGHT VOTING — the usual manner of election of directors in which each share of stock entitles its holder to cast one vote for as many different directors as there are vacancies being filled. Thus, if there are seven vacancies, the owner of 100 shares may vote 100 shares for each of seven persons. *Compare cumulative voting.*

STREET CERTIFICATE — a share transferred without designating a transferee by name; this certificate may be further transferred by delivery only, without indorsement.

STRICT LIABILITY — a modern common law principle imposing liability (regardless of whether the defendant is at fault) as a matter of public policy.

SUBCHAPTER S CORPORATION — *See S corporation.*

SUBJECT-MATTER JURISDICTION — the authority of a court to decide the issues in a particular case.

SUBLEASE — a lessee's lease of her leasehold interest to a third party; a sublease is for a time less than the full term of the leasehold (if not, it is an assignment rather than a sublease).

SUBPOENA — a court order requiring a person to appear as a witness, generally at a deposition or at a trial.

SUBPOENA *DUCES TECUM* — a court order requiring a person to appear as a witness and to bring specified documents.

SUBROGATION — the right of an insurer, once it has paid the insured for a loss, to proceed against third parties responsible for that loss (exception: no subrogation on life insurance payments); a surety's or guarantor's right to reimbursement from the debtor for any amounts the surety or guarantor must pay the creditor.

SUBSCRIBE — to agree to buy shares of stock at a specified price.

SUBSTANTIVE LAW — a body of law defining rights and obligations within a single area, such as contracts or torts.

SUBTERRANEAN RIGHTS — the exclusive rights of a landowner to oil, minerals, and other substances found beneath her land, including reasonable use of percolating (subsurface) waters. (This last right is also often considered a riparian right.)

SUMMARY JUDGMENT — a pretrial judgment on behalf of a civil plaintiff or civil defendant; awarded if the judge decides that (a) there is no general issue as to material (potentially determinative) facts, *and* (b) when the law is applied to these facts, one party is clearly entitled to a judgment in his/her favor. Summary judgment is generally granted or denied in response to a motion for it; it may be awarded on all or just part of a lawsuit.

SUMMONS — a document served on the defendant, along with the complaint, and notifying the defendant that he must file an answer or other response to the complaint within a certain period of time (e.g., 30 days) or else be subject to a default judgment.

SUPERSEDING (INTERVENING) CAUSE — a tort defense based on the lack of either causation in fact or proximate cause (foreseeability); an intervening cause, subsequent to and not resulting from the defendant's acts.

"SUPREMACY" CLAUSE — a provision in the U.S. Constitution, Article VI, Section 2, stating that the federal Constitution, laws made in pursuit of the Constitution, and treaties are "the supreme law of the land."

SURETY — a person who agreed to be liable for another's debts, even if the creditor has not exhausted all remedies for collection; the surety is primarily, not secondarily, liable (as is a guarantor).

SURPLUS — an excess of net assets over stated capital; capital surplus may be used in the calculation of dividends.

SURVIVORSHIP, RIGHT OF — in certain types of joint ownership (e.g., joint tenancy, tenancy by the entireties), when a co-owner dies his/her interest passes equally to the surviving co-owner(s), who have a right of survivorship.

SYMPATHY STRIKE — a strike called, not to gain benefits for strikers, but to assist other workers and/or unions.

TANGIBLE PERSONAL PROPERTY — personal property that may be physically possessed.

TENANCY — 1. the right to possess, and/or actual possession of, real property (a lease) without having title (ownership). 2. a form of co-ownership of property. *See also joint and periodic tenancy.*

TENANCY AT SUFFERANCE — (lease) tenancy continuing after a lease has expired, with most states holding that the leasehold implicitly becomes a periodic tenancy.

TENANCY AT WILL — (lease) tenancy that either lessor or lessee may end at any time, although most states require a termination notice.

TENANCY BY THE ENTIRETY — (co-ownership) no longer recognized in many states, tenancy held by a married couple; similar to a joint tenancy, with a right of survivorship and four unities (owners received their interest at the same time, from the same source and in equal interests (e.g., amounts), with each having a right to possess the whole); however, unlike a joint tenancy, can be terminated only by death, divorce, or agreement by both owners.

TENANCY IN COMMON — (co-ownership) shared tenancy with two or more co-owners who have the right to possess the whole; the three other unities (same time, same source, equal interest) are not required, and there is no right of survivorship (interests pass to one's heirs); if a conveyance with two or more persons is unclear, it is treated as this tenancy, not a joint tenancy.

TENANT — 1. a person possessing, or having the right to possess, real property without having ownership (a lessee of real property). 2. a co-owner of property owned by more than one person.

TENDER — to offer or make available.

TENDER OF DELIVERY — to offer or make available goods in conformity with the terms of a contract of sale.

TENDER OFFER — general invitation to all shareholders to purchase their shares at a specified price.

TESTAMENTARY GIFT — a gift specified in a will, effective (property is transferred) only upon death; this gift is revocable until the testator/testatrix dies.

TESTATOR — a man who has executed a will.

TESTATRIX — a woman who has executed a will.

THIRD-PARTY CLAIM — a claim bringing a third party into an existing lawsuit; for example, A sues B, who files a third-party claim against C for all or part of the damages A claims from B.

TIPPEE — a person who receives corporate information from an insider so that she may invest in (or sell) its securities.

TITLE — 1. a section of a code devoted to a single subject matter. 2. legal, formal ownership rights—broadly, the right to possess, control, and benefit from property; other types of title (ownership) are more limited in scope.

TITLE INSURANCE — insurance against defects in title to real property.

TOMBSTONE ADVERTISEMENT — a limited informational notice of anticipation concerning an issuance of securities.

TORT — a private wrong against a person or his property. Aside from certain limited circumstances, all torts arise from either an intentional, wrongful action or a negligent action.

TORTFEASOR — a person who commits a tort.

TRADE ACCEPTANCE — a draft drawn by seller of goods and presented to the buyer for her signature (acceptance); its signing effectively makes the instrument a note receivable of the seller and a note payable of the buyer.

TRADE FIXTURE — a fixture placed on leased premises by a tenant for use in his business; unlike the situation with other fixtures, the tenant can continue to treat a trade fixture as personal property.

TRADE NAME — a name denoting the business entity itself.

TRADE SECRET — any formal process or method of operation used in the production of goods and services, needed by an employee to perform her job, and meant to be held in the employee's confidence.

TRADEMARK — a distinctive symbol, word, letter, number, picture, or combination adopted and used by a merchant or manufacturer to identify his goods.

TRANSFER WARRANTY — *See warranty on transfer.*

TRAVELER'S CHECK — similar to a cashier's check (the same bank is both drawer and drawee); a negotiable instrument signed by the purchaser when obtained from the bank and later used as cash upon a second signature (indorsement) by the purchaser.

TREASON — the only crime defined in the U.S. Constitution: "Treason against the United States shall consist only in levying war against them, or adhering to their enemies, giving them aid and comfort" (Article III, Section 3).

TREASURE TROVE RULE — a common law principle, followed in most states, that a non-trespassing finder has title to money or other treasure buried for so long that it is unlikely a prior owner will return for it. (Otherwise, a landowner usually has the rightful claim.)

TREASURY STOCK — shares issued and later repurchased by a corporation.

TRESPASS TO PERSONAL PROPERTY — the intentional tort (often a crime; e.g., conversion or criminal trespass) of unjustifiably interfering with the plaintiff's possessory interest (e.g., use) in personal property; not generally as serious as the intentional tort of conversion.

TRESPASS TO REAL PROPERTY — the intentional tort (and usually a crime) of unauthorized entry onto the plaintiff land, either by a person or by something the person caused to enter the land; also occurs when presence on the plaintiff's land becomes unauthorized, but continues.

TRIAL — the proceedings before a competent court (or other tribunal) in which a civil or criminal case is heard and decided.

TROVER — a court action to recover damages for wrongfully converted property.

TRUST — 1. an arrangement where property is transferred to a trustee, who administers it for the benefit of another party, the beneficiary. Trusts can be *inter vivos* (taking effect during the creator's lifetime) or by will (testamentary trust). *See also constructive trust, resulting trust, and voting trust.* 2. a relationship requiring a high degree of loyalty.

TRUSTEE — 1. a person who administers property for the benefit of another party. 2. a person occupying a position of trust; a fiduciary. 3. in bankruptcy, a person who acquires title to the debtor's property (the estate) and administers the estate by collecting and liquidating assets, as well as deciding claims; the trustee has numerous powers and is in charge of distributing the estate to creditors.

TRUSTOR — a transferor of property to a trustee for the benefit of a third party. Also called a "settlor" or "creator."

TYING ARRANGEMENT — an agreement requiring the purchase of one product in return for a contract involving another product; often a *per se* violation of antitrust laws.

ULTRA VIRES (Latin) — "beyond the powers" (of a corporation).

UNAUTHORIZED SIGNATURE — a signature indicating that the signer has authority to bind another person when such is not the case.

UNCERTIFIED SECURITY — a security for which no certificate has been issued.

UNCERTIFIED SHARE — a share for which no certificate has been issued, but the ownership is shown on stock books maintained for that purpose by the issuer.

UNCONSCIONABILITY — the superior position of a party in a contract is used to be grossly unfair to another party in that contract.

UNCONSCIONABLE CONTRACT — a grossly unfair contract brought about by the superior position of one of the parties.

UNDERWRITER — one who provides an outlet for the stock of an issuer and may guarantee to furnish a definite sum of money by a definite date for an issue of bonds or stock; the underwriter acquires securities intending their overall distribution. In insurance law, the insurer.

UNDISCLOSED PRINCIPAL — a principal/agency relationship in which neither the fact of agency, nor the identity of the principal, is disclosed to third parties acting in the belief that the agent is the real party in interest.

UNDUE INFLUENCE — taking advantage of another by reason of a position of trust in a close or confidential relationship.

UNENFORCEABLE CONTRACT — an agreement that, for some legal reason, is not enforceable in a court of law.

UNFAIR COMPETITION — broadly, an intentional tort encompassing such activities as infringement of intellectual property and interference with contracts or prospective economic advantage; more narrowly, the intentional tort of trying to "pass off" goods or services upon the public as if they were the goods or services of another, more reputable business or product; also, usually a crime.

UNFAIR LABOR PRACTICE — any activity by a labor union or management that is prohibited by the National Labor Relations Act or an amendment to that act.

UNIFORM COMMERCIAL CODE — a comprehensive uniform law covering most commercial transactions (e.g., banking, sale of goods).

UNIFORM LAWS — laws uniformly adopted by most or all states in order to reduce uncertainty about the law in other states and to reduce differing interpretations and enforcement of the law (e.g., Uniform Commercial Code).

UNILATERAL CONTRACT — a contract based on the exchange of a promise by one party for an action of another.

UNILATERAL MISTAKE — a mistake by one of the parties, but not both parties, to a contract; not grounds for cancellation or rescission.

UNION SHOP — a business entity that requires (e.g., because of union "rules") that a worker, in order to remain employed, become a union member within a specified period of time after being hired. Some states outlaw union shops. *See also right-to-work law.*

UNLAWFUL BOYCOTT — 1. *See secondary boycott.* 2. a *per se* violation of antitrust laws: an agreement among supposed competitors that excludes other businesses from dealing in their product(s).

UNLIQUIDATED DEBT — debt about which there is a good faith dispute as to the amount due; an obligation not reduced to a specific amount due.

UNSECURED CREDITOR — a creditor without security for a debt who has only the debtor's express or implied promise to pay.

USAGE OF TRADE — a regular practice or method of dealing, observed with such frequency as to become part of the transaction or contract of the parties.

USURY — a charge of interest in excess of the rate allowed by law.

VENUE — the geographical area in which an action is tried and jurors are chosen.

VERDICT — the formal decision reached by a jury in a civil or criminal case.

VERTICAL MERGER — a merger in which the merged businesses operated the same type of business, but at different levels (e.g., manufacturer merges with his supplier of raw materials); generally permitted under antitrust law.

VERTICAL PRIVITY — privity among persons up and down, that is, on different levels, of the chain of distribution and consumption.

VESTED — settled; accrued; fixed; definite; more than an expectation based on contingency; a present right or interest that is or will be definitely enforceable.

VICARIOUS LIABILITY — responsibility for another party's actions because of the relationship between the two parties (the acting party and the vicariously liable party). *Respondeat superior* is the most important type of vicarious liability.

VICTIMLESS CRIME — a crime sometimes considered to have no specific victims, just society as a whole (e.g., prostitution, gambling).

VOID — of no legal effect from the very beginning; not even susceptible to ratification.

VOID CONTRACT — an agreement having no legal force or effect; null from the very beginning.

Voidable — capable of being void; a voidable instrument may have some validity until an appropriate action is taken declaring the instrument void.

Voidable Contract — an agreement subject to being declared of no legal effect as a result of action (e.g., disaffirmance, nullification, a lawsuit) by one of the parties.

Voidable Title — a title received by a buyer subject to cancellation by the seller.

Voir Dire — a jury selection process in which the judge and/or the attorneys for both sides question prospective jurors; the information provided may be used to determine whether persons can be kept off the panel "for cause" (e.g., bias) and whether a peremptory challenge (rejecting a potential juror without offering a reason) should be exercised.

Voluntary Bankruptcy — proceeding initiated by debtor under Chapter 7, 9, 11, or 13 of the Bankruptcy Code.

Voluntary Intoxication — *See intoxication.* Generally, not a defense for crimes or torts.

Voting Trust — a combination of shareholders accomplished through transfer of voting shares to a voting trustee for the limited purpose of voting on matters to come before a shareholders' meeting.

Waiver — voluntary relinquishment of one or more of a person's known rights (e.g., rights in a contract). A written waiver does not require consideration; other waivers may. *See also estoppel.*

Warehouseman — a person engaged in the business of receiving and storing goods for hire (UCC Article 7).

Warrant — court order, such as a search or arrest warrant; *see also stock warrant.*

Warranty — a guarantee. *See also implied, limited, and presentment warranty.*

Warranty Deed — a deed in which the grantor warrants good, clear title to the grantee. The usual covenants are possession, quiet enjoyment, right to convey, freedom from encumbrances, and defense of title as to all claims.

Warranty of Fitness — an implied warranty that goods being sold are fit for the buyer's use or purpose.

Warranty of Merchantability — an implied warranty that goods being sold are fit for the ordinary purpose for which goods of that class or kind are sold.

Warranty on Transfer — a warranty made by any person who transfers a negotiable instrument and receives consideration; it covers title, signature genuineness and authorization, lack of material alteration, lack of knowledge of insolvency proceeding (against maker, acceptor or (for unaccepted drafts) drawer), and lack of good defenses against the transferor (the last one can be qualified); it is given to the immediate transferee and, if the transfer is by indorsement, any subsequent holder who takes the instrument in good faith.

Waste — property damage beyond ordinary wear and tear by a person in rightful possession of the property; the damage harms another with an interest in the property (e.g., a landlord, a co-owner).

Watered Stock — stock issued without consideration or for cash, property, or services less than par value.

White-Collar Crime — a nonviolent crime, perpetrated by a person in a position of trust, against a business or government.

Will — an instrument, executed by a testator/testatrix according to the formalities required by state statute, setting forth how that person's estate is to be distributed after his or her death.

Winding Up — 1. action by the corporation, after dissolution, to liquidate assets and distribute the proceeds—first, to creditors; second, to preferred shareholders; finally, to common shareholders. 2. in partnership law, the liquidation and termination process for a dissolved partnership. *See liquidation, 2.*

Without Recourse Endorsement — *See disclaimer, 2.*

Without Reserve — the stipulation that an auctioneer may not withdraw goods from the auction.

Workers' Compensation Statute — a law, found in all states, requiring many types of employees to relinquish their right to sue their employers for accidental death, injury, or disease arising from or during the course of their employment; in exchange, the employees gain the right to receive financial benefits (according to a statutory schedule of amounts) regardless of fault.

WRIT — a written court order requiring the performance of an act or giving authority to have it done.

WRIT OF ATTACHMENT — *See attachment.*

WRIT OF *CERTIORARI* — *See certiorari, writ of.*

WRIT OF EXECUTION — after a judgment against a debtor, a court order that a sheriff or other authorized official seize and sell the debtor's nonexempt property.

WRONGFUL BOYCOTT — *See unlawful boycott, 2.*

WRONGFUL DISCHARGE — *See abusive discharge.*

WRONGFUL DISHONOR — dishonoring, by a bank, of a customer's check without good cause (e.g., insufficient funds, improper or missing indorsements).

YELLOW DOG CONTRACT — an unlawful agreement in which the employee, as a condition of employment, agrees not to join or remain a member of a union.

ZONING — legislative action, usually at the municipal level, regulating the use of real property, including the types of construction permitted within different zoning districts.

INDEX